More Praise for *The Prosecutors*

"*The Prosecutors* reads like a tornado. The writing jumps off the page and propels each of the extraordinary cases with immediacy and vigor. Non-fiction doesn't get more compelling than this."

—John Lescroart, *New York Times* bestselling author of
The Oath and *The Hearing*

"*The Prosecutors* is a gritty, absorbing, and—I found—authentic look into the sights, sounds, and smells of a big-city prosecutor's office . . . A valuable insider's account that is a must-read for lawyers and those fascinated by true crime and our justice system."

—Vincent Bugliosi, author of *New York Times* bestsellers
Outrage and *Helter Skelter*

"[A] remarkable book."
—*The Denver Post*

"Riveting . . . an insightful look at how local justice is dispensed."
—Ray Locker, Associated Press

"Enlightening . . . *The Prosecutors* represents a worthy endeavor."
—*San Antonio Express-News*

"An eye-opening read and a perfect gift for a law student."
—*East Bay Express* (California)

"Delsohn does a deft job of highlighting the complexities of the cases that he encounters . . . The perennial struggle between the DAs and defense attorneys will appeal to those junkies who can't get enough of bloody crimes and courtroom drama."
—*Publishers Weekly*

"As an insider's view of an urban prosecutor's office, [*The Prosecutors*] does an excellent job."
—*Library Journal*

Gary Delsohn is a senior writer for *The Sacramento Bee*. A recipient of the Alicia Patterson Foundation Fellowship, he is a past Knight Fellow at Stanford University. His work has been featured in Salon.com, *The Denver Post*, and the Denver *Rocky Mountain News*. Mr. Delsohn lives in Sacramento, California. This is his first book.

Visit www.Garyl

THE
PROSECUTORS

Kidnap, Rape,
Murder, Justice:
One Year Behind the
Scenes in a Big-City
DA's Office

GARY DELSOHN

A PLUME BOOK

PLUME
Published by the Penguin Group
Penguin Group (USA) Inc., 375 Hudson Street, New York, New York 10014, U.S.A.
Penguin Books Ltd, 80 Strand, London WC2R 0RL, England
Penguin Books Australia Ltd, 250 Camberwell Road, Camberwell, Victoria 3124, Australia
Penguin Books Canada Ltd, 10 Alcorn Avenue, Toronto, Ontario, Canada M4V 3B2
Penguin Books India (P) Ltd, 11 Community Centre, Panchsheel Park,
New Delhi–110 017, India
Penguin Books (NZ), cnr Airborne and Rosedale Roads,
Albany, Auckland 1310, New Zealand
Penguin Books (South Africa) (Pty) Ltd, 24 Sturdee Avenue, Rosebank, Johannesburg 2196,
South Africa

Penguin Books Ltd, Registered Offices: 80 Strand, London WC2R 0RL, England

Published by Plume, a member of Penguin Group (USA) Inc.
Previously published in a Dutton edition.

First Plume Printing, August 2004
10 9 8 7 6 5 4 3 2 1

REGISTERED TRADEMARK—MARCA REGISTRADA

The Library of Congress has catalogued the Dutton edition as follows:
Delsohn, Gary.
The prosecutors : a year in the life of a District attorney's office / by Gary Delsohn.
p. cm.
ISBN 0-525-94712-4 (hc.)
ISBN 0-452-28554-2 (pbk.)
1. California. District Attorney (Sacramento County)   2. Prosecution—California—Sacramento
County.   3. Public prosecutors—California—Sacramento County—Biography.   I. Title.
KFC1158.D45 2003
345.794'5401—dc21

2002153860

Printed in the United States of America

To Eilene and Norman Delsohn, my mother and father, who gave me endless love and inspiration. To my wife, Linda, who has always been there to let me express them; and to my children, Joseph and Amanda, who filled me with the reasons to want to.

Contents

Acknowledgments | ix

Chapter 1. Easy In, Easy Out | 1

Chapter 2. It's Going to Be a Tough Year | 17

Chapter 3. I Want Twelve Americans | 47

Chapter 4. Child Killer | 64

Chapter 5. On with the Show | 80

Chapter 6. Suspicious Story | 107

Chapter 7. Southside Punks | 121

Chapter 8. Dead Bang Winner | 137

Chapter 9. Great Bodily Injury Resulting in Death | 160

Chapter 10. Trial by Jury | 170

Chapter 11. Kidnap, Rape, Murder, Justice | 187

Chapter 12. Closing Arguments | 204

Chapter 13. Serial Killer | 217

Chapter 14. Doctor on Trial | 236

Chapter 15. Major Participant | 247

Chapter 16. Life or Death   267

Chapter 17. One Less Case   280

Chapter 18. L.A. Blues   296

Chapter 19. Decision Time   314

Chapter 20. Long Time Coming   330

Chapter 21. The Frosts   345

Chapter 22. Epilogue: The Sacramento District Attorney   360

Acknowledgments

JOURNALISTS are always on the outside looking in. No matter what we cover or how well-placed our sources, we rarely get to break through the walls and spend real time inside the institutions we follow.

I first met Jan Scully, the Sacramento County district attorney, shortly after she took office for the start of her first term in 1995. My assignment at *The Sacramento Bee* was to find interesting people and write Sunday profiles about them. The new forty-four-year-old district attorney certainly fit that bill. She had recently won an election in which few had given her much of a chance. Nine days later, she became a widow and single mother of two small children. Steve Scully, her husband, died of a heart attack while swimming in his health club pool.

I wrote a long story about how she was coping with the new job and the death of her husband. She thought the resulting article was fair and over time we crossed paths occasionally on other stories. When I finally approached her about spending a year as a fly on the wall inside her office, she was intrigued with the idea and at least open to it.

She is a politician, cautious by nature, and she thought about it for a couple of months. Finally, she invited me in to pitch the idea to her top lieutenants and the answer came back a few weeks later: I could spend a year inside the office with a few ground rules that were later spelled out in writing.

I wouldn't write anything for my newspaper during the year; no one from her office would be quoted in the book unless they agreed to be; personnel matters and anything else the district attorney believed "necessary and expedient" would be off-limits. Finally, I would follow the same code of conduct governing county employees and from time to time I would apprise the district attorney of how the work was progressing. That last part was unnecessary, since she never asked me anything more than what I was following and whether I was getting what I needed.

On January 2, 2001, I showed up and was later given a small office in a corner of the second floor where I could write. I was allowed to go wherever I pleased. There were more than a few people in the office who thought Scully was insane to let a reporter wander around freely, and other pockets of resistance made themselves evident from time to time. But for the most part people were extremely open and accessible. Prosecutors and investigators freely discussed the most sensitive aspects of their cases in front of me. I was allowed to sit in on meetings with victims, defense attorneys, judges, police, and witnesses. I was almost never told something was off-limits and after I had been showing up for a few weeks, most of the resistance that I was aware of had disappeared. I was given extraordinary access to the inner workings of the office. Not once was I asked to show anyone what I was writing. I am convinced the unfettered access given to a working journalist by a district attorney was unprecedented.

There are so many people to thank in this undertaking, my only fear is leaving someone out. First and foremost is Jan Scully. She believes the district attorney's office is conscientious, does the right thing the vast majority of the time, and that it's actually to the DA's advantage if the public has a more accurate, complete, and realistic picture of how it works than is possible from following daily coverage in the news media or watching the latest hot show on television. She was as gracious and hospitable as I could ever have imagined. Cindy Besemer, her chief deputy, was equally helpful and candid.

John O'Mara, the longtime head of Major Crimes, doesn't talk to reporters much, but he indulged me for an entire year. There was not a single question he wouldn't answer, barely a meeting I wanted to attend where he said no. He's as dedicated and hard working as an[y] vant I've encountered during twenty-eight years in journ[alism] grateful for his assistance in making this book possible.

I took up countless hours of time from Steve Harrold, Dawn Bladet, Steve Grippi, Mark Curry, Tom Johnson, Tim Frawley, Rob Gold, Mike Savage, Todd Laras, Marge Koller, Paul Durenberger, Andrew Smith, Ernest Sawtelle, Kerry Martin, Anne Marie Schubert, Robin Shakely, Albert Locher, Frank Meyer, Jeff Rose, Don Steed, Marv Stern, Laurie Earl, Rod Norgaard, Chris Ore, and Jennifer Moncrieff.

Many others were helpful in answering my questions, including Ed Dudensing, Jennifer Sawtelle, Jean Williamson, Donna Gissing, Lori Greene, Jennifer Kennedy, Eric Kindall, Dale Kitching, Rick Lewkowitz, Noah Phillips, Jeff Ritschard, Albert Roldan, Karen Maxwell, Katie McGarry, Donnelle Slivka, Andrew Soloman, Mike Wise, Kevin Greene, Kit Cleland, Dick Margarita, Russ Dietrick, Nancy Ramirez, Dave Brown, Heidi Smith, Rick Yenovkian, Marcia Christian, Giovanna Flaggs, Daniel Oforlea, and Ahmanal Dorsey.

DA investigators Dave Duckett, Shawn Loehr, Ray Antar, Bob Bell, Teresa Kahl, Jason Gay, Mark Rall, and Gary Wagg were exceptionally generous with their time and information.

Administrative assistants Diane Richardson, Vineeta Chand, Georgeanna Fox, Debbie Ward, Paula White, Micki Dunaway, and Jan Pina did me more favors than I could count and I greatly appreciated every one of them. Jack and Becky Frost, two of the most decent people I've ever met, were gracious above and beyond the call.

I owe an enormous debt of gratitude to my agent, David Black, who believed in this book and stayed with me as we searched for the best way to tell and frame the story. His assistants, Joy and Jason, were always willing to do what they could to make life easier for me and I thank them for it.

Brian Tart, editor in chief at Dutton, was a constant source of enthusiasm, insight, and good ideas. He did a fantastic job of helping me shape and polish the manuscript; there is no way the book would have been possible without him. Amy Hughes and Anna Cowles, also at Dutton, were inspiring, supportive, and at all times wise and helpful.

My editors at *The Sacramento Bee*, Rick Rodriguez and Joyce Terhaar, were kind enough to allow me to take a year-long leave of absence. A very special thank you must go to Peggy Engel, executive director of the Alicia Patterson Foundation, for her tremendous backing and for the foundation's invaluable assistance in getting this project off the ground. Jim Risser, one of the very best and most generous journalists I have ever known, and Paul Seave are two friends whose early support also proved to be worth more than they know.

Others whose generous assistance proved valuable were Greta Fall, Morrison C. England Jr., Jane Ure, Lloyd Connelly, James Long, Gerald Backarich, Michael J. Virga, Glenn Powell, David Simon, Richard C. Park, John Lippsmeyer, Jan Karowsky, Barbara Bedow, Betty Williams, Sue Nelson-Campoy, Lou Blanas, John McGinness, Jim Cooper, Craig Hill, Lori Timberlake, Marci Minter, Lance McHenry, Clark Fancher, Bill Nicholson, Ed Newton, Nick Rossi, Jamie Lewis, Bill Kelly, Mike Smith, Dave Lind, Ray Biondi, Bill Roberts, Toni Winfield, Rich Overton, and Jody Handley.

A writer needs supportive friends whose encouragement and enthusiasm can pull him through the long, lonesome moments of working on such a project and I am blessed in that regard. My heartfelt appreciation to Marjie Lundstrom, Sam Stanton, Andy Furillo, Deborah Anderluh, Steven Magagnini, Nancy Vogel, Mary Lynne Vellinga, M.S. Enkoji, Cathy Ferarro, Becky Boyd, Saul Moses, Cynthia Hubert, Mike Brady, Steve Wiegand, Mareva Brown, John Farrell, Amy Pyle, Aurelio Rojas, Dana Parsons, Suzanne Weiss, Wynne Racine, Robert Nemzin, Tom Bell, and Barry Kaliner.

Thanks to Jack Golan and Greg Lang. Kevin Clymo, Pete Harned, Linda Parisi, and Don Heller are all able defense lawyers who helped put perspective into the book. My brother, Steve Delsohn, who's been down this road many times before and knows what to expect, was a constant source of encouragement and good advice. The rest of my family provided me sustenance in ways they're probably not even aware of.

To say that I owe perhaps the biggest thank you of all to Linda Townsdin, my dear wife of twenty-seven years, is a massive understatement. Her sound judgment, guidance, love, and encouragement kept me going from start to finish.

Justice, justice shall you pursue. —Deuteronomy 16:20

1 | Easy In, Easy Out

That went sour downtown. That went real sour downtown.
—Rick Brewer to Carlos Cervantes

NOTHING could go wrong. That's what Rick Brewer told everyone. With a crew he could trust, Brewer knew there was a pile of cash waiting to be slipped into his empty pockets. A mean-eyed twenty-four-year-old parolee with a drug-addict girlfriend and three young children to feed, Brewer knew from experience that the Bread Store, a popular sandwich shop and bakery about a mile east of the California Capitol in Midtown Sacramento, was an easy target.

On November 23, 1996, just before 6:00 P.M., as the day's cash was about to be emptied from the registers and placed into a floor safe that could not be opened until the owners arrived the next morning, Brewer, a Latino, and an accomplice identified by witnesses as a tall, thin black man, slipped in through an open back door and held up the place. Between the registers and the employees' wallets they stole $1,903.42. Brewer's getaway driver was his sister, Angelina, who waited in the alley in her white Jeep Cherokee. The tall black man was Michael Smith, a paroled felon whose crime of choice was robbing small Sacramento motels. The stocky, slump-shouldered Brewer, wearing a child's skeleton mask from Halloween and carrying his beloved Mossberg pistol-gripped twelve-gauge shotgun, scared the shit out of the employees who were closing up. No one was dumb enough to give the robbers any trouble. Not with Brewer and his ugly brown-and-black Mossberg—it measured a menacing twenty-eight inches from its finger-sculpted grip to its deadly muzzle opening—staring them in the face. It was a snap—easy in, easy out.

A month later, Christmas was coming. Brewer and his girlfriend, Marichu Flores, liked to party and get loaded. Their favorite drugs were cocaine and marijuana. Flores liked crank too. She used it heavily when she was pregnant with her then five-month-old son, Rick Brewer, Jr., and the baby suffered from drug-induced tremors when he was born.

The couple was not in the Christmas spirit, however. They'd been fighting even more than usual. Worn out and depressed, Flores had checked herself into a county mental health facility for some peace. When Brewer called to find out when she'd be coming home, he got belligerent at the nurse's stonewalling and threatened her. "I have the same thing the cops have," he barked into the phone, apparently referring to a gun. The nurse reported the threat and because he was a paroled felon, police came to search for the weapon. They couldn't find it, but a few days later caseworkers from the state's Child Protective Services agency came and took away his three children. Brewer ran for his shotgun, retrieved it from its hiding place, and was about to chase the CPS workers down the stairs of his apartment complex when Smith, who was with him at the time, stopped him. Brewer had already served time in state prison for dealing drugs and had no job skills or prospects. He was mad at the world. His kids and lady were gone. He was broke. Why not hit the Bread Store again?

Brewer didn't want to use his sister this time. Smith's cover was blown because he had refused to wear a mask in the first robbery. Brewer wanted a new crew, people he could control more easily. Because he and Flores had lived in Southside Park before they moved a few months earlier to an apartment several miles north, he was familiar with a lot of the young wanna-be gangsters in the area. Southside is a rough part of Sacramento that sits on the southern edge of downtown. The new office towers and a downtown mall are achingly close by, but the only common ground between the impoverished streets of Southside and the shiny buildings a few blocks north is at lunchtime, when the secretaries and state office workers put on their running shoes and jog around the well-worn track at the park's edge. At night, Southside Park itself is a haven for drug dealers and gangbangers, despite a couple of new housing complexes sponsored by the city and a few brave urban homesteaders.

Brewer knew the scene. He had plenty of punks to enlist from the collection of unsupervised teenage males who used the park to hang out and get wasted. Because everyone in the neighborhood knew Brewer had been to the joint and wasn't reluctant to kick someone's ass when necessary, many of these punks both looked up to him and were afraid of him. None of them would give him any shit.

"Easy in, easy out," he told sixteen-year-old Carlos Cervantes, a sweet-faced kid who liked to steal cars and was among Brewer's South-side admirers. When he wasn't smoking dope, Cervantes would sometimes play touch football in the park with his two younger brothers. He could run like a track star and dreamed of becoming a professional football player, but he was too little and undisciplined to have a chance.

"Wanna make some money?" Brewer asked him a few days before Christmas. "You down for a lick?"

"Yeah, man, I'm down," Los, as his neighborhood buds called him, assured Brewer. He didn't want to appear weak in front of him.

For a wheelman, Brewer chose Bobby Dixon, a twenty-three-year-old parolee who was only three weeks out of state prison for grand theft auto. Brewer had grown up with Dixon, a tall, skinny black man who, like Carlos, could barely read or write but had an uncanny talent for being able to bust into a locked car, get it started, and rip it off in less than five minutes. Brewer, whose father and grandfather had each served time in state prison for robbery and drug-related crimes, felt he could trust Dixon. If they got caught, Brewer knew Dixon would keep things quiet with the cops. Dixon knew how things worked. He'd served almost two years of a three-year sentence for the auto theft and a prior purse-snatching. On November 29, 1996—six days after Brewer first robbed the Bread Store—Dixon was released on parole and came to live in Southside with his grandmother. He needed cash. He could be depended on. Brewer considered him rock-solid loyal. Dixon wasn't too bright, but he understood what a snitch's life was worth.

Brewer was the only one in the group who had a car that ran, a ratty old 1976 Cutlass, but he wasn't about to use it in a robbery. They needed some wheels, a G-ride they could dump right after the job. It was up to Dixon and Cervantes to find one. The term G-ride came from the gangsta rap music Brewer and his pals liked to listen to while they drank malt liquor and hung out in the park. Dr. Dre, Snoop Dogg, Ice Cube. That was their language, the slang of the streets. A gangster's car was his G-ride, a robbery was a lick. Everything was cool.

Three days before Christmas, Dixon and Cervantes were walking around the neighborhood when they found their G-ride parked outside a dive not far from the park called the Monte Carlo Club. The black, four-door 1992 GMC Jimmy was sitting in the alley. It was a snap to jack. Dixon smashed the driver's side window, got in, and, using a screwdriver he kept in his back pocket, started tinkering with the steering column until the engine started. Dixon told his pals that when they finished using the G-ride, he planned to get some help and take the motor out and put it into his own dead 1976 Buick Skylark.

As soon as he got his hands on the Jimmy, Dixon was driving the hot truck like a wild man around the streets of his neighborhood. He'd burn rubber and peel down the street, try to take a turn on two wheels. He did doughnuts, accelerating and slamming the brakes so the car spun in a circle. He wanted everyone to see his new ill-gotten toy. Less than a month out of the joint for the same crime and he's showing all the punks in the street how he makes his own damn rules. Fuck the cops. It was a game to Dixon and his boys.

Brewer wanted a couple more guys to go in and help him loot the place and make sure the employees followed his orders without a fuss. Rickie Martinez and James David Glica were sixteen-year-old gang-bangers who knew Brewer from when they used to visit their girlfriends in the apartment complex Brewer and Flores lived in. Martinez was a short and stocky wiseass who didn't do much except drink, say *motherfucker* a lot, and chase girls. His mom, Rhonda Ybarra, tried desperately to keep an eye on him and make sure he stayed in school, but she had too many of her own problems to make it happen. She had a steady job with the state but lousy taste in men. She freely admits drinking and drugging too much while Rickie was growing up. Rickie's dad used to slap her around and spent time in state prison for a variety of crimes, most having to do with drugs. She remarried another felon who drank and abused her and Rickie.

Martinez had been in and out of several juvenile offender facilities for crimes that included possession of a loaded .38-caliber handgun at school, stealing cars, throwing rocks at a moving car, assault, and robbery.

Glica was different. He was bright, curious about the world. He was a talented artist, good enough to be a professional illustrator. His father is a minister who also worked for the Sacramento Opera Association, but Glica and he were not very close. J.D.'s parents divorced when he was about twelve, and his mom moved with the kids to Arizona to get her son away from his gang associations in Sacramento. He moved back to town to stay with his dad, who is gay—a fact that often landed J.D. on the short end of fights trying to stick up for him when he did attend school.

Unhappy and on his own most of the time, Glica had a temper. He had been arrested for seriously beating a twenty-five-year-old man who simply came up to him on a street in Davis, a college town fifteen miles west of Sacramento, and asked him if he knew where a party was. On the afternoon of December 23, 1996, Glica and Martinez wandered over to the park to hang with their homies. Brewer asked if they wanted to "pull a lick downtown." Neither had the balls—or the inclination—to say no.

Trevor Garcia, twenty-three, a year younger than Brewer, was dough faced and pudgy. He was a doper and acute diabetic whose parents were divorced. He and his dad had moved about a year earlier from the Bay Area to the same apartment complex Brewer and Flores lived in. Affable and more laid back than the others, Garcia had no menace in him. He needed insulin shots twice a day and also had to take medicine for high blood pressure and to regulate his kidneys. He wasn't an angel, but Garcia had no criminal record. Twice in recent years his kidneys had failed and he'd had to be rushed to the hospital. He was a follower, without much ambition of his own. Broke most of the time, on welfare, Garcia hung out at Brewer's a lot, catching a buzz and chilling over video games. He liked "40s," tall cans of cheap Olde English malt liquor. One or more of the large beers would knock out most people. Despite his poor health, Garcia seemed able to drink them all day.

Brewer had been pitching him about the job for more than a month, even before the first robbery. "I was down," Garcia would say later. "I didn't want to be a punk."

Brewer mapped things out. He told everyone he'd been peeping the place for a while. Dixon would stay in the G-ride. He'd sit in the alley with the motor running. The other four would force whatever employees were in the store to the floor and make sure no one moved. They'd empty the registers while Brewer did what he did best: scare the crap out of people. He'd wave the Mossberg in the air and freak out everyone with his new disguise: a red devil mask with horns, fake hair, and a deranged open-mouthed smile. He gave Garcia his old skeleton mask. Glica was to cover his face in a red T-shirt. Martinez got a nylon stocking somewhere and would use that to shield his identity. Dixon didn't need a mask because he wasn't going in. Everyone would wear gloves so no one could identify them or the color of their skin. That way they'd also leave behind no prints.

That was the plan. Easy in, easy out.

By the time dusk rolled around, everyone but Brewer and Dixon had been drinking heavily. With Dixon at the wheel, they got into the Jimmy and made sure everyone knew their assignments. It was about 5:00 P.M., a typically cold and damp December day in the California capital. They had a few stops to make and planned to get to the Bread Store by six o'clock, just before the cash went into the floor safe. Two days before Christmas, they figured there'd be a lot more money now, even better than Brewer's Thanksgiving take. Everything was good.

Everything but the G-ride. It was a piece of shit. When they tried to start it and pull away, the battery was dead. They still had some time, so Dixon ran around the corner and pulled the battery out of his car. Within twenty minutes, they were ready to get moving but Lisa Lopez, Cervantes's seventeen-year-old girlfriend, had wandered by. She'd been hanging around the park with a few of the neighborhood girls and was screaming at Cervantes to get out of the car. Carlos got out of the Jimmy to talk with her, calm her down. Dixon's sister, Faye, was so disgusted with Dixon that she had called the cops and said her brother was driving around like an asshole in a stolen truck. Lisa didn't want Cervantes to be with him when the cops picked up his sorry ass.

"The police know about the car, Los. Don't go," she said with tears in her eyes.

Brewer yelled to his boy. "Los, come here." Cervantes went over. Brewer's dark eyes narrowed. "You ain't gonna go, Los?" Cervantes looked at Lisa, looked at Brewer. "No, man," he said. "I'm cool." The others in the Jimmy called him names: pussy, punk, bitch. Fuck you, they yelled at him. But Cervantes was out of the car, out of the plan.

Now they were in a hurry. Dixon drove with Brewer in the passenger seat, his devil's mask and the Mossberg on the floor between them. Garcia was behind Dixon. Martinez sat behind Brewer. Glica, holding the red T-shirt he'd wrap around his face, was lying down in the back of the Jimmy. They stopped at a nearby gas station, where Glica jammed his feet against the back window several times until he managed to kick it out. If he had to, he could escape from the Jimmy in an instant. They put in a few bucks and were off.

By the time they got to the Bread Store it was 6:25 P.M. Most of Sacramento and its sprawling suburbs were preparing for the holiday. Tomorrow was Christmas Eve. Some of the nearby stores, like the Beat, a hip record emporium and café a few doors down, were busy with Christmas shoppers.

Brewer told Dixon to cruise past the front of the store on J Street so he could peer inside. The Bread Store's large picture windows were decorated for Christmas; employees' names had been painted on them, along with red and green Christmas stockings and wreaths. SEASON'S GREETINGS, it said on the glass. Check out the alley, Brewer told Dixon. Four or five men were inside with brooms, sweeping the floors, closing up for the night. One was gathering old bread that had gone unsold, putting it in bags so it could be taken to nearby homeless shelters. Pulling the Jimmy into the alley, Dixon and the others saw that the back door had been left open again, just as it had during the first robbery. Dixon parked the Jimmy next to a wall around the corner and everyone else got out.

Brewer was first in. Swinging the Mossberg through the air in a wide, circular motion, the way old rock-and-roll star Pete Townshend of the Who wound his arm across his guitar for show, Brewer yelled for the three employees in the back baking area of the store to hit the floor.

Martinez and Glica were next, storming to the front of the store, where the registers were kept. "Where's the safe?" they demanded. "Where's the fuckin' money?" Garcia, stumbling out of the Jimmy and falling to the ground, was last in. He heard one shot, then he was inside and shouting with the chorus. "Where's the money? Where's the fuckin' money?"

Dung Dao and Kelly Range, employees who had been sweeping out the back of the store, and Josh Christian, who was wiping off the muffin counter in front, managed to make it out the main door on J Street. Dao ran from the back of the store to the front, yelling, "Get out, get out. Run, run." Once out the door, he kept running until he bumped into a man and woman walking their dog about two blocks away and pleaded for them to call for help. Range and Christian raced next door to the Beat. Frantic, they grabbed the glass door to the store with so much force it shattered. Call 911, they shouted to a clerk. There's a robbery in progress.

That left only employee Hector Montelongo in the back. A quiet thirty-one-year-old bread baker from Mexico, Montelongo tried to get away by running up some stairs to offices on the second floor. When he realized he couldn't make it up there fast enough to escape, that the robbers had seen him, he meekly came back down and hoped for the best. Glica kicked him and ordered him to the ground. Montelongo spoke broken English. He had a wife and three small children at home. He was sure he was going to be robbed and killed. He slipped his wallet out of his back pocket and was able to hide it under some clutter on the floor before one of the robbers made him get up and go to the front of the store. When he stuttered that he didn't know anything about any money, that all he did was bake bread, Martinez sprayed him in the face with a can of Mace Garcia had given to him earlier that day.

The robbers and Montelongo were in the front now. The only other employee in the store was Jason Frost, the twenty-three-year-old assistant manager. Everyone was yelling, "Where's the money? Where's the fucking money?"

Glica and Martinez rummaged through the Bread Store's cash registers. When they realized they were empty, they crashed them to the floor. They were scattered on the floor in pieces as Brewer zeroed in on sandy-haired Jason Frost, who was behind the counter, near the floor safe.

"Where's the money, motherfucker?" the man in the devil mask demanded. "Open the fuckin' safe." The Mossberg was in Frost's face. He had nowhere to go.

Trapped between a wall and the bread counter on three sides and with Brewer behind the counter with him demanding the cash, Frost muttered something about the money already being placed in a drop safe. Christian had placed it all in plastic sandwich bags and slipped it into the floor safe only minutes before the robbers came in. It couldn't be opened until the owners showed up the next morning. "I don't have a key," Frost—working at the Bread Store to gain experience for what he hoped would be the day he ran his own restaurant—said to the man in the devil's mask.

Range and Christian were across the street, looking into the store window, when they saw the stocky man in the devil's mask, his hands, neck, and face covered so thoroughly that they would later say they believed he was black, fire point-blank at Jason Frost. His sweater and body somehow opened wide all at once.

The young man, an eight-inch hole in his right abdomen spouting blood and exposing his intestines and bowel, melted to the floor. The shooter racked the Mossberg again, dropping the spent cartridge in the process. Garcia was in the store now, too, shouting for money while Brewer placed the still-smoking weapon on Jason Frost's left side. Frost was already mortally wounded; the enraged man in the devil's mask fired again. The wound was smaller this time, but the gun was again fired at extremely close range. Lying in a pool of blood, his internal organs partially exposed on the cold tile floor, it's hard to imagine any conceivable reason that Jason Frost should have been fired upon again.

Putting the muzzle of the hot gun directly on Jason Frost's left buttock, Brewer, pouring a lifetime of rage into this defenseless young man's already devastated body, squeezed the trigger a third time. Two days before Christmas, Jason Frost was reduced to something that barely resembled a human being. His body lay in pieces. Forensic experts would say later it was unusual to examine a crime scene where a shotgun is fired three times and no pellets are found on the floor, in the walls, or ceiling. Jason Frost's blood, skin, and muscle tissue seemed to be splattered everywhere in the area behind the bread counter. The lead pellets were found deep inside his flesh and organs. So was cardboard wadding from the shells.

By the time the cops and paramedics arrived, the robbers had fled. They got no money. Jason Frost was on the floor, in shock and barely alive.

As the robbers sped from the scene, Dixon kept asking Brewer what had happened. Why had he heard gunshots? How much money did we get? A little less than a mile from Southside Park the Jimmy died again, so they ditched it. Brewer hid his weapon in some bushes—he would return later to retrieve it—and they ran the rest of the way to the park. When they saw a young Asian man about to get into his car near an alley, Dixon went up to him, slammed his fist into the man's face, and demanded the keys. The man resisted, so Dixon and his pals kept running.

Just before the robbers came into the store, Frost had telephoned Megan Gould, the girl he was living with and planned soon to propose to, to say he'd be right home. Worried when he failed to show up, Megan went to the Bread Store to see what was keeping him. She still had a few Christmas presents to wrap and place under the tree, but she'd finish when she got back with Jason. She saw the half-dozen squad cars and yellow police crime-tape blocking off the front entrance and almost passed out.

In Yuba City, a small town about thirty-five miles north of downtown Sacramento, Jack Frost was just sitting down to watch the San Francisco 49ers play the Detroit Lions when the telephone rang. Jack and his son loved the 49ers. They had suffered through some of the usual father-son tension that often went along with a boy's teenage years, but their relationship was good now, getting better all the time. Jack felt the two had cleared up most of the crap between them the summer before, when Jason spent time helping his dad run a boat-rental business up in Lassen National Forest, where the family had a cabin. This was the last *Monday Night Football* game of the season and Jack was looking forward to watching it, but he was much more excited about the next night, when he'd be in Sacramento having Christmas Eve dinner with his son and his girlfriend. Becky, Jason's mother, had drawn a bath and was looking forward to relaxing in it after a day running errands and finishing her Christmas shopping. The next night would be the first time Jack and Becky visited Jason since he and Megan had moved in together a few months earlier. Jason loved to cook and he was planning to serve a Christmas goose for his mom and dad. When the telephone rang, they thought it was Jason wanting to go over some final details for their dinner. It was the police telling them their son had been shot.

The next night, when Steve Harrold, head of the Sacramento

County district attorney's Gangs unit, heard from a detective friend about the shooting, he immediately drove down to police headquarters to see what he could find out. Assistant district attorneys usually don't get involved in a case until detectives come over to the DA's office and tell prosecutors what they know and ask for written authority to file charges. Harrold had just finished prosecuting two gang members from the area for murdering an innocent bystander during a drive-by shooting. He suspected some of the same crowd could have been involved in this one. If that were true, he wanted to be in on this from the beginning.

On January 3, 1997, Jason Frost died. Megan and his parents had been at the hospital the whole time, through ten surgeries. At times they even believed he'd pull through, although it was hard to imagine the shape he'd be in if he had. A few days later, when he might have been thinking about getting married and spending his honeymoon in England, which he'd been reading about in the weeks before his death, Jason Frost was cremated.

The day after the robbery and shooting, an anonymous call had come into the Sacramento Police Department's tip line. The caller was Jamie Salyer, a parolee who said some guy by the name of Rick Brewer was involved. He knew Brewer well and occasionally hung out with him. Salyer later told the cops he was pissed at Brewer because after the first robbery a month earlier, Brewer had shown up at his mom's house, looking for Salyer, and wound up locking himself in the bathroom while he and Michael Smith split the proceeds.

Police went to the apartment Brewer and Flores shared to see what they could learn. Since she paid the bills and was named in the lease, it was up to her whether she let them search without producing a warrant. She said yes, signing a police waiver. Brewer told the cops he didn't live there. After they'd looked in a bedroom closet and found several of his jackets and pairs of shoes—one pair had what appeared to be white baking flour splashed on them—he admitted that, yes, he was staying there with Flores.

Detectives found the Mossberg concealed under the bottom drawer of a bedroom dresser. In a black Oakland Raiders jacket—the Raiders were Brewer's favorite football team—they also found two shotgun shells that fit the gun. Brewer's sister had removed some of his clothing from the apartment, but she missed a few key items. Brewer was arrested for violating his parole—felons aren't allowed to possess guns—but denied knowing anything about the Bread Store robbery.

Harrold was having Christmas-night dinner with his parents when Detective Toni Winfield paged him to say a search of Brewer's apartment had led to what she believed was the weapon used to shoot Jason Frost. It wasn't a murder weapon yet because Jason was clinging to life, but it was only a matter of time. Harrold left the dinner and went back to the police department. He wanted to be there when Winfield started interviewing Brewer and other potential suspects.

Dixon had already been booked into the county jail for a parole violation as a result of his sister notifying the cops about his antics in the stolen Jimmy. The others were arrested within days. Some of the neighborhood punks, interviewed at their homes or at school with no parents around, admitted to detectives that they'd heard the robbers talking about their plans before the crime and afterward about the lethal results. They identified the crew and pointed out the suspects in pictures the cops showed to them.

Dixon lied. He told Winfield he knew nothing about the stolen Jimmy or the robbery and shooting. Glica and Martinez, waiving their rights to have a lawyer present, consented to long interviews with detectives. Both refused to snitch on anyone else—"Snitches end up in ditches," Glica told Sacramento Police Detective Rich Overton—but they admitted what they said were their own minimal roles. Brewer refused to talk. Cervantes told the cops that Brewer let him know sometime after the robbery that things went "real sour downtown."

Garcia lied, too, but Harrold would eventually offer him a deal: Testify truthfully against your pals and you can plead to manslaughter and get off with twelve years instead of the life without parole for first-degree murder everyone else is looking at. Others in the district attorney's office would later question the generous deal, but Harrold thought Garcia could pull the case together and make it work. Brewer, the prosecutor felt strongly, deserved to die.

Steve Harrold, forty-nine at the time of the shooting, is a native of Sacramento born into wealth and privilege. He grew up at country clubs and exclusive men's clubs where his politically connected grandfather and father, owners of one of the largest Ford dealerships in northern California, often held court of their own. For kicks, the wiry prosecutor now likes to compete in hundred-mile runs so punishing, his toenails fall off. He's about five nine, divorced, a ladies' man with two daughters in their twenties who seem destined for great things. Like a lot of career prosecutors, he spent so much time at it over the years, he woke up one day and realized he didn't have much of a marriage left. His daughters live in Berkeley and in New York City, but he still manages to dote on them constantly. A supervisor who doesn't try that many cases himself and often enlists a co-counsel to do much of the heavy lifting when he does, Harrold isn't one of the district attorney's storied trial lawyers. He's a career prosecutor, a good one and an affable gentleman whom virtually everyone in the office likes. His detractors say he may be heavier on flash than substance, but he loves his job. Victims like the Frost family say Harrold's compassion and humanity saved them from going mad.

For all his blue Republican blood, Harrold loves to mix it up with the gangbangers and the punks who commit their own crimes one day and may later hold the key to cases he and his four gangs deputies prosecute. He's comfortable talking their language, and like the personable car salesman his father and grandfather were, he manages to find common ground with everyone.

Assistant DAs don't get to choose their clientele. In an urban prosecutor's office, witnesses you build a case around are often just a shade less unsavory than the defendants you're trying to put away. It's blue-collar law. To succeed, a prosecutor has to be willing and able to deal with all kinds of people. If you're a lawyer looking for civility and intellectual rigor, you go to work for the attorney general or the feds. Maybe you get a job for one of the countless state agencies that surround the Capitol. You go into private practice. If you want real blood-and-guts trial work and the feeling that you're doing someone some good, that you're bringing some measure of relief to a battered family and getting at least a few bad actors off the streets, this is where you want to be.

Murders. Rapes. Sexual assaults against children. Beatings. Robberies. Dope deals. Burglaries. Career criminals and criminals trying to create a career of crime. This is it. Every day of the week, every week of the year. It slows up once in a while, but it never stops.

Every part of a district attorney's office has it own peculiar challenges. In Domestic Violence, victims recant and wind up convinced it's the prosecutor who's the enemy, not the son of a bitch who beat them up. Sex assaults against children break your heart. Homicide prosecutors talk about "twofers": put some asshole away for life because he murdered another piece of shit who'd been in and out prison a half-dozen times before he got taken out for good. Sometimes you get a case like the Bread Store, with a solid family, a righteous victim. Any DA who's being straight will concede those are the cases they get the most worked up about.

All the Bread Store defendants have some gang affiliation in their backgrounds, but Harrold learns early this isn't the gangs case he thought it might have been when he first got the detective's call. It should go to Major Crimes, where one of the homicide prosecutors assigned to the legendary John O'Mara, who runs the section, would try it.

But Harrold was so taken with the Frost family and the love they had for their son, that he was determined to keep the case.

This case, as one article in *The Sacramento Bee* put it, was a simple robbery gone bad. A bakery stickup. Easy in, easy out, turned into anything but. Harrold didn't realize at the time that many of the issues raised in this case as it crawled through the system would be emblematic of the hazards prosecutors must navigate when they try murders anywhere in America: using a snitch; felony murder where the guy who drives the getaway car is just as guilty as the triggerman; dealing with self-serving testimony from accomplices; the fragility of juries; personal animosity among attorneys; arguments about the death penalty; evidence not fully disclosed. Because of the personalities of the attorneys and serious misconduct by one of them, there would be drama and crises no one could possibly have foreseen until the moment they floated to the murky surface.

There is regret in almost every case a prosecutor tries: a life sentence isn't enough, it should have been the death penalty; a victim's family looks to the DA for justice only to feel like victims again from the ordeal of going to trial; any sense of satisfaction is fleeting because even in victory there is another case eating away at you and demanding to have its day in court.

In 2001, O'Mara, District Attorney Jan Scully, and all the Sacramento prosecutors would be confronted with an extraordinary array of cases that would test the office on a daily basis: a prominent doctor would be suspected of murdering his daughter by throwing her out a window; a Ukrainian immigrant with a history of spousal abuse would spark an international manhunt and terror in the local Slavic community after his pregnant wife and six other family members, including his own three-year-old son, were slashed to death; the son of a criminal supervisor in the state attorney general's office would face a potential death sentence in the kidnap, rape, and strangulation of a twelve-year-old girl he abducted from a street near her house while he was on LSD. The sensational case would force the district attorney's office to weigh a potential plea agreement some would suspect was on the table just because the defendant was white, middle class, and had a father with connections.

There would be much more to confound prosecutors over the coming year, including a notorious murder from 1975 involving the kidnapped newspaper heiress Patricia Hearst that would resurface and subject O'Mara and the district attorney to fierce second-guessing and criticism over earlier decisions to not file charges. Nothing would cast a bigger shadow over the office in the coming year than Hearst herself, the once notorious Symbionese Liberation Army, and Myrna Opsahl, a forty-two-year-old churchgoing mother of four gunned down during a politically motivated bank robbery in which her killers were never brought to justice.

The bright, ambitious men and women who prosecute criminals in Sacramento, the capital of America's largest state, will trudge most mornings and afternoons to the county courthouse, rolling their heavy case files across the street with them, to muck around in the sordid underbelly of their community. Each criminal complaint they file will be labeled an affront "against the peace and dignity of the People of the State of California," and they will do their best to restore some of that peace and some of that dignity, knowing that it's often impossible to succeed fully. They'll do much of their work far from the gaze of ordinary citizens, who, unless they're called for jury duty, would have little reason to step inside and join this highly combative, shadowy netherworld in which prosecutors live. They'll dispense with thousands of cases and deal with countless victims and families, an endless array of witnesses and defendants. Inside the courtroom and, more often the case, outside the courtroom, they will exercise their extraordinary power and authority to alter lives forever.

2 | It's Going to Be a Tough Year

Most people are aware that a district attorney, by whatever label he is known, prosecutes those charged with crime, but not many fully appreciate the awesome power vested in the office.
—Martin M. Frank, *Diary of a D.A.*

THE first weekday of a new year is usually filled with hope and promise. By the time John Matthew O'Mara shows up at his office, punctual as ever at 8 A.M. on Tuesday, January 2, his desk is littered with homicide reports, pictures of murder victims, and a stack of videotaped police interrogations of suspected killers. This year at the district attorney's office in Sacramento, California, seems a lot like the previous year.

Crime in Sacramento is not a new phenomenon. In the late 1840s and 1850s, Sacramento was staging ground for the Gold Rush. It had a reputation as a boisterous and rowdy place miners came to so they could buy supplies before hiking up into the Sierras in search of fortune. More than a hundred years later, it is a rapidly growing community in the California heartland, far from the idyllic beaches of Los Angeles or the iconic architecture and topography of San Francisco. Until a few decades ago, when earthquakes and jacked-up real estate prices in those more familiar parts of the Golden State began to push people into the great Central Valley and its biggest city, Sacramento was still a relatively small town. Dominated by rice farms, hop growers, and state workers, the Sacramento of twenty years ago was a slow-moving place. It bustled with activity when the Legislature was in session for six months a year but seldom drew attention for much of anything else. In the summer, when temperatures of 100 degrees were customary, the whole town seemed to take a siesta. Winter months were dominated by wet, cool weather. Thick tule fog would sometimes lie over the city for weeks before being burned off by the sun. Or it would rain so long or hard in the winter and spring, the Sacramento and American rivers, as well as the countless creeks that fed them, would breach their levees. Floods, and the mud and damage they left behind, would be all anybody wanted to talk about.

By the time Sacramento lured a professional basketball team from Kansas City in 1985, the region was in the midst of a building and population boom, fueled in large part by cheap and plentiful real estate that has yet to slow down. For whatever reason, even in its quieter and more obscure past, a metropolitan area now crowded with more than 1.2 million people of all social and ethnic backgrounds has always seemed to have more than its share of bizarre and brutal crime. And for much of the past two decades, the absolute worst of it has passed through John O'Mara's office.

As the longtime head of the Homicide and Major Crimes division of the Sacramento County District Attorney's Office, O'Mara has reviewed more than two thousand murders in his storied career. In each of those homicides, every time the detectives came over to try to convince him to file charges after they had a suspect, O'Mara alone decided whether the cops had collected enough evidence for the DA to accuse someone officially of being a murderer. "The Sell" is what detectives call the not always pleasant ritual of going over to O'Mara's office and trying to get him to see a case the same way they do.

"Whaddya got?" O'Mara says this morning while alternately fiddling with his wire-rimmed reading glasses and tugging at his thick salt-and-pepper mustache. In this pitch, two sheriff's detectives want him to feel as good as they do good about the confession they've gotten from a meth freak by the name of Ryan Kanawyer. The skinny dark-haired kid told them he used a shotgun to blow away his grandparents inside their exclusive gated subdivision because they got tired of throwing money at him and said he couldn't have any more.

"A confession is nice," O'Mara tells Sheriff's Detective Will Bayles, "but that doesn't mean there won't be some big problems down the road." As usual, O'Mara has questions, lots of questions, as he stares at the detective and his partner.

"What about the other kids who were with him? Did they see Ryan with the shotgun? Whose gun was it? Did they know what he was up to? They any sharper than he is? Do they have records? Did you search his place? What were the circumstances of the search? Have you talked to the woman at the guard's gate?"

Bayles has some of the answers, but he has to confess that no one has talked to the security guard yet.

"No?" O'Mara says while thumbing through some paperwork the detectives brought over. "You're shitting me. This is Monday. Grandma and Grandpa were killed a week ago Wednesday. Why not? Have you pressed the other kids? I don't care what sonny boy told you. You know Goddamn well they were in on this. No way they take a ninety-minute ride with this whack job—a sawed-off tucked into his pants—and see him get out of the car with the gun, then wait at the fuckin' Taco Bell and not know what he's up to. If you guys haven't worked them over pretty well by now, we're fucked. They're gonna be all lawyered up next time you see 'em and they won't say shit."

This is how it always seems to go. The cops come over with a case and O'Mara grills them as if the cheap imitation leather chairs across from his desk are the witness stand and they've just been sworn in. He wants them to know arresting a bad guy—police work—is just part of the program. Being able to convict them in court is the prosecutor's job.

"Tell me about the confession," he continues. "Did the kid go down to the police station willingly or did you bullshit him? Did you arrest him or take him against his will? Because even if you didn't, his defense attorney will sure as shit claim you did and then that nice neat, wrapped-in-ribbon confession you're telling me about—that puppy won't be admissible."

Despite being less than fully satisfied, O'Mara signs the complaint charging Kanawyer with first-degree murder and the detectives shuffle out. They want to pay a visit to the suspect at the county jail before arraignment to see if they can get some of O'Mara's questions answered. Most of the cops he's worked with in his more than two decades in the job consider O'Mara a ball breaker of gargantuan proportions. Many of them have refused at various times to come over and talk to him or ask for advice until they've felt sure their cases were locked tight. If they should come over early, they were certain that once he started busting their balls, they'd snap and tell him to go fuck himself.

O'Mara genuinely believes most of the cops are not very bright or if they do get a confession, they stop working. Such cases are always in jeopardy because if a smart defense lawyer can show the confession was obtained improperly and get it tossed out of court, which they always tried to do, the DA will lose the case.

After the detectives have left, O'Mara comes out of his office. Frank Meyer, a homicide prosecutor to whom O'Mara will assign the case, is pulling some warmed-up coffee out of the office microwave. A thin, nervous prosecutor who's making a career comeback after being banished to workmen's comp fraud a few years back for some perceived show of disloyalty, Meyer happens to live in Rancho Murieta, the community southeast of downtown where the murder occurred.

"These guys just don't get it," O'Mara tells Meyer. "No way do you rob Grandma and Grandpa with a shotgun without killing them. As soon as you get to the gate at Rancho Murieta, the guard calls ahead, you've been ID'd and you get arrested. How can these other people in the car not know about the shotgun? That doesn't even pass the straight-face test."

Ray Biondi, who retired from the sheriff's department after thirty-one years, including seventeen as chief of Homicide, calls O'Mara a dinosaur, because he just wants to be a prosecutor and not a judge.

"I learned over the years that if John said the case was a piece of shit, it was. No one reviewed a case like John O'Mara. John knew every single detail better than we did. You didn't always want to admit it, but it was a great learning experience for a detective to realize that whatever John said about your case was right. I'd stack O'Mara up against any prosecutor in the country on any measure you use."

Most of the people who run Major Crimes or Homicide divisions in large prosecutors' offices use the position as a stepping-stone to become the elected district attorney. Or they fraternize with the right person on the governor's staff—or someone who knows the right person on the governor's staff—and get themselves appointed to the bench. Whenever the subject of trying to become a judge would come up, O'Mara would demure that the job held no appeal for him. All they do is sit up there and referee, he believed. "When they carry me out of here and I retire, this is the only job I'll ever have. I got no fuckin' interest in any of the rest of it."

After the cops shuffle out, O'Mara will usually close the door to his tiny, cramped office, lean back in his oversized leather chair, and study their reports. He'll make the call on his own. If it's clear cut, he may immediately assign the case to a deputy and let him or her review all the evidence. Sometimes, he tells the cops they need to go out and do more investigative work. If he decides to file, which he usually does after giving them a hard time, he'll have his secretary type up a criminal complaint. When she's finished, he'll sign his name and charge someone with violating *Title VIII of the California Penal Code, Crimes Against the Person, Chapter One, Section 187: Murder . . . the unlawful killing of a human being, or fetus, with malice aforethought.* Depending on how he finally sizes up the case and the possible outcome of a trial—if the charge isn't negotiated beforehand with some type of guilty plea—O'Mara's decision will cause a defendant to be tried on charges that could send him to prison for life or to death row.

He makes the decision about who should be assigned to prosecute every murder, often reserving the toughest or most complex cases for himself. There's little rhyme or reason to how he assigns cases. He looks at a "cheat sheet" that lists everyone's workload and sees who's light. If a sensational, particularly high profile murder comes in, he likes to spread those around so each of his eight deputies has a chance to get some public recognition and experience the big case.

For more than two decades, with the coming and going of elected sheriffs, appointed police chiefs, and five elected district attorneys, John O'Mara has run the Homicide and Major Crimes unit of the district attorney's office. In the past several years, as District Attorney Jan Scully— she began her third term in 2002—has pushed him to take on more day-to-day authority over felony, intake, and other units in her office, O'Mara has emerged as the heart and soul of the place. She's the boss, but O'Mara is clearly the dominant voice and personality in the office.

In capital cases, there has always been an elected district attorney to sign off on O'Mara's course of action and stand behind it to the public. But for more than twenty years he's been the one person in all of Sacramento County who actually decided whether to seek the death penalty.

Neither Scully nor the four other DAs O'Mara has worked under has ever overruled him in a capital case. O'Mara alone makes the life-or-death decision based on what he feels is appropriate. When he's asked to explain what makes a capital case, he paraphrases what the late supreme court justice Potter Stewart once wrote about obscenity. It's a hard thing to define, O'Mara says, "but I know one when I see one."

Due to his disposition toward privacy and his distaste for blowing his own horn in the news media, he's virtually unknown to the public at large. Even when he tried cases all the time, he rarely gave interviews or made himself available to reporters. He did his talking in the courtroom.

His office in a corner of the fourth floor feels like the hub of the place. Deputies knock and come in for advice about how to handle a touchy piece of evidence or a recalcitrant witness. A defense attorney will call, saying he has some information he wants to share in hopes of knocking a first-degree murder down to a second. Cops come in with updates on murders, to ask for affidavits they'll need to take to a judge so they can get a search warrant, or they sit on the fake leather chairs and lay out a case from start to finish. He's in at eight o'clock every day, takes a half-hour lunch break at noon after a quick stop in the room with the vending machines, and is usually gone by five or five-thirty. He's not in trial these days, so there are few late nights and working weekends.

There are prosecutors who behave as rigid, fire-breathing ideologues, firm in the belief they're doing the Lord's work keeping the capital city safe from depraved killers. O'Mara is not one of them. He's a career prosecutor in the classic sense of the term. It's a job, he tells everyone who tries to probe his motives. Most days, he'd rather be alone on the five acres of grassland he lives on beyond the southern suburbs, sipping Coors Lights and using his hands to build fences and barns, cut the grass, or keep watch over the two dozen or so Barbados sheep, old goats, and ducks he keeps for no other reason than he seems to like them.

Despite his curmudgeonly personality, he lives in a bright, cheery house whose walls are covered with family pictures, oil paintings of California landscapes, and large, striking pencil drawings of animals and family members sketched by his brother, Tom, who lives a few miles down the road.

It's a house for a family. O'Mara and his wife, Patsy, raised their two children here. Remnants of those hectic, noisy days are everywhere. The elaborate Victorian dollhouse he took months to build when his daughter was small. The pool table his son still plays on all night long with old friends when he comes home to spend the summers. Patsy died in 1998 from lung cancer just as O'Mara was to try one of his biggest cases, a thirteen-year-old murder of a young woman abducted from a shopping center while buying last-minute items for Christmas Eve dinner she was planning for her parents. Connor is off in college in San Diego, and Molly lives in Colorado, where she skis and waits tables at a restaurant in Vail. O'Mara rattles around his property mostly by himself and enjoys it that way.

After more than twenty years of mucking around with murder, O'Mara relies on his gallows humor to help him get through the day. It's often on display during the office ritual known as the Four o'Clock Follies, when attorneys return from court and sit around on the couch and chairs outside O'Mara's office riffing back and forth about what happened in trial that day, what some fool defense attorney tried to pull off, how a witness tanked, what a judge ruled. Or he'll watch an interrogation tape alone in his office and chuckle cynically when detectives make their inevitable speech to some murder accomplice or knowing witness about this is the time to come clean and tell us what you know.

To an outsider not familiar with the ways of the men and women who prosecute serious crime for a living, it might be shocking to see the head of Homicide watching a police tape about a heinous murder and laughing like some adolescent at the Cineplex for the latest summer comedy. It's partly a self-defense mechanism, a way to blow off steam and put some distance between what you do and who you are. If you do this kind of work and let every killing and tragedy invade your heart and soul, you'll go mad. To say nothing of probably not having the guts to leave the house in the morning for fear of what's out there.

In the Bread Store case, Harrold wrote a long memo arguing that Brewer deserved the death penalty. The murder was senseless, Harrold argued. It was carried out execution-style. Brewer was extremely violent, bound to kill again, even in prison. O'Mara disagreed. Brewer was a badass but didn't have a prior record of violence. While the killing was heinous and unprovoked, O'Mara thought life without parole was an appropriate disposition for the DA. *I disagree with Steve,* he scribbled in the margins of Harrold's memo before passing it on to Scully for review. The district attorney didn't seek the death penalty on Rick Brewer.

In February 2002, the Ninth Circuit Federal Court of Appeals overturned four death cases in three weeks, including one from Sacramento. A month later, the appeals court overturned a Sacramento case after finding that a prosecutor, who worked under O'Mara at the time, didn't adequately disclose to the jury a deal made with a snitch, and a woman was ordered freed after serving sixteen years of a thirty-two-to-life sentence.

"What is the point of getting a death penalty case and then fifteen years from now we're going to have to try it all over again?" O'Mara said. "We can't find half the witnesses by that time. There's nothing wrong with life without parole if that's really what it means. Life without parole. Hell, we have six hundred men on California death row. Something like twelve women. We put three on death row a week and it takes fifteen years to get rid of one. This isn't Georgia or Texas or Florida, where people are really likely to get executed."

That such extraordinary life-or-death power has resided for so long with one individual has never bothered Sacramento's contentious defense bar enough for anyone to challenge the DA's policy or its record in capital cases. Even the most pugnacious defense lawyers in town have never suggested O'Mara has abused his authority.

That doesn't mean he won't abuse people in his own office. If they knock on his often-closed door and hear the muffled "Come in" from the other side, they'd better be prepared for him to challenge whatever they say or do—and to toss it right back.

"He loves to see people squirm," says Don Steed, a tough ex-cop who became a prosecutor and did homicides for O'Mara for years before O'Mara exiled him downstairs early in 2001 to run the DA's Intake unit. The intake deputies were agreeing to file too many bullshit charges that would only get thrown out later. Scully and her chief deputy, Cindy Besemer, were tired of hearing complaints about Intake, the first point of contact between cop and prosecutor, from felony trial supervisors who were forced to work and eventually toss the bad cases. They put the division under O'Mara's umbrella of divisions that he ran, an umbrella that seemed to keep getting bigger, and essentially said: Okay, smart guy. It's yours. Fix it.

O'Mara sent his old buddy down there—Steed probably knows him better than anyone else in the office—and most of the problems were gone in a couple of weeks. Steed, who had been sulking in Major Crimes after a failed campaign to get himself elected to the bench, had the balls to tell the cops no.

If Steed's not happy with his new position, which he isn't, well, O'Mara can't help that. The problem needed to be fixed and he knew Steed could fix it. O'Mara can be a prick, any cop or sheriff's detective who ever worked homicide in this town, will raise his right hand and swear. "Your wife was an angel," Detective Stan Reed told him when O'Mara's wife died in 1998 and Reed was paying his respects at her funeral. "Yeah, but I'm still an asshole," O'Mara shot back. They both knew he was right.

Aside from his reputation of being a ball breaker, O'Mara is known by judges, defense lawyers, cops, and deputies in the office as someone who plays it straight all the time. He's certainly not alone in his commitment to the principle of honest and full disclosure to defense lawyers, for instance, but in large part because of O'Mara's ethics and his long-held power and sway within the DA's office, the Sacramento district attorney over the years has not suffered the embarrassing history, say, of Los Angeles, for bad judgment and blowing big cases. Sacramento hasn't had its own version of the O. J. Simpson debacle, no Menendez brothers fiasco, Rodney King or a host of other infamous blunders that led Steve Cooley, the current DA in Los Angeles County, to campaign in large part on a pledge to reverse the L.A. district attorney's record of blowing big case after big case.

It's no accident that the office has been highly regarded around the state in the years he's been there or that in 1996, the California District Attorneys Association named O'Mara California Prosecutor of the Year. Lawyers in the state attorney general's office, who handle criminal appeals of cases from district attorneys all over the state, are quick to say they've been as impressed with Sacramento's quality of work over the last twenty years as they were with any other DA's office in California.

In many ways, 2001 will be a typical year. In the prelim unit that is part of O'Mara's domain, where new prosecutors hold as many as five or six probable-cause hearings a day before judges who'll determine if there's enough evidence to warrant a full-blown trial, no more than four young deputies working in court at any one time will rip through 2,934 cases during the year—an inconceivable number, considering each one requires sitting down with cops and witnesses to sort out conflicting or confusing evidence and testimony. They'll take 306 negotiated guilty pleas that will make it unnecessary to assign a felony deputy for an actual trial. Many more will be disposed of at the trial level under pressure from judges demanding that cases be settled, before a single juror is selected. O'Mara and the other top officials in the office pay close attention to prosecutors' won-and-lost records and how often they go to trial. Ambitious prosecutors are always jockeying to move to more glamorous and fulfilling assignments. They're looking to rise up the civil-service job rankings that bring higher pay and prestige and offices with a window. The best ones all seem to want to get to Major Crimes, the top of the mountain for most prosecutors. For all the talk prosecutors like to engage in about how their number-one priority is to seek justice, not just win trials, it's numbers—trials completed, trials won, and trials lost— that mean everything. It doesn't take long for the gun-shy prosecutor with a knack for settling cases before going to trial to be tagged with the kind of "no-balls" reputation he or she never lives down.

Several thousand more cases will be negotiated out in a unit of the district attorney's office called SCR, or Superior Court Review, where *not* going to trial is the aim. Courtrooms where these cases are negotiated resemble some loud, exotic Middle Eastern bazaar. Prosecutors and defense attorneys in dark suits take the place of merchants hawking their wares. Instead of haggling over spices and hand-woven rugs, it's jail sentences and terms of probation that are bartered over. Thousands of cases are disposed of in this way each year. They have to be or the system would collapse under its own weight. It all happens so fast, if you look the other way for an instant, it's easy to miss a case.

Overall, about 13,000 felonies are brought to the Sacramento DA's office every year. It will file on 11,000 to 12,000 of them. A typical year will see as many as 30,000 misdemeanors come in; the DA will file charges on about eighty percent. The vast majority, as many as eighty-five percent of felonies and misdemeanors, will be settled before trial.

The ones that aren't settled, where the crime's too serious to offer a deal and the defendant wants to take his chances at trial, are more than enough to keep an office of 180 attorneys and a like number of investigators and other support personnel cranking for much of the year.

For someone at it as long as O'Mara, Sacramento can feel like one giant crime scene, yellow police tape around its borders, evidence technicians dusting for prints, searching for physical evidence, examining blood spatter, scrambling through bushes, and diving into lakes and rivers for murder weapons. Every street corner is an interrogation room where cops give the bad guys their bullshit and the bad guys give the cops theirs.

When he drives through the California capital, he's reminded of murders the way some people are reminded of parks their kids might have played soccer in, houses where friends used to live, schools they once attended, fields they might have tossed a ball in while growing up.

About to turn fifty-five, John O'Mara—onetime Catholic altar boy, son of a San Francisco Bay Area homebuilder, and law student almost as a lark—has more than held his own during nearly twenty-five years of prosecuting murder cases. But as he limps off the elevator the morning of Tuesday, January 2, his sore right knee acting up again, and pulls himself into the oversized, plush leather chair at his desk that a former DA insisted on buying him as a reward for his long hours and hard work, he's in a dark mood.

It's been several years since O'Mara went across the street to slay a dragon before a judge and jury. But no one can recall the last time he was faced with so much second-guessing about a major case as he's getting, one simply known around the office as "the SLA case." It's Patty Hearst revisited, twenty-seven years after the fact.

The year 2001 will be one of his most difficult. He and Scully will be the ones forced to squirm under tough, nonstop second-guessing from the victim's family, officials in Los Angeles, the Sacramento Sheriff's Department, and the news media. The old SLA case looms over him like one of those January Sacramento thunderclouds that can blacken the sky and dump enough rain in an hour or two to overflow the creeks, clog sewers, and fill hundreds of streets and intersections with dark water. There is no avoiding it anymore, even if he wanted to. He knows he is going to get dumped on.

In the first few weeks of 2001 a spate of front-page articles in some of the state's leading newspapers reveal behind-the-scenes pressure being applied to the Sacramento DA's office to finally file charges in the 1975 suburban Sacramento bank robbery and murder that involved Hearst. The newspaper heiress had become an object of national obsession a year earlier when a group calling itself the Symbionese Liberation Army kidnapped her at gunpoint from her college apartment in Berkeley.

The ragtag collection of middle-class revolutionaries made international headlines when they abducted Hearst, whose grandfather happened to have been William Randolph Hearst, the newspaper tycoon and American icon immortalized in the classic film *Citizen Kane*. The kidnapping and subsequent SLA crime spree were one great irrational last gasp of the Days of Rage emanating from Vietnam War protests, the Kennedy assassinations, the murder of Martin Luther King, Jr., urban race riots, and a government often at violent odds with its middle-class children.

Springing up from a movement of white California college kids who worked on behalf of the rights of black prison inmates in the state, the SLA became one of the most bizarre and closely followed dramas of the 1970s. Locked in a closet and psychologically brutalized for fifty-seven days, waiflike Patty Hearst was transformed over a period of weeks from the naïve nineteen-year-old daughter of one America's wealthiest and most influential families to machine-gun-toting revolutionary. The country was divided over whether she was brainwashed or willingly assumed her new identity and political beliefs, but at some point she seemed to have thrown in with her captors. She assumed the revolutionary nom-de-guerre "Tania," after a guerrilla who had fought in Bolivia with Communist rebel Che Guevara.

Hearst, whose parents acceded to the terrorists' demands and put $2 million into an ill-fated program to feed California's poor, in a series of SLA communiqués publicized around the world came to disavow everything about her privileged upbringing. As a consequence, the world has never been quite sure what to make of her. The day before six SLA members, including those who had kidnapped her, were killed in a fiery shootout with Los Angeles police and FBI agents that was captured on live television, Patty strafed the front of a Los Angeles sporting goods store with machine gun fire to help two of her captors, Bill and Emily

Harris, avoid getting arrested for shoplifting. She helped rob banks to finance the SLA's perverse People's Revolution, eventually providing information about a string of California bombings that could be tied to the group. In one such robbery that occurred in the Sacramento suburb of Carmichael, Hearst admitted that she had driven a switch car used in the getaway, and described how Emily Harris, aka Yolanda, aimed a shotgun at a Sacramento mother of four and accidentally blew a hole in her side that killed her. "Oh, she's dead," Harris supposedly told her comrades, "but it really doesn't matter. She was a bourgeois pig anyway. Her husband is a doctor." Over the years, Jon Opsahl, fifteen at the time Myrna Opsahl was killed, would come back to that statement again and again, obsessed with the cavalier disregard shown for his mother's life.

Geoff Burroughs, the Sacramento deputy district attorney who ran Major Crimes at the time, wanted to prosecute the suspects in 1975 after they were arrested in San Francisco on other charges, including a bank job there. Following a lengthy investigation, Burroughs concluded there wasn't enough evidence to back up Hearst's story. Only one of the suspected Carmichael bank robbers, Steven Soliah, was charged, and he was found not guilty in a botched federal bank robbery trial.

At the urging of Sacramento Sheriff's Department homicide detectives who couldn't stand the fact that the case had never been prosecuted, particularly after Hearst detailed the crime in her 1982 autobiography, O'Mara reviewed the evidence again in 1990–91. He convened a grand jury and called a reluctant Hearst as his star witness. But again, a determination was made—by him, this time—that the case wasn't provable. Now, with 2001 barely a few days old, new pressure is being applied to the office to bring the killers of forty-two-year-old Myrna Opsahl to justice.

The case took on new urgency due to the surprise and sudden arrest in the summer of 1999 of Kathleen Soliah, an SLA sympathizer, and Steven Soliah's sister, who Hearst had said participated in the robbery and was inside the Carmichael branch of Crocker National Bank when Mrs. Opsahl was killed. Kathleen Soliah had been armed with a 9mm handgun, according to Hearst, and a backpack filled with ammunition that, in her haste, she spilled throughout the bank and parking lot. Soliah's job, according to Hearst's account, was to fill up the money bags.

A little more than a month after the TV show *America's Most Wanted* ran a segment on the twenty-fifth anniversary of the SLA shootout in Los Angeles, federal agents in St. Paul, Minnesota, acting on a tip from a viewer, arrested Soliah. For the past twenty years, she'd been living there under the name Sara Jane Olson. She'd married a doctor, had three daughters, and had become a soccer mom. She was a community volunteer, reading to the blind, getting involved in various liberal political causes. She ran marathons and acted in a local theater company. Newspapers in the Twin Cities often gave favorable reviews to her performances. She was hiding out in the open. Within a day or two of her arrest, veteran Sacramento Sheriff's Detective Bob Bell and a partner met with O'Mara and again urged him to reopen the case.

Authorities in Los Angeles were most anxious to get hold of Soliah, who, shortly after being released on $1 million bail raised by friends and supporters, legally changed her name to Sara Jane Olson, a name inspired by a Bob Dylan song she loved. The Los Angeles district attorney's office had open charges against her that she had planted bombs under police cars in August of 1975. The city's police department had never let go of the notion that someone should be tried and sent to prison for risking the lives of its officers and innocent civilians who could have been killed had the bombs gone off. Authorities believed she and her boyfriend at the time, James Kilgore, planted the bombs in retaliation for the L.A. shootout. Soliah's best friend, Angela Atwood, was among those who had lost their lives. Soliah organized a protest in Berkeley a few weeks after the shootout and, with the TV news cameras rolling, appeared to be speaking directly to surviving SLA members when she proclaimed, "Keep fighting. I'm with you. We're with you."

While the bombs under the LAPD patrol cars didn't detonate—one planted on a car parked outside a crowded restaurant missed the mark when a firing pin slipped one sixteenth of an inch off its target—they were loaded with a hundred heavy-duty construction nails and considered extremely deadly. Police were expecting to find Soliah when they raided two SLA safehouses in San Francisco on September 18, 1975, but she had already become a fugitive. Hearst, the Harrises, and Wendy Yoshimura, another SLA associate, were arrested instead. Soliah was gone. She stayed gone for two decades.

With Soliah suddenly in custody in the summer of 1999 and the Los Angeles district attorney's reactivating its case against her, the situation in Sacramento was now different. The FBI had only partial fingerprints of Soliah on file while she was a fugitive, but when she was captured, a full set of major case prints were taken. Now they could be matched to a full palm print found and filed twenty-four years earlier on the padlock to a garage SLA members had leased in Sacramento to hide stolen and rented cars used in the Carmichael robbery and other crimes.

Bell, the detective who'd been working the case, had retired from the Sacramento Sheriff's Department and was now a DA's investigator working in Major Crimes. Within days of Soliah's arrest, he called members of the Opsahl family to tell them it was possible a new case would soon be developed against Mrs. Opsahl's killers.

"I spoke by phone with the victim's son, Roy Opsahl," Bell's notes from July 19, 1999, say. "Opsahl advised this detective that he was misquoted in the papers where he was saying that he did not wish this investigation to go forward. I explained to Opsahl the circumstances surrounding the legal difficulties concerning this case and added, however, that the circumstantial evidence was very strong. Roy Opsahl concluded by indicating that he, too, wished to have this investigation go forward if there were any viable leads at all."

By January 2001, it has been eighteen months since Soliah's arrest. Dr. Trygve Opsahl, the dead woman's husband, and Jon, one of her four grown children and also a physician, have come up for a meeting with District Attorney Jan Scully and her top staff. They want to know whether Olson's arrest will finally bring their mother's alleged killers to trial. Prosecutors in Los Angeles have been telling anyone who will listen that Sacramento has been sitting on a murder case involving Soliah and others that is much stronger than the case they had. They have offered to hold off prosecuting Olson if Sacramento goes ahead and tries her and other SLA members in the more serious Opsahl murder. O'Mara and Scully are convinced L.A. is taking the highly unusual step of pushing the Sacramento case in favor of their own because the Los Angeles case is weak and prosecutors there are looking for a way out.

After being notified and briefed by the L.A. prosecutors, Jon Opsahl has accused the Sacramento district attorney's office of being too timid and incompetent to try his mother's murder. He has become convinced after listening to L.A. prosecutors Mike Latin and Eleanor Hunter lay out the details that Sacramento has the more compelling evidence. O'Mara is not at all eager to meet with the Opsahls, since he figures they are doing L.A.'s bidding, but Scully tells him this is one meeting she will not let him skip.

The district attorney relies on O'Mara and other top deputies in the office to keep her steeped in the details of the county's most controversial and high profile cases. By her own admission, Scully is the politician, "the face," as she has put it on more than one occasion. Tall and thin with brown hair she wears short, Scully is the liaison to the community, the county board of supervisors who set the district attorney's budget, and the various special interest groups and victims' advocates who want to influence local criminal justice policy. She's the top law-enforcement official in the county and while people in her own office questioned whether she was up to the job when she first ran in 1994, she has grown to the point where when she runs for a third term in the March 5, 2002, primary election, it will be the second time in a row Scully will run unopposed. In an office where part of the culture is for prosecutors to walk around believing they can do a better job than whoever holds the top position, that's a highly significant accomplishment— even more so, given Scully's history.

Scully was forty-four, a sex-crimes supervisor for eight years and not thought of as one of the DA's star prosecutors, when she decided to run for the top job against Steve White, an unpopular incumbent. Nine days after she was elected over White and another supervisor with a strong record trying big cases, Steve Scully, her husband of eight years and the father of her five-year-old daughter and seven-year-old son, had a heart attack and died while swimming laps at his health club. Scully hadn't even been sworn in yet and suddenly she was the DA-elect and a single mother. The shattering loss left her both tougher and with an even greater appreciation of how a victim responds to loss, and with a commitment to balance her demanding job with her very real demands at home. She has since remarried a Sacramento oral surgeon, but neither voters nor most people in her office seem to begrudge her for making sure she doesn't devote so much time to her job that her family suffers.

Scully wouldn't consider meeting with a crime victim's family—especially one as angry as the Opsahls—without the line prosecutor at her side to answer questions and explain the intricacies of the case. Even though he's never filed charges in the 1975 robbery and murder, O'Mara arguably knows more about the case and all of its strengths and short-comings than anyone.

O'Mara expects the meeting, which has been set for February 8, to get ugly. He expects that somehow the family will use whatever's said between them as more fodder for its pressure campaign.

Jon Opsahl has already said he was amazed when he learned of the Sacramento evidence from Los Angeles prosecutors. His refrain ever since has been that O'Mara may have a great reputation as a tough prosecutor, but that's because he's a "cherry picker." He only takes cases he knows he can win. On a big, high-stakes case like this, the Opsahls are convinced it takes far more able and sophisticated prosecutors, like the ones in the Los Angeles District Attorney's Office who've romanced the Opsahls almost from the time Soliah was arrested. If not L.A., maybe the California attorney general or United States attorney would step in. To Opsahl, the evidence against those he believes murdered his mother seem like more than enough to file charges and hold someone account-able.

Hearst has admitted in her autobiography, in interviews with the FBI, and in testimony to O'Mara's grand jury that she was part of the robbery team. She said she waited a short distance away in a switch car, a rented white Volkswagen van, and drove the thieves to safety after another get-away car, which Hearst said was driven by Bay Area radical Wendy Yoshimura, was abandoned.

Myrna Opsahl came into the Crocker Bank carrying a heavy portable adding machine that would tally up her deposit from the Carmichael Seventh-Day Adventist Church, where she was a volunteer. One of the robbers, James Kilgore, held open the door for Mrs. Opsahl and two other women, according to Hearst. As soon as they got inside the bank, the SLA members put on ski masks and yelled for everyone to get down on the floor.

Bill Harris and Steven Soliah waited outside the bank, according to Hearst's account, in their stolen blue Ford Mustang with the recognizable license plate 916LBJ. The numbers are Sacramento's area code, the initials belong to former U.S. president Lyndon Baines Johnson. Although they weren't identified until months later, the license plates on the Mustang, stolen off another vehicle in a college parking lot, were found to have fingerprints on them belonging to Kilgore and Steve

Soliah. Harris and Soliah were outside, according to Hearst, because Bill Harris, aka Teko, boasted he was the best shot and could easily pick off the "pigs" if they showed up while the others were inside. Steven Soliah was the second-best shot and still nursing five broken ribs from a car accident. Inside the bank, according to Hearst, were Kilgore, Kathleen Soliah, Emily Harris, and Mike Bortin, who remains married to Soliah/Olson's sister, Josephine.

Emily Harris, the most high-strung member of the group, was angry that the men were always in charge, according to Hearst, so she insisted on being boss inside the bank. She also ignored the others who told her not to carry the twelve-gauge shotgun, which had a hair trigger. During dress rehearsals, Hearst said the shotgun kept accidentally firing dry, before it was loaded. Emily Harris, at the same time she loudly counted off the seconds from a stopwatch, according to Hearst's account, pointed the twelve-gauge at customers and barked orders. She apparently told Mrs. Opsahl and others to get down on the floor but for some reason, Mrs. Opsahl didn't respond right away. Harris jerked the gun in her direction to get her to move, and according to Hearst, it accidentally fired. Mrs. Opsahl was hit in the left side. She might have survived had she gotten immediate medical care, but she was allowed to bleed for some twenty minutes while the robbers collected their loot.

While his wife was trapped in the middle of this unfolding robbery, Dr. Trygve Opsahl made his morning rounds at a nearby suburban hospital, where he was employed as a surgeon. His mother's death traumatized Jon, who for a long time used to call out for her when he came home each day, refusing to believe she was dead. When he saw a station wagon that looked like hers, he expected to see her driving. He has two brothers and a sister, but for some reason he says he seemed to take his mother's death the hardest. He learned later that his father, who came to the hospital emergency room to find his wife lying dead on a gurney, cried himself to sleep every night for a year.

United States Attorney Dwayne Keyes considered calling Hearst as a witness in the federal case against Steven Soliah, but elected not to. She was a convicted felon, of course, already found guilty for participating in an SLA bank robbery in San Francisco, and facing possible accomplice charges in Carmichael as well. She and Soliah had also been lovers, so it would have been logical to suspect she might try to protect him in some way. Her account of the Carmichael robbery differed in some very impor-tant details from those of several witnesses who insisted Steven Soliah was among the robbers inside the bank barking orders and waving a shot-gun. Either Hearst or the other witnesses were mistaken. After spending hours going over the incident with Hearst, who insisted her version was correct and said she'd be willing to testify against her onetime lover, Keyes wrote a memo to his file that said he considered her version of events to contain "possible deception" and "outright untruthfulness."

For the Sacramento County Sheriff's Department and the Sacramento District Attorney's Office, the Carmichael bank robbery is one of those hideous failures that just won't seem to go away. Four different elected Sacramento DAs have examined the case since 1975. For a variety of reasons, each elected not to file charges. The primary stumbling block is fairly straightforward and easy to understand. California law requires corroboration when an accomplice to a crime testifies against other ac-complices. Without strong evidence—physical, circumstantial, or from witnesses or other accomplices—Hearst's testimony might prove explo-sive but wouldn't necessarily result in a conviction. And without some insider sorting everything out for the jury—and Hearst has always been seen as the only possible insider who could and would be willing to do it—the district attorney's office has believed the rest of the evidence doesn't carry enough weight to make the case work. This has been the official opinion of the Sacramento County District Attorney's Office since 1976. "Everyone wants to make a big deal about what I did or didn't do in '90 and '91," O'Mara says, "but this goes back a lot farther than me."

The Sacramento DA's official opinion was initially spelled out in an internal memorandum dated June 7 that same year. Its contents and conclusion would be cited time and again over the next twenty-five years as the principal explanation for not filing charges in the case. It was written to "FILE" by Geoff Burroughs. "Two primary considerations exist in assessing the likelihood of a successful prosecution," wrote Bur-roughs, who's retired and still lives in Sacramento and is occasionally in touch with O'Mara. "Firstly, Patricia Hearst is obviously an accomplice. Therefore, in order to use her testimony we must produce corroborative evidence . . . and our evidence fails to meet the standard required of corroborative evidence."

O'Mara never held out hope that other SLA members could be induced to testify against their old partners, thereby corroborating what Hearst has said. They still cling to their antigovernment beliefs and have given plenty of signs over the years that they're unwilling to rat out their co-suspects. Yoshimura testified before the O'Mara-led grand jury under a grant of immunity on March 18, 1991, and admitted she participated in the robbery. She also accurately described what Hearst said she was wearing that day and the disguise that witnesses attributed to a woman driving the getaway car Yoshimura was in. But when it came time to say who else participated, Yoshimura said she couldn't remember.

To make Hearst an effective and credible witness, O'Mara has always insisted she'd have to be willing to spend days, if not weeks, in preparation for her testimony, going over every detail from an old case and life she has tried for nearly three decades to put behind her. She wasn't willing to do this in 1990, and as 2001 gets under way and people outside the office are clamoring for charges to be filed in Sacramento, O'Mara's seen little to change his mind about her willingness to do the work necessary to sell a jury and stand up under fierce cross-examination in court from the other side.

O'Mara is being second-guessed even by some of his colleagues. Mark Curry, a prosecutor on O'Mara's homicide team, has tried to argue that someone from the Sacramento DA should feel out Olson and the prosecutors in Los Angeles, to see whether a deal could be struck. O'Mara's made no overture to Hearst in ten years, so his belief she's less than genuine about testifying effectively is based on past experience only.

"How do you know Sara Jane Olson wouldn't make a deal?" Curry asked a few of his colleagues more than once. "She has three kids. She's married to a doctor. She has a hell of a lot to lose. I'd just go in fresh and see if you could hook someone up and get the case moving. I don't get John's approach."

O'Mara feels certain such overtures are a waste. He believes that Olson and the others, while they've disavowed the violent tendencies of their youth, would never help the DA prosecute a case against their old comrades. As fresh evidence, O'Mara can point to a series of conversations between investigator Bell and Stuart Hanlon, a Bay Area attorney and longtime friend of Olson's who also represented her for a time. Bell's official report from a conversation he had with Hanlon says the lawyer told Bell that Soliah insisted she was not a member of the SLA and had had no role in any bank robberies. Despite ample evidence to the contrary, she swears she wasn't even in Sacramento at the time. Hearst wrote in her book and said in her grand jury testimony that Soliah/Olson climbed over the teller counters and took the cash. She also kicked a pregnant bank employee, who later miscarried, in the stomach. In Hearst's telling she took great pride in boasting to her accomplices that she was able to get all the cash from the drive-up teller's window.

In the typical fashion of the small town it was at the time, Sacramento sheriff's officials concede they abdicated their role in investigating the bank robbery and murder. They stepped aside and let the FBI take over. Given the agency's obsession over the SLA's antigovernment rhetoric and misdeeds, prosecuting someone for Mrs. Opsahl's murder was almost an afterthought.

The Opsahl murder occurred in a different era. In 1975, a sheriff in Sacramento didn't have the clout to stand up to the FBI, especially on a case that was part of one of the biggest manhunts in the agency's history.

"It happened in our jurisdiction and we didn't even investigate," says Bell, who worked the case originally as a sheriff's homicide detective. Bell, who has lived with the Opsahl murder for more than twenty-five years, has also been the strongest local advocate for reopening it and finally filing charges. Like Curry, he, too, believed O'Mara was being overly cautious in not moving to file charges following Olson's arrest in 1999.

The air is cool and clear the morning of February 8 as the Sacramento prosecutors wait for the Opsahls to arrive. The fog, for a change, is gone. The winter rains have let up and the sun is shining brightly, almost blinding as it sits low on the horizon. The temperature outside is no more than 45 degrees. Inside the district attorney's office, Scully's personal assistants are scurrying around nervously. Diane Richardson and Vineeta Chand are arranging and rearranging chairs around Scully's inner-office conference table. Scully and her assistant, Besemer, want the meeting small. The two women have been friends for years, ever since working together early in their careers. Besemer has always been the bad cop in the office to Scully's good cop.

"Better keep O'Mara at safe distance," Besemer says, as if she knows what's coming. "If he goes off, it'll be better if he's a few chairs away."

"Remember, don't let this go on forever," says Robin Shakely, who used to prosecute child homicides but has been handling Scully's press relations since deciding she needed a break. "Let's hear them out, explain our position, and say Jan has another appointment. Not too many elected DAs would even participate in such a meeting."

Jon and Trygve Opsahl, Myrna's now-elderly husband, sit across from one another. Trygve's second wife is with him, as are two advocates for victims, including Genelle Reilly, a member of the statewide group Justice for Homicide Victims. The guests are in their seats, and after Scully thanks everyone for coming and says it's good to open up this dialogue, she tries to set the tone right away. She alludes to "a very politically sensitive situation" where prosecutors in one jurisdiction—Los Angeles—are conducting a public relations campaign to influence how prosecutors in another jurisdiction—Sacramento—handle a case. "As hard as it is at times, we're not going to make a decision based on politics," she tells the visitors. "We're going to make it on our own experience and what we have to work with."

She turns it over to O'Mara, who starts out slowly and calmly. Instead of the rumpled khakis, plaid shirt, and Sperry Top-Siders he wears most days when he's not in court, he's got on a black-and-white herringbone suit, starched white shirt, and bright, patterned tie. His shaggy hair is combed so it rests behind his ears; it appears as if he's trimmed his mustache. He tells the family he first got involved in Mrs. Opsahl's death in 1989, after two different district attorneys had examined the case and elected not to prosecute. There always were two issues, he says: if someone could be found to corroborate Hearst's testimony and how twelve people off the street would feel about her. Would they believe her enough to convict four or five people of murder?

Biondi, the sheriff's homicide chief at the time, took the case to Steve White, who was then DA, O'Mara tells the family. A grand jury was convened; O'Mara ran it. Witnesses were located and subpoenaed, but none wished to cooperate. "They didn't want to snitch or rat off anybody," he tells the Opsahls. "Their politics hadn't changed at all. Maybe they no longer believed in violence or advocating the violent overthrow of the U.S. government, but they really didn't believe coming in and testifying was a good idea at all."

As for Hearst being willing to testify back then, O'Mara says, "The impression I want to leave you with is this: There was a wrangling that went on for the better part of a year. George Martinez, her attorney in the Bay Area—he was initially saying she will never testify at all. Biondi got her unlisted number in Connecticut and called her out of the blue. That didn't make her happy but Martinez changed his mind and said she will testify.

"I got nickel and dimed to the point where I saw her the afternoon right before she was going to testify before the grand jury. Martinez was like a pulling guard in football. He is gentlemanly, but he's always standing between you and the witness."

The Opsahls sit patiently, listening to O'Mara's every word. Jon Opsahl is beginning to fidget some in his chair. He's here to listen, but he wants to get some things off his chest.

"She had to call her children in Greenwich, Connecticut," O'Mara goes on about his attempts to sit down with Hearst and go over her testimony. Preparing a witness is essential to any prosecution or defense effort, particularly in an old case. O'Mara never got to do it.

"She had to lie down. She had to have lunch. I grew up on the Peninsula and Martinez grew up on the Peninsula. We had to talk about that. It was all very calculated. I got maybe forty-five minutes to an hour of decent, quality time with her. If you read the transcript, it sounds okay. But it was me feeding her from her book. She wasn't interested. She was there only because she wanted a presidential pardon. That's why she came. I asked the grand jury what they thought and to a person they said she was not a credible witness. To a person. She was just a little rich girl who was there because she had to be and had no real interest in the proceedings."

There's another issue he wants the Opsahls to be aware of. "One of the significant things about this case is the lawyers involved are very good lawyers," O'Mara says. "I have to recognize that they're good. They're not the usual public defender or indigent defense panel lawyers we usually go up against."

Contrary to what the Opsahls may have been told, O'Mara assures them the district attorney's office hasn't abandoned the case. Bob Bell works on it at least half time. He's given Los Angeles prosecutors everything from the Carmichael case so they can use it against Olson.

"We're looking at all the physical evidence. The science has made great strides. There are things we can do with this evidence now that we couldn't do in 1975 or '76. But I want to go see Patty Hearst testify. I've asked people in L.A. to get me a seat in that courtroom. If she's a credible witness, I will reconsider the decision I made in '90–'91. If the jurors find her credible, she can be a credible witness even though she was not in the bank. If we believe Patty, the person who pulled the trigger was Emily Harris. It's first-degree felony murder. If you commit murder in the act of committing a robbery, everyone is guilty. The problem in my mind with prosecuting all these people is everyone's got a shot at cross-examining. The next guy gets to ask all the same questions. For Patty Hearst to go through cross-examination from four different attorneys—I don't think she's going to make it. I think we have a better chance of getting Patty Hearst successfully through cross-examination if we limit the focus. We ought to go after Emily Harris alone."

O'Mara is talking more quickly now. He's defensive. He wants to let the Opsahls know he's not some lightweight who doesn't know what it takes to try and win a tough case, no matter what the assholes in L.A. might have suggested to the family.

"I've done two cases that went on six or seven years," he says. "If I charged these people today, it won't go to trial for two years. That's just how it is in cases like this. But I want to start out with a reasonable certainty that I'm going to win the case.

"I know [the L.A. prosecutor] Mike Latin has said he'd be willing to come up here and prosecute this case if we don't. That was a gratuitous statement. The DA of this county is not going to say we have a hundred and eighty attorneys and none of them can do this case."

He's running out of steam. He can tell, like jurors who sit through a closing argument that goes on too long, that Jon Opsahl's patience is wearing thin. The doctor has been taking notes on a yellow legal pad as O'Mara rambled on. It's time now for the victim's forty-two-year-old son to talk.

"I was fifteen at the time my mother was murdered," he says slowly. "I didn't know what the word *indict* or *acquit* meant at the time. I guess I just had faith in the system that it would do its job and the bad guys would wind up in prison. But when it didn't happen, we just went on with our lives and I guess I learned to accept the fact that these people would just get away with my mother's murder.

"Kathleen Soliah changed her ways. She developed her life in a way that mirrored my mom's. I was kind of wishing Soliah had never been captured, because it opened up all these wounds again.

"But what do you mean there was no corroborating evidence? Your excuses are not acceptable to me. It's your job to prepare Hearst to be a credible witness. That's a difficult case down there, but they are compelling her to be credible. Bortin has confessed. It's unimaginable you wouldn't want to go after him. He's confessed!"

Yeah, Bortin supposedly confessed to some guy he knew, O'Mara will tell Opsahl when he stops talking. They were sitting in a park not long after the robbery and Bortin told this guy, Charles Deutschman, he participated in the robbery. That Bortin was inside the bank when Opsahl was murdered. When Deutschman first came forward with his story in 1981, he tried to sell it to the FBI for $100,000, though, so his credibility is pretty well shot. No prosecutor worth a damn would dream of calling him as a witness, but O'Mara didn't expect L.A. to have explained such obstacles to the Opsahls.

"It's hard for me to accept there's been an ongoing investigation," Opsahl continues. "You want to see how Patty Hearst does? Why not just file the charges and then see? Patty Hearst was on *Larry King* the other night and she said she will testify in Los Angeles. It's your job to bring Patty Hearst in and make her a credible witness. You haven't done a thing."

Larry Fucking King, big fucking deal, O'Mara wants to say. A trial is not an interview with Larry King. With Opsahl's crack that O'Mara hasn't done a thing on the case, there is suddenly another character at the table. It's the dark, brooding O'Mara. The John O'Mara usually reserved for slothful cops or hostile witnesses has been sprung from its cage.

"Are you of the opinion that if Patty Hearst never existed, this is a prosecutable case?" O'Mara demands of Opsahl. The prosecutor is leaning across the table and waving his right hand at him as if he's trying to shake a bug off it. "That's what L.A. has said and in my opinion, this is nonsense. She has to be at the top of her game to make this work.

"You have to know, too, the ballistics evidence is promising, but no one knows how this is going to play out. Can you get a jury to accept how much lead was used in those pellets manufactured over three days in 1974? You have to know the lead used with Winchester is similar to every bullet in America. You need to know this. Has anyone told you these things?" O'Mara was referring to recent FBI tests that showed pellets removed from Mrs. Opsahl's body matched ammunition seized in SLA safehouses in San Francisco when Hearst was arrested, but he's never been as sold on how the science would hold up in court as some others in the office.

The head of Major Crimes doesn't pretty up his speech. He's not exactly enjoying this, but he's glad to get it out. When he gets angry, he pokes his head out over and over like a chicken scratching for feed.

The voice gets louder. He's almost shouting. His face has turned crimson. He's jabbing his index finger—hell, he's jabbing his whole hand—at the younger Opsahl. He leans his body across the table to get closer. Everyone else sits silent and stunned. John O'Mara, head of Homicide, the man entrusted to do justice by murder victims and their families, is tearing into the son of a woman murdered in one of the highest-profile unsolved homicides in California history. Scully, looking poised and preppy in her dark blue pants suit, sits and watches. She's seen this kind of show before and is oddly content to let it go on. She knew what could be unleashed in this room. The elder Opsahl and his second wife sit and watch too. They're not sure what to make of the madman gesticulating wildly in front of them.

"Not everyone agrees with me on this," O'Mara says. "This is a judgment call, okay? I'm not saying I can't make a mistake, but I'm a serious person. You don't know a thing about me. I've read a lot that's been said in the L.A. Times and the Chronicle, but I don't shy away from tough cases. When I was bringing witnesses in this case to the grand jury in 1991, that was my night job, okay? My day job was prosecuting a mass murderer who cut up a dozen prostitutes and didn't leave clues. I don't shy away from people I don't identify with. Check my reputation. You're implying that I haven't prosecuted this case because I didn't feel like it, that I sat around and left early every day because I wanted to go home and have supper with my family."

That last point is a particularly sore one with O'Mara. Everyone in the office who's been around awhile knows his marriage with his late wife and his relationship with his two kids suffered during the years he was trying tough case after tough case. They were his self-destructive years, he says now. Strung out on murder cases like a junkie on heroin. "I'm trying to cut down to once a week," he jokes today. "You get older and that's what happens."

Jon Opsahl doesn't care about any of this. All he's interested in is seeing his mother's killers brought to justice. It's understandable. His mother was murdered twenty-six years ago while depositing church funds in the bank. Her killers were never charged even though everyone believes they've known for decades who was responsible.

"Why not file charges to put pressure on people to testify?" Opsahl asks O'Mara. Not backing down. "If it doesn't work out, you can always drop them. I read about charges being dropped every day. At least you'd be doing something. You're doing nothing."

O'Mara shifts his weight in his chair as if he's coiling in preparation to burst out of it. The expression on his face, the way his eyes narrow and his head tilts as if he's straining to bring their target into focus, reveal what he's thinking: I'm talking to a fucking fool.

"You think people are going to roll over like a big fat dog because we file charges?" O'Mara asks the doctor and his father. "We have fifteen-year-olds at Juvenile Hall who are no taller than this table who won't rat off their partners. They'd rather take twenty-five to life than do it. You think it's going to happen with these people?

"This isn't politics or me shying away," O'Mara continues with his closing argument. "I wish I could deputize you, sir, and we could prosecute murder cases together, because you seem to think that any eighth grader with a little knowledge of basic civics can prosecute a person for murder, and that the only thing standing in the way of this case moving forward is big fat stupid John O'Mara. But that ain't the way this works. This is not television. *This is real*."

Even the young doctor doesn't know what to say. His face is pinched and tight, as if he's swallowed a glass of his own bile. There's a long moment of quiet where everyone waits anxiously for the next assault, not sure which side it will come from.

"I didn't mean to attack your work ethic or your integrity," Opsahl says, pulling himself back up in his chair. "I'm sorry if you took it that way. But I have to tell you, it's no wonder to me that Patty Hearst hasn't cooperated with you if this is how you treat people."

It's time, Scully knows, to break this up. "John gets a little passionate at times," she says with a half smile. "But I have to tell you. I have total confidence in him. I have a lot of first-rate prosecutors who have won many tough cases, but none approaching the numbers that John has done. No one in the state's better at trying hard murder cases. You have to believe me. If this case can be tried, John will try it and he will bring in the right verdict."

This will seem like a curious statement a few months later, when Scully decides that if her office tries the Opsahl case she wants someone other than O'Mara to prosecute it. She'll say she wants two younger deputies to try the case with O'Mara in the background, supervising and advising, when the attorneys need it. She'll say it's because he's too valuable to her in too many other areas to have him tied up with a case of this magnitude for several years. O'Mara and others in the office suspect the real reason has more to do with Scully wanting to remove O'Mara from this picture because she knows—in the same way he's come to know—he's an obstacle to it moving forward.

For now, though, Scully goes on to tell the Opsahls that she's glad the family and her office have finally sat down and talked. As a district attorney who stresses comforting and being responsive to crime victims and their families almost as much as she does prosecuting the criminals who have harmed them, Scully says this much time never would have passed without a meeting between her staff and the family had she been in charge during the long life of the case. That's the one genuine point she feels embarrassed about, that it's taken this long for someone in the district attorney's office to sit down with the family and have a heart-to-heart talk. She understands why it never occurred, but later, when emotions have calmed, she'll say it's O'Mara's fault for failing to reach out to the family. Had that been done, she's convinced, things wouldn't be so polarized today.

Father and son don't say much. Everyone can sense the meeting is over. All the Opsahls want to know right now is where's a good place to eat before they head home to southern California. No one knows what to say next. Finally, Scully pushes her chair back from the table and stands. Good-byes are being exchanged, but before the group gets on the elevator, Shakely hustles the Opsahls into her office, which is two doors down from Scully's. She shuts the door and tries to do some damage control before sending the Opsahls back out into the cool Sacramento air. John's not that bad, she reassures them. He's a great prosecutor. If it's doable, John will do it. And he'll kill himself to do it right. She knows Opsahl will have more choice words to share with reporters about the Sacramento County District Attorney's Office and its Homicide chief. Shakely is hoping to mitigate matters at least a little bit.

O'Mara skulks off, spent and sullen. His shoulders droop; so do his dark eyes. He retreats to his office and shuts the door, wanting to be alone. He's sorry he went off like he did but—hell, he figures, they ought to know him by now. It's another example of why he could never be DA. He can't say what people want to hear just because it would be easier.

O'Mara knows he'll hear from the Opsahls again, but not because they want to sit down with him. The pressure will increase as L.A. gets closer to its trial. He flatly told the Opsahls there is no way L.A. will start its trial on April 30, the latest planned date, and he turns out to be right. The trial, in fact, will be delayed about a dozen times over the summer and fall. Finally, in a spectacle that involves Olson changing her mind several times about what she finally intends to do, the onetime-radical-turned-soccer-mom will plead guilty in Los Angeles to aiding and abetting attempted murder for attempting to blow up L.A. police cars. In exchange, prosecutors will drop the attempted-murder and conspiracy-to-commit-murder charges. O'Mara will have to abandon his plan to wait and see how Hearst does on the witness stand in Los Angeles. He'll have to make his decision without the Patty Hearst dress rehearsal.

In a few days, O'Mara does hear from the Opsahls. After the far more temperate father sends O'Mara a card thanking him for his time and devotion to the case, his son blisters him in an e-mail to the Sacramento Sheriff's Department media office. The younger Opsahl accuses O'Mara of lying to him and not having the guts to prosecute. He says O'Mara has bungled the case and adds, "John O'Mara may have respectable win/loss stats, but that's easy when you're a cherry picker." O'Mara seems amused by the insult. For the next week, O'Mara tells everyone whose path he crosses that the truth is finally out: "I'm a bungling cherry picker without the balls to try this big case."

He spends the next couple days on the phone ordering books written about and by Hearst, every little magazine or paperback about the SLA and its record that he can track down. Dozens of them. No matter how

turgid or dated. He'll shut the door to his office and read one after another until his eyes roll around in his head. He makes plans with Bell for
the investigator to take several clerical staff down to L.A. with a Ryder
rental truck and bring back copies of every piece of paper L.A. has assembled as evidence in its case against Olson so he can see if there is
anything in it that can help Sacramento. More than twenty-five thousand
pages will arrive in due time and he'll keep the door locked and read
every sheet that's not duplicative or a waste of time. It's such a mess, in
no particular order, he's convinced L.A. threw all the discovery up in the
air just to fuck with him after he resisted their pleadings to file.

A few weeks into the documents and he realizes there's very little in
them that wasn't available ten years ago. He'll order four copies, more
than a hundred thousand pages of shit: one for him, one for the file, and
two for defense lawyers when they ask for discovery of Sacramento files,
which by this time he knows that he will. He knows, too, that it won't be
possible to evaluate the case thoroughly until he or someone else spends
weeks, months, digging into original evidence files and learning what
and who are still available and in a position to be helpful in court.

O'Mara came out of that hideous meeting with the Opsahls reminded yet again how big cases have a life all their own. How outside
factors like political and community pressure can force a prosecutor's
hand. Despite what he told the family, he knows it's all but inevitable
he'll recommend to Scully that the office file charges for the April 21,
1975, murder of Myrna Opsahl. The only questions are when, against
whom, and which Sacramento County assistant district attorney will get
the dubious honor of being assigned to try the case. He'll spend the
coming months reviewing the evidence, knowing he won't have to make
any final decisions until later in the year, after the Olson case is resolved.

3 | I Want Twelve Americans

If a Presbyterian enters the jury box and carefully rolls up his umbrella and calmly and critically sits down, let him go. He is cold as the grave. —Clarence Darrow, "How to Pick a Jury"

WHILE the Opsahls find their way out of Scully's office and O'Mara retreats into his, across the street at the courthouse it's finally time to start the long-awaited production known as the Bread Store trial. With four defendants sitting in the county jail, the trial can be a logistical nightmare. It already has a tortured history. The crime happened December 23, 1996. It's more than four years later and jury selection is only now starting in February of 2001. Twice the case was set for trial, and a judge assigned, only to be delayed for nearly a year each time. Trying to find dates on the calendar that will work for two assistant district attorneys and four defense lawyers in a courthouse woefully short on judges—at the start of 2001, eight judgeships are vacant, not yet filled by the governor—is like trying to put together a Rubik's Cube while blindfolded.

Choosing the jurors, whose lives will be put on hold for much of the year, draws very little attention from the media, but it's the questions asked in these early mornings and afternoons that many lawyers believe determine a trial's outcome.

Prosecutors know they can present a near-flawless case and one juror can screw up the whole thing. One holdout can send the foreman out to inform the judge the panel cannot reach a unanimous decision. A hung jury, in most instances, means the prosecutor will have to try the case again. If the jury hangs up again, it's always a tougher call on whether to retry it. A case rarely gets better the second time around. It's like over-ripe fruit; it takes on a stench if it sits too long.

Jury selection is the place where a trial attorney's every bias is laid bare. The best prosecutors, the ones who've tried a lot of cases, tend to have the fewest hot-button rules on whom they'll let into the box. To the extent they can figure this out ahead of time, they'd prefer twelve rea-sonable people who can get along with one another. An assistant DA looks for people he likes, figuring the jurors will in turn like him. Or at least listen to him. You steer clear of bona fide whack-jobs, free thinkers, cultists, people who take pride in being apart from the crowd. Prosecutors don't like religious zealots. They don't want prison and jail guards. Corrections employees need to get along with convicts to sur-vive in their job, so they tend to identify with them. Each side in a crim-inal trial is allowed twenty peremptory challenges the attorney can use to dismiss a juror without having to say why. About the only characteris-tic that's supposed to be taboo is race; lawyers aren't allowed to dismiss jurors because of their ethnicity, but both sides do.

Prosecutors want people who identify with the victim. They don't want jurors who may bond with the defendant. "If they say 'yo,' I dis-miss them," Marge Koller, a homicide prosecutor who tries a lot of gang killings, says of one of her few cardinal rules. At the same time, if some of your witnesses are gangsters, you can't have an all-white middle-class jury from the suburbs. They'll take one look at the punk who's ratting out your defendant and dismiss him, which is exactly what the defense will want the jury to do. All the blather about jury-selection gurus notwithstanding, picking a jury is more art than science: going with your gut, using common sense.

In early jury questioning for the Bread Store, a woman refuses to promise to tell the whole truth and nothing but the truth when the judge tries to swear her in, even though she insists she can be fair. That's a vow she'll take only before God, not some guy in a black robe. The DAs send her home. A prosecutor gets nervous after a trial starts when the normal-looking heavyset Hispanic woman she allowed in the box is sud-denly off by herself during breaks thumbing through a Bible. Bad sign. DAs want joiners, people comfortable in the group dynamic. No Henry

Fondas who convinced everyone else to acquit in the film classic *12 Angry Men*. Those heavily principled types will trip you up every time.

Dawn Bladet, Steve Harrold's co-counsel in the Bread Store case, is a feminine, independent-minded career woman who can argue circles around most lawyers she meets in court, male or female. Bladet instills fear in opposing counsel. Defendants get shaky in her presence. She'll get right up next to them while addressing the jury and wave an intimidating finger in a defendant's face. If she doesn't like opposing counsel, and she often doesn't, she lets them know it. Harrold took to calling her the Diva during the trial for her pouty demeanor when things didn't go exactly her way. Juries seem to respond positively to her aggressiveness. Yet she doesn't want women on a jury when the defendant is being tried for murder.

Women are "too softhearted and sympathetic," she believes, and most women in the office would agree with her. "You want men on a murder trial jury. They're more analytical and clear eyed in how they look at these guys. You don't want some weepy woman on there to get feeling all sorry for the tough life the defendant's led and blow your case."

If someone's been on a jury before, the prosecutor is pleased to learn he was foreman. That's means the other jurors respected him. The law forbids asking if the defendant in the case was found guilty, but the smart DAs ask whether the juror was on the winning or losing side and how the vote came out: if you lost eleven to one, you're dismissed. If it's close, prosecutors consider it a toss-up. They look for any little advantage they can find.

Until they've been around awhile and have tried a lot of cases, prosecuting attorneys usually rely on the old rules of conventional courtroom wisdom. They avoid jurors in so-called "helping" professions: teachers, nurses, social workers. They don't want anyone who might be inclined toward sympathy, unless it's toward the victim, her family, or the DA. If a trial goes on very long, nurses, teachers, and social workers could start feeling sorry for the defendant.

Defense lawyers love the lone wolf, anyone independent and headstrong. They adore government bashers. People who make a snide remark in their questionnaires about hating to pay taxes or that the government's only out to rip them off. Prosecutors hate people like that.

Defense lawyers are looking for that one not-guilty vote that will hang up everything and force the DA to bring the case again or drop it. To the defense bar, people with strident points of view can be a godsend.

In his memoir *Roughing It*, Mark Twain, a onetime correspondent for the now-defunct *Sacramento Union*, wrote what still stands as one of the most dead-on assessments of criminal juries in America. Update the circumstances and the observations still hold.

> I remember one of those sorrowful farces, in Virginia, which we call a jury trial. A noted desperado killed Mr. B., a good citizen, in the most wanton and cold-blooded way. Of course, the papers were full of it, and all men capable of reading read about it. And of course all men not deaf and dumb and idiotic talked about it. A jury list was made out, and Mr. B.L., a prominent banker and a valued citizen, was questioned precisely as he would have been questioned in any court in America.
>
> "Have you heard of this homicide?"
>
> "Yes."
>
> "Have you held conversation upon the subject?"
>
> "Yes."
>
> "Have you formed or expressed opinions about it?"
>
> "Yes."
>
> "Have you read the newspaper accounts of it?"
>
> "Yes."
>
> "We do not want you."
>
> A minister, intelligent, esteemed and greatly respected; a merchant of high character and known probity; a mining superintendent of intelligence and unblemished reputation; a quartz-mill owner of excellent standing, were all questioned in the same way and set aside. Each said the public talk and the newspaper reports had not so biased his mind but that sworn testimony would overthrow his previously formed opinions and enable him to render a verdict without prejudice and in accordance with the facts. But of course such men could not be trusted with the case. Ignoramuses alone could mete out unsullied justice.
>
> When the peremptory challenges were all exhausted, a jury of twelve men was empaneled—a jury who swore they had neither heard, read, talked about, nor expressed an opinion concerning a murder which the very cattle in the corrals, the Indians in the sagebrush, and

the stones in the streets were cognizant of! It was a jury composed of two desperadoes, two low beerhouse politicians, three barkeepers, two ranchers who could not read, and three dull, stupid, human donkeys! It actually came out afterward that one of these latter thought that incest and arson were the same thing.

The verdict rendered by this jury was, Not Guilty. What else could one expect?

The jury system puts a ban upon intelligence and honesty, and a premium upon ignorance, stupidity, and perjury. It is a shame that we must continue to use a worthless system because it was good a thousand years ago. In this age, when a gentleman of high social standing, intelligence, and probity swears that testimony given under solemn oath will outweigh with him, street talk and newspaper reports based upon mere hearsay, he is worth a hundred jurymen who will swear to their own ignorance and stupidity, and justice would be far safer in his hands than in theirs. Why could not the jury law be so altered as to give men of brains and honesty an equal chance with fools and miscreants?

"All I want are twelve Americans," Harrold says during a break in jury questioning. "People who work and pay taxes. People with common sense and their feet on the ground. Not people with uncommon sense who are off in the clouds."

When it comes to juries, DAs in Sacramento know they're lucky. The jury pool—potential jurors are taken from drivers' license numbers—is solid in California's capital. The county is a healthy mix of urban and suburban. Jurors are pulled from the full county. It's not like downtown L.A. or Washington, D.C., where minorities dominate the pool and you're stuck with a lot of people inherently suspicious of a criminal justice system still run by white people who arrest, prosecute, and judge minorities. Because of its large share of state government workers, Sacramento per capita is one of the better-educated communities in the nation. Movies and consumer products are sometimes tested in Sacramento before they're trotted out to a national audience because marketers see Sacramento for what it is: a middle-of-the-road "normal" community. It's not the People's Republic of Berkeley, with a bunch of government-hating radicals. It takes some work, but it's possible to assemble a relatively clear-headed, good, reasonable jury in Sacramento County.

Harrold is known around the office as a prosecutor who likes the big show, someone for whom every trial takes on the elements of a lavish production. Rob Gold, who successfully completed a year-long, three-prosecutor, two-defendant capital murder trial that was one of the most complex cases in the history of the office just as Harrold was trying to get the Bread Store trial going, says Harrold is like one of those hotshot Hollywood directors who only make one movie every four or five years. When they do, it's always a big deal. Usually, it turns out pretty well.

For more than two years, if someone mentioned the Bread Store to a prosecutor in the office, he'd roll his eyes and groan: "That ever gonna be done?" About the worst rap someone can get in a DA's office is you don't go to trial or when you do, you don't turn it quickly enough.

O'Mara likens the job to flipping pancakes. Let them pile up too high on the plate and they get cold. Prosecutors who go six months or longer before standing up and arguing to a jury are ruthlessly ridiculed. One supervisor in the office issued the lowest blow of all when he said, "Shit, by the time this thing's over, the Frosts won't remember they had a son."

Between the death of Harrold's father and a defense lawyer's heart attack and surgery, several years' delay were granted. Harrold did manage to get the case through a lengthy preliminary hearing. He got the result he wanted when a judge ordered the defendants held over for trial, but the proceeding took so long that it gave rise to some of the same snide whispers heard around the office in the midst of Harrold's last high-profile trial a few years earlier.

In that case he prosecuted four gang members who beat a *Sacramento Bee* photographer nearly to death. John Trotter, the photographer, is a small, thin man who was out taking pictures on a pleasant spring day in Sacramento. Sensitive to critics of newspapers who say there are not enough people of color in them unless they're in handcuffs, Trotter was shooting photos of a little African-American girl enjoying the weather when thugs came up to him and demanded his cameras and film. They knocked him to the ground and viciously stomped and kicked him in the head. Beaten unrecognizable, he suffered some permanent memory loss and was out of work for several years. Harrold was so concerned with Trotter's well-being that—just as with the Frosts—he and Trotter struck up a close friendship. His emotional attachment to the victim, the lengthy trial, and the fact that he enlisted another attorney in Gangs—

Kevin Greene, one of the few African-American prosecutors in the office—to try it with him and do most of the heavy legal work made him the target of office sniping. It didn't seem to matter than the main perpetrator in the beating was found guilty and sentenced to life in prison.

His detractors say Harrold likes the spotlight, but doesn't want to put up with the rigors of trial without some help. Everything's a big emotional spectacle with the guy. He tries a case and adopts a friend. The rest of us just try the cases one after the other. Everything's a big fucking deal with Harrold. They'd like to see him try one of these alone, like they do.

He did the Bread Store prelim alone and then enlisted Bladet, a fiery redhead, as co-counsel for the trial. But the length and profile of the prelim, a usually perfunctory obstacle most prosecutors try to execute quickly without a hitch, just reinforced the office critics.

After arrests are made and charges are filed, a criminal defendant is entitled to a preliminary hearing to determine if there's enough evidence to warrant a full-blown trial. Other states use grand juries to much the same effect, but California legal tradition has embraced the prelim more often than it has the grand jury, which is a tool of prosecutors, easily manipulated and much loathed by defense attorneys.

In the prelim system, a defendant can waive his right to the hearing and proceed directly to trial, but few do. Depending on how it's presented, a prelim can require the DA to tip his or her hand about the People's case. That's why it's usually an advantage for the defendant to go through with it, even though the odds of a judge siding with the defense and against the prosecution at this stage are slim. All the DA has to do is show "probable cause" that a crime was committed and that there's a reasonable likelihood the defendant committed it. Judges issue hold orders on scant evidence, usually requiring little more than a cop's word or an investigator's recounting of what happened.

In 1990, at the urging of the California District Attorneys Association, voters approved a sweeping "Victims Justice Reform Act" known as Proposition 115. It made it even easier for a prosecutor to put on a prelim. The measure made a number of remarkable changes in court procedure, including transfer from the lawyers to the judge of most voir dire questioning of jurors during jury selection—this was supposed to speed things up—and something known as "reciprocal discovery." This, for the first time, required defense attorneys to give prosecutors all evidence they intend to present at trial. Before 115, only the prosecution had to share its evidence before trial.

But the change that received the most attention, and was most notable to people who watched trials or monitored the criminal justice system, was the so-called "hearsay" or 115 prelim. Hearsay evidence is almost always inadmissible at trial. A witness, no matter who he is, can't get on the stand and, for example, testify about something he has not witnessed or about which he has no firsthand knowledge. At a 115 prelim, experienced police officers can testify what others told them about a crime. The change in law was sold to voters as an efficiency measure. It's also designed to spare victims and victims' families from being dragged to court more than necessary. The prelim on a murder charge can usually be done in a morning.

Odds are overwhelming the judge will issue a hold order and the DA will still have time to order lunch at the Thai place by the courthouse before noon crowds converge. After lunch, a prosecutor assigned to the prelim unit, where that's all they do, may race through another two preliminary hearings in just the same manner. If you're in a full trial, there is barely time for a sandwich at your desk while preparing for the next court session.

To Harrold, the Bread Store cried out for a live, full-blown, non-hearsay prelim. According to cops, six people were involved to one degree or another in the planning or activities that led to the robbery and subsequent shotgun killing of Jason Frost. A dozen punks from the neighborhood had told cops they heard the defendants plan the robbery and talk about it later. Most of them looked up to defendant Rick Brewer, who was believed to be the shooter and organizer. These witnesses were kids when the crime occurred. None had a lawyer present when the cops interrogated them. Most were alone when questioned, without their parents. They were interviewed at school, in their living rooms while their parents were away, at the park. To a kid, each one told the cops what they had heard the defendants say about the robbery, the gun, masks—virtually everything that occurred.

Harrold knew that as court witnesses go, they posed problems. By the time they were put on the stand and sworn to tell the truth, their cronies would have pressured and intimidated them. They'd be scared to testify in open court with Brewer and his co-defendants giving them hard looks. Their statements to the cops were videotaped. Harrold wanted to see how the witnesses would hold up in a courtroom. If they changed stories, he could confront them with their earlier statements, which he'd also do at trial. He wanted a test run of his case. Attorneys who try a lot of cases don't have such luxuries. A supervisor like Harrold who gets to pick and choose when he goes to trial can be far more deliberate. With four attorneys trying to juggle their schedules, the prelim stretched across ten months of 1998.

The proceeding itself consumed nearly forty days of court. Bigtime murder trials are done in half that time. Harrold called every witness and presented every piece of evidence, as if it were the real deal and not just what the word says: a preliminary to the real deal.

"Being a gangs prosecutor, it's always been my position, and others obviously disagree with me, that we have to put the witnesses on at the outset. Witnesses are going to disappear. They're going to go to the penitentiary. They're going to change their stories. None of the witnesses are friendly to us. They're all hostile. I want them to know my style. If they fuck with me, I'll fuck with them right back. How can this not be a big production? Do I have a personal stake in this case? Yeah. You're goddamn right I do. I know the motherfucker who got Jason Frost and I know all the other shit he pulled. I've already prosecuted his father and grandfather and I'm prosecuting his sister. Shit, I'm looking at the mom next. I'm sure she's a piece of shit."

Aside from all the crap being said about him in the office for the big production and his need for a partner, now that the trial is finally about to start, Harrold is being second-guessed on a deal he made with Trevor Garcia, one of the robbers. He offered Garcia twelve years in prison in exchange for a promise to testify truthfully against the others. O'Mara and Bladet each thought Harrold was far too generous, that they could have gotten a stiffer sentence and still had Garcia's testimony.

"I probably wouldn't have made that deal," O'Mara, who supervises Harrold and his unit, says as jury selection moves along. "But I'm a fairly realistic person. I know if I force my way of thinking on what an appropriate deal is down supervisors' throats or down the throats of the deputies who work for me, it doesn't work out very well. The person trying the case has to have a certain comfort level with it. They have to believe in what they're doing."

Bladet, whose large round eyes may lull a defendant into thinking she wouldn't possibly hurt him, can be sweet and sentimental outside the office and courtroom. Inside, she's ice. Ask her a dumb question or one she thinks she's already answered and she looks at you with a face of disgust that makes it clear she thinks you're an idiot. Harrold might do the same thing, but he'd feel sorry for you. Not Bladet. It's not enough for her to win. She enjoys rubbing it in. She'll slaughter you and charm you with a flirtatious smile that seems to say: We both know I'm pretty fuckin' good, now get out of the way while I kick your ass. She'd fit in well at Major Crimes, where O'Mara has created a culture where every show of weakness is pounced on.

She can infuriate a defense attorney, because she's never willing to let one get away with anything. Harrold's too much of a gentleman to go for the throat. He can't stand to make it personal. Bladet will, at one point or another, attack every one of the defense attorneys in the Bread Store, just as she attacks Harrold on occasion. Not a bad trait for a prosecutor, and if you're Steve Harrold, it's why you risk more shit from your colleagues and bosses and practically beg her to try the case with you.

Harrold also knows there's some truth in all these criticisms. Sure, he's close to the case. He's emotionally involved. The deal with the snitch is a huge risk. Harrold could get his ass handed to him if the jury thinks he gave away too much or Garcia doesn't come off as credible. They're going to know he snitched to save his own skin.

By the time jury selection is completed and both sides begin to argue pretrial motions about exactly what evidence will be allowed in, Bladet is beginning to fear there will be just one prosecutor on the case after all and it will be her.

It is the last Friday in February. The first witness won't be called for three more weeks. She and Harrold are walking into Courtroom 9 for what he considers the ultimate indignity. Karol Martin Repkow, a public defender assigned to represent Brewer, has filed a recusal motion. She is demanding Harrold be removed from the case for what she claims is prosecutorial misconduct. She refrains from using that term directly, but a list of Harrold's supposed transgressions certainly adds up to misconduct if true. The other defense lawyers, Jan Karowsky, Jon Lippsmeyer, and Bob Peters, aren't joining Repkow's motion, but they're certainly not doing anything to disavow it.

The nerve of that fucking bitch, Harrold's thinking as the judge enters the courtroom. Bladet, meanwhile, isn't sure what to think about Repkow's motion. Nothing that the defense lawyer put in writing makes her anxious. It's what isn't in the motion that is making her stomach hurt. She's concerned that Harrold has exposed the prosecution in a way that could prove extraordinarily embarrassing if the defense picks up on it and somehow the story gets out. Harrold could be off the case, she is thinking, but not for the reasons listed in Repkow's motion. Bladet is already imagining how she'll do everything alone if Harrold gets bounced in this morning's hearing.

If nothing else, Repkow knows removing Harrold from the case at this late date will delay it indefinitely. Delay is the stock and trade for public defenders, any DA will swear, unless they really believe their client is innocent. Then they want a trial immediately and won't waive any of the quick trial provisions of the law. They'll demand to start within sixty days of the prelim, as their clients are entitled to, if not sooner. But if your guy's locked up and you don't hold out much hope that a jury of twelve will turn him loose at trial, what's the rush?

She also must know her motion will infuriate the usually easygoing Harrold. That he'll take as highly personal any on-the-record questioning of his integrity and sense of fair play. This isn't the Four o'Clock Follies outside O'Mara's office, where everyone gets tarred and feathered. This is in court, transcribed, permanent.

At the public defender's office, Repkow is known as one of the true believers. She takes on some of the toughest cases, the most disenfranchised clients, death cases, serial rapists, you name it, and she conducts herself in trial as if anything goes. She'll hit above the belt, below the belt, in the back. She'll try a case and offer a phantom murderer in her closing without having put on a shred of evidence to support her claim.

These are just some of the reasons that over at the district attorney's office, Repkow is known—not the least bit affectionately—as Karol Reptile. Or simply, The Reptile. Tall and thin, with long gray hair that hangs past her shoulders, Repkow is one of those trial lawyers—and there are some on both sides—who make the battle personal. The district attorney she squares off against is evil to be prosecuting her client, so virtually anything she can do or say to win the case is fair game. At least that's the perception at 901 G Street, the address of the district attorney's office.

In court or out, Repkow likes to wear tight, form-fitting tops and snug jeans that show off her trim figure. Anyone spending time around the courthouse can't help notice her at breaks or when she's not in trial and she's standing in front of the building where the public defender is housed, chain-smoking furiously. She sucks on her cigarettes so intensely, it's as if they pump life—not tar and nicotine—into her lungs.

Don't stoop to her level, Harrold tells himself as the hearing begins. Unlike Bladet—whose dislike for Repkow is already so intensely personal, she'd like nothing better than to lay into her—Harrold is forever civil. Colleagues in the office tell him he should go for Repkow's throat, but it's not his style. He feels sorry for the woman. Anyone with as many extracurricular distractions keeping her from what could otherwise be a solid legal career as she seems to have, needs help. Harrold is determined to keep things on a high plane.

Allegation number one from Repkow is that Harrold ordered witnesses in the case to talk only to him, to stay away from defense lawyers and their investigators. His response to this charge is measured and calm.

"My standard admonition with respect to people, witnesses, people affected by these cases that I've encountered over the years, is when I am questioned on that point, I tell them it's up to them whether or not they want to speak to anybody," he tells Judge Morrison England, Jr. "And I leave it with them. I would never, ever advise anyone that they not cooperate or discuss a matter with anyone."

"Phenomena number two," as Harrold calls it in his response: Repkow accuses Harrold of somehow engineering things so sheriff's deputies and prosecutors assigned to Juvenile Hall blocked a defense investigator from interviewing Carlos Cervantes, one of the DA's key witnesses, in November 1997. Harrold says this allegation surfaced and was aired during the preliminary hearing in 1998. He reminds Repkow and the judge that officials at Juvenile Hall did in fact block access to Cervantes. Word had gotten out at the Hall that Cervantes had implicated Brewer and the other defendants when detectives interviewed him in the days and weeks following the crime. Cervantes was later made available, but at the time, Juvenile Hall officials were concerned for his safety. He was isolated for his own protection, Harrold says. "For counsel now to allege, assert, argue, whatever, that we've been playing hide-the-ball, that we are biased, that we are unfair, simply is not founded, based in part on that fact alone."

Harrold is most incensed about her next two claims. He doesn't scowl or raise his voice, but his face shades toward crimson when he answers. Harrold has lost his objectivity in this case, Repkow alleges. He believes Brewer is "evil"—no shit, Harrold and Bladet are thinking. He's also been overheard calling the defendant an "asshole."

Harrold's also too close to the family of the murder victim, Repkow's motion goes on. He spends time with the Frost family during the Christmas season, the anniversary of their son's death. "This," Repkow's motion states, "is one more indication of Mr. Harrold's very personal involvement, which we contend interferes with his ability to fairly and objectively prosecute this case." As further proof of Harrold's loss of objectivity, Repkow notes a longtime social relationship he's had with Toni Winfield, a Sacramento police detective who was assigned to the case the night of the robbery and shooting.

"This one's a baffler," Harrold tells the judge. "To the extent I have engaged the Frosts personally, to the extent that I encounter them during the Christmas season each year, we do get together in part because of the anniversary of this horrendous event. I am guilty of that. And I believe and I state on the record that it's the least I can do.

"And I would also indicate for the record because it just strikes me as so bizarre that someone would question the extension of oneself to a victim, a person's compassion. Heaven forbid, should something occur with respect to a loved one of Miss Repkow's, for instance, I would extend myself to her in much the same way if I was involved in the prosecution of the case."

On her last point, that Harrold's ethics have lapsed because he's linked socially to a detective in the case—the implication is he can't be objective because he's smitten with Toni Winfield—Harrold talks to Repkow in code. Rumors about Repkow's behavior while visiting clients at the jail and her relationship with a confessed killer she's representing, a lifelong criminal named Fred Clark who's facing the death penalty, have been circulating around the jail and courthouse for weeks. There's been talk about Repkow being in trouble at her office over this, nasty rumors about phone sex at the jail, love affairs with an inmate, a sheriff's department investigation of her, allegations that she's been caught smuggling contraband to inmates she represents, the possibility of criminal charges. So far it's just rumors and talk in the stairwells, but Harrold, who disclosed his relationship with Winfield in a February discovery memo to the defense, is trying to send Repkow a message of his own: How dare you, of all people, question my ethics?

"My friendship with Detective Winfield exists in the open, in public," he says. "It is honorable. It is legitimate. It is healthy. It is not tawdry. It is not untoward. And it is never clandestine." Harrold, who is divorced and has two grown daughters, has dated a lot of women since his marriage fell apart. Winfield is one of them. The two are nothing more than close friends today.

When it's her turn to speak, Repkow seems surprised Harrold is taking it so hard. "When I see evidence there is a personal relationship between a prosecutor and the detective in the case," she says, "it's my job to ask questions."

Repkow suggests to Judge England that he hold an extended hearing on the matter, but he's heard enough. "There'll be no hearing," he tells her dismissively. "Mr. Harrold has conducted himself like a professional at all times. Motion denied."

Harrold feels vindicated. Bladet breathes a deep sigh of relief. She knows her co-counsel and boss had given the defense a huge opening it could exploit to great advantage, but Repkow is so focused on the personal issues she never even raises it.

After his rebuttal of Repkow's motion, Bladet is back at the office telling everyone Harrold is "my hero" for how he stood up to her. Just a few weeks earlier, she was cursing some of the decisions he'd made that she felt needlessly jeopardized the case. In a stinging ten-point memo she gave to him as he prepared his response to Repkow, Bladet insisted he'd better have some clear and convincing answers for Judge England during the recusal hearing. She was trying to think like a defense lawyer, anticipating an attack she'd make if she were on the other side.

Her concern centered on Trevor Garcia. If Harrold didn't say the right things and the defense attorneys did raise the right issues, England would have to explain the DA's behavior to the juries in such a damaging way they might not be able to call Garcia, the People's star witness. Or, if the judge were inclined, Harrold might have to bow out of the case altogether.

Garcia was in the store when Frost was shot. When the case came to the district attorney, O'Mara charged Garcia with first-degree murder along with the other defendants. But Harrold eventually decided Garcia was the best of the bunch for a deal. None of the others would rat out Brewer, for one thing, so to get the shooter, the DA needed an insider. Bobby Dixon was arguably the least culpable criminally, since police maintained he had only driven everyone to and from the robbery. But Dixon couldn't get out of bed in the morning without lying about it. His story changed so many times when he was interviewed by the cops that the other defense lawyers would have no problem picking him apart on cross. Harrold chose Garcia because he wasn't armed. He had no criminal record. Nor was there any evidence that he ever struck or menaced anyone inside the store. More than anything, Harrold and Bladet thought he was believable and that a jury would conclude the same thing.

In May 1998, during the preliminary hearing, Harrold and Winfield first interviewed Garcia in the county jail about a possible deal. Harrold took no notes. He instructed Winfield to make or keep no record of the meeting or tentative offer. This is routine in dealing with snitches. If the DA feels out a guy about a possible deal in exchange for incriminating testimony about an accomplice and there's a written record of the meeting, at some point it has to be turned over to the defense. That's done when a deal is made, but if it's turned over and a deal isn't made, the DA has risked someone's life for nothing. In this case, Harrold, when he knew he had to finally disclose this to the defense, had Winfield write up her recollection of the initial meeting more than two years after it happened, relying only on her memory.

"Nondisclosure or sealing of 5/98 interview content until deal is made is reasonable protection to witness," Bladet wrote in her memo to Harrold. "However, what is justification/reason for prosecutor to direct law enforcement not to memorialize or preserve the content of the interview at a time when it is fresh in the mind of witness and interviewers?"

"Now that the content of that interview may not ever truly be known or recalled," point two asked, "why has the defense not been prejudiced by not having access to information which may be utilized to impeach a material witness in the case?"

She was worried Harrold might have to be called as a witness in his own case, since he was a participant in the Garcia interview only now being disclosed. The defense would be nuts not to call him, if for no other reason than to embarrass the prosecution. At the very least, he'd better be able to explain why a report of the interview was finally written in September 2000, six months after a deal with Garcia was struck, yet still not turned over to the defense until the following January.

How does the report finally handed over have any meaning at all, Bladet asked in her memo, since it's based on recollection obviously rendered faulty with time? Why should Garcia still be allowed to testify, given Harrold's sloppy handling of the issue? Why should the judge not inform the juries that the district attorney's office violated discovery rules? Lastly, Bladet demands to know how her co-counsel—her boss in the Gangs unit—can avoid testifying on the issue.

Bladet was looking at a potential train wreck. When she figured out all the implications of what Harrold had done, she was livid. She could not believe how vulnerable Harrold had made his own case. Nor was she reluctant to talk about Harrold's faux pas. It blew through the office in a hurry. Cindy Besemer, chief deputy, number two in the office behind Scully, is the office heavy. Get on her bad side and you might find yourself doing lead in misdemeanors, advising young prosecutors on the tricks of trying DUIs. Besemer already believed Harrold's gangs unit kicked too many cases down to the felony teams simply because he didn't like them. She thought he'd grown a little too comfortable in the supervisor's chair, that he handpicked cases he and the unit could look good on and passed on the troublesome ones.

Besemer was also close to Bladet, having hired her at the California Attorney General's Office when Besemer was a supervisor there. They liked to think of themselves as mentor-protégée. It was safe money around the office that every time Harrold did something sloppy in the case, Besemer got an earful.

Bladet had never wanted the assignment to begin with. Very few attorneys in the office like to prosecute a case with someone else. If you're tough, you go it alone unless there are compelling reasons not to. Plus, this was her boss she was teamed with. Given her temperament and outspokenness, it could be career suicide to be in court every day for ten months on a complicated case with your direct superior. Now, by the time the recusal motion was filed, she was figuring she'd wind up alone on the case—her first murder—anyway. "I'm thinking to myself, he's going to get recused. He's going to get sanctioned by the judge."

"I should have taped it and put it in a safe somewhere," Harrold will say months later about his failure to memorialize the initial deal discussion with Garcia. "It's the first time he's selling his story. I don't want it recorded so if there's no deal, you don't get him killed."

The Garcia meeting becomes late discovery. The defense could argue it's tainted because of the long lapse between the time Winfield participated in the meeting and the time she wrote about it in a memo. The district attorney's office has long insisted that cops and sheriff's detectives videotape virtually every important interview in a case, yet here's one of the most crucial early meetings and there's no record. And it's all connected to the very relationship—Harrold and Winfield—that Repkow argues tainted the DA's case in the first place.

Once Besemer learned of Bladet's concern, there were discussions in Scully's office about taking Harrold off the case. The district attorney was worried about a story coming out in the media that a supervising prosecutor who's worked a high-profile case for four years was sloppy enough to jeopardize the outcome. A news story about the DA and a top detective, by their own actions, causing evidence to be destroyed or covered up wouldn't look good, but reporters never found out about the internal conflict.

Bladet can't believe it when the recusal motion comes and goes and none of this is mentioned. At the very least, she figured an airing of Harrold's actions would render Garcia unusable as the prosecution's main witness. All Bladet could think was no one went after it because Repkow knew she'd have to put Winfield on the stand to question her about it. And if she did, Bladet figured, Repkow must have been afraid the tough cop would somehow find a way to let the court know some of what Repkow had going in her life as the trial was getting off the ground. This was all kept quiet for now, but it would only be a matter of time before Repkow's secrets were exposed.

4 | Child Killer

Foul deeds will rise,/Though all the earth o'erwhelm them,
to men's eyes

—*Hamlet*

YOU'RE only as good as your last case, O'Mara likes to say, which in early 2001 raises some pretty interesting questions about Mark Curry. The year before, he had won the DA's Brian Hintz Outstanding Prosecutor Award, named for another bright prosecutor in the office who was murdered by a troubled nephew. Curry won in large part for his dogged prosecution of Mariet Ford, a former University of California football star who seemed to have it all until his pregnant wife and three-year-old son were found bludgeoned to death in their comfortable suburban-Sacramento home. The killer tried to obliterate the evidence by dousing the victims with gasoline and setting fire to their bodies and the house.

Due to some lethargic and less-than-complete detective work by two sheriff's detectives who were later reassigned out of homicides for their performance in this and several other murders, the case that soon focused on Ford was largely circumstantial. Still, Curry got a guilty verdict by hammering at the defendant's story until it was so weak, the story and defendant were sunk.

Mariet Ford, it turned out, didn't have it all. He only wanted people to think he did. He was miserable at home. The happy husband and father who loved his job were a façade. He couldn't stand the fact that he wasn't a bigger success. He hated it that his modest income kept him from being able to live more extravagantly. He had numerous extra-marital affairs. He told detectives he was thrilled to be expecting a second child, but he was really bitter that his wife was pregnant again. He wasn't what he appeared to be, which is exactly the kind of case Mark Curry loves.

Curry grew up in a small town about two hundred miles north of Sacramento wanting to be a cop. From one of his first summer jobs as a lake ranger to the time he entered law school, he's been fascinated with puzzling out things, looking beneath the surface and learning what's actually going on in someone's life. Whenever he can, he likes to take on the homicides that require some prosecutorial detective work.

He took every one of Ford's lies and tied it to his character. He was able to convict him of second-degree murder and arson. By trying to present Ford as an upstanding citizen who loved his job and was happily married, Ford's lawyer allowed Curry to introduce evidence to show otherwise. Ford was sentenced to forty-five years to life. He's still protesting his innocence.

Curry's next big case didn't work out as well: he convinced a jury to convict an innocent man of murder. It was December 1999. The forty-year-old prosecutor was looking forward to some rest and time at home with his wife and two small children after a demanding trial. "Hey, Curry, remember me?" a voice on the other end of the phone said not long after Curry found satisfaction in the front-page headlines about a guilty verdict for David Quindt. "You just convicted the wrong guy."

The murder in question was one of the most heavily publicized of 1998. Riley Haeling was an eighteen-year-old who dreamed of opening a school for students with learning disabilities like the dyslexia he had struggled with his entire life. He'd been asked by the father of a girl he knew from the neighborhood to spend the night at her house and keep an eye on her while her parents were at the hospital with their son. The son had been beaten over the head with a baseball bat after interrupting thieves in the backyard who had come to steal the father's high-grade pot plants. Because the family didn't want police to know about the marijuana plants, they said the beating was a mystery to them and took place down the street, not at their home. With Riley and fifteen-year-old

Jennifer Salmon asleep on the couch early the next morning, a second set of thieves kicked in the front door and, in the chaos that followed, fired their guns wildly. Riley threw his body over Jennifer, taking five bullets to her two. Detectives said he gave his life saving his friend. The news media called him a hero, a good kid in the wrong place at the wrong time.

Quindt, a twenty-four-year-old with a history of minor scrapes with the law, was somehow implicated. His friend, who also was charged but was to be tried separately, had bought some freshly cultivated marijuana the day after the crimes. Quindt owned guns and tried to get rid of them after the shooting. He also bore an uncanny resemblance to a police artist's sketch of one of the shooters. Jennifer Salmon, who made a full recovery from her wounds, positively identified him in court.

"He shot because he was angry," Curry told the jury in Quindt's case. He said the young man had been involved in the first robbery and came back to finish the job. "Therein lies the motive for both of these crimes," Curry argued. "It is over money."

Curry's telephone tipster was Brian Lutz, who a few years earlier had given Curry some inside information that helped him successfully prosecute a murder where the victim was shot for the wheel rims on his car. Curry met with Lutz and, over the next several months, unraveled his own case. When he went to the county jail to see Quindt, who was about to be sentenced to life in prison without parole, the young man broke down and hugged the prosecutor after Curry told him he would soon be freed. He thanked Curry for saving his life. Curry and DA investigator Shawn Loehr soon put together a whole new case against four new defendants, one of whom confessed to doing the shooting.

What was frightening was the fact the new defendants' names had never surfaced before in the sheriff's department's lengthy investigation of the crimes. When Curry contacted the two lead detectives to get their help after the tipster's call—the same detectives who had worked the Ford case with him—they told him they were too busy with new cases to assist.

"Curry's so good, he convicted an innocent man" went the joke in the DA's office. "Anyone can convict someone who's guilty. It takes real talent to do what Curry did." Riley Haeling's mother, understandably distraught when she learned that the two men she believed had killed her son were not responsible, thinks the world of Curry and was in court every day when he eventually tried and convicted the new defendants, just as she had been for the first trial. "No one has more integrity than Mark Curry," she said. "He did the absolute right thing."

At the DA's office, no one was terribly upset that Quindt was convicted or spent fourteen months in the county jail for a crime he didn't commit. "DA time," prosecutors call it. Quindt, who twice attempted suicide while he was in jail protesting his innocence, admits he was a gangbanger punk before his arrest, which led an untroubled O'Mara to blithely predict, "He'll be right back in it within six months."

Curry suffered no career repercussions from the Quindt case. Quindt threatened to sue the county and public defender's office, but holds no grudge against Curry. He even calls the prosecutor from time to time to ask if he can use him as a job reference. "I have nothing against the DA," Quindt said. "He was just doing his job. I was doing a lot of things at the time I shouldn't have been doing."

In early 2001, Curry is one of two prosecutors promoted to supervisor status after scoring high on a promotional exam. The boost brought him a pay raise to more than $100,000 a year. When Don Steed was banished to Intake, Curry also got Steed's old window office next door to O'Mara. He has a new assignment too. It was one he asked for because he figured it would quench his appetite for tough, challenging cases. Curry is the DA's child-homicide prosecutor. If someone under eighteen in Sacramento County is shot, drowned, suffocated, dies mysteriously in a crib, is put in a closet as punishment and starved to death, or comes down with a cold that develops into a fatal case of pneumonia, Curry gets a call.

He's a member of the countywide child-death review team comprised of doctors, social service workers, officials from the county Child Protective Services agency, and others who meet once a month and review each of these deaths. Police and hospital reports are sent to Curry, who has two small children of his own and talks seriously from time to time about wanting to move with them and his wife to a smaller town, where there is more room to breathe and less crime. He begins an immediate review when a death seems suspicious. He sizes up the case. Maybe he urges the cops to go out and do a little more investigative legwork. When he's made up his own mind about whether the child died as the result of an unfortunate accident or something more sinister, he walks into the office next to his and runs it all by O'Mara, who makes the final decision on whether to file.

Child homicides are among the most difficult of all murder cases to evaluate and prosecute. In an adult homicide, a bullet ripping through someone's body tells cops a lot about the killer's intent. You don't shoot someone in the head, for instance, because you want him to stop crying or you're angry he wet his pants. Children are killed in less obvious ways.

Very few child homicides, where a baby-sitter, parent, or some other caregiver kills a child, are the result of gunshots. Babies are slammed, shaken, slugged, choked, drowned, scalded, made to drink bleach, asphyxiated. The signs can be harder to read. Intent lies somewhere in the shadows. Several caregivers may be in the picture. A deputy district attorney must become a medical scientist, interpreting arcane scientific evidence well enough to understand it and explain it to a jury of computer programmers, secretaries, retired military men, teachers, laborers—average citizens. Just getting the medical experts who testify in your case to speak in language anyone can understand will take the communication skills of Bill Clinton. Most medical experts who testify in criminal cases don't fully comprehend what a prosecutor needs to win a case. Not all prosecutors have the patience or diligence to master the science so the law and medicine can be combined to kick the hell out of a defendant.

In some child homicides, the signs of abuse and torture are clear cut. A ten-month old baby, say, has such severe head injuries that the membranes covering and protecting her optic nerves have literally been shaken loose from her skull and grossly discolored. Or there is such violent bruising along her spine that the coroner can confidently testify that this child was shaken to death by an adult. That, no, the baby didn't fall off a thirty-six-inch-high table and suffer fatal injuries when his head hit the floor, as a janitor watching his girlfriend's baby claimed in another Sacramento case. The jury didn't buy his story and quickly came back with a guilty verdict.

Another case in the office from 2000 involves a foster mom who admitted she put the two-year-old victim in a scalding hot bath to get her clean. With the child in agony from third-degree burns on much of her body, the defendant rubbed over-the-counter burn ointment on her skin. Of course the baby should have been rushed to a hospital emergency room, but the foster mom had reasons for behaving the way she did.

Maybe she thought this could save the child. Maybe she's borderline 5150, the section of the mental health code that allows people to be locked up if they're a danger to themselves or others. The toddler died from toxic levels of lidocaine in her body because the ointment was rubbed directly on skin already burned raw.

When little Isabel Tison's death comes into the Sacramento County district attorney's office in January 2001, Curry is in the middle of a capital trial that involves an admitted murderer who dismissed his public defender—Karol Repkow—and pleaded guilty so he could, as the defendant put it, face his punishment as quickly as possible. David Scott Daniels, a charismatic African-American from San Francisco who could be pretty likable when he wasn't strung out on crack cocaine, said he wanted to get everything—his trial and his life—over as quickly as possible. It wasn't a hard or particularly demanding trial, but it was Curry's first capital case that made it all the way to court.

"Whaddya think, Mr. Curry?" the defendant starts to ask Curry one morning at the lawyers' table. Because Daniels was representing himself, there was no defense attorney there to make sure such a direct conversation between prosecutor and defendant didn't take place.

"Do I think the judge will give you the juice?" Curry finishes the question. "Is that what you want to know? I'm not sure. He could." After a three-week trial, the judge did just that. Curry had his first capital conviction, though some of his colleagues joked he didn't have to work very hard to get it.

With Curry temporarily distracted by the Daniels case, Isabel Tison's death, for a variety of reasons, isn't referred to homicide. Had the case landed on Curry's desk, where it was supposed to, his suspicions would have gotten the better of him and he would have moved it forward. He would have leaned on the sheriff's department to aggressively track down all their leads and call in the child's father, a well-known thirty-five-year-old diet doctor, for questioning.

Jason Gay, the cherub-faced sheriff's deputy who responded to a hospital emergency-room call shortly after Dr. Dennis Tison brought in his daughter with serious head injuries, was highly skeptical about Tison's behavior and explanation of how his daughter was injured. Gay had never worked a case like this and wasn't sure exactly how to proceed. Nor was he getting much help from his bosses, some of whom at times exhibited what Gay found to be an uncomfortable level of interest in Dr. Tison's legal problems.

As in the Mariet Ford case details about the doctor's story changed from one telling to the next when he met with sheriff's deputies. In one account, Tison said he was in his upstairs study a little after 4:00 P.M., checking his stocks on the Internet, reading news reports, while Isabel sat atop his crowded desk. Suddenly, he said, "she leapt like a cat" through a screened open window and fell what he first said was thirty feet down to a redwood deck in the backyard.

In another version, Tison was reading the newspaper at the time, getting his daughter ready for a shower. He said he turned off his computer after she fell, before leaving for the hospital. When he told the story again, the computer was shut down by accident—either Isabel pulled the plug or Tison kicked it out.

At almost fourteen months, Isabel was just learning how to walk. She loved sitting atop the desk in his study. She was playing with an old wallet and some keys she enjoyed batting around while he was on the computer. Tison said she kept trying to get up on her feet, so he kept a close eye on her. Pushed flush against the wall and directly next to a window he said he had opened on a day when the high temperature reached the low fifties, the desk was crowded with plastic vertical file folders, a phone, speakers, papers, a computer keyboard and monitor, and assorted other items.

Among those: a sheathed army bayonet he said he used as a letter opener and a laser-sighted Smith & Wesson five-shot .357 Magnum revolver. It was loaded and had a speed loader attached for extra-fast firing. Tison said he took the weapon with him whenever he left the house. One of four guns listed on a concealed-weapons permit that the sheriff's department had given him, he said the gun was for protection. The way he ran his three diet clinics required him to keep and dispense a lot of diet drugs that are amphetamine based, so he believed he was an obvious potential target for drug thieves.

Tison said he instinctively lunged for Isabel, but grabbed nothing as she tumbled through the screen. He said he was drinking a beer at the time, his second that afternoon, and it spilled on him when he reached for the child. Everything on the desk went flying, he said, though when detectives got there and searched the house nothing on the desk was disturbed. Nor were there any markings on the desk, which had a thin layer of dust on the surface, to indicate Isabel had been on it. In a point Curry would dwell on as the case developed, no empty glass or beer bottle was found. To Curry, that meant the doctor took the time to tidy up the place before he rushed his gravely injured daughter to the hospital—all without ever dialing 911. It also meant he'd probably had more to drink than he was admitting.

Tison said he made no attempts to clean anything up after she fell. Screaming Isabel's name, he ran downstairs and found her sprawled on the deck, some nine and a half feet from the window. She was still conscious, bleeding from the nose, with the window screen on top of her. He put her over his shoulder, found his keys, and raced to a nearby hospital in his Mercedes-Benz. He called several times to say he was on his way.

Medical personnel at the hospital said Tison smelled as if he'd been drinking. They said he was extremely belligerent. As a result of his behavior, they called the Folsom police and asked an officer to respond. At 7:50 P.M., Tison agreed to be tested for blood alcohol. This was three hours after the doctor first telephoned Mercy Folsom Hospital to say his daughter was injured and he was bringing her in. He had demanded that a trauma unit be set up. When he was told that the hospital doesn't have such a unit, that he should call 911 so dispatchers could send the Flight for Life helicopter, he started barking orders and insisted on driving to the hospital anyway. On the way, he called again and for a second time was told to call 911 because the hospital couldn't give his daughter the care he insisted she needed.

Once at the hospital, doctors did finally call Flight for Life. Isabel was flown to the trauma center in Sacramento run by the University of California at Davis Medical Center, one of the best in the state. Her brain badly swollen, Isabel died in surgery.

While she was in the operating room, Tison was asked to blow into what's known as a "portable alcohol screening" device. He said he'd had only one beer and spilled part of another on his clothing, but the PAS reading came up .075—just under the .08 that is legal intoxication. Tison told detectives that, even though he's a large man—six feet four inches tall and 215 pounds—it doesn't take much alcohol to jack up his blood alcohol levels. That's just my metabolism, he told them. Weeks later he said the high reading resulted from his spraying a shot of Binaca breath freshener into his mouth just before the test.

The Folsom cop who gave Tison the breath test said in his report that, based on how rapidly the body metabolizes alcohol, Tison likely consumed at least four beers before arriving at the hospital. Since he tested .075 at 7:50 P.M., the patrolman said, when Tison got to the hospital he was probably a .12.

When Curry and Gay sit down in early March to take stock of the investigation, they know they're dealing with a suspect most people on a jury would consider an oddball but not someone who would willfully murder his own daughter.

Gay tells Curry he and his colleagues got Tison's signed consent to search his two-story, four-bedroom suburban house while Isabel was still in surgery. They found dozens of guns, assault machine guns, assault rifles, survival gear, and an attack Doberman in the backyard. Pantry shelves were lined with hundreds of bottles of prescription pills that Tison dispensed to his patients. The doctor liked to collect Nazi regalia. He had a pistol he said had belonged to Hitler. A Nazi flag was on display in one room. The screen that the baby supposedly fell through was sitting up against a chair in the living room. A crime-scene technician said it appeared to have a child's hand marks on it.

"Did you seize the screen?" Curry asks Gay, thinking this is basic stuff, Crime Scene Investigations 101. No, Gay tells him sheepishly. Same answer when Curry asks if the baby's clothes were saved so they could help show how much bleeding she did. Did the cops get the shirt Tison was wearing, the one with blood on the front? Negative, says Gay. Curry's wondering exactly what the detectives do have.

"There's not much evidence at the scene," he tells Gay. "Ultimately what gets these guys is their mouth. If he's smart, when you call him and ask him to come down to talk, he'll say, 'I better get my lawyer.' But if you play it exactly right and seem sympathetic and you're just trying to wrap up loose ends and have some questions to ask, the guy just might come in on his own."

"He's extremely egotistical," Gay says.

"Good," says Curry. "Good for us. Because he probably thinks he can fool us."

"I was playing the Columbo role pretty strong," says Gay, who has the kind of sweet, baby face that would make it hard for anyone to think him dangerous. "He probably thinks I'm his friend. I've been treating him as the grieving father. I haven't come on strong at all."

Gay mentions several small blood drops on the doctor's redwood deck, one the size of a quarter, almost ten feet out from the window. The doctor said that's the spot where the baby landed, a long way from the house if she simply fell out the window without being pushed or thrown. When Gay tells Curry that Tison was being helpful and tried to wipe up the blood with a paper towel, Curry's face starts to fall. He comes back to life when Gay tells him he told the doctor, That's okay, let me do that, and Gay used the paper towel to wipe up some of Isabel's blood. Not exactly textbook evidence collection, but at least it was collected. This would be vital later, Curry knew, and he was relieved to hear there was some of the baby's blood collected and stored—even if he does learn later that the area was never roped off, protected, or methodically searched as a crime scene.

Curry can't believe how sloppy the cops are in some of these serious cases. If he feels like giving them the benefit of the doubt, he'll say they're stretched thin, working a bunch of cases at once. Or he'll buy into O'Mara's belief that they're lazy and often inept. Unlike his boss, though, Curry is diplomatic. He knows how to get along with just about everyone; he can always find a way to compliment a detective or one of the DA's own investigators, even when he might be thinking something else. He knows at some point he'll need these guys on his side, no matter how badly they may have botched things.

"At least you collected it," he reassures Gay. "You didn't throw it in the garbage. Any jury will understand. This is a grieving father. You can't just go around accusing people, yet you have to be suspicious. That's your job. It's what you're paid to do."

The important thing now, Curry says, is getting the doctor to come in for an interview. "If you think he's going to hink up about coming in, ask him as many details as you can over the phone. What exactly were you doing when she fell? You say you were drinking. When did you start? How many beers did you have? What happened to the beer you said you spilled? Did you clean it up? The computer was turned off when we got there. How'd that happen if you said you ran downstairs in a panic and immediately got on a cell phone and headed for the hospital? Who closed the window? Are you sure that right after she fell you rushed to pick her up and went immediately to the hospital? You didn't wait around to see whether she'd improve? All the little questions. Then when you think you have answers to all those type of fact questions, turn the gas up.

"It's possible that everything he told you is true, that it can all be explained by an accident," Curry says to Gay. "But it doesn't add up. I've got one just about the same age as him. I can see how it happens in an instant. They're crying or throwing a tantrum and they won't stop. You're busy, exhausted from a hard day, and you snap. You lose your temper for that one second and you slam her. Then the cover-up starts. He'd been drinking. He was trying to get some work done. He gets pissed because she won't let him. He slams her head on the desk and maybe he throws her out the window to make it look like an accident. Or he takes her out there and lets some blood drip on the deck because that's his story. I don't know exactly what happened in that room. But his story makes no sense.

"We gotta make sure no one hears about this," he continues to brief Gay. "What we're looking at could leak out and he'll never talk to us. He'll get all lawyered up and then we're done."

Because Gay was a detective on the sheriff's child-abuse team, when he wanted to run the Tison incident by a deputy district attorney, he went to the equivalent unit at the DA's office. That was Marv Stern's Special Assaults and Child Abuse team. Given Gay's skepticism about the case, it was not a wise move. The case had homicide written all over it. It should have been treated that way at the sheriff's department from the start and been assigned to homicide detectives there. On the very night of the incident, Gay wrote in one of his reports: "Victim sustained major head trauma and died as a result of 'shaken impact syndrome.' [Dr. Tison] is suspected of causing the injuries to victim based on medical evidence and statements made by the suspect." A county pathologist consulted by Gay said as far as he was concerned, this was a homicide until he saw compelling evidence to the contrary. Although he had once worked in Homicide and was considered one of the district attorney's most capable prosecutors, Stern advised Gay to go slowly. Don't interview the doctor or his wife—she'd been out shopping for houses when Isabel fell—until final autopsy results are in.

That could take up to three months, time that is crucial in a homicide investigation. Had the suspect not been a doctor—one who also claimed to have powerful friends at the sheriff's department—it's highly unlikely Tison would have been handled so delicately. The initial autopsy findings showed possible shaken-baby syndrome. Everyone who came into contact with Tison the evening of Isabel's fall was suspicious.

The case started eating at Curry almost as soon as he heard about it. Why the hell hadn't it been sent to homicide on Day One? Did it have anything to do with the fact that Tison, who was quoted often in *The Sacramento Bee* and *The New York Times* as a leading expert on using drugs to lose weight, claimed to have friends in high places? Tison had gotten rich prescribing and dispensing the diet drug known as Phen-Fen before the U.S. Food and Drug Administration, declaring it unsafe, banned it. He had patients at the sheriff's department.

The doctor made a habit of dropping big names when he talked to Gay. Sheriff Lou Blanas was an old friend, he said, even though this turned out to be untrue. So were sheriff's department captains John McGinness and Christine Hess, another exaggeration. McGinness, is Blanas's handpicked successor to be the next sheriff when Blanas retires. As former longtime spokesman for Blanas and his predecessor, Sheriff Glen Craig, McGinness has a very high profile in the community. He appears in the news as a talking head on countless cases and issues. When Tison started throwing around McGinness's name, Gay began to feel uncomfortable.

"Did John McGinness get ahold of you by chance?" Tison asked Gay when they talked on the telephone shortly before 1:00 P.M. on January 17, five days after the baby died. Gay taped the call and included a verbatim transcript of the conversation in his files. "I talked to him yesterday," Tison told the detective. "He's a good friend of mine. He told me he was going to call you and talk to you about different things. I'm sure he'll be in touch." Gay also taped Tison asking him this: "Well, I'll ask you straight out. Do you see anything that doesn't fit?"

When Gay and Curry finally get together to talk about the case, Gay tells him that he suspects Tison has been trying to exert influence on Gay's inquiry. McGinness and other high-ranking sheriff's officials asked Gay on several occasions how things were progressing, something McGinness said he did only because he heard complaints about how the sheriff's department was handling the case. Tison was one of those guys who, if he met you and you were someone whose name he thought would come in handy, he'd tell people you were pals. He seemed to be doing that with Gay. The doctor had been given an award a few years earlier by former sheriff Glen Craig for his role in rescuing a distraught man who tried to kill himself by jumping off the Bay Bridge in San Francisco. Tison was kayaking in the Bay when the man jumped and he pulled him to safety. His estranged wife at the time claimed the rescue was a fake, designed to win her back. The incident nevertheless landed him on the *Today* show and brought him a heroism award given out by *Star Trek* actor William Shatner. When the locals honored him as well, Craig, Blanas, and McGinness were all in attendance.

Tison called McGinness some time after the ceremony and asked whether he would like to buy into his season-ticket plan for the Sacramento Kings basketball team. McGinness said he thought it was an odd phone call, since he barely knew the guy, and politely declined.

"He has some very powerful ties in the community," Gay tells Curry when they're discussing the pressure Gay feels. "They put a gag order on the case in our department. I keep getting calls from higher-ups asking how it's going and I tell them to remember where they're working and to let me do my job. It's not a comfortable feeling."

O'Mara tells Curry it's going to be tough making a case against the doctor because three months have gone by and he still hasn't been formally interrogated. Curry doesn't mind. He likes the tough ones best.

Investigators at the district attorney's office also were suspicious over exactly how Tison got a concealed-weapons permit from the Sacramento Sheriff's Department for one of the weapons listed on his permit: a Heckler & Koch SP89 9mm semiautomatic assault weapon. Why would a doctor need an assault weapon? Curry wondered. In any case, the permit was revoked soon after Curry started asking questions. Sheriff's officials told Tison the permit was being pulled because he had sold his house and moved one county over to Placer, where much of the region's nouveau riche live. The sheriff's office never did revoke the permit Tison's wife, Elena, had for her handgun, which employees at the diet clinics said she liked to wear in a shoulder harness even while in the office.

Like a number of detectives at the sheriff and police departments, Gay was interested in the more predictable hours and working conditions that go with being a DA investigator. He and his wife had a new baby he wanted to spend time with, so he put in an application at the DA's office soon after Isabel died. Given the heat he was feeling while working the Tison case as a sheriff's detective, he was delighted when Tricia Hacker, head of investigations for the DA, offered him a job. By that time, Curry was fully engaged in the Tison case, and Gay was more than happy to press hard now that he was on the same side as Curry and was being encouraged by him.

The initial autopsy report showed hemorrhaging behind the child's optic-nerve sheath, a strong indicator of shaken-baby syndrome. When a child is shaken violently, the covering of the optic nerve that extends from the back of the eyeball, sending signals from the retina to the brain, is reddish-purple in color. The optic nerve sheath usually is grayish-white in tint. Medical literature suggests the hemorrhaging isn't found as the result of a simple fall. It takes quite a violent shaking to produce it. To be certain of their findings, county pathologists ordered additional tests on the baby's eyes and brain. Those were sent to a neuropathologist at the University of California Medical Center, Dr. Claudia Greco. Wait for those results before bugging Dr. Tison, Stern told Gay when he came to see him. Stern admitted later that failing to kick the investigation up a notch was probably not appropriate in light of the doctor's behavior and Isabel's injuries.

When word began to circulate at the sheriff's department that Curry and others at the DA were critical of the department's lack of haste in the matter, Stern stopped by O'Mara's office one morning to take the blame for not demanding more urgent action. If anyone was at fault for things not moving quickly, Stern conceded to O'Mara, it was him. Don't blame Gay or the sheriff's department.

About a week after Isabel's death, Gay had talked with Dr. Donald Henrikson, one of the county's forensic pathologists. Henrikson had performed the initial autopsy on Isabel, and Gay wrote his own report of their conversation. Henrikson told him that he was extremely skeptical of Tison's story. Henrikson went through a number of possibilities, according to Gay's report, and as soon as Curry saw Gay's write-up a few weeks later, he thought, Oh, shit, that's not a good thing to have done.

It was Gay's recording of a conversation he'd had with the doctor, not the doctor's own official report. Because it was now part of the written police file, it would have to be handed over to the defense in discovery.

Lawyers on both sides, defense and prosecution, are careful to avoid having anything put in writing they don't want to see turned over to their adversary. It's a game they each play, particularly in the early stages of a case, when both sides are looking for experts who support their point of view about what happened. No sense putting it all in writing and leaving it open to discovery. O'Mara and Curry worried that this could come back to undermine the case, if indeed there was a case.

Tison told doctors at the emergency room the baby fell thirty feet, but the actual distance from window to deck was about twelve feet. Was he trying to make the fall sound worse than it was, or was he just confused? Other odd qualities about the incident made Gay even more suspicious. How could Tison possibly let his daughter play on a desk, next to an open window, that had a loaded gun and a bayonet on it? Tison was said to be a collector, and there were several dozen other rifles and weapons in the room. This is where she played? What's with this guy? Curry thought. He's a doctor?

In his first full interview with detectives, Tison breaks down, crying one minute, sobbing uncontrollably about losing "Daddy's little girl"—"I special-ordered this one myself," he says of Isabel—and snaps out of it just as quickly. When he does, he's suddenly sharing details of the $950,000 home he and his wife, Elena, four months pregnant when Isabel was killed, are buying.

Elena Tison swore her husband would never hurt their child. But as Curry would learn months later, Mrs. Tison was extremely concerned about some of her husband's habits.

In one of a series of e-mail messages from Elena to Tison that members of the Sacramento County High-Tech Crimes Task Force were able to extract from Tison's computers after Curry subpoenaed them, Elena reveals another side of her husband, as well as significant strains in their marriage.

"A need to work till midnight, but drinking and driving, waking up the baby, calling me names," she wrote. "That is my limit. Don't you realize I only get upset because I love and miss you and worry about you? Isabel needs you, too, but not the drinking you. . . . You should have seen her face last night when you were yelling at me and grabbing her. She is confused . . . and she is learning this and may either seek out relationships where she is yelled at or drinks herself.

"I have said before, I am not experienced with alcoholism. I really thought becoming a father would make you want to quit . . . But please understand this, I AM NOT YOUR REASON FOR DRINKING. I AM NOT LAZY AND I AM NOT LEAVING MY HOME AND I AM NOT LETTING YOU HANDLE OUR DAUGHTER WHEN YOU ARE DRINKING. If you will not get help, our relationship will diminish and as Isabel grows she will understand for herself. There is nondrinking daddy and drinking daddy. She will never fault me for not staying with you because you keep drinking. She saw you push me, yell, and she could feel me shake and cry. I only hope she forgets."

Long before he gets his hands on this highly incriminating piece of e-mail, Curry is convinced that Tison—just like Mariet Ford—is not all that he had presented himself to be. Curry is worried a jury might never get to hear much of this stuff. A judge could very likely rule it inadmissible because it would prejudice a jury's opinion of Tison. Curry would argue just the opposite, that such character information says a great deal about Tison and whether he is capable of what Curry believes he's done. It also establishes that Elena Tison, who had told sheriff's detectives her husband would never harm either her or their daughter, was concerned about what might happen to Isabel if Tison was drinking when he was taking care of her.

Curry knows a jury would have a hard time looking at Tison and believing he tossed his baby out a window or willfully hurt her in a way that led to her death. It's not something a civilized man, an educated career man, would do. He knows he'll have to find out more about this guy if he's going to prove his case. O'Mara, the great skeptic, is still not convinced Curry will dig up enough to justify murder charges. O'Mara's somewhat peeved at Curry because Curry's been whispering about his handling of the Opsahl case. But as spring starts to creep into the northern California air, O'Mara's content to let Curry continue taking a run at the strange diet doctor.

5 | On with the Show

Defendants Glica and Martinez, along with Richard Anthony Brewer and Bobby Marion Dixon, are each charged with a violation of Penal Code Section 187 (a) that on or about December 23, 1996, in Sacramento County, they did willfully, unlawfully, and with malice aforethought, murder Jason Frost. —The court clerk

A T 9:45 A.M. on Monday, March 19, more than four years after Jason Frost was murdered, more than four years after a hunch took Steve Harrold away from the holidays with his family and the last Christmas he would spend with his father, the supervisor of the DA's gangs unit is finally standing before a jury and getting ready to present the People's case. Spring comes early to Sacramento and the Central Valley. The azaleas and camellias are in bloom. The Sacramento River, ten blocks to the west of the courthouse, is running high and fast from the winter rains. The air is warm, nice enough to sit out on the courthouse steps and smoke a cigarette, as jurors, court employees, and those with business inside will do throughout the day.

Opening arguments in a murder trial are a little like Opening Day ceremonies at the start of baseball season. There's lots of pomp and circumstance. The gallery is full. If it's a big case, colleagues come to watch. You're nervous. You put on your best suit; in Harrold's case a smart thousand-dollar blue-and-white pinstripe of worsted wool. Bladet is equally striking, her long red hair set off against her dark blue suit. The black pumps are appropriate for a business meeting. Every time thirty-six jurors and eighteen alternates are ushered in or out, the prosecutors stand, hands folded politely in front of them, facing the men and women who'll decide their case in part based on how they feel about the attorneys arguing it. They could be a bride and groom's mother and father in a wedding receiving line. Every chance they get to connect with the jurors, they take.

The four defense attorneys look fresh and relaxed. The battle fatigue from weeks of pretrial motions has vanished.

On the right side of the courtroom gallery are friends and family of the defendants. They usually have more than enough seats to choose from, but two of the three juries and their alternates take up thirty-six of the fifty or so spots. One jury will sit in the box. In the very back, behind the men and women who will decide their loved ones' fates, is defendant James Glica's dad, dressed in his Sunday best. Two young wives, one of whom met her defendant husband while he was in jail on the murder charge, sit on the edge of their seats looking anxious. Next to them is a guilt-ridden mother who sobs during breaks about how much she loves her son; she feels terrible about all the drinking and drugging she did while he was growing up. A hard-eyed grandmother is here for the man the cops and prosecutors call the ringleader, the shooter. She's confined to a wheelchair and says she's there because she loves her grandson, that he was a good boy. She remembers how much Rick Brewer liked going to the movies with her when he was a kid. He's being framed, she tells someone out in the hallway, by the same DA's office who framed his father and grandfather before him.

"That's Rick B's grandmother in the wheelchair," Harrold whispers a few minutes before court convenes. "She's fucking with me. Giving me the evil eye. Man, I ought to just go up to her and slap her in the fucking head. The bitch. You can see where all this shit started—with that woman."

The left side of the gallery is reserved for friends and relatives of the victim, Jason Frost, a handsome and mischievous twenty-two-year-old who liked to play practical jokes on his sister and told his mom he'd wait one more year before asking his sweetheart to marry him. He figured the Bread Store, where he was assistant manager, was a good apprenticeship for a career in the restaurant business. Jack and Becky Frost will occupy two of these seats almost every day. The years of prelims, motions, delays, and arguments over evidence have become part of them. It's what they do, their daily ritual. They'll make the hour drive every day down congested Highway 80 from Grass Valley, a quaint little town in the Sierra foothills where they rent a small house. Most Wednesdays, Becky will stay home so she can baby-sit Ayla, her year-old granddaughter. She was born a few months ago and complications in her mother's pregnancy made Jack and Becky fear they might also lose Shauna, Jason's sister, the baby's mother and their only other child. Shauna will come to court only a handful of times. She loved her brother dearly but can't stand to be in the same room with the men accused of taking him from her.

Jason's gentle features are apparent in Jack's big, round face: the deep-set eyes, the thin lips, the quick, somewhat wry smile. Jack Frost, whose income from his current job as a substitute high school teacher will plummet because of all the days he's in court instead of working, does not look healthy during this trial. He's far too heavy, putting on extra weight after years of eating to push down the unspeakable pain of losing his son. Becky, who runs the floral department at a supermarket where they live, is softer, sweet, a quiet woman by nature. Unlike Jack, she feels her emotions. She cries a lot. Her neck and back get sore. She has nightmares. As the trial begins, she's wary of just about everyone in the room but Harrold and Bladet.

The Frosts' loss is on display for anyone in the courtroom to see. Students on field trips will come in to watch. A journalist from abroad will sit in to observe how a murder trial is conducted in America. On one morning early in the trial, a very loud retired man who watches trials as a hobby will sit down next to them, see that there are six bailiffs in the courtroom, and nearly shout to Jack, "Man, this must be one of those really big trials. Like Perry Mason or something." Jack and Becky will sit there and politely say, "Yes, it's a murder trial. Our son was killed." Marcia Christian, victims' advocate from the DA's office, will sneer at the old man and want to hit him over the head with his cane for being so crass.

The Frosts will walk out when the testimony gets too graphic. They can't listen to the coroner's testimony about Jason's surgeries and setbacks. There will be a time or two when Jack thinks he'd better leave or he'll jump out of his seat and attack one of the defendants. His rage is just below the surface. Once during the prelim, when Brewer's attorney lost some long-argued motion, Jack allowed himself a slight smile. When he looked up, he noticed Brewer had been staring at him. "Fuck you," Brewer mouthed. Jack had to take a deep breath. He knew if he got up and did anything stupid, like grab Brewer by the throat or hit him over the head with a chair, the bailiffs would be on him and he'd end up in jail.

Six sheriff's deputies are in the courtroom to make sure everything is orderly. They guard the main door, stand near the entrance to the jail tank where the defendants are held before and after each court appearance. They ring the attorneys' table, keeping close tabs on the defendants.

Two court attendants, a petite woman with long braided hair, and a very large African-American man who's ready with a warm smile or a menacing scowl of intimidation—whatever the situation requires—are on hand to assist the judge and juries. They hand out notepads, pens, and tissue when someone in court for the victim or the defendants sheds a tear. A court reporter is hunched over her computer so she can take down every word. The judge's clerk, an elegantly dressed woman, will read the charges, swear witnesses, and perform whatever tasks the judge needs performed.

The four defendants are brought through a private secured hallway. Their arms and legs are chained, but this is always done before the juries are seated so no one associates guilt with the chains and the funny little bunny-hop a shackled man must dance to move forward. They're allowed to change from the soft-soled sneakers used in the county jail into their own shoes: work boots, loafers, dress brogues, stored off to the side of the lawyers' table. They're neat and groomed, shaved, in V-neck sweaters and button-down shirts. The two youngest defendants look almost angelic. James Glica, his eyes rimmed by studious-looking wire glasses, will scribble throughout the trial on a scratch pad, drawing elaborate pencil etchings that offer proof of what his family says was his chance for an art scholarship before he hooked up with these guys.

Brewer's intense and focused. No matter how much grooming he does, and both the prosecution and defense know this, he can't lose his menacing demeanor. This pleases Harrold and Bladet. It helps the juries believe the DA's claim that everyone from the neighborhood who was interviewed by the cops or subpoenaed to testify is terrified of Brewer.

Above it all, on his pedestal, surrounded by flags and the county seal, sits the judge, Morrison England, Jr. A large man with a round, expressive face that at times makes it hard for him to hide his thoughts and feelings,

England was a star offensive lineman when he was in college at the University of the Pacific in Stockton and had a chance to play for the New York Jets. He instead took a coaching job at California State University at Sacramento so he could still be around the game and also attend McGeorge School of Law, which is in Sacramento and part of his Stockton alma mater. He was admitted to the bar in 1983 and was in private practice, concentrating exclusively on civil law, until Republican governor Pete Wilson named him to the Sacramento bench in 1996.

"Mr. Harrold, are you ready for the People?" the judge asks. "Ready for the People," Harrold says. He's out of his chair, facing as many jurors at once as he can. He will open first for Dixon. Bladet will open next for Brewer. Glica and Martinez will come last, and Harrold will open for them too. Right now, he's at center stage, nervous, anxious, and grateful this day is finally here.

An opening statement is a blueprint, an overview of the case. It tells the jury where the attorney plans to go. If it's done well, it's delivered in a conversational tone. It's not evidence, but don't tell the jury that. Don't do anything that invites them to tune out. In any trial, especially a long one like this, there'll be countless opportunities for jurors to daydream. The opening should pack a wallop. For Harrold, whose veins flow with the blood of a natural-born salesman, it's a come-on, a tease.

"Acquaintances of defendant Dixon's from the Southside Park neighborhood told the authorities," Harrold begins, "that Dixon had confided in them or that they overheard him say upon his return that night, and in the days following, that he had committed a store robbery on J Street, that he drove Richard Brewer, Trevor Garcia, Rickie Martinez, and James Glica over near the Bread Store, that he dropped them off nearby, that someone among them had a twelve-gauge pump shotgun, and that while he was sitting in the Jimmy waiting outside he heard a boom, they came running out of the business, and that Brewer was carrying the shotgun."

Yet when Detective Toni Winfield interviewed Dixon on January 7, 1997, Dixon initially told her little more than that he grew up in Southside Park and his only knowledge of any robbery at some Bread Store place was that he heard about it on the news.

Dixon waived his rights to an attorney, Harrold says, and agreed to talk, but he doesn't know anything about no Jimmy. Oh, maybe he saw one parked near the park and he touched it. Then, "I ain't going to lie, I was up in the car. We was touching everything up inside the car."

He first says he doesn't know who stole it. Then he says he and Carlos Cervantes were with Little Rickie and Little Rickie split and he stole it.

Does he know a guy named Rick Brewer? Winfield asks him. "Only time I met him was last night" in jail.

Later he says he did meet Brewer at the park. That Brewer said something about, Hey, I heard you guys got a G-ride. Then: "I was not there when it happened. I was not there. I didn't know it was going to go down. I didn't know nothing. All I know is the only time is, what I did leave out was this, when them cats left, me and Carlos went to the gas station with them." He said Brewer was driving and Cervantes and Dixon were left behind on foot.

These were answers—word by word—that were ending Bobby Dixon's life. Had he told the truth, like Garcia did after only a few minutes, Harrold might have made him the plea deal.

"When listening to the various statements of defendant Dixon, you will hear his many different versions of his involvement in these events and you will be able to make an educated assessment of the credibility of those statements." Harrold's ready to close the deal, but he has one more little item to sell: Trevor Garcia, robber, punk, doper, snitch, star witness.

"He will testify that prior to December 23, Brewer had shown him the twelve-gauge Mossberg pump shotgun on one or more occasions and that through December he used, on occasion, methamphetamine, crank, with Brewer, Martinez, and Glica.

"Significantly, Garcia will testify that in early December 1996 Brewer told him that he, Brewer, had done a lick, robbery, with his sister and a fellow named Michael Smith and had gotten away with a good amount of money. Brewer told him that the lick involved an easy way in and an easy way out, without being much more specific. Brewer at that time wanted to know if Garcia was down for it, to which he replied that he was."

In their opening statements, attorneys for Dixon, Glica, and Martinez all admit their clients participated in the robbery. They know the evidence is overwhelming. Glica and Martinez confessed to being inside the store. What the attorneys are doing from the start is trying to lay the groundwork for leniency, something less than L-WOP, Life Without Parole. Jon Lippsmeyer, representing Glica, goes first.

"A seventeen-year-old boy in the wee hours talks to detectives. I'll tell you what I did, nothing else. I remember I got drunk. All I did was run in. I didn't have the gauge. I didn't pull the trigger, I can tell you that. I didn't even have a gun."

Jan Karowsky's next. "The evidence will disclose that my client, Rickie Martinez, is guilty. The question you folks will have to answer in this trial is guilty of what."

Skillfully, without using the words, these two defense attorneys are raising the possibility of jury nullification, something courts have ruled is not legal. Jurors are instructed in the law, told they must follow it closely, but they come up with an alternative because they don't think the law is fair as it pertains to the case. Lippsmeyer and Karowsky know their guys will die in prison if they're convicted of first-degree murder as charged. First-degree murderers don't get paroled in California. But they genuinely believe it's unfair. Their clients are a couple of dumb kids, they maintain. They made a very bad choice to participate in a robbery with a volatile guy like Brewer, who they knew was armed. But they're not killers. They don't deserve life in prison. Brewer, sure. Not their guys.

"Rickie Martinez looked like a kid at the time of this robbery," Karowsky tells the Glica-Martinez jury. "He acted like a kid. When he was caught and confronted by the police, he admitted his participation. Rickie Martinez was in the interview room close to four hours. Within the first five minutes after being confronted, he admitted his participation as a kid who is caught committing a crime."

He was honest with the cops, Karowsky says. He just wouldn't give up the shooter. His mother and girlfriend came into the interview room and asked him to name the shooter and he refused. "He was dominated by and fearful of the shooter," Karowsky says.

Harrold is waiting for this next part. He knows it's coming.

"Trevor Garcia, like every other defendant in this case, is facing the penalty of life without possibility of parole," Karowsky says. "Trevor Garcia, facing that, agreed to cooperate."

Bob Peters, attorney for Dixon, does his opening the next morning.

He's got a warm, self-deprecating manner. He resembles the aw-shucks country lawyer he wants the jury to think he is. He accidentally kicks out the plug for the overhead projector he's using and jokes that it must have something to do with California's energy crisis, which has dominated the news in recent weeks.

"What did Bobby do?" Peters drawls to his jury. "Bobby was involved in stealing a GMC truck with Carlos Cervantes. He and Carlos stole that truck from the Monte Carlo Club. There is no doubt about that. He did that."

Bobby needed an engine for his dead Buick Skylark, Peters says. "Stealing a car so you can get the engine for your car is certainly not an honorable thing to do. It's nothing to be proud of. But that's what he did." Harrold and Bladet know what he's up to. Admit the little stuff; make the jury believe you and maybe they'll cut your guy some slack when it matters.

"He didn't participate in any plan to rob the Bread Store. He did not wear a mask. That's the evidence you're going to hear. He waited in the truck. He said—and the evidence you're going to hear is—he was not aware they were going to rob the Bread Store when he waited there in that truck."

Bladet and Harrold don't care for Peters. They think the country-boy act is pure bullshit. And they're still incensed from an earlier offer Peters made to them about his client. Before the trial, Presiding Judge Richard Park hoped to avoid the logistical nightmare of a three-jury spectacle that could tie up one of his best judges for the better part of a year. Park called prosecutors and Peters together in Park's office to see if a settlement could be reached for at least one defendant. O'Mara would have to approve, so he was also at the meeting, which ended badly when Peters said his client would be willing to plead right then and there, as if this was some big giveaway, to grand theft auto.

Peters's offer was so insulting the prosecutors didn't even run it by the Frosts. Why offend them? Harrold and Bladet would delight in kicking Peters's ass and making Bobby Dixon out for the lying two-bit con they knew he was. Peters, like any good defense attorney, was undeterred.

"The rumors and stories were flying around the neighborhood," he tells the Dixon jury. "Everyone was talking. Some kids were so interested, they clipped *Sacramento Bee* articles and pasted them on their walls. The truth became rumors and the rumors became the truth in the neighborhood. Then came the detectives. They wanted to solve the case.

"Witnesses," Peters goes on, "were coerced and intimidated into saying what the detectives wanted to hear. The witnesses would tell Mr. Harrold one thing, what he wanted to hear. When my investigator went to interview them, these witnesses would tell him something else."

Like the rest of them, Peters wants to confuse the jury. He wants them to think there is more going on than what the prosecutors are trying to present.

"After Mr. Brewer robbed the Bread Store two times and committed murder there," he goes on, "there were two employees of the Bread Store at his apartment when the police came. It gets curiouser and curiouser.

"Now, we know this guy here, Trevor Garcia, made a deal with the prosecution," Peters says as he puts a piece of paper on the overhead projector so the jury can see "Agreement to Cooperate," the contract Harrold signed with Garcia. He points them to the section that says Garcia's first-degree murder charge will be reduced to manslaughter if he cooperates and testifies truthfully.

"Whether the deal goes down," Peters says, "depends on whether the prosecution approves of his testimony in this case." He then puts the DA's original complaint on the visualizer, with the defendants' names all in a row. He runs a felt tip pen through Garcia's name. "Because he made a plea bargain, we gotta take him right out of here."

How fair is that? Peters is asking. Garcia is clearly more of a planner and instigator than my guy. Garcia and Brewer talked about this in early December.

"They met and planned this thing. There's no doubt whatsoever Trevor Garcia planned the robbery of the Bread Store. Before it happened, when he lived with Brewer. There was no doubt Trevor Garcia went inside the Bread Store. There was no doubt Trevor Garcia put on a mask. There's no doubt Trevor Garcia is guilty of first-degree murder."

Harrold's out of his seat. "Your Honor, may I approach?"

All six attorneys saunter over to the judge and lean close to his right side, farthest from the jury, to hear Harrold. He wants Peters to ease up. He says he's carrying his attack of the Garcia deal too far.

Back in their places, Peters says: "The bottom line is Trevor Garcia, because of credits he's received for time served and good time, he will be out in five and a half years. The evidence does not and will not show Bobby Dixon guilty of first-degree murder beyond a reasonable doubt. We know once you've heard that evidence, you'll agree."

Peters did a good job, but he also gave the prosecutors a gift. He put Dixon in the car outside the Bread Store. His own attorney puts him at the scene, admits he stole the Jimmy. Harrold and Bladet need not lift a finger on that point. They can accept all the bullshit they think he slung around the room in exchange for that little present.

At 9:00 A.M. on the trial's second day, the opening argument everyone is waiting for is about to begin. Dawn Bladet stands to address the jury and open against Richard Brewer. To the Frosts, he's evil personified. They're convinced the other defendants went along and had a hand in their son's death, but Brewer's the devil who brought everyone together and pulled the trigger.

Because jury selection and the pretrial arguments about evidence took so long, Bladet's been champing at the bit for weeks. She can't wait to tear into Brewer. She's furious that rules of evidence won't allow her to include a picture of Jason in her opening. A few days earlier, she wandered back to O'Mara's office to see what he thought about "sneaking it in."

O'Mara told Bladet the judge wouldn't allow a photo of Jason unless there was a compelling reason to present one. If there was some question of identification, for instance. Prosecutors like showing the jury autopsy photos so jurors can appreciate the damage inflicted by the defendants, but most judges view this as overly prejudicial. Bladet knows O'Mara's right, that the defense attorneys will scream and holler if Jason Frost's photo is presented to the jury.

"Fuck it," Bladet told O'Mara. "I'm going to just put it up there and see what happens. It's not fair these assholes can sit there all cleaned up and looking innocent and the fucking jury can't even see a picture of Jason. I'd like to put the goddamn autopsy pictures up there so the jury can see what these assholes did to him."

The picture she wants to use is a sweet shot of Jason sitting barefoot on the front steps of his apartment building, a smile on his warm, friendly face as he reads a Fodor's travel book. He's planning a trip to England, looking to his future. It's a powerful image in a murder trial, and when Bladet tells O'Mara the defense lawyers already have the picture, that it's in the discovery binders she and Harrold put together for the court exhibits, O'Mara says, What the hell, go for it. It's not like the judge will declare a mistrial or anything.

Before Bladet can begin, Repkow has a few points she wants to raise with the judge, outside the jury's presence. First, she wants the judge to rule that neither Bladet nor Harrold can mention Brewer's sister's involvement in the first Bread Store robbery. Not before evidence is presented later in the trial. Repkow insists there be no mention of her in the opening. She wants Angie Brewer "sanitized" from the opening, because to allow her in would unduly prejudice the jury against her client right from the start.

"That's part of the case," England tells her. "He was with someone and who was that someone? He was with his sister. I see no reason to sanitize that fact."

Repkow's also not happy that Michael Smith, who was already convicted for his role in the first Bread Store robbery, is on the DA's witness list. The prosecution has said he won't be called to testify, since his credibility is nil, but just having him on the list makes Repkow nervous. The judge offers her no relief.

Repkow is already showing her colors and how she plans to conduct her defense. She asks the judge to forgo the customary reading of the charges by the clerk before the opening arguments. She says it's unnecessary; jurors have heard them before. They were listed in the jury questionnaire, and the district attorney will no doubt repeat them in her opening. "My fear," she says with a straight face, "is the jury will take it as a reminder that these charges are very serious."

"And why shouldn't they?" England asks with a stern look on his face as he cuts her off. "That's what I want to do. Remind the jury that these are very serious charges."

Bladet groaned audibly when Repkow asked that the charges not be read. It won't take long for the jury to learn what the judge and everyone else in the courtroom already know: these two women can't stand each other.

"It was Christmastime a little over four years ago," Bladet begins, "that Jason Frost lost his life at the hands of"—she turns, points and gets right in his face, wagging her right index finger as she does—"this man, Richard Anthony Brewer."

Where Harrold is the gentleman, pacing, laying out his points as if he were a college professor giving a lecture called "The Night Jason Frost Was Killed 101," Bladet is a street fighter.

"This is not the first time Richard Brewer robbed the Bread Store. Only, that time he arrived right around six. That robbery was much more profitable for him. This time, the stolen car Mr. Brewer was using broke down. So he was late."

Just like in the recusal motion against Harrold in February, when she was stunned that none of the defense attorneys raised what she considered the real issue, no one says a word when Jason Frost's picture goes up on the screen of the PowerPoint presentation Bladet is using. The jury now has a mental image of the man Brewer is accused of murdering to go with the live flesh-and-blood image of Mr. and Mrs. Frost sitting in the courtroom.

The night of the crime, Bladet says, the police had no suspects. Descriptions of the shooter that came from witnesses inside the store were of a tall black man in a devil's mask. His skin was covered. He wore gloves. No one saw his face. But police got an anonymous call from someone the prosecution would produce as an early witness, a guy by the name of Jamie Salyer. He called the police department's Crime Alert line and said the man in the devil's mask was Richard Brewer. Salyer is best friends with Brewer's cousin, David Estacio. On the night of the first robbery, Brewer took the cash to Salyer's mother's apartment. He was looking for Estacio, who wasn't there yet. He went into the bathroom, counted and divided the money. When Salyer found out, he was pissed that his mother's house was now implicated in the crime, even more so, the cops said, because neither he nor his mother got a cut. She points again to Brewer, who is wearing a yellow V-neck sweater and stares at her throughout.

Two days later, on Christmas Day, she says as the PowerPoint flashes a picture of Brewer and Kelly Range, the Bread Store employee and his old friend, sitting at the kitchen table at Brewer's girlfriend's apartment, police came by to talk with Brewer. Marichu Flores, whose apartment it was, allowed them in and gave them consent to search. Now she clicks the remote mouse on her laptop computer and that ugly Mossberg is on the screen. Police searched the apartment and found it "in a very personal place," she says—hidden beneath the bottom drawer of a dresser in Brewer's and Flores's bedroom.

She continues to take the jury through the night of the crime. Brewer confronted Frost and demanded money. "Jason's behind the counter," she says as the jury sees a slide of the exact spot where Frost was shot. "He's trapped. There's no way out of that area. Jason is trying to tell him, 'I don't have a key. I can't get the money'. The next thing Hector Montelongo hears is a shot. Then he hears Mr. Frost moan. He's lying on his side and his intestines are coming out of his body. Ten surgeries. The holes defendant Brewer created in Jason Frost's body were significant." She holds up a five-inch by seven-inch piece of paper to show the jury exactly how big. It is a grotesque image, which is exactly what she wants the jury to imagine. "The buttocks wound was at such close range, the wadding from the shotgun shells was removed from his body."

She's into the conspiracy element now. To prove first-degree murder with special circumstances, which would land the defendants in prison for the rest of their lives with no chance at parole, the prosecution must show the murder was committed in the act of robbery. Brewer told his cronies, Bladet goes on, that he knew of an easy-way-in, easy-way-out lick. "When the subject of guns came up, defendant Brewer said, I've got the gun taken care of. If we get caught, keep it on the downlow because they're gonna come to your place. Don't tell them nothing."

When it comes to Trevor Garcia and the role he'll play in the trial, Bladet says, "He is just another piece of the People's case," knowing, of course, he is more than that. He is what holds together the prosecutors' case, but she wants jurors to reach that conclusion on their own. Now she undersells him.

She goes through other physical evidence that she and Harrold intend to introduce: a shotgun shell matching those that killed Frost found in the pocket of a coat in Brewer's closet; shoes in his closet that had flour on their soles, gathered from walking through the back of the bakery on his way to the front of the store, where the money was kept, where Frost was gunned down.

"I'm pleased to represent Mr. Brewer," Repkow starts when it's her turn to open. "I thank you on his behalf for the enormous commitment you've made to serve as jurors in his case."

An opening statement, Repkow says, repeating something defense attorneys almost always offer, is not evidence. It's just an attorney's blueprint, what she hopes to prove. "Like a book cover, you can read the book and find out what was inside didn't match what was outside."

Curiously, she begins with the November 23 Bread Store robbery, but in a moment it's apparent why. Two men robbed the Bread Store in that first incident. One of them was Michael Smith, a tall black man. In the second robbery, employee Hector Montelongo described the shooter as a tall, thin black man. "He actually said not that he saw gloves but that he saw black skin. Ladies and gentlemen, it was not Mr. Brewer who participated in these robberies. He is obviously not black and he does not fit the description of the man seen at those robberies."

Rick Brewer allowed the police into his apartment. He didn't resist. He let them search. It was the only legal way police could search the apartment. They had no warrant. They had no warrant because they had no probable cause to believe Richard Brewer had committed a crime. Bladet knows it was Brewer's girlfriend who gave the cops consent to search, but she says nothing. Her time will come to present that fact as evidence.

The cops found the neighborhood kids the DA will call to testify and led them around by the nose, Repkow says. They force-fed them information and coerced them to spit it back, to tell them what they wanted to hear.

"I ask that you pay really close attention to what they say. That may sound funny, because they are prosecution witnesses. But the prosecution will say they are reliable witnesses. Their statements conflict. Their statements are long and thick and I'll have to go back and forth with them. It may get a little heated and it may be a little frustrating. But don't tune them out and assume they're saying what it is the DA is representing that they're saying.

"That brings me to Trevor Garcia." She says Garcia's lawyer approached the DA with an offer to testify in exchange for leniency, and in March 2000, with the trial originally set for August of that year, the district attorney's office accepted.

"Keep in mind that when Mr. Garcia approached the DA, Mr. Garcia made himself the deal of a lifetime. His lifetime. He's a very young man. Since he's been in custody four years, he has a little over six years to do. Then he'll get out. He'll have a life and he'll still be a very young man.

Keep in mind the enormous motivation for Mr. Garcia. He'll do just about anything to have another chance at a life. Including testify against Mr. Brewer—and the law directs you to view the testimony of someone like Mr. Garcia with caution, and for good reason."

Please, Repkow asks the jurors, set aside your emotions. Look hard at what the DA says is true and what the evidence says is true beyond a reasonable doubt. "Keep in mind, Jason Frost's family is here and they've suffered a great loss and have to deal with it a long time. And they deserve our respect and sympathy. But you have to set your emotions aside. I ask that you listen carefully to all the evidence. Insist on solid evidence for the proof. I submit you will find they have not proved guilt beyond a reasonable doubt. Not with respect to Mr. Brewer. He's not guilty. Thank you very much."

Back at the office, Harrold's satisfied. Peters put his own client in the truck at the scene. Later, Harrold will play videotapes for the jury of Glica and Martinez confessing their roles when the cops got to them. There won't be much their lawyers will be able to say to that evidence. It was a good two days' worth of openings. It went about as expected. Then the unexpected happened.

About a week after the openings, early on the last Thursday morning in March, Harrold gets an anxious telephone call from Repkow. She's having a personal dispute with her superiors at the public defender's office and needs a week's delay in the trial to sort things out. Because she doesn't want to raise it with the judge, Repkow asks Harrold if he'll make up some excuse and ask England for the break. She's too distracted to devote full attention to the case, she tells Harrold. He's sympathetic by nature, but the last thing he wants is a delay just as the trial is starting. You're on your own, he tells her, and hangs up the phone. He can't believe she'd ask him to do this after skewering him just a few weeks ago in that bogus recusal motion.

Rumors had been circulating around the courthouse for weeks that Repkow was about to be fired for any one of several transgressions that range from smuggling contraband to clients, falling in love with a confessed murderer while she was representing him, or being recorded at the jail having phone sex with him even though there are signs posted everywhere at the jail that phone conversations are monitored and recorded.

Harrold's scared to death the public defender will fire her, requiring a new lawyer to be appointed. Judge England would have no choice but to sever Brewer's trial from the others while a new lawyer got acquainted with the case. Brewer would have to be tried sometime off in the future, by himself. That would mean the Frosts would have to go through this whole ordeal twice, which is exactly what Harrold and Bladet were determined to avoid when they decided to try all the defendants together in the first place. Brewer couldn't be retried until the others, assuming they're found guilty, were sentenced. It would stretch things out interminably.

Harrold knows, too, that Brewer understands the system. During a jailhouse visit, a deputy overheard him say, "I know exactly how to make this whole thing start over." He also knows Harrold gets tapes of his monitored conversations, so he saves some choice comments for the prosecutor about how he hopes he dies or maybe he should stick a black dildo up his ass.

A three-jury trial that *The Sacramento Bee* has virtually ignored, calling it a "simple armed robbery gone bad," is suddenly a train wreck waiting to happen. The prosecutors' minds are in a fever with possibilities, none of them good.

Harrold's so nervous, he can't sit still. "How could she do this?" he says while pacing in O'Mara's office. "What if the *Bee* gets onto this and writes a story? Paulino [Duran, the chief public defender] will have to fire her."

Repkow's superiors have been concerned about her behavior for some time. Several months before she asked for the delay in the Bread Store trial, they stripped her of all her other assigned cases after officials at the jail contacted them and said Repkow had been caught smuggling contraband to two clients. One of the clients, Fred Clark, was a confessed murderer awaiting trial on capital homicide charges. It was Clark, in many lurid and sexually frank phone calls recorded by the jail, to whom she had pledged her undying love at the same time she was blasting Harrold for what she said were his ethical lapses.

Sheriff's Captain Bill Kelly, who ran the county jail at the time, said Repkow's behavior became a problem in the summer of 2000 when her office assigned her to represent Erin Rae Kuhn. The woman was accused of murdering her pregnant seventeen-year-old niece and the baby she was carrying by knocking the niece out and then cutting the fetus from her womb and trying to take it as her own. It was a bizarre, sensational case, and Repkow represented her only a short time because the killings had taken place outside Reno, Nevada, where the trial was eventually moved.

Lawyers who are the attorney of record for inmates at the jail have special rights not extended to other visitors. They have what the jail refers to as "pass-through privileges," which means they can pass legal documents and other court-related material directly to an inmate without having the packages checked or screened.

While visiting Kuhn at the county jail, deputies said Repkow was discovered smuggling in magazines, cigarettes, a Bic lighter, and other fairly innocuous material. Kelly said the jail has a zero tolerance of such infractions, because inmates often begin smuggling relatively innocent matter into their cells to gauge how the staff will react. Then, Kelly said, the inmates up the ante. They're always testing the system.

Kelly notified Paulino Duran, the public defender, and Doug Welch, Repkow's direct supervisor, about the incidents. Both men, according to jail reports, assured him they'd talk to Repkow and make certain nothing similar happened again. A short time later, she was visiting Clark and jail officials said she brought him pornography. This caused even more consternation on the part of jail officials, due to Clark's behavior. He made a dildo out of wet, rolled-up newspapers and plastic and would penetrate himself while masturbating to the pornography Repkow allegedly brought him, according to jail incident reports. When other inmates learned about this, Clark, whom jail memos from June 2001 describe as "arguably the most problematic inmate within our facility," became the target of their taunts. Guards say he then claimed it was deputies who had brought the grotesque nine-inch-long dildo into his cell, held him down, and raped him with it.

He shared his allegations with the local NAACP chapter and at one point, chapter head Ida Sydnor notified the sheriff's department and said she was going to hold a press conference on Clark's allegations. The organization told sheriff's officials it planned to use Clark as another example of what Sydnor claimed was routine mistreatment of minorities while in custody. Sheriff Lou Blanas, whose department operates the jail, went with Captain John McGinness to meet with Sydnor and told her they were checking out abuse allegations inside the institution. Several deputies who were found to be too rough with inmates, they told her, were likely to be fired. But they also told her that Clark's claims were unfounded and that he was the last inmate the NAACP should consider making any kind of cause célèbre.

Johnnie Griffin, Jr., a local defense lawyer who had been a prosecutor for both the Sacramento DA and the U.S. Attorney's Office, took up Clark's cause and filed a $2.5 million claim against the county—it's a precursor to a possible lawsuit—alleging that Clark had been sexually assaulted by jail guards and injured as a result. "Unequivocally," Kelly, the jail's captain, was quoted in the *Bee*, "the allegations raised by Frederick Clark are false. Any injuries that Fred Clark had were inflicted by himself."

Clark was in custody at the jail on a no-bail murder charge because in a videotaped statement given to Sacramento homicide detectives on November 11, 1999, he admitted stabbing to death Reverend Ed Sherriff, a popular gay minister who had been found murdered in his home a month earlier. Clark, who faces a possible death sentence if convicted, says he went to Sherriff's home to "smack his ass up" for making homosexual advances to Clark's young nephew and other young men who had complained to Clark, who in the summer of 2001 was thirty-nine years old. He went to Sherriff's with two other men, one of whom tried to choke Sherriff to death. When he wouldn't die, Clark says he went into Sherriff's kitchen and grabbed a knife. The men decided to steal Sherriff's cars and other belongings only after they killed him, Clark said on the tape.

"I whacked Ed's ass with it," Clark admitted to Detective Toni Winfield. "That's just the way it is. Maybe about ten [times]. I don't know for sure. He had crapped all over hisself when Adam was choking him. I hit him. I think it was pretty much the kill shot. After that happened, I couldn't leave the dude alive. I already stabbed him once. That's when I stabbed him four or five times in the neck, in the back of the neck."

During the time jail officials were growing more and more frustrated with Clark, and increasingly concerned that he was a danger to inmates and staff alike, Repkow, who had represented him for a time, was apparently falling in love with him.

On February 24, the very morning after she argued her recusal motion against Harrold, Clark calls her collect at her house and the two engage in what can only be described as fully consummated telephone sex. Jail recordings of their phone calls show them doing this on numerous occasions.

"What you got on?" he asks in a deep whisper. The call, lasting forty-four minutes and nineteen seconds according to the jail's digital log of the literally several thousand telephone conversations that take place and were recorded between the two, begins at 7:30 A.M.

"Underwear," she says, explaining that she's just woken up.

"Maybe I should strip down to my underwear," Clark's heard to say.

"I think you should," she says back in a sultry voice. "That would be wonderful. Then I'd take these off."

How Clark has telephone access at this hour, let alone the privacy to engage in this type of talk, remains a mystery. But in the sheriff's administrative offices inside the jail, a computer software program that tracks inmate calls has what seems like an endless list of conversations recorded between the two. Some are only a few seconds. Some never get started because for one reason or another, he has to hang up. Others go on for more than forty-five minutes. In many, they pledge their total devotion to each other. He swears his undying love. She tells Clark she loves him, too, with all her heart, and always will, no matter what. They talk about marriage. At one point in a conversation, he asks how she feels about prenuptial agreements. The talk is often excruciatingly banal. Once, when she asks him what he's wearing, he laughs and sounds angry: "What the fuck you think I'm wearing? I'm in fucking jail. I'm wearing an orange fucking county jumpsuit. What would I be wearing?"

In a call recorded April 28, she cries about being under tremendous pressure at work and says her career may be in jeopardy. "When it comes to my personal safety, fuck your trial," he shouts into the phone. "I don't give a shit about your motherfucking trial. I'm going to revert to penitentiary style. Anybody who isn't for me is against me."

Her voice grows weak, pleading, and she says, "Please don't talk like that." She's in tears and says she's fighting for her "professional survival. It's real hot right now and I have to get past this place."

"Your career? This is my fucking life I'm talking about. I don't want to become a casualty of your job. I want to be a priority in your life."

Repkow and Clark were involved in other shenanigans too. On Saturday, August 11, about 11:00 P.M., a guard at the jail was making his rounds and observed Clark turning his cell light on and off. Clark was being videotaped in his cell around the clock by this time and the guard noticed he was talking to another inmate who was in a nearby dayroom with a phone to his ear.

Deputies raced outside the jail to see whom Clark's light display might be meant for, and discovered Repkow and a short man with a ponytail drinking wine, standing beside a red Toyota 4 Runner on the parking-garage roof of ABC Bail Bonds, a building catacorner to the jail that faces Clark's cell.

A deputy approached Repkow, and, according to the sheriff's report, "Repkow stated that she understood that it was illegal and was wondering why she was unable to have any social visits with inmate Clark." By this time, Repkow had been barred all access to the jail unless she could prove she was the attorney of record for whoever she was visiting. After being removed from the Clark case, she had for a time signed in as the criminal defense investigator in his case, even though another deputy public defender had been assigned and was not using her services.

Three sheriff's deputies were on the garage roof and put handcuffs on Repkow while they ran a check on her for possible warrants and tried to learn the identity of the man who was seated in her vehicle. It was Tommy Clinkenbeard, a colleague at the public defender's office who in a few weeks would plead with his bosses to assign him to the DA's case against a Ukrainian émigré accused of murdering seven members of his family.

"I opened the door of the vehicle and asked Mr. Clinkenbeard to step out of the vehicle," says the incident report written the next day by Sheriff's Deputy Bradley Rose. "Clinkenbeard immediately said: 'If you put handcuffs on me, I am going to fucking sue your ass.'"

Rose said he had Clinkenbeard turn away from him "for officer safety" and then cuffed him. Because he smelled strongly of alcohol, Rose said, he administered three sobriety tests to the deputy public defender. Clinkenbeard was intoxicated "but not to the point where he would be a danger to personal and public safety," the deputy's report said. Clinkenbeard told Rose he had had one glass of wine with dinner an hour earlier and that he and Repkow were on the roof of the building to watch a meteor shower.

The two were detained while deputies checked to see if they were wanted. Repkow came up clean but there was an infraction warrant for Clinkenbeard for riding on the city's light rail trains without paying. Reports were written and both attorneys were released.

It turned out Clark was talking to an inmate in the dayroom who had Repkow on the phone. "He wants you to go stand under the light," the inmate, identified as Michael Gage, is heard telling Repkow on a recording of the call. "What?" Repkow responds with a giggle. "Go stand under the light? Okay. I can do that and tell him I love him."

"He sees you," Gage tells Karol, and she giggles some more. "He says it's all good."

On the morning that he gets his call from Repkow, Harrold has no idea how dirty the story will get, but he's beside himself with anxiety nevertheless. He paces back and forth between his office at one end of the fourth floor and O'Mara's at the other. He's been back to O'Mara's office a half-dozen times before lunch.

"Fuck it, John, if Karol's going to get fired or something, this could all blow up and end up in a mistrial for Brewer at the very least," he tells O'Mara. "Whatever she's got going is going to take more than a week to sort out. I don't see how the judge can utter any magic words and make this all go away. Damn it!" he shouts. "Welcome to the Bread Store. This has been the situation with this case from Day One."

Judge England has scheduled a hearing for the next morning regarding Repkow's request for a week off. There's not much Harrold and Bladet can do between now and then but fume and imagine what's going on. O'Mara lets them vent and tries reassuring them it will all work out fine in the end, but at the moment, he's distracted with his own worries in the SLA case and his ongoing review of boxes of evidence piled everywhere in his office.

On the morning of Friday, March 30, the scene outside Judge England's courtroom is more hectic than usual. Harrold and Bladet stride up the courthouse steps and take a seat on the hard wooden benches outside Courtroom 9. Three of the defense lawyers in the Bread Store case look as anxious and every bit as confused as the prosecutors. Kevin Clymo, a giant bear of a man who was once married to Repkow, has shown up but no one knows why. Is he representing his ex-wife in whatever grievance she has with the public defender's office, where Clymo was a star before he left over a dispute he had with his bosses?

At 10:00 A.M., Betty Williams, a bailiff assigned to the trial, strides out of the courtroom and says the judge wants to see all the lawyers in chambers.

About forty-five minutes later, the attorneys, except for Repkow, who's not here this morning, come out of the locked courtroom with glum expressions on their faces. Don Manning, Repkow's boss at the public defender's office, is among them. He won't say a word about what's going on, only that it's a private personnel matter and he's not allowed to comment.

Afterward, when they're in their offices across the street, Harrold and Bladet silently ride the elevator to the fourth floor, set their briefcases down, and pace resolutely over to see O'Mara, who wants a full accounting of what suddenly appears to be the trial's unraveling.

"I said in camera and on the record that I am very concerned about Mr. Brewer's consciousness of all that is going on with his attorney," Harrold says. "Don Manning said on the record she hasn't been able to concentrate on this case for two weeks. Well, in the past two weeks, she gave an opening statement, which was not good, and she picked a jury, which was terrible. They [the Court clerk] got on the phone right then and there with fifty-four jurors, telling them the schedule was being changed. I do wish my judge was a little more astute in getting to the bottom of this. He keeps playing the 'Well, she has personal problems.' I'm thinking we're going to need to amputate this part of my case."

"This can't go on very long," O'Mara says of the Repkow-inspired delay. "The judge can't keep fifty-four jurors in line forever. At the same time, he's got to sever Brewer or make it go."

Harrold knows enough about Repkow and the desperation she must be feeling right now to believe she'll fight to keep the case, whether she's fired or not.

"Repkow would resent the hell out of being severed out," he says. "If she gets fired and doesn't stay on this case, she has no work. She thinks it's all hanging in the balance on what the judge does."

On the following Monday, the judge has another closed meeting in his chambers scheduled for 10:00 A.M. All the attorneys are inside the courtroom telling stories, waiting for the in-camera hearing to begin, wondering what's going to happen and how come the news media hasn't picked up on any of the funny business.

The spectacle of uncertainty is getting harder to overlook since this morning's session has drawn an even bigger crowd of strange legal bedfellows. Don Manning is back. So is Bert Lahr, another supervising deputy public defender. Mark Millard, newly assigned by the court to represent Clark, has joined the huddle of lawyers standing around, whispering, waiting. All anyone would have to do is walk past Courtroom 9 or stick his or her head in and they'd know something very unusual was taking place.

It seems that Millard and Clymo are here today because, as Millard says, he has "a mystery client that may be impacted by these proceedings." He and Clymo want to make sure the client doesn't get dragged into the Repkow mess in the Bread Store. That client, of course, is Clark, who Clymo and Millard fear may somehow be penalized in his case if the Repkow matter gets a full and open hearing.

Manning tells Judge England behind closed doors that Repkow has a conflict of interest with the public defender's office. The office no longer believes she can competently serve as Rick Brewer's attorney. Neither Manning nor Repkow, who is here this morning, ever go into much detail with the judge, resting on attorney-client privilege and what they cite as Repkow's right to privacy in a county personnel matter.

When Bladet and Harrold get back to talk to O'Mara, no one can quite believe what's happening. For one thing, no one's quite sure what's happening. The judge has had numerous closed meetings in his chambers. Sometimes he's in there only with Repkow and her bosses.

"A lot of this is going to happen in camera," Bladet says, but her real concern is: can the judge keep Repkow on the case, avoiding a mistrial or delay, and can Brewer knowingly agree to ignore the concerns of the public defender's office, stay loyal to Repkow, and keep her as his lawyer if even he doesn't fully know what's going on?

"Brewer can't conceivably give a knowing waiver, because he doesn't have full knowledge," she says. "Brewer can't be fully apprised of the situation, because the PD says it's just now beginning its investigation into Repkow. Brewer could say three, six, nine months down the road, if he keeps Repkow, that he didn't know all this and wants to appeal based on the fact that he didn't know enough to make an appropriate decision. What a fucking mess. Or if we go down the line and he gets a new lawyer and he bitches and moans, You took my lawyer for no good reason, he'll say through the new lawyer that jeopardy attached and you can't try me again."

If Brewer wants to keep Repkow despite the fact her superiors in her own office are saying she's not competent to represent him, Judge England will need to be very careful to make sure he establishes a clear record that Brewer knows what he's doing. Brewer will have to say he understands the position of the public defender's office, but that he still wants Repkow as his lawyer. Which is going to be difficult, since no one believes Brewer's being told the full story.

At 1:30, the judge calls everyone in for another private session. In the brief moments he's on the bench stating his request to meet in his chambers, his pain is expressed clearly on his face. England's large mouth turns down into an exaggerated frown when he's upset. He talks low, almost in a whisper. He's doing his best to keep this case intact. He's not sure he can.

Repkow goes into the cell defendants wait in, adjacent to the courtroom, and talks to Brewer before the in-camera session. Then Repkow, Peters, Bladet, Harrold, Karowsky, Lippsmeyer, Millard, Clymo, and Manning all walk behind England's bench and assemble inside his chambers.

After ten minutes, the extraordinary session is over. The bailiff opens the courtroom and tells another bailiff to bring in the defendants. Much to the relief of the attorneys on both sides, no news reporters are in the courtroom.

The judge doesn't come back to the bench until 2:00 P.M., giving everyone a few minutes to squirm anxiously in their seats. When he sits down, he says—with the court reporter present to transcribe—that he wishes to recap the past few days' events for the record.

On the afternoon of March 29, a solemn Judge England begins, Ms. Repkow came to his chambers and asked him for a week's continuance. The judge said Repkow indicated she had a personnel dispute with her superiors and needed one week to clear it up. At 1:30 P.M. the following day, Manning came to see the judge and echoed Repkow's concern and said she would be ready to go by April 9. At that time, England ordered all the jurors excused.

Three days later, the judge met with all the attorneys again. On the final day of the week-long delay, England said he talked to Paulino

Duran, the public defender, and Duran concurred Repkow would be ready on the ninth. The judge was promised there would be no additional disruptions.

But instead of being ready to go on the ninth, Repkow and Manning came to see Judge England in chambers again that morning. Manning said the office was declaring a legal conflict of interest in the case and was asking to be removed. "At that time," the judge says, "Ms. Repkow made no comment and asked for more time." Millard and Clymo also said Repkow's situation might harm their "mystery client." Repkow told the judge she disagreed with her superiors at the public defender's office; there was no conflict that would keep her from continuing to represent Brewer.

The judge, in open court, asks to hear from Don Manning. "That was our belief at the time," Manning says. "It is best for our office to ask to be relieved because we do not believe Mr. Brewer can get effective counsel if we remain on the case. That is our position. That is the position of our office, regardless of whether Ms. Repkow agrees. We cannot sit here as an office without raising the issue of effective assistance of counsel."

Karowsky asks to be heard and he suggests the judge issue a gag order on the matter. "In light of the grave consequences attached to this hearing and this trial" is Karowsky's reason. "We have three juries, fifty-four jurors. I am concerned about the potential of any word getting out that might taint and otherwise prejudice the case."

No reporters are around, so there's no worry something will leak out. A spectacle is occurring in Courtroom 9, but for all intents and purposes, the doors might as well be locked.

Now it's Clymo's turn. "The public defender is on notice in this case that Mr. Millard and I represent a capital defendant. I don't believe there is any mistake on that case. I would ask the court to vigilantly monitor any closed proceedings so if there is a discussion or circumstances in that defendant's case, you would allow the defendant who is the subject of that discussion to be present." Millard tells the judge he's worried that something about the Repkow matter could somehow come back and harm their client in the other case.

Out in the hallway afterward, Karowsky is fuming. He's appalled at the performance of the public defender's office. He can't believe Duran hasn't shown up in court.

"If I were an appointed public defender," he says, "and I had to go to the board of supervisors and explain why we're spending a ton of money and there may be something in my office that caused us to spend even more, instead of sitting around in meetings all day deciding how many staplers the office needs, I'd sure as hell be over here representing that office. This is a bureaucrat who has his head stuck somewhere other than where it should be. He sends two low-level people over here? He doesn't even send the chief deputy? I don't understand that."

At 10:30, the judge calls everyone in again. He goes on the record. He says he's conducted "fairly extensive research in this whole issue. This is a little bit different than the normal conflict-of-interest issue. No such conflict exists at this time between Mr. Brewer and Ms. Repkow." He's not sure what the public defender's concerns are exactly, and he's not certain of Repkow's employment status at the moment, or "how it might affect her emotional and psychological well-being and how that may affect" her representation of Brewer. "The court doesn't find that the concern of the public defender rises to the level of a legal conflict of interest," England declares. "Ms. Repkow has conducted herself in all phases of this trial in nothing but a professional and courteous manner since Ms. Repkow was appointed counsel. The court has not seen or heard anything that would indicate in the slightest bit there has been or will be an inappropriate conduct from Ms. Repkow."

The case is intact. It sounds to Harrold and Bladet as if the judge will let her continue to represent Brewer, even if she has to resign from the PD or is fired.

England turns to Repkow and asks if she'll be ready to go April 9. "Yes," she says. "Is there any issue that will affect your ability to represent Mr. Brewer?" he wants to know. "Not at all," she assures him.

Does Brewer, who's seated to Repkow's left, understand what's taken place? "Pretty much all of it," Brewer tells the judge.

"They do not feel Ms. Repkow will be able to effectively represent you in this case," England explains to the defendant. "There are issues Ms. Repkow may have to deal with concerning her employment that may distract her from representing you."

Brewer says he understands that. "Their concern," the judge goes on, "is her attention may be divided among other things." Brewer nods. "It is possible," England continues, "if you proceed with your current counsel, Ms. Repkow, she may be distracted for some time. Their position is that Ms. Repkow may not be able to devote full time to your case. That's what the public defender's office is saying. Ms. Repkow is saying it's not the case.

"Are you comfortable," he asks Brewer, "with the decision you made in this matter?"

"With Karol representing me?" Brewer asks.

"Yes, absolutely," England tells him.

"Yes," says Brewer.

The case will move forward, all four defendants tried together.

Back at their office, everyone wants to know the latest. Besemer comes to see Harrold and Bladet right away.

"This was the first time in a long time that I had butterflies before a hearing," Bladet says. "The judge told Brewer this even changes the possibility of him being convicted and Brewer said he understood. The PD covered their asses. They said, We're not condoning this. We don't think you should do this but the judge made a good record. Brewer said all the right things. We're home free."

6 | Suspicious Story

Everyone lies. If they say they don't lie, they're lying.
—Dr. Dennis Tison

THERE have only been a few occasions when John O'Mara thoroughly second-guessed one of his people. He figures it's rarely worth the trouble, because the deputies tend to stay pissed forever. As a cop years before, Don Steed had teamed up with O'Mara on a notorious Mexican Mafia murder-ring case that lasted seven years and ran the length of the state. In 1994 he was a prosecutor seeking seek the death penalty against a twenty-six-year-old prostitute who became known in the press as "Batgirl" for the bat and vampire tattoos she wore on her neck and upper left arm.

Michelle Cuminsky, a former prostitute at the infamous Nevada Mustang Ranch brothel, stabbed one of the men she saw regularly thirty-two times, stuffed his body in a closet, and made off with his 1975 Mercedes and other belongings. On the eve of trial, the woman's two lawyers—death-penalty defendants are assigned two lawyers, one for the guilt phase and one for the penalty phase—called O'Mara. They wanted to meet with him in private, without Steed. O'Mara said sure, he'd meet with them alone.

"I was furious," Steed said seven years later, still not over the slight. "I think it showed a lack of confidence in me, that somehow I wasn't a match for those two attorneys, when I thought I could more than hold my own against them. John had that meeting and told me to dismiss the special against her so she'd plead. It still bothers me."

O'Mara said it's his job to meet with defense attorneys if they approach him, and in the Batgirl case, "they'd been seeing each for some time, so I'm not sure we could prove the robbery as the special. There were other problems too. The victim was a righteous guy, but he was in his fifties. The killer's twenty-three or twenty-four. Some jurors would be bothered by that relationship. I thought twenty-six to life was a good disposition. I still do. It had nothing to do with my confidence in Don. I'm the supervisor, so they wanted to approach me. I'm open to it if they call and make the overture."

Such second-guessing by O'Mara is rare, though. Although he remains skeptical, he's allowing Curry to pursue the Tison case as he feels he should. As often happens, Curry's weak case keeps getting stronger.

He is becoming more confident he will be able to convince O'Mara to file murder charges against the guy. If Don Heller, Tison's lawyer, had called O'Mara early on and felt him out about a possible plea for, say, involuntary manslaughter, which carries a prison term of no more than four years, he might have listened. Now Curry believes if he can just get him charged and arrested, Dr. Tison's case is going to trial and he can convict him of murder.

Curry's living with this one full-time. One night, working at home after his two small kids were asleep in bed, he was considering Isabel's size. The police and autopsy reports said the little girl weighed twenty-three pounds and was thirty-one inches tall. Still having trouble conjuring up a precise mental picture of Isabel and the force it must have taken to get her through the window and to land so far from the house, Curry crept into his daughter's room. She was sound asleep in her bed. He looked at the ruler etched onto the wall that parents use to track their children's growth. Thirty-one inches tall suddenly made more sense. It was an eerie moment that brought the case a little too close to home.

O'Mara isn't suffering through the case like Curry. It's not his. When he tried his own complex murders, O'Mara would become even more distant and removed from the rest of the world than usual. He would literally forget to eat, shedding sometimes as much as thirty pounds off his slightly round frame in a six-month trial. He'd grow a beard. The good ones almost have to wall themselves off from the rest of the world, like some actor immersing himself in the role of a lifetime, so they can in-habit the case and make every single detail about it their own. As if they woke up with the killer on the day of the crime and followed him around and got inside his head and were right there by his side as he plunged the knife, fired the gun, swung the machete, or whatever fucked-up way he chose to end one person's life and in turn set himself up to become a lifelong tenant of one of the state of California's penal institutions. This one is Curry's obsession. O'Mara is content to let him see what he can turn it into.

That's not to say he doesn't encourage him in his own way. O'Mara's seen enough defendant statements over the years to know when things don't add up. He doesn't believe the doctor's story any more than Gay or Curry do. It's just taking him a while to believe a prosecutable case might be made of it. But he also knows if anyone in the office can turn it into something, Curry can.

"This guy needed to be interviewed right from the get-go," O'Mara tells Stern on the day Stern comes in to explain the advice he'd given to Gay. "A bungled interview the day after is better than no interview at all, in my opinion. If these child-abuse detectives can't do their jobs, they ought to take the case to homicide or someone who can."

"You can't expect them to do the right thing," Stern says, dismissing the notion as silly. "You can't expect the Child Abuse guys to go over to Homicide and say, We can't do the job. Can you help us?"

"Maybe so," O'Mara tells him. "But Tison is a smart son of a bitch. He's had almost sixty days to meditate on this thing. You can't waste that kind of time and expect to have it come out the way it's supposed to. This happens time and time again with these people."

If anyone's to blame for the slow pace, Stern says it's him. But O'Mara's not placated. "The best we can hope for at this point in time is that the guy is so smart he thinks he can outsmart everyone. That he'll still talk to the detectives without a lawyer. We'd certainly oblige him if he's a dumb enough son of a bitch to think he can pull it off."

Tison will begin to learn this lesson when he shows up at the sheriff's department to be questioned about two months after his daughter's death. He's alone: no wife, no lawyer, no friend. Just Dr. Tison and his ego.

He's directed up the elevator to a series of small interview rooms. Gay leads him into one and the doctor eases his large frame into a thin metal chair. Gay sits down next to him. How 'bout a soda or some water? A cop interviewing a murder suspect in one of these rooms should never be construed—if you're the suspect—as a friend. Murder suspects fall for it time and time again. A soda would be great, Tison says. Thanks.

He's terribly sorry for his loss, Gay says, apologizing for wanting to ask Tison all these unpleasant questions. That's okay, Tison says. "You guys are just doing your jobs." Both of them seem relaxed.

"This is not an accusatory interview," Gay reassures the doctor. "And you're certainly not under arrest. I just want to make sure I understand everything that happened the night Isabel died, in chronological order, so I can put it all together and write a final report and close the case."

In the next room over, sitting in front of a row of VCRs and color televisions, Curry and two detectives will watch the interview as it happens on closed-circuit TV. The setup allows Gay to ask his questions, and after making up phony reasons to take a short break—How 'bout a glass of water, do you need the bathroom, I have to make a quick call— he can stick his head inside the surveillance room and ask Curry or the other detectives if he's missed anything.

Eighteen minutes in, and the doctor's sobbing. "She was the light of my life," Tison wails. He doesn't see any tears, but Gay offers to find him a tissue and goes next door to get it. Now he and Curry and the detectives are watching Tison alone in the interview cubicle. Gay grabs a box of tissues from the surveillance room and goes back in. The detective asks Tison to run through what happened the afternoon of January 12.

"I was checking the mutual funds and she got on the side of the filing cabinet and just started standing there and she just dove and hit that screen and I lurched forward to grab for her," the doctor says without taking a breath. "She just went with the screen and downstairs and everything went tumbling off the desk."

He talks about the trip to the hospital, his frustration that doctors and nurses weren't moving quickly enough. He remembers taking the screen off the window a few weeks earlier to clean it. Maybe he put it back wrong, he suggests to Gay. Maybe that's why she burst through it so quickly. He admits he was drinking and tells Gay he can't help but blame himself for what happened, even if it was just a terrible accident.

"I've not had a drop since," he says. "I can't walk by those liquor departments at the supermarket. My stomach turns, because that's in the back of my mind. It always will be there. When I grabbed for her, if I hadn't had those [beers] would I have grabbed her?"

Curry is next door taking it all in. Here's a guy being asked about the death of his daughter, questions that clearly suggest the cops don't believe his version of events, and he's calm as can be. None of the questions annoy him. He never once looks at the detective, as Curry and Gay know they would if they were in his shoes, and says, "Fuck you guys. I'm a doctor. I'm a respectable member of this community. I've just been through a parent's worst nightmare. My baby is dead and you're asking me questions like you think I killed her. How dare you suggest I killed her. This interview is over. You got more questions, call my lawyer!"

Curry's taken aback, too, when Tison mentions his education and experience in psychiatry and one of the lessons that stayed with him over the years. "Everyone lies," Tison tells Gay. "If they say they don't lie, they're lying." What's that all about? Curry wonders. The guy's not even a psychiatrist. His résumé and Web site list his residency in psychiatry at the University of California at San Diego, but Curry called the school and learned Tison quit his psychiatric residency after eighteen weeks.

Tison seems as if he has all kinds of time to kill. He's in no hurry at all. He tells Gay about all the problems he and his wife have had in trying to close the deal for that new $950,000 house they intend to buy. Odd behavior for a guy in his position, Curry's thinking next door.

How 'bout a break? Gay says. He steps out and goes next door to where Curry is watching. The prosecutor has been taking notes, much of the time sitting with his back to the TV screens, not watching the doctor answer.

"You're doing a good job," Curry reassures Gay, "but the guy's impossible to keep on track. He keeps wanting to change the subject. Get him to answer what we need to get from him. Get him to tell you everything he did while he was upstairs. Did he go in the bedroom? Why did he shut off the computer? Where was the screen after she fell? What exactly was he looking at on the computer when she fell? How did she get up on the desk? How long was she up there?

"Unless we get him in some inconsistencies, we don't have a case. There's something about that computer that he's covering up."

Gay says he can't believe how put-on Tison is. "When he wipes his eyes, there are no tears. It's for effect."

It goes like this for three hours. Then the doctor can't resist. Before he leaves, he has a question. "In all honesty"—he looks intently at Gay—"I mean, this story is suspicious. I mean, do you see any signs of abuse?"

Gay feeds him another line of bullshit—a detective's prerogative in a homicide investigation. "I don't think there's any glaring problems with the case," he says, but the final determination is up to others.

"If this would have been an interrogation, I would have maybe come across a little more gruff," Tison says as they're wrapping up. "I would have brought an attorney. I—I just—I have nothing to hide."

Call me anytime if you have any more questions, Tison says to Gay, adding that he's anxious to get finished. He admits, though, that when he returned one of Gay's calls a few days ago and Gay answered the phone, "Child Abuse. Detective Gay," it unnerved him. Tison says he never connected Isabel's death with any kind of abuse.

The guy loves to talk, Curry's thinking. I'd shut my mouth if I were him.

In a case like this, it's going to be the details that add up to make it go. Curry will read an interview transcript ten times and then read it three more times a week later. He'll catalog all the statements a defendant makes that don't add up. He'll put into a separate binder copies of everything he has ever heard or read that sheds light on Tison's character and integrity. He'll get pictures of the desk she supposedly fell from and every other aspect of the room she was in blown up and he'll stare at them through a magnifying glass. He makes lists of more questions he wants to ask Tison. No detail is too small.

Did you turn off the computer? How? Where's the plug? Where's the bottle of beer you said you had? Did you go through the garage when you left or right out the front door? Where were your dogs? What did you do with the screen? What exactly were you doing on the computer when she fell? If you say you always leave the computer on, why was it off? Did you shut the window before you left? Where was the newspaper? I thought you were reading the newspaper? When did you have your first beer? Did you pick her up with both hands or just sling her over your shoulder with one? Why can't we find that beer bottle, Doctor? What did you do with it?

He'll finish and then ask the same fifty questions again to see if you trip up and get one or more of the details wrong. Why would an innocent man lie even about the most trivial fact? Curry keeps prodding the detectives and investigator who work the case with him. He could never understand why an innocent man would lie; he hoped a jury would see things the same way. You're innocent, Curry has always believed, you tell the truth about everything. If you're lying about where you put the beer bottle or whether there even was a beer bottle, you're hiding something.

"You take a case like this and you watch the video of his statements to the detectives over and over again," Curry tells someone in his office. "You really listen to what he said. Every word. He said he had a beer and took it upstairs and was drinking it when Isabel fell. Where the hell's the glass? He told the detective he spilled the beer on himself. When did that happen? Gay never asked the question. It proves to me he did something other than what he told us. That's the kind of thing that can convict someone."

Curry is not one of those prosecutors given to self-doubt. Once he makes up his mind about a case, and he made up his mind about Dr. Tison long ago, he pursues the defendant with a stubborn relentlessness that even some in his own office say can border on obsession. Not all prosecutors are as confident of the rightness of their approach on a case, especially a murky case like this one, but the most aggressive prosecutors like Curry need that sense of certainty to keep pushing. As the gray and foggy days of winter turn to Sacramento's typically early spring, where an eighty-degree afternoon in March is not unheard of, O'Mara is also warming to the case. Curry's persistence and daily updates have convinced his boss that Tison is probably a fileable case, though he's still not sure about the appropriate charges or whether a jury will agree Dr. Tison is a child killer.

Curry thinks O'Mara's being overly cautious. "We have the advantage that the jury is going to be sympathetic to us right off," Curry says one morning. "Babies don't fall out of windows. The photos will impress them. The evidence of what was on the desk and how it looked when the detectives got there. Nine out of ten people will see that and say it can't happen the way he says it did. If I can show the jury all the lies he made, then they start to think everything is suspicious."

To Curry, it's the Mariet Ford case all over again. A supposedly upstanding citizen portraying himself one way to the world and acting in an altogether different and sinister way when he's behind closed doors.

He made that case, too, when others in the office doubted he could put all the details together to convince a jury that the impressive looking professional sitting in front of them was really an impostor.

"If there's a gap between the time Tison says he got off the computer and the time he called for medical treatment, and I think there is, don't you think every juror is going to think that from his point of view he had some pretty compelling reasons not to immediately seek treatment for his daughter? At the very least, the jury will think he's reckless. A physician who's been drinking, he has a loaded handgun right on the desk where his daughter is playing. He's a doctor and he knows minutes are crucial and he doesn't call 911. I'll prosecute this guy for anything I can get him on just to make sure he loses his medical license. But I think he's good to go for the murder. I really do."

Tison is a hell of a lot smarter than the typical murder defendant prosecuted by the district attorney's office. He's not some reckless gang-banger or thug off the street. He's a physician. Tison graduated from law school. He's quoted in *The New York Times* as a weight-loss expert. The *Bee* has regularly portrayed him as a leader in the field. Dr. Tison appears to have standing in the community. He's made a small fortune with his three weight-loss clinics and by shrewdly playing the stock market. But his story doesn't add up.

Curry's not surprised when Gay calls in mid-April and says Tison has agreed to come downtown to the sheriff's department for another interview. At this point, he has yet to hire a lawyer. Curry again hides out next door and is considering joining in this time. He wants to see how it's going. If he doesn't think Gay's getting it done, the doctor will meet the determined prosecutor who wants to put him in prison for much, if not all, of the rest of his life.

"I want to make sure that you understand you're not under arrest," Gay tells Tison in his best nonthreatening voice. "You're free to leave, all that stuff. I'll try to get this done as quickly as possible. I know you have to go."

"Oh, no problem," Tison says.

Tison starts making small talk about how he's refinancing the house he just bought, the one his wife was out looking at when Isabel died. He even offers Gay advice on how to beat the mortgage lenders at their own game by using the Internet. If he's nervous and feeling the pressure of another interrogation, he keeps it hidden.

"I refuse to pay points. So I get these rates off the Internet and go in to mortgage brokers and they hate me. I ask 'em, 'Can you match it?' If not, I'll go with the Internet person. And our credit's so clean, it's not a big problem."

"They probably don't like educated people like you," Gay says. Then, before Tison can go off on another tangent, Gay starts in with the questions.

Tison says he had just fed Isabel a dinner of carrots and peas, fixed her a bottle of baby formula, and decided to take her upstairs so he could take a shower with her. She loved to play with a new fish radio he bought her. She was playing with some keys and an old wallet Tison says he gave her on the one bare corner of his desk when suddenly she's on her feet and through the window. Even though he's been trained in trauma medicine, he admits he ignored an essential tenet that says never move a person with spinal or head injuries until they can be stabilized. He scooped Isabel up in one arm, he tells Gay, used the screen to fend off his Doberman with the other, tossed her over his shoulder, and figured the best thing to do was rush her to the hospital. His wife, Elena, called just after Isabel's fall and Tison told her it looked as if Isabel would be okay. She was moving her eyes and legs; she followed him with her eyes. She was awake. "I thought, Thank God she is okay. Rubber girl survives. But I wasn't going to wait for 911 regardless."

The conversation is all over the place. Tison's back to financial matters. He'd be living in San Diego, where he went to school, but his wife doesn't want to move back because she's jealous of all the tall, thin, beautiful women living in La Jolla. You couldn't make this shit up, Curry thinks. No one would believe it.

Tison tells Gay the type of Internet service he has and how he always leaves his computer on. Odd, Gay says, that the computer was shut off when we got to the house. Why's that, Doctor? Tison says Isabel must have pulled the plug or maybe the doctor himself unplugged the machine when he lunged for his daughter. Curry is convinced this is impossible. The computer box was jammed into a corner of the floor, almost touching the wall plug and desk. There was no room for anyone to get in there and accidentally pull out the plug. Maybe I kicked it out when I reached for her, Tison offers. Curry has studied the crime-scene pictures. It couldn't have happened this way.

It's time for a break. Gay says he has to make a quick telephone call. The doctor is left alone while Gay and Curry confer next door. Cops use this trick to great advantage. They'll be sweating a suspect in an interview room and then leave him alone with the hidden camera and video rolling. The bad guy could ask three times if he's being taped. The cop will say, No, you don't see any recorder in here, do you? If the detective is lucky and the suspect is even dumber than he appears, the guy will get bored and look right into the spot in the ceiling where the camera's hidden and say something like "Man, I told that bitch she'd be dead if she kept fucking with me."

It doesn't happen often, but it has happened. Tison has made a terrible mistake by agreeing to talk without an attorney, but he's not foolish enough to confess to an invisible camera.

Keep going for the details, Curry tells Gay. Pin him down, Jason. Don't let him change the subject. You're doing great. Curry wants to get the investigator's blood moving, to pump him up like a coach would a player.

Back in the room and as soon as the two are seated, Gay once again lets the conversation drift to something Tison wants to talk about: his new house, the health benefits of drinking lots of water. Curry's next door twisting in his chair.

Anytime a child is killed, Gay says to the doctor, the case file gets thick, so after they spoke last time, Gay consulted a district attorney just to make sure everything was in order. His name is Mark Curry. He makes it sound as if Curry is new to the case. "It's no reflection on any improprieties," Gay says. "What it is a reflection of is there's a lot of information. And we have to go through each piece." Fine, Tison says, and soon after Gay leaves to "make a call and get Mr. Curry over here," Tison and Curry are face to face in the little room.

"Hi, Mr. Tison," Curry says as he enters the room and extends his hand. He figures he'll fuck with him a little right from the start by not calling him doctor.

"Hi, nice to meet you," Tison says back.

"Likewise," says Curry.

These guys are about as happy to meet each other as two rabid dogs who haven't eaten for a week. Curry can't stand the thought of Tison, who he is, how he lives, or what he likely did to that little girl. If Tison has any clue at all what's going on here, the sight of Curry should make him ill.

"The reason I'm here," Curry says, "is just because of the fact it's an accident, apparently, and we review every case very thoroughly." He's reviewed several cases where small children drowned in buckets of water and the death-review team he's on discussed ways to avoid such accidental deaths in the future. Curry wants Tison to relax, to think the district attorney's office views the tragic death of his young daughter as an accident. Maybe if we talk it through, Curry seems to suggest, we can put this case behind us and come up with some good ideas on ways to avoid babies being flung out of windows.

"And so," Curry continues to reassure him, "I've taken a kind of cursory look at it and reviewed everything. And this will probably be the last time you're interviewed by an official about what occurred. And then, um, the case, uh, goes up to the sheriff's department and could be closed once it's deemed an accident."

"Okay," Tison—this doctor, this guy who finished law school—says. Okay, Mr. Curry, you seem like a nice guy. Let's get these questions out of the way, call it an accident, and go our separate ways. "What can I tell you?" he asks.

After a few minutes of preliminaries, Curry gets to the point.

"I think you waited around hoping that she was gonna be all right," he says. "And all of this still could have been an accident, if you see what I'm getting at here." He thinks the doctor threw the kid out the window or slammed her head on the desk or floor and then tried to cover up with the story about a fall, but he knows he doesn't have to prove that to bury him. You don't always have to be that explicit with a jury. You take what the evidence and the defendant give you.

"And she started showing signs that her condition was worsening, then you made the decision," Curry continued. " 'I gotta get her to the hospital.' And please, Doctor, if that is true, and it was an accident, you need to tell us that. Because you're digging yourself a hole right now."

Tison remains calm. He insists that isn't what happened. "I would give my life for my child. I would not hang around that house. I don't care how guilty. I don't care how suspicious. I don't care what the penalties are. If my daughter was hurt, I would take her immediately to the hospital, not worrying about the penalties for myself. I would give my life for my daughter."

More back and forth. Tison holds his ground. It's time to rattle him and see if he breaks. "You know," Curry says, "I'm gonna be honest with you. I don't believe you about the Binaca thing."

"Okay," is all Tison can say. His shoulders are slumped, his energy drained. These three hours with Gay and Curry are much more tiring for him than the first session with Gay. Though he sticks to his essential story, that she was playing on the desk and inexplicably lunged for the screen, Tison comes out of this more wounded. Curry will walk back to the district attorney's office confident O'Mara will charge the guy. In addition to the county pathologists who can testify that Isabel's injuries are suspicious, that they don't seem to have resulted from a fall, Curry has found two other experts who have studied the police reports and other evidence and come up with similar conclusions.

One has told Curry the baby had to have been propelled from the window at a speed of five miles per hour to have landed as far from the house as she did. If she went through the screen on her own, she would have landed much closer. The other, a child development expert, has told Curry, after viewing the videos of the baby provided by Tison's lawyer, that she wouldn't have been strong enough or agile enough to stand up as quickly as Tison alleges and jump through the window. Both have submitted written reports and will testify if there's a trial.

"And by the way," Curry tells Tison as they're about to call it quits. "We did check on your residency thing. You know, you probably shouldn't put that on your Web site. If you didn't get a residency, you shouldn't advertise that you did. Seems a little misleading. Don't you think?"

Again, all Tison can say is "Okay." They thank one another for their time and Gay shows Tison to the elevator. The next day, Tison's Web site no longer says he completed a psychiatric residency at UC San Diego. He also hires a lawyer—finally—Don Heller, a former federal prosecutor who seems to know everyone in town, is friendly with reporters, and loves to talk to the press. Curry can't understand why he didn't hire someone known more for his trial skills than his public-relations acumen and political connections. This one, he's thinking during a six-mile run at lunch along the Sacramento River, is going to trial.

Curry knows he has more work to do. More details to amass and master. So on a very hot morning in late April, the prosecutor assembles a group of deputies, crime-lab technicians, crime-scene investigators with video cameras, and quietly stages what surely must have been the strangest-looking incident in the relatively short history of the suburban neighborhood the Tisons lived in when Isabel was killed.

He has subpoenaed the desk Tison says he was working on when Isabel fell, a desk now in his new house, and it's being delivered to his old residence on a quiet street overlooking the bluffs around Folsom Lake. Detectives carry the desk to the second-floor bedroom Isabel was in and re-create everything to perfection. Using crime-scene pictures, they place the desk in its original spot near the window. A phone, gun, horizontal files, tape dispenser, and stapler are all placed carefully on the desk exactly all as they appeared in the crime-scene photos. This alone takes more than two hours.

Once everything is in place, a crime-lab technician spends much of the rest of the day tossing from the window two babies, a rag doll that weighs the same twenty-three pounds as Isabel, and a much lighter doll deputies borrowed from the local fire department. Each fall or push is videotaped and measured. The dolls are thrown out with a screen engaged, with a screen partially engaged, and with no screen. Each time the baby lands with a thud close to the house. Isabel's blood was found on a spot on the deck nine and a half feet from the house. The only time the twenty-three-pound Raggedy Ann doll Detective Mary Lee Cranford says she spent five hours preparing lands anywhere near that far is when the crime-lab technician puts much of his weight behind the toss and heaves it. By the end of the day, when the last of the thirty-five thuds has attracted neighbors who are walking through the wooded area behind the houses, it is a surreal scene. Neighbors staring, crime technicians tossing babies out the window, half a dozen deputies and other officials in the yard watching, measuring, taking photos. Curry has borrowed a camera from the district attorney's office and is taking his own photos.

The throws don't prove much of scientific value. It's hard to imagine a judge allowing testimony about them to come in as evidence. The experiment is too crude. It does affirm Curry's suspicion, however, that the baby didn't go through the window as Tison said she did. He knows in court he'll have to present bona fide experts who've done more precise work. And he knows O'Mara is still not convinced the guy should be charged with murder. He's getting close, but he's not there yet.

7 | Southside Punks

In the courtroom, man, she's a real bitch.
— Carlos Cervantes, about Dawn Bladet

BY the middle of April, the Repkow controversy is behind them, but both Harrold and Bladet know it can come back almost anytime and upset the trial. By mutual agreement, Repkow has left the public defender's office. Much to the prosecutors' relief, Judge England has appointed her to continue representing Rick Brewer. Now they hope she doesn't do something nuts until the trial is over, but they're not taking bets.

Right from the start this morning, though, a problem crops up. Peters, Bobby Dixon's attorney, moves for a mistrial as soon as England finishes informing the lawyers that he's dismissed a Dixon juror for being tardy. The Dixon jury is losing people quickly. One woman is disqualified because the judge learns she was discussing the case with an alternate on one of the other juries. Another juror is thrown off because, even though she said on her questionnaire she doesn't know anyone in law enforcement, it turns out she works for a state social services unit where officers, wearing guns and badges, track down welfare cheats. She told England when it came to his attention that she didn't think they were law-enforcement employees, but the judge thanked her and said her services were no longer needed.

"This is obviously a logistical nightmare to get all three juries and all the parties here at the same time," England says. He denies Peters's motion.

The defense attorney is not happy. A lot of colds and flus are going around, he tells England, and he's fighting a bit of a bug himself. With the lawyers' quirky personalities and the demeanor of the various defendants and everything else that can go wrong with so many jurors and alternates, England sometimes must feel more like a well-paid baby-sitter than he does one of the most respected members of the Sacramento bench. Sometimes, that's all a judge really is. He or she tries to make sure no one gets too pouty or temperamental. That all the people who are supposed to show up to participate on any given day are in court ready to go. Rumors are abundant around the courthouse that England's headed for the federal bench, and there are days when it's impossible to avoid wondering whether he wouldn't enjoy the change of scenery right now.

The prosecutors should breeze through their first couple witnesses, but Harrold does the questioning. He asks the same thing a number of times, enunciating as if he's talking to a small child. Josh Christian, the first noncop witness in the case, is called to describe what happened the night of the robbery. Christian is a competent artist and he drew a picture of the man in the devil's mask that Harrold used in the prelim. Sketched with Magic Marker on a large poster-sized piece of white paper, it's a menacing image that Harrold has on an easel facing the jury. He wants the jurors to see Brewer as the devil. As he's questioning Christian, Harrold puts Jason Frost's photo on the visualizer so the jury can see once more that the victim was a real person. It's a nice contrast with the devil drawing, the face of good versus the face of evil. No one objects.

Much of Harrold's questioning has to do with the minutiae of the crime scene. It's necessary so nothing is left to the jury's imagination. But some of them start to drift off as he goes over and over every precise detail: How far were you from the counter, what's in each room of the store, where are the registers located, tell us again where the bread is prepared, walk us through the closing ritual. Harrold leaves out nothing.

Lippsmeyer is first to cross-examine Christian, and the defense attorney scores one point in his rambling set of questions when he gets him to admit that the drawing he did is not all that accurate. The mask didn't look exactly like the image drawn by Christian. Big deal, Harrold figures. The jurors have seen it. He knows the devil image is one they won't forget.

It's Repkow's turn. Under her cross-examination, Christian admits a few things that the prosecution wishes he hadn't: He's not sure how tall the shooter was because he didn't get a clean look at him. He's not certain how many robbers came into the store, four or five.

"Sometimes our memory can be distorted if we go over and over an event in our minds," Repkow says. "Do you agree with that?"

"Oh, yes," Christian answers. As for the shooter, he admits he didn't see any white skin coming out of his gloves or protruding beneath the mask. As far as he could tell, the man was black. This is Repkow's case right here. Harrold and Bladet know it's weak, since even his own accomplices put Brewer in the store. She'll maintain Brewer couldn't have shot Jason Frost because the eyewitnesses said the shooter was a tall, thin black man. Brewer is Hispanic, white skinned, about five feet nine inches tall, and stocky. It couldn't have been him. She wants the jury to remember there was a tall, thin black man involved in the first Bread Store robbery. His name was Michael Smith.

The trial is moving slowly, but no one at the DA's office is surprised. For one thing, it's a Harrold production. Bruce Moran, a criminalist with the DA's crime lab, will testify about the murder weapon and his tests showing that the shotgun shells that killed Frost did, without question, come from the Mossberg found in the apartment Brewer was sharing with Marichu Flores. No shotgun pellets were found at the scene, he tells the juries, because "they were retained by the target." In other words, the shotgun was placed so close to Jason Frost's body that the hundreds of buckshot pellets that normally could be expected to be showered everywhere all went directly into the young man's torso.

With Moran on the stand, Bladet bends down to grab the brown-and-black Mossberg from its resting spot beneath a lawyer's podium. She hands it to the tall, talkative expert on firearms and ballistics. Demonstrating how the gun works—load, cock, chamber, fire, extract, and eject—Moran pumps the weapon and produces a blood-curdling metal-against-metal sound. All thirty-six jurors and their alternates are sitting upright, focused completely on Moran and the pump-action weapon, just as Bladet and Moran hoped they would when they discussed his testimony in their office a few days ago.

John Parker, a Sacramento homicide detective, testifies about the Crime Alert call that came in and says Brewer was involved in the robbery and shooting. Parker was among the detectives who went to Flores's apartment and was allowed in when Brewer opened the apartment door after they knocked. Flores gave her consent to search the place and two of the detectives went into the bedroom, but they didn't find a weapon. It was only after Parker went in after them and searched again that he saw the Mossberg hidden beneath the bottom drawer of a bedroom dresser. Parker also testifies about the two shotgun shells he found in the pockets of a silver-and-black Oakland Raiders jacket hanging in the bedroom closet, shells Moran testified earlier had been cycled through the Mossberg. They had the fine metal engravings on the shell casing that could only be made by having been placed into the gun, chambered, and extracted without being fired.

On the afternoon of May 1, Bladet intends to call Flores to the stand. Brewer's girlfriend, the mother of two of his children, is a dark-eyed beauty whose face wears the tired, blank look of someone who's seen too much too soon. A drug addict and petty criminal herself, she'll testify how Brewer's sister, Angie, came to her apartment one night and smashed a bottle against the side of her head to indicate how the Brewer family felt about her and her cooperation with authorities. Next time, Flores testifies, Angie Brewer said she'd come back with a gun.

Flores is kept waiting all morning and for an hour or so after the lunch break, and she kills the time by sitting on one of the hard wooden benches outside Courtroom 9, staring off into space. She is alone. No one says a word to her. She just sits and stares, waiting to be called by the bailiff inside the courtroom where her lover, roommate, and father of her children is the focus of everyone's attention.

As always seems to be the case in a long, complicated trial, before Flores can take the stand, there are housekeeping issues to resolve.

First, two of the punk gangbangers, Chris and Will Stephens, kids from Southside Park, show up to testify. They've been subpoenaed as part of the district attorney's effort to show that the crime participants talked openly of their plans before the fact and how the whole thing "went sour downtown" afterward. The two teens are expecting to be called today but murder trials are rarely on schedule, so Harrold has them appear before the judge to be ordered to return at another time. If they don't show up, he wants the judge to remind them, they'll be arrested. They are thin, handsome boys. Jurors will say later how they looked at them and felt a profound sense of waste, as if these boys had been discarded somehow. That it was just a matter of time before they'd wind up in these rooms as defendants. "Where are their parents?" one of the jurors would ask when the trial was over. "That's what I wondered. Could they read? Were they developing any skills they could use, or were they just being led down this path that the defendants in this case followed? My heart broke for those boys."

The Stephens boys live near Southside. Once they do testify, they'll be reminded on the stand of what they told the cops in the weeks after the robbery: that they saw the robbers together the day of the stickup, that they heard them talk about "doing a lick," that Brewer said he had "the guns taken care of," that they saw Dixon driving the Jimmy right before the robbery. They saw Brewer, Glica, Martinez, Garcia, and Carlos Cervantes in it. Will Stephens, the older of the two brothers, will be reminded that he told the cops he saw a twelve-gauge shotgun in the Jimmy when Brewer got out to talk with him. He saw a ski mask too.

"We're going to do this thing, so don't tell no one," Will Stephens told the cops Brewer said to him. "If we get caught, keep it on the downlow, because they'll be coming to your place. Don't tell them nothing."

An hour after seeing the Jimmy in front of his house, Chris Stephens told the cops he heard news reports of the robbery and shooting and that later than night, when he again saw Brewer, he heard Brewer say, "Everything went sour downtown."

When they come into the courtroom side by side this afternoon, expecting to be called to the stand, the brothers are all swagger and machismo. They're dressed in red T-shirts. They strut up the aisle to stand before Judge England with the false confidence they might show in the park if someone they don't know shoots them a hard look. They have to try to look tough. It's one thing to have spilled their guts to Detective Richard Overton when no one was around. Despite the defense allegations that Overton bullied the kids to talk, it's hard to feel threatened by the big, pasty-faced detective who's so rumpled and unkempt, he can't keep his shirttails in his pants.

This is the courtroom. Rick Brewer is sitting at the defense table to stare holes through the brothers.

The judge explains to the Stephens brothers that their testimony will not be needed today, that the proceedings are behind schedule. They need to return in a week or so.

"Man, this is bullshit," the older Stephens brother says, loud enough for everyone to hear. Two beefy deputies rush over to the boys as they face the judge. Spit out your gum and take off your hats, they're ordered. "You'll address this court with respect," England says with authority. When one of the boys bumps a deputy—he was rocking back and forth as part of the show but the contact appeared unintentional—the beefier of the two deputies looks at the boy like he's a piece of shit. Brush up against me again, the deputy says, and you'll be arrested.

They get the message. This is Judge England's world, not some alley by the park. But it is a message they could forget. When they do come back and testify, they can't remember anything. They told the cops what they wanted to hear just to get the interviews over and get on with their lives, they'll say. It was what the prosecutors expected and warned jurors about in the opening arguments.

What Harrold and Bladet must do throughout the trial is show that Overton is a professional, not some bully who pushes kids around and coerces statements out of them. And that these Southside punks, all of whom fear and look up to Brewer, have good reason to say one thing to the cops, where no one was around the eavesdrop, and quite another in the courtroom.

As soon as the blur of elbows and red that was the skinny Stephens boys leave the courtroom, Repkow moves for a mistrial. Bladet had put autopsy photos of Jason Frost on the visualizer this morning while the pathologist was testifying about the exact nature of Jason's injuries and his cause of death. It seems the photos of Jason laid out on the examining table, his body purple and bloated from the rampant infection that ultimately killed him, had not been presented to the defense earlier in discovery. Motion denied, England says. The pictures were germane to the testimony.

Jack Frost is alone in the gallery today. Becky has stayed home to baby-sit her granddaughter, the one joy in her life right now. Jack came in late. Neither one could stand to be there when the autopsy photos would be shown. Bladet had warned Jack about the photos and the pathologist's testimony even as she forgot to warn the defense. When Jack does show up, he's agitated. Becky's not here to calm him and Jack's anger is out there, on the surface.

Finally, at 2:30 in the afternoon, with all the hot blood and fever that has passed through the courtroom this warm, sunny day in May, Marichu Flores is escorted in to testify.

Soon after she's sworn in, Bladet confronts her with the lies she told Detective Toni Winfield when Winfield interviewed her after the robbery. For starters, she told Winfield that on the night of the incident she and Brewer were home throughout the evening. They watched two movies on video, *Sunset Park,* which they had taped off the TV, and *Eraser,* a rental. The only time Rick left was around 5:00 P.M. for a few minutes, to take out the trash.

Bladet knows from the thousands of pages of police reports and discovery documents that Winfield, ever the thorough detective, interviewed Flores a second time while she was being held in the county jail on a misdemeanor traffic warrant. The charge was nothing, just a way to sweat her a little bit and see if she'd give up Brewer. On January 8, 1997, the day after Winfield's first interview with her, Flores told a different story.

She told Winfield how Brewer's sister had intimidated her and had also come to the apartment the day after the robbery and removed some clothing that belonged to Brewer. She informed the detective that she and Brewer used to live in Southside Park before moving into their current apartment a few miles away. She still lied about such incidentals as the shotgun, claiming she had never seen Brewer with it, which Winfield found impossible to believe. She was a little more forthcoming on some other points, especially after Winfield said she was preparing to have her charged with a Section 32 of the California Penal Code, accessory to robbery and murder. That made Flores think a little harder about whether Brewer had left the apartment on the night of the robbery.

Flores had been placed in a holding cell after Winfield grew frustrated with her lies. Two hours later, after sitting in the cell and contemplating felony charges she faced for protecting Brewer, who had been abusing her and her children in the days before the stickup, she said she was ready to tell Winfield the truth.

Brewer did leave their apartment in the evening, she suddenly recalled, and it was for more than just a few minutes to throw out the garbage. It was more like twenty-five minutes. When he came back, there was nothing unusual in his demeanor. When she asked why Flores had lied earlier, Winfield got a blank stare. Bladet has no trouble getting to the heart of it when she finally has Flores on the stand.

"You were purposefully withholding information from the police because you thought it would harm Mr. Brewer," Bladet says to her, waiting for a response.

"It wasn't that I was lying for Mr. Brewer," Flores answers in a soft voice. "I didn't want you guys thinking . . ." She trails off, which is okay with Bladet. The jurors will fill in the rest.

Bladet bangs away on other points, trying to show jurors Flores still cares about Brewer and would have no trouble lying for him. One day she was subpoenaed to testify in this trial but failed to show up. For several days, she was nowhere to be found. Investigators went looking for her to no avail. She didn't call the DA's office or the court to say she was having problems. Bladet assumed she was on a drug binge, but she lets Flores know that on the day she ignored her subpoena, jail visitor logs show she went to see Brewer at the county jail.

Bladet finishes by getting Flores to admit she has become close to Repkow. They talk every now and then, three or four times in the last month, by Flores's reckoning. They talk during breaks. Repkow shows her transcripts. Is an investigator present when you meet with Repkow, or is it just the two of you? Bladet asks. The implication is clear, even if it's never spelled out for the jury. Bladet wants jurors to think Repkow has coached Flores to testify in a way that will help Brewer. He is, after all, the father of her children. Jurors don't like testimony from either side that seems too rehearsed.

When Repkow steps up to cross-examine the witness, Bladet expects the worst. The defense attorney tries to question Flores about the time she was arrested for beating up a boyfriend, but Bladet loudly, and with a snap in her voice that sounds like she's scolding a small child, objects on relevancy to this case. England sustains. His large, round face once again seems to reveal some of his innermost thoughts. He can't help but smile just a little at how Repkow and Bladet carry on. He calls them over to the bench for a brief sidebar conference, where he tells them to keep in check their personal dislike for each other.

As soon as Repkow is back at the defense table, she asks Flores if it's okay to call her Mary from time to time.

Bladet can't believe her ears. "Objection," she shouts in her coldest, sternest voice.

"We're in a courtroom, Your Honor," Bladet says. "I don't think it's proper to be that informal, but if that's the nature of your relationship . . ."

"I would ask that the district attorney's comments be stricken," Repkow snaps back. The judge immediately calls for another sidebar conference. Jurors are smiling, stifling a giggle, squirming in their seats, as all six lawyers lumber up to the side of the judge's podium for yet another scolding from England. He tilts his head down and looks at them as if they're players on the college football team he helped coach before he went into law, who were unable to follow directions and run the play that was called. They're lectured again about behaving and keeping their personal feelings to themselves.

Flores finishes up talking about her depression, her battle with addiction, her use of antidepressants, and the overall tough life she's led. It's all Repkow can do. Try to make her sympathetic. Make Bladet into a witch. It appears futile. Bladet sits there and listens. She knows it's not working. Repkow never gets Flores to explain her lies to the cops and never even raises the notion that Brewer didn't live at the apartment or that he was there for all but a few minutes on the night of the robbery and shooting. Better yet, Bladet and Harrold are thinking, when Flores is done, the jurors know Flores offered the juries no alternative to the notion that the shotgun belonged to Brewer. No one could have brought it in. He wasn't hiding it for anyone. It was his.

"He's living there," Harrold crows the next morning in the office, knowing Flores helped their case even though she was hostile. "That was their bedroom. The kids were in foster placement. No one else put the gun in there."

As for Bladet's escalating battle with Repkow and the judge's frequent admonishments to clean it up, Harrold seems amused more than anything. "The Diva's feisty. It's not my style," he says.

Although this is the thirty-four-year-old prosecutor's first homicide, on matters of the law, Bladet doesn't have many equals in the DA's office. She spent three years as an appellate lawyer in the California Attorney General's Office honing that part of her craft. When it comes to dealing with the variety of people a prosecutor encounters in a case, she can be rough, but she always seems to get her way.

Cervantes pegged her right when he told an investigator for the DA's office that when he met her in prison he thought Bladet was real sweet. "But in the courtroom, man, she's a real bitch." It's a tag she's proud of and does nothing to dispute, though she admits it can make it hard to have much of a personal life. On more than one occasion when she met a man she liked in a social setting, she told him she was a secretary so she wouldn't scare him off.

Bladet went to see Cervantes a few times at the California State Penitentiary at Folsom just as the trial was about to begin. He was serving his final months for auto theft, a favorite pastime of his at Southside Park. Cervantes was in the Jimmy with Brewer, Dixon, and the others on the late afternoon of December 23, 1996, all set to "kick it" downtown, as he told Detective Overton, when Lisa Lopez, a senior at McClatchy High School, came running up and shouting for him to get out and stay out of the car.

When Cervantes is escorted into court the morning of Monday, May 21, for his first day of testimony, he's scared shitless. His friends are on trial for felony murder, not him. They're facing life sentences. He's due out for the auto theft in a few weeks.

He owes Lisa Lopez his life and now another woman is trying to get him to do something even tougher than walking away from Brewer, whom he's known for years. Bladet needs Cervantes to snitch off Brewer and his cohorts in open court. To testify that he had been in the Jimmy all set to go. That he knew what everyone was up to the day the Bread Store was robbed and Jason Frost was shot. That he ran into everyone later and heard Brewer say how "it all went sour downtown." With Brewer and the other defendants sitting at the defense table staring at him again, Bladet is expecting Cervantes to put the first big nail in his buddies' coffins. And she's not a woman to take no for an answer.

Two investigators from the district attorney's office drive out to Folsom every day he's to appear in court, and get Cervantes. On the first day, they spread the word he has to come downtown for some phony paternity test, but when you're in the joint and guys with guns and badges come and take you away in the morning and bring you back at the end of the day, word travels fast. Everyone knows where you've been. You're out being a snitch. You've been at court selling out your homeboys.

Cervantes's nervous eyes are darting everywhere at once as he sits in the witness box. He practically shakes. His gaze doesn't lock on anyone for long. On a few occasions, never in front of Brewer and the others, he'll break into tears. He knows he's going to be back on the street in a month or so wearing a snitch jacket. Even if he were tempted to lie on the stand and say he never told the cops a thing, he knows he's fucked when Bladet tells the judge she first wants to play a five-hour videotape of Detective Overton's interrogation of Cervantes down at Sacramento police headquarters the morning of January 13, 1997.

Showing the video is important for several reasons. Bladet and Harrold know the defense is going to make an issue of how the cops got information from the Southside punks. They're claiming Overton in particular was underhanded. That he taped the interviews but kept turning off the machine so he could threaten the young boys and have no record of it. The witnesses were kids. Lawyers for the defendants want jurors to think the cops played dirty. That they made threats. Intimidated the boys to give up their homies and say a bunch of things they were not certain of. Showing the long tape in its entirety is the best way to defuse this. Both prosecutors have watched the tape so many times already and reviewed the transcripts so often, they can practically recite the interview verbatim. It is essential to do it again in court. Overton was nothing if not professional. Jurors can see and hear for themselves.

The prosecution also wants to show the tape because the jurors will see how scared Cervantes was to tell the cops anything. He was not a witness who was eager to rat out his pals, as the defense will later claim of Trevor Garcia. Trevor was an actual participant. He went into the store. He yelled for money. The DAs cut him a very big break in exchange for very specific testimony. Cervantes made no such deal. He had nothing to gain, everything to lose. He was testifying because he'd been convinced that telling the truth was the best avenue available to him.

Bladet doesn't know how he'll act on the stand. When she went to see him at Folsom a few weeks ago and flirted a little with him, he said he was prepared to speak the truth once more, even if Brewer was in the courtroom to menace him. But Bladet has no assurance he'll do that. She has no leverage over him as she and Harrold have over Garcia. They have a contract with Garcia and his lawyer. Garcia tells the truth or he's good for felony murder just like the rest of them. Cervantes tells the truth or he lies; it's up to him.

The video shows another side of Cervantes that Bladet and Harrold want jurors to understand. He was loyal. Rick was his buddy. He told Overton he'd first met him a few years earlier when some bigger dudes were roughing him up at the park. Brewer stepped in and kicked their ass. He was scared of Brewer. He also had genuine affection for him, and no matter what he might say in court or how tough and unfeeling he might act on the stand, Bladet wants jurors to see that Cervantes has a heart. That it's tough for him to say anything that will help send his buddy to prison for the rest of his life.

As soon as Bladet hits "play" on the VCR and the tape's image is projected onto a screen, jurors see a scared, skinny kid who seems to be at Overton's mercy. The detective's been at this game a long time. The tape shows him waiting a good fifteen minutes before telling Cervantes why he's in custody and advising him of his rights. Overton asks him a bunch of questions first, like Who does he live with, where does he stay? Does he know this guy or that guy? Has he ever seen Brewer? Ever hang with Dixon? He shows Cervantes a picture of Dixon and says he knows that Cervantes has talked to Dixon, but Carlos is playing dumb. "I probably seen him on the street, but we ain't bumped heads before," he says.

This goes on for a good quarter hour before Overton bothers to tell Cervantes he's in custody on a warrant for a "10851," auto theft, and reads him his rights. There is no intimidation on the tape. Harrold and Bladet hope jurors will see that the guy's a pro. When he's sitting down man-to-man with Carlos Cervantes—man to boy, really—he uses a few tricks of the trade without bullying the kid. He runs a solid interrogation with someone who's not exactly forthcoming.

"So, having the rights in mind, do you wish to waive them and talk to me about whatever it is you know about all this?" Overton asks on the video the jurors are watching.

"About what?" the kid says.

"About what we're investigating here?"

"What are you guys investigating?"

"Well, we're investigating a car that may have been stolen."

"Stolen?"

"Uh-huh."

"A car?"

"Yeah."

"A stolen car?"

"Yeah. Maybe you have some information on it; maybe you don't."

"I don't—I don't steal cars no more."

"Okay. That's cool. So you don't mind, then, talking to me about it?"

"Talking about what?"

"About a stolen car."

"I don't steal cars no more."

"I know, but you don't have—you don't—it's okay to talk about it?"

"Uh, if you want."

"Is that all right with you?"

"Yeah. I ain't tripping."

Overton gets a call, or so he tells the kid. He really goes next door, where another detective is watching on closed-circuit television and making sure the VCRs are recording it all. When he comes back, Overton tells Cervantes what the cop in the other room just reminded him about. Hey, Carlos, he says, it's cool you are willing to talk about a stolen car, but I also want to talk to you about this robbery your name came up in.

"My name came up . . . ?" Carlos asks him as the jurors follow along.

"Yeah," Overton says.

"I.was in the robbery?"

"Well, that's—that's—that's the information we're getting is that—"

"Me?" Cervantes can't believe his ears.

"Yeah," Overton says, even though he knows Carlos never participated in the robbery. It's yet another abject lesson in why suspects should never waive their rights and never talk to the cops. Not without their lawyers present.

"Could be wrong," the detective goes on. "I don't know. That's why I'm talking to you, because I don't want to take somebody else's word for it. I want to give you an opportunity to set the record straight. Okay? So is that okay, that we talk about that robbery too?"

"Huh? I don't know nothing about a robbery." Everyone in the courtroom can see Overton has the kid by the balls. He's got him convinced the only way he can clear himself from felony murder is to give up his friends.

Overton gets him to say how he spent Christmas and backtracks from there. Cervantes tells the detective that he went to Downtown Plaza "the day before Christmas Eve" and then went to Lisa's and watched some videos.

The rest of the interrogation follows along classic lines. The kid's asked whether he knows anything about Dixon and a stolen car. Not really, though he saw him in a car, but not until Christmas Day. Overton knows he's fudging. The car was abandoned December 23, after the shooting. Cervantes says he didn't even talk to Dixon about the car because he looked inside and saw the steering column had been peeled away. He knew it was hot.

"Hell, no," he insists when Overton asks if he ever rode in it. A few minutes later, he admits Bobby did give him a ride home. But Cervantes wore gloves and made sure he didn't touch nothing inside because he knew it was hot.

"Okay, where did he say he got it from?" Overton asks.

"I didn't ask him all that."

"Well, yeah, you did."

"Huh?"

"Yeah, you did."

"Huh?"

"Yeah, you did."

"I did?"

"Yeah."

"I did? I asked him? I told you I asked him?"

"You're gonna tell me."

"Huh?"

"You're gonna tell me where he told you he got it from."

"How come?"

"Because you know."

"I don't know."

"We've already talked to Bobby. He already gave it up. I want you to do the same thing. You—you need to do the right thing."

It's the classic cop lie. You may as well tell us because the other dude did. Cervantes falls for it.

He starts out telling the detective Dixon stole the car from outside some dive club but before long, Cervantes admits he stood watch while

Bobby jacked the Jimmy. He gives that up just because Overton tells him he's talked to witnesses who put him there. Another lie, but cops can do that during criminal interrogations.

A couple minutes later, as the tape rolls on, Overton asks the kid, "What can you tell me about that robbery-homicide?" This is after Cervantes has told him he'd read about Brewer's arrest in the newspaper in connection with a robbery and killing at the Bread Store.

"Huh?"

"What can you tell me about it?"

"Oh, I don't know nothing about that."

"Okay."

"I'm not lying or nothing."

"Hold on. Hold on," Overton tells him in a soft, unthreatening voice, like he's simply asking for a favor from a friend. "You need to come completely clean here, Carlos. I'm gonna be straight with you, guy. We know you were there."

"Where?"

"Hold on. Hold on. I—I know you were—"

"Where was I?"

"Hold on."

"I wasn't in no robbery."

"Yeah, you were. Yeah, you were."

"I wasn't there," Cervantes says, and tells Overton to call his grandma. He was at her place when this happened. Call her, he says.

"Carlos. Listen to me. Just listen to me. We've talked to everybody. We've talked to Rick Brewer. We've talked to little Rick. We've talked to Trevor. We've talked to J. D. We talked to Bobby. Everyone's given it up. I'm not saying this is easy. But you gotta do the right thing because the truth is the truth."

Overton hardly seems an authority on the subject, since he's blatantly lying himself. He's talked to all those people, but no one gave up Cervantes because Overton knows he wasn't there. He knows the kid bailed when his girlfriend got in his face. Doesn't matter. Overton needs Cervantes to nail the others. If he's stupid enough to think they've made him on the robbery and shooting, he's going to do exactly what Overton wants.

"We can't change anything," the detective says. "That young man is dead. I need to hear from you what it is you did, because there were six people there; only one person pulled the trigger. I need to know who that person is."

He starts to cry. Overton gives him a Kleenex. The detective is his friend now. He knows it's hard, but, Hey, Carlos, you're not going to tell me anything we don't already know. It's just best for you if you're truthful.

"You need to tell me whose idea this was."

"Rick."

"Rick who?" Overton asks.

"B," Cervantes says, as if can't utter his full name. Brewer told him he'd been "peeping the place for some time," that it was an easy mark. The jurors are riveted. They're watching the tape, reading along on a transcript. All thirty-six jurors and the alternates turn the page at once when it's time.

He's sobbing like a baby now. This is exactly what Bladet wants to jury to see. Cervantes is afraid; he hates himself for giving up his friend. This is the real deal, she's thinking. He told Detective Rich Overton the truth when the two of them were alone in that room within days of the crime. Now, if Trevor Garcia comes off anywhere near as well as Cervantes does, the prosecutors know they're just about there.

8 | Dead Bang Winner

All we gotta do is present it and stay out of the way and twelve morons will convict these assholes. —John O'Mara

THERE is no such thing as too much evidence. No matter what they say about the thrill of a good court fight against an able adversary, prosecutors want it all. They dream of DNA, unimpeachable eyewitnesses, freely given confessions. While they're at it, how about throwing in a videotape of the bad guy pulling the trigger or knocking over the liquor store? A menacing outburst by the defendant in court would be nice. Then the most pathetic collection of bleeding-heart ignoramuses ever assembled into a jury box, as Mark Twain might say, couldn't possibly vote the wrong way.

DAs want the perfect case, one that's utterly impossible to mess up. They want the hundred-percent certifiable DBW, the Dead Bang Winner.

It's hot the morning of June 18. Summer has arrived in the California capital. There have already been a few 100-degree days. It hasn't rained for more than a month and won't again until October. The city sits upstream of the Sacramento River Delta, and the otherwise stultifying summer heat is often moderated by a delicious afternoon and evening Delta breeze that blows through the city as cool marine air from the San Francisco Bay is pulled into the Sacramento Valley by the hot air rising above it. The brown ozone that collects on particularly hot days has not made an appearance yet. People are flocking to garden and landscaping stores; families and beer-drinking college kids spend weekends floating in yellow rafts down the ice-cold American River. The pleasure boats and water skiers are starting to line the deep Sacramento River that supplies much of the state with its drinking water and slices north to south through the city.

In Major Crimes, not much out of the ordinary is happening. A pizza deliveryman got his head blown off the other night while making a delivery in a seedy part of town. The homicide detectives at the sheriff's department are pretty sure who did it. They come and tell O'Mara about a shotgun they pulled out of someone's house that had brain matter stuck to the end of the weapon. They're still trying to nail down enough details to make it a prosecutable case. The dirtbags they've been interviewing are giving all kinds of conflicting stories. Detectives are still not sure what they've got.

O'Mara's feet are up on his desk. He's watching some fat guy with an accent fry up crepes on the Food Network. Things are slow for a Monday. Deputies are sitting around on the chairs outside O'Mara's office listening to Paul Durenberger's horror story about a drive-by shooting case that is falling apart day by day. It was hard enough from the start, a gang killing where no one wanted to testify or could remember what happened. Some Laotian gangbangers were hanging out by an all-night convenience market. Words were exchanged. What else is new? One group of assholes leaves and the other group of assholes stays. The assholes who leave come back and shoot the place up, wounding some of the assholes who stayed. A young man by the name of Pa Sang Saelee was killed and four years later the People of the State of California are spending the public's hard-earned tax money to subpoena witnesses, interview thugs, get them all in court so an Attorney 5 who may be at the top of the scale and is paid $102,195.79 a year can square off against an Attorney 5 who makes the same amount for the public defender's office or an equivalent hourly wage working on the Indigent Defense Panel. They spend four weeks presenting evidence, calling witnesses, arguing, cajoling, and pleading with the jury in a case where evidence and witnesses are scarce. On day fifty-three, after Durenberger has just put on his penultimate witness, a bad case becomes a genuine nightmare.

Lori Teichert, the defense attorney, who, everyone in the DA's office agrees, is a nice woman and a decent lawyer who shouldn't be trying homicides because they stress her out too much, goes to the judge, crying in chambers, and says she's got a conflict. She's concerned for her personal safety and needs to be taken off the case. Durenberger's back to square fuckin' one.

Durenberger looks for commiseration from his colleagues, but all he gets is another lecture from Professor O'Mara on the inadequacies of court-appointed defense lawyers. He could put these little talks in a binder and label it *Law School Is Interesting, but Here's How This Shit Really Works.* It's a perfect day for something unusual to walk in the door. People have too much time on their hands to pontificate about virtually everything.

Midmorning, just such a case appears. The men and women in Major Crimes have a man by the name of Arthur Gene Lane to thank for this Dead Bang Winner. He's a tall, skinny man in his mid-thirties with no hair. An octopus is tattooed on his head.

Sheriff's detectives Marci Minter and Lori Timberlake drop off a videotape in O'Mara's office in the morning and don't say much more than: Watch it. Known around the sheriff's department as Cagney and Lacey, the department's only two-women homicide detective team, Minter and Timberlake got on the Lane case after the warrants officers— cops and prosecutors call them "the Knuckle Draggers" because they're all giants—arrested Art as he was getting off a Greyhound bus at the downtown station. Seems a friend of Artie's was at a wedding somewhere up in Nevada with him a weekend back and he was talking more than he should have been. But, hey, Art's a people person. He makes music and writes poetry he says is full of hope and promise and love. Music he told the cops that could have made him a star if all this hadn't happened.

He's at the wedding, getting loaded, having a good time. He's telling this friend how he frantically telephoned 911 about his girlfriend after he said he found her hanging from a rope attached to the ceiling in his garage. But the funny thing about it, Art goes on, the story wasn't quite the way he first told it. When this friend heard Art say the truth was hiding on a video stashed in the tent he lived in behind his mother's house in an industrial part of Sacramento, the friend split from the wedding, raced down to Art's mom's place and got her permission to rifle through his stuff. Tammy, his friend, found a videotape with the label "Blair Witch Project" taped to it. Something told her to pop it into a VCR.

While Art's mom, Harlene, was out buying groceries, she watched that video. Tammy must have been horrified at what she saw, but she couldn't have been shocked. Tammy had known Art for a long time. She knew the stories he told about drowning a girlfriend's three-hundred-dollar puppy in the bathtub after it got on his nerves, about the explosive devices he liked to set off in high school. She knew Art so well, in fact, she told the cops she left the wedding and went to get the video because she understood how dangerous Art could be when he was off his medication. He scared her. She had to see this tape for herself.

There's a prologue to the video, though, and it's best to consider this story in context. The detectives also left O'Mara a copy of a tape recording of a 911 call a very distraught and emotional Art Lane made on the afternoon of May 21, when the woman he said was the love of his life tragically decided to end it all.

They had just eaten lunch with his mom. Nancy Paul, his twenty-seven-year-old girlfriend, went outside to smoke a cigarette, Art told the operator. When Art, who's three years older than Nancy, returned to the garage that he also lived in and used as an art and music studio, God damn it all if his old love-filled heart didn't just start to burst from sorrow and grief. There was Nancy hanging from a rope.

"Oh, my girlfriend's dead," he says to the operator in a high-pitched, mile-a-minute squeal. He's hysterical.

The operator's voice is sturdy and calm. She needs his address.

"Seven three zero nine Power Inn Road," he says in a panic.

"Is this a house?"

"Yes."

"And what is your name? What is your name, please?"

"My name's Arthur."

"Okay." The operator gets back to the matter at hand. "What do you mean she's dead? What happened?"

Arthur has accelerated from zero to sixty in an instant. He is talking as quickly as a human can and still be understood. "I broke up with her and she went out in the garage. She told me she was going to smoke a cigarette. When I come out there she's hanging from the fucking—from the fucking ceiling."

He shrieks. He wails. He loved her so much. He doesn't know what to do. She looks like she's already dead.

"Okay, listen, we've already got the ambulance on the way," the operator reassures him. "Did you cut her down?"

"Yes."

Put her flat on her back, she tells him. Put a hand on her neck and a
hand on her forehead. Tilt her head back.

Arthur's beside himself. He's losing her. He can't do everything the
operator says and still hold on to the phone, for Chrissakes.

She tells him to put down the phone, which he does. He's unnerved;
she can hear him hyperventilating even though the phone is on the
floor.

"She just isn't responding to me at all," he yells into the phone after
picking it back up.

"Do you know CPR?" the operator asks.

"No," he shouts. "I don't want to hurt her."

Now the operator is yelling.

"Stay calm with me."

"I'm trying," he says but, damn, it's hard. He loved her so.

"Just let me breathe." He takes several deep and noisy breaths, the
kind they teach in Lamaze classes to expectant mothers. Maybe he
learned it on a Buddhist meditation tape.

The operator is in there with him. She's busting her butt trying to
save his girlfriend's life. "Give her two big breaths of air like you're
blowing up a big balloon," she says.

He says okay and repeats her instructions as if to ensure he heard
them right. "Two breaths of air." He's racing against time. He drops the
phone again. She can hear his valiant attempts to breathe life into her.
He's trying so hard.

"Good," she tells him when he comes back to the phone, as if she
were praising a two-year-old who's finished his oatmeal. "I heard you do
it. That's real good."

You can hear the paramedics coming through the garage door. It's too
late. Nancy Paul, twenty-seven, mother of a seven-month-old daughter,
is dead.

Arthur is inconsolable. He's crying, wailing how much he loved her.
"She came into my life. Now she's gone."

Two Sacramento sheriff's patrolmen arrive. They're very sympathetic.
They ask a few questions about why she'd want to hang herself. Arthur

tells them she was strung out on meth, that she was very depressed. Her best friend died a few weeks ago. She went into a total tailspin. Nancy and that best friend figured in another case this summer, in fact. They were drinking at a sleazy bar called Yolanda's when some badass gave them a ride somewhere and flashed a gun. Don't worry, he told them, it's not for you. Later that night, the guy who the gun *was* for got popped. Nancy and her friend were supposed to be witnesses at a future murder trial. That's how it is sometimes in the small criminal circles that the Homicide team's clientele runs in. Everyone knows everyone else, and everyone's a bad night or a bar fight away from being a corpse, a witness, or a defendant on a 187.

Besides Lane carrying on so, the deputies, God bless 'em, did get a little curious about a video camera that was propped up on a tripod and aimed at the spot where Nancy's body had been hanging. She was wearing bluejean shorts and a red tube top when the paramedics showed up. Lane said they liked to tape Nancy's seven-month-old son, his band, stuff they did around the house. You know, he told the detectives, the things any normal family does with a video camera.

"All I ever did was try to help that girl," he said. "I took her off the street and tried to give her something she never had. Then to open the door and see that."

They buy the whole package. Her death is ruled a suicide, despite some suspicions expressed in the investigative report filed by a coroner who was called to the scene. He disagreed with what the deputy at the county jail would later say at the prelim, that Art Lane was just another inmate. The deputy coroner wrote in his report that Arthur Lane was one strange dude.

"The only thing that caused concern for this investigator," David Santos, deputy coroner, wrote, "was the deceased's boyfriend. He reportedly had a criminal past and was or had been on parole. Although there was no evidence that any attack had occurred, the boyfriend came across as a suspicious character. This is based on appearances alone."

No shit, O'Mara thought. The guy's suspicious. Octopus tattoo on his head. More ink on the rest of his drug-ravaged body than a naval battalion. Deep-set eyes as dark as dirt. A diabolical grin. The meth rant. Yeah, he might be a little suspicious.

Santos's instincts were better than the sheriff's officers, you could say that much. But it didn't change anything. It went down as a suicide and no one paid any attention. Never even made the papers.

The case was closed. Nancy Paul was officially ruled to have died the way anyone who knew her would have predicted: by her own hand, with a body full of illegal drugs. She was a drug addict who turned tricks. The way Arthur Lane must have figured, who'd care if she were dead or alive? She was the kind of victim DAs see a lot in their murder cases. The kind juries will vote to convict on, if the evidence is there, but not the kind these same juries muster up much sympathy for.

A lot of criminal defendants are stone-cold idiots, too dumb to put their hands in their pockets if it's cold outside. Arthur Gene Lane is smart, creative enough to write his own music and poetry, but taping a homicide and bragging about it to friends at a wedding—a prosecutor couldn't ask for much more than that.

Tammy, the friend who left the wedding and found the tape, confronted Art's mom with what was on it when she returned from the store. "I did not believe it," Harlene said in her statement to detectives, "so I had to watch the tape for myself." Tammy hit the "play" button one more time.

There's almost ninety minutes of feverish sex of every stripe and variation imaginable. Arthur is resplendent in all his tattooed glory: a gang name in giant Roman letters across his back, serpents and dragons on the arms, the octopus on his shaved head. They have sex over and over and over again. They use toys and all kinds of assorted props and aids. The meth must have given them both superhuman stamina. Just when you think they can't possibly move another muscle, he lifts her in his arms and appears to carry her somewhere. Everything is captured on videotape. Her skinny legs are wrapped tight around his waist. He kisses and pets her. She strokes him back. They seem to be in love.

This is not the part of the video Timberlake and Minter told O'Mara to watch. No one would want to witness these two having sex. O'Mara speeds through the sex scenes, wanting no part of any of them. Maybe whoever actually gets the case will have to watch them to see if there are other bits of evidence, but not O'Mara. He's paid well, more than $120,000 a year, but it ain't enough to watch this.

When the sex is done, Arthur is seen carrying Nancy into the garage. She's obviously stoned. She has trouble maintaining her balance. He holds her up and in a nimble move he jumps up on the chair with her. He's gentle. He's still stroking her hair, petting her face. He kisses her, whispers into her ear words that the microphone does not pick up. Both her arms and legs are wrapped tightly around him. You can see that she feels safe. It's a loving embrace.

After they're both steady on the chair, he reaches up one of his heavily tattooed arms and pulls down a thick black climbing rope shaped into a hangman's noose. It's hanging from a heavy wooden beam that's part of the garage ceiling. He slips the noose gently over her neck. Her long brown hair is messy, so he's having a hard time slipping it over her head. She drops her neck back obligingly, gathering up her hair and pulling it into a pony-tail. She helps him place the noose on her neck. He continues to kiss and pet her. It's a Hallmark video for the kinky-sex-and-meth crowd.

Arthur is heard reassuring her that they're in this together. She's not worried. Their bodies are pressed tight together as he hugs her one last time.

Then he snaps. The evil Arthur is in the room. He jumps off the chair and kicks it out from under her. You can see the terror in her eyes as her feet drop toward the floor and she begins to choke. For one final instant, she knows. Nancy Paul grabs her throat and tries to loosen the rope's tightening grip. She gasps for air but there is none.

"I'm gonna die," she manages to say.

Not yet, though. Arthur miscalculated. Nancy's feet are touching the ground. The rope is too low. Staring into the camera as if on a director's cue, he grabs one of her flailing legs at the ankle. Then the other. He pulls them toward him. He has her by both feet now. He yanks left, then right. He leaves nothing to chance. He tugs two, three times. She's fully extended, legs out. The black rope is tight around her pale neck. She appears to be dead. He looks back at the camera again and again, as if to seek its approval.

She may be finished but he isn't. Arthur Gene Lane stares into the camera, the one on the tripod that the deputies found curious.

"Poor fucking baby," he says with mock, exaggerated concern. "Poor fucking baby."

He lets go. She's hanging lifeless from the rope. "Get a fuckin' load of that," he tells the camera, impressed with his work. "That'll make a grown man out of ya."

Art's film found its way into the detectives' hands because Tammy had a friend, a guy by the name of David Shipman, who went to high school with Donald C. Enloe, a records officer and reserve deputy with the Sacramento Sheriff's Department. They've known each other nearly thirty years.

Shipman called Enloe and said he had a tape that appeared to show a murder being committed. Enloe got the tape, called a communications officer, and told him what his old friend had said. The officer told Enloe to watch the tape and evaluate it for himself. He did, calling the guy back and telling him it's the real deal. This is a bona fide snuff film. The tape quickly was sent to Sergeant Craig Hill, head of the sheriff's homicide squad, who got O'Mara to prepare an arrest warrant for a judge to sign. Hill assigned the case to Minter and Timberlake.

A team of warrant detectives staked out the Greyhound station and waited for Lane to show up. His mom had told them he was planning to stay in Carson City for five days, so they had no trouble picking him up. He got off the bus and gave them no resistance. They told him there was a warrant out for his arrest on a minor parole violation and they needed to take him downtown for a chat. Plus, they said, they wanted to ask a few questions about Nancy's death. He was helpful. He told them he had a loaded .380-caliber handgun in his backpack. He knew he was in some kind of trouble for again violating his parole. He knew they had him on a 12021a, Felon in Possession of a Firearm.

On the video O'Mara is watching, because the women are in an interview room alone with him, Lane is chained to a desk before the interrogation begins. They just need a few more details about Nancy's state of mind so they can close the books on her suicide, they tell him. And by the way, Timberlake asks, did you do anything at all to help her kill herself? Hell, no, Lane says. He'd never do anything like that. He finds the question insulting.

"Suicide is a fucking cheap way out," he insists. "All you have to do is ask someone to help you. That's why I hurt so bad, because all I ever tried to do is help that girl. I took her off the street and tried to give her something she never had. If you care about people, you'll let them help you work your problems out."

Okay, the detectives tell him. Can we get you anything? Are you thirsty? Are you cold? It's cold in here, isn't it? They're his friends. They care about his well-being. They want to make sure he's comfortable.

This goes on for a while. Art seems to be feeling okay, despite the fact he knows he can go back to the joint for violating parole. He keeps muttering to himself, telling the detectives the main thought on his mind was poor Nancy. Why'd she have to kill herself? It just isn't right, he told them.

The detectives get up to leave. "We'll be right back, Arthur," one of them says reassuringly. He gets out of the chair he's been sitting in and, as much as the shackles attached to his wrists will allow, stretches away from the desk and tries to sit on the floor. Timberlake and Minter are back in less than a minute. One of them is wheeling a metal cart with a television and VCR on top of it.

"What's that?" Lane asks suspiciously, nodding his head up toward the TV and VCR.

"Just something we want you to take a look at," Minter says.

O'Mara should have known the detectives' performance was too good to be true. Minter has one of those questions she always seems to ask that make prosecutors nuts. She wants to know if Lane ever has blackouts.

Sure, he tells her, all the time. He'll pass out and when he wakes up he can't remember much of anything.

"Fucking fantastic," O'Mara groans. The detectives insert into Lane's octopus-covered globe the only alibi he can come up with, save for temporary insanity. Why do the detectives always seem to bend over backward, O'Mara is nearly shouting, to give the guy some kind of an out? Maybe it makes sense when the cop is trying to soften the guy up to talk. But Lane was already soft as warm butter. There was no need to sweet-talk this guy.

Timberlake flips on the VCR and TV. The tape is cued to the exact moment that Arthur jumps off the chair, kicks it out from under Nancy, and she says she's going to die.

Arthur Gene Lane is cooked. All that's left is to package him up and ship him off to some very high-security correctional institution. "What the hell can I say to that?" he asks the detectives while pointing to the macabre images on the TV screen.

"My life is pretty much over," he says on the video. "That fucking sucks. I can't believe anyone found that. I was trying to figure out what to do with that to make it go away. You just need to kill me right now and get it over with. My life is over."

Some of the people in O'Mara's office said the boss was in a foul mood when he came to work this morning. Connor, his nineteen-year-old son, has been home for summer break from college for a day or two and already he's borrowed his dad's old Suburban and returned it with the battery dead and the radio not working. But he can barely contain his glee while watching Lane sell himself out. O'Mara claps his hands together and lets out a giant belly laugh when Lane erupts in anger over people not respecting his privacy.

"I can't believe someone got into my shit. That was my own private collection. That ain't right to go through someone's shit and find a skeleton in their closet." Only a man who's been institutionalized and spent time in the joint, as Lane has, thinks like this. He's caught on video hanging his girlfriend after lying to the cops that she committed suicide because Lane—God's gift to women everywhere—broke up with her and she figured life was no longer worth living. That was his story. Now they got him dead to rights and all he can come up with is Shit, what a fucked world we're living in. People get into your shit when you're not around and fuck you up. O'Mara can't stop laughing.

Realizing he's finished, Lane goes ahead and tells Timberlake and Minter he killed Nancy after he learned that she had "traded" her seven-month-old daughter to some pervert for a bag of speed. Art said Nancy told him the guy performed oral sex on the infant. When Nancy told him what she had done to get some dope, he said he decided then and there she had to be eliminated.

"I stand behind what I did one hundred percent," he says to the detectives. "I fulfilled my mission in life. I don't care what anybody says. I did it for that child because that baby was going to grow up just like her mother."

O'Mara has reviewed more than two thousand murders in his career. He's never seen one actually committed on tape before. Still, as he ponders the case and considers who to assign it to for prosecution, this guy seems familiar to O'Mara. Lane, he will say later, is as dangerous as anyone he's seen come through Major Crimes in a long, long time. It's as bizarre a murder as he's ever handled. While it's probably not a capital case because it will turn up later that the guy has a long history of psychiatric problems that would cause at least one juror in the penalty phase of a capital trial to feel some sympathy for Lane, O'Mara wants to bury this son of a bitch for life. He wants first-degree murder and special circumstances. He wants him L-WOPped.

"This guy is institutionalized up the ying-yang," O'Mara says when the VCR is off. "He feels really good about killing her and he's fucking furious someone went through his shit. This is a prison murder. He did it because of the reason they kill guys in prison. In his mind he's killing a child molester. It's a righteous act."

Lane said his original plan was to get Nancy Paul drunk and loaded on downers, put her in a warm bath, and watch her drown as she fell asleep. She'd slip quietly into the water. But Nancy was so used to taking drugs she never passed out. When she started to nod off, she'd hit the water and wake up. He wasn't an idiot. Lane told the detectives he knew that if he held her head down and drowned her that way, his marks would be on her head. Maybe she'd struggle and scratch him, leaving his DNA under her nails. It was risky. He had to go to Plan B. "It was going down one way or the other," Lane told the detectives. "If that didn't work, it would have been a sledgehammer or whatever. I was just trying not to go that route."

But why did he tape it? Minter and Timberlake wanted to know. Hell, it was ruled a suicide. If there had been no tape—or if he had kept his mouth shut—he would have pulled off the perfect murder.

"That was the mean part of me that was hurt by what she did," Arthur tells the detectives. "I wanted to see the look on my face. It was such a hard thing to do. I wanted to understand myself in a way too. Now you know me too. Now the whole world will know me. That was not my intention. As sick as it seems, my intentions are good. My parole agent cared about me. He's going to be so disappointed. I let him down."

For good measure, he tells the detectives he found the guy who molested the baby and put a bullet in his head, tied him to some rebar, and dumped his body in the Sacramento River.

Lane refuses to give up details of the other murder, so no one's sure early on if he's telling the truth. Later, as it turned out, the story was determined to be false. Prosecutors learned this because a few weeks after Lane's arrest, a man came by the district attorney's office to say he used to pay Nancy for sex and that he was the baby's father. Police originally thought the baby's father was Art's brother. The man who came to the DA's office says he wants to adopt the baby. A few days later, he comes back with his wife and she says, Yeah, my husband was going to that prostitute, it's his baby and I forgive him and we both really want to adopt her.

Before the world knows the full story, before some extremely confident prosecutor looks at a jury and presses the play button on a VCR and shows a jury how Arthur Lane murdered Nancy Paul, before the DBW to end all DBWs is taken to court and Lane is sent away for the rest of his life, the case must be assigned. O'Mara isn't sure who should get it. Everyone in the unit seems to want it.

The head of Major Crimes doesn't feel like taking chances with this guy. He's tired of sitting in his office and supervising deputies while they have all the fun. It's been a long time since he tried a case. No more cooking channel for a few days. O'Mara pores over the file, he goes to the Department of Corrections and inspects Lane's prison records. Reads his fat psych report, which talks about explosions as a kid, drowned puppies, years on psychotropic medication. O'Mara looks up his record and doesn't see anything all that heavy. The worst entry on a long rap sheet filled with drug and robbery charges is a 1995 conviction for conspiracy to commit attempted murder while using a gun. That's a felony strike under the state's Three Strikes and You're Out sentencing law, which means the penalty for the next strike is doubled. Even without the special, this guy's probably good for fifty to life on the first-degree murder.

O'Mara calls one of the detectives and tells her a few loose ends need to be tied up. Lane had a tape of some of his music in the backpack detectives turned over to his mother. O'Mara can't believe they didn't seize it to see what it sounded like. Maybe it would offer some insight into Lane's warped thinking. He videotaped the murder, maybe he wrote a song about it too.

Prosecutors will intercept his mail later at the jail, and some of his letters are doozies. He writes to a friend and says he killed Nancy because he couldn't stand her anymore. He sends countless letters to his mom with drawings and Hallmark card–type poems. "Each day without you goes so slow/It's hard to count the time," goes one. "So I just wanted you to know/You're always on my mind." A hand with a wristwatch on it is reaching out with a bunch of flowers in an obvious show of affection. In that same letter, Lane says, "I'm a lost cause. This one will break me," and he asks his mom: "Why do I seem to have such piss poor luck with girls?"

O'Mara tells Minter over the phone to try to retrieve the tape of Lane's music, but it's never found. The closest anyone comes is Bob Bell, a former sheriff's homicide detective who now is a DA investigator, who will track down a friend of Lane's who says he heard the tape and that at least one of Lane's songs contained yet another confession.

"And I want you to go interview his sister, his mother, his brother," O'Mara tells the detective on the phone. "We need to know more about these so-called blackouts. You know what's going to happen. He's gonna change his mind about all this. He's not going to plead guilty. The bottom line will probably work out the same, but we're probably gonna take three trips down to the end of the block and the end of the field before we get there."

The big question remains: Who gets the case? O'Mara decides he won't take it. He's bored from reading case files about the SLA and puts more of his own time into the Lane murder than usual, but he knows it wouldn't be right for him to keep one this easy.

Laurie Green, a short, intense woman who used to be in Homicide but now supervises the Domestic Violence bureau, put in her bid with O'Mara as soon as word of the case started to spread through the DA's corridors. He told her she was nuts to even ask. She wanted one of her folks to get it because it was, after all, a domestic-violence-type case. So what if Arthur lived in a lean-to behind his mother's duplex in the middle of a city industrial zone? His environment was domestic, his case violent. With two or three prosecutors close enough to hear it all, O'Mara demanded to know how Green could have the audacity to lobby for another murder case when the last three assigned to her deputies were pleaded out short of trial. It's not manly for prosecutors to make deals in murder cases unless the deal sends the guy away forever or there is no other way. O'Mara was not about to tolerate some no-muss, no-fuss plea deal on a DBW murder that the fucking janitor could prosecute.

Andrew Smith makes it known he wants the case. A brashly confident homicide prosecutor who never seems to sweat the rigors of the job, he would love an easy case bound to generate national publicity. A murder on video? Who could pass it up? Smith's considered first rate, so O'Mara knows he'd do as good a job on the special as anyone in the office.

Ernest Sawtelle doesn't want to make it appear that he wants it too badly, because he knows if he does, O'Mara, who ribs him endlessly about his anal-retentive personality, will never give it to him. But he's had a few tough cases back to back and he'd love one where he doesn't have to deal with lying witnesses, forgetful cops, or murky evidence. O'Mara can't decide. You don't just give this to someone. You have to have some fun with it first.

So, in what some in the office said was a stroke of genius and others decried as an example of the type of monumental bad taste O'Mara displays from time to time, the Major Crimes bureau chief reaches for something new. It would seem highly insensitive to an outsider, but when you deal with murder day after day, you can find something perversely humorous where less desensitized souls would only see tragedy.

O'Mara decides to have an essay contest. Write a memo and explain in five hundred words or less why you should get the case. Anyone in the building is eligible, as long as you have a law degree.

The office responds immediately and enthusiastically to O'Mara's challenge. The summer intern in Major Crimes starts off the contest by writing how he would "live and sleep with this defendant (although I would make sure I hid all the rope in my home) and I would empathize with this victim day in and day out. Assigning this case to me would tell the public that this office is a well-oiled machine and that we have so much confidence in our success that we would allow our *interns* to try such a significant case."

Laurie Earl, a former public defender who has been a prosecutor about six years and just came over to Homicide after a stint in the Domestic Violence bureau, makes her pitch by writing that "Arthur potentially suffers from a mental disease or defect that could have prohibited him from understanding the nature and quality of his actions. Clearly a person who truly understood that placing a rope around someone's neck and then causing them to be suspended in midair could be life threatening would never do such a thing."

In the type of stab-your-colleague-in-the-back-to-get-what-you-want-or-have-a-laugh behavior familiar in most large offices filled with smart, ambitious people, one essayist can't resist slamming some of his fellow prosecutors.

"As for Ernie [Sawtelle], do you really trust him on a case where they will probably try a mental defense? Have you seen this nut job's office? It looks like a scene from a Pledge commercial. Anybody who keeps his phone in his desk and carries his lunch of cottage cheese and fruit in an Ann Taylor bag with handles has no business in a mental defense case."

Lots of fine candidates, O'Mara thinks. He's in a quandary trying to decide who gets this bizarre case. He can imagine several of the candidates coming back from court each day with sidesplitting stories about the defendant, his lawyer, and a host of other characters. Suddenly, though, the answer appears.

Steve Grippi is an accomplished trial attorney and longtime employee of the office who oversees a team of young prosecutors. He's done his stint in homicides under O'Mara, and when Jan Scully was first elected and announced to the press and public that she was rearranging the office so O'Mara would no longer have final say on murder cases, Grippi led a group of attorneys who worked for him into the new district attorney's office to let her know she was about to make a dreadful mistake. Scully said she only wanted O'Mara more available to help her on the exact types of responsibilities that are his now—overseeing other bureaus, trying fewer cases so he could review and supervise more attorneys—but she backed down. Grippi has tried a good many cases in his career and is well regarded around the DA's office and down the street at the public defender's as someone with integrity, skill, and an abundance of common sense. He's also known as an occasionally hotheaded Italian whose not-so-infrequent outbursts are a source of amusement to everyone except him and whoever is on the receiving end. He no longer has anything to prove as a trial attorney, and he wrote his essay more as a joke than out of any real desire to spend a few weeks in court with Arthur Lane. He made O'Mara laugh so hard when he handed him his entry that he had no choice but to end the contest on the spot and declare Grippi the winner.

"Another Opportunity to Tube My Career—": Grippi's entry was written in the name and voice of a veteran district attorney who many in the office—no one more than O'Mara, who has feuded with this lawyer on a number of occasions—consider an unstable crackpot with an extremely high and unrealistic opinion of himself.

"It is my understanding that you are accepting applications for the prosecution of the case of *People* v. *Lane*, you sycophantic bastard," the essay began. "As usual, you don't have the balls to make a decision in the manner of a true leader like the ones I fought under in Nam. Perhaps if you would take the time to remove your lips from the butt of every punk assistant district attorney that thinks he/she is ready for the job, you would realize that I am the only man for the case.

"Has Andrew Smith ever got a ten-thousand-year sentence? Has Ernie Sawtelle ever kept his own victim/witness on the stand on direct for six full days? Has Tim Frawley ever smoked three packs of Winstons during one morning recess? I am clearly the only man for the job."

When O'Mara announces his decision, there are some hurt feelings. In Domestic Violence, some deputies are upset because O'Mara attacked their track record on homicides. Several of the prosecutors in his unit are disappointed because with so many dog cases that come their way, they all feel they deserve an easy one that is virtually impossible to screw up. Or as Sawtelle puts it in a tone of disbelief: "We finally get a case that's not just the same old garden-variety homicide and he assigns it outside the unit. What a shit!"

Grippi doesn't care what any of the losers think. He's glad to get an interesting case. Supervising young felony trial attorneys wears you down after a while. Instead of spending all day reviewing cases as they come in, assigning them, and then answering the deputies' questions, now he would do all that *and* try Arthur Lane. His first real test won't come until November, when a preliminary hearing is scheduled. But given how he got the case and how truly dangerous both he and O'Mara believe this particular defendant is, he knows there will be more work to do than it first appeared to make sure this one comes out right.

For one thing, there's the question: Should I show the video at the prelim? When word filters out around the office that Grippi does plan to show the tape of the prelim to the judge, the whispers and doubting begin. For a workplace capable of being as collegial as the district attorney's office can be, where prosecutors love to sit around and exchange stories on how their cases are going, offering advice and ideas about ways to proceed in this or that trial, there is also an inordinate amount of second-guessing and backstabbing that goes on. Even someone as solid and accomplished as Grippi, whom many in the office consider a likely successor to O'Mara in the prestigious job of running Major Crimes when O'Mara eventually retires, isn't immune. The burden of proof at a prelim is low. All the DA has to do is show a judge there is probable cause to believe some defendant may have committed the crime in question. Throw a funny glance at a cop, and a district attorney can almost find a judge willing to sign a hold order.

The hanging video obviously meets the probable-cause threshold, but prosecutors like to save the best and most dramatic evidence for trial. Why waste it on the judge when you can cart the video out before the jury, push "play" on the VCR, and walk off victorious? The case will actually turn out to be far more complicated than that by the time it comes to trial in the summer of 2002, but Grippi knows he could get by at the prelim with very little in the way of direct evidence. He can put on the cops who investigated the case and have them recount what witnesses, and eventually Lane, told them. Any judge in the country would issue a hold order on this defendant and order him to stand trial.

When word starts to circulate around the building that Grippi does plan to play the video in prelim, the second-guessing is rampant. It is the kind of whispered second-guessing that takes places in the hallways on all the big cases, but Grippi thought about it, did some research, and decided he had to put on the video at the prelim.

He knows the judge will have no problem with the 187. All Grippi has to show is malice aforethought, a prerequisite in the crime of murder. In a prelim, where all you're asking is that a defendant be "held to answer," there's not even the need to show intent for a 187. Malice is proved when someone takes another person's life unlawfully, deliberately, and without provocation. Or, as the penal code says, "when the circumstances of the killing show an abandoned and malignant heart." Which seems to apply amply to the Lane case.

Nor would Grippi have a problem showing probable cause on the 12021—possession of a handgun by a felon. When he was arrested at the bus station, Lane had the loaded pistol in his backpack. He even volunteered it to the warrant detectives when they asked if they could search his backpack. These are perfect DBW circumstances. Grippi could get the hold order in fifteen minutes. The lying in wait—that is another matter.

Grippi and O'Mara want the special. Grippi knows he has to show the judge that lying in wait doesn't have to mean what it sounds like it would mean. A killer doesn't need to hide behind a bush or a car to lie in wait to murder someone. He can lie in wait by concealing his purpose. The penal code also calls for "a substantial period of watching and waiting for an opportune time to act" and "immediately thereafter, a surprise attack on an unsuspecting victim."

What about the three minutes or so that Lane had Nancy Paul on the chair, when he was caressing her and making her feel safe before putting the rope on her neck and kicking out the chair? Was that "substantial" enough under the law?

Lane's defense lawyer, conceding the murder charge from the start, would argue it wasn't substantial enough, but Grippi finds several California cases that seem to buttress his claim. Each of the cases involved killers who were in plain view of their victims before and while the murder was being committed. It was their plan—their purpose—that was concealed, not them. In one such ruling, a California appeals court upheld that notion in a case involving a couple that had a domestic dispute and had a child together. After they broke up, the defendant knocked on the victim's door and lured her to the front yard, saying he wanted to talk to her. Then he shot her to death. "The defendant never actually concealed his presence from the victim," Grippi wrote in his motion. "The court found that it was enough that the defendant concealed his purpose from the victim by luring the victim to the front yard to talk. Again, the court found it necessary that the defendant use the concealment of purpose to obtain a position of advantage."

Grippi figures the only way the judge will buy his argument is if he sees the video. The judge needs to see Lane lure Paul to the chair, apparently under the guise of participating in some type of sexual act. He needs to see him solicit her help in placing the noose around her neck so the defense can't argue that he was merely assisting her commit suicide, which is a crime but not murder. Grippi wants the judge to see the victim look as if she feels safe, being caressed by Lane in an apparent demonstration of affection. The judge needs to see him act gently toward the victim, as if he were her lover, not her killer. He needs to see how she appears content and secure right up until that very moment where his true purpose is revealed and he jumps down off the chair, kicks it out from under her, and takes her life.

The news media have a short attention span. Robin Shakely, the district attorney's press spokesman, took calls from reporters around the world when the case broke and rumors about a possible murder on video surfaced. On the day of the prelim, with Grippi showing the video in open court, no one from *The Sacramento Bee* or any of the local television stations bothers to show up. Surely, Grippi figures, the press would have come had they known his plans, but neither he nor Shakely was talking publicly about the case, so very little was reported about it.

Two people who did want to see the video were Nancy Paul's elderly mother and sister. Everyone in the courtroom tries convincing the women, particularly Nancy's mother, to change their minds, but they insist. The judge invites them into his chambers before the hearing to tell them that the tape is extremely graphic and disturbing. Are you sure you want to see your daughter being killed? the judge asks Shirley Paul, who already wears a lifetime of hurt on her pale, wrinkled face. Are you sure you want to have that image planted in your memory forever?

Grippi recommends against it. Minter, the homicide detective, tells Nancy's mother everyone is concerned for her health. Minter puts her arm around the old woman and says she wouldn't watch it if she were her. Giovanna Flaggs, the Victim/Witness advocate from the DA's office who worked the hearing, tells Mrs. Paul she won't even watch the video. While it's on, Flaggs looks at her shoes. But she does her best to comfort Mrs. Paul, patting her on the shoulder, gently rubbing her back, holding a box of Kleenex to wipe away the woman's tears.

"This is the day. I'm going to see it. I don't care what happens," Shirley Paul proclaims. "I'm not going to let him get to me. I'm going to get him in my own way. I'm okay."

Even a boorish bailiff doesn't affect this strong woman. The fat, bald deputy assigned to the courtroom this morning doesn't know exactly what case is being heard as the prelim's about to begin, but the court attendant said a few minutes earlier that it was a homicide. There's hardly anyone in court besides the victim's mother and sister. Still, when the court attendant tells him that he would have to find a video recorder and television for the hearing, the bailiff says loudly: "What? For the prelim? Must be one of those good cases."

All he has to do is look around and even he might figure out the two sad-looking women in a corner belong to the victim. Instead, when he finally hooks up the VCR and TV and it is the court reporter's turn to make a comment about how odd it is to go to this much trouble just for a prelim, he bellows again: "We're going to the movies."

This is all part of the unavoidable preliminaries for the prelim, as far as the victim's family is concerned. They were in court at 8:30 A.M. as instructed, but the whole thing doesn't begin until two hours later. When Grippi shows up, the detectives aren't there yet and the calendar judge tells Grippi that there are only two judges available to hear a prelim this morning. Grippi comes out into the hallway and tells the family as tactfully as he can that he considers the two available judges idiots. "Even our misdemeanor people don't go there," Grippi says of one. "He's a flake. We could be there all week," he says of the other. "The assigning judge even said to me, 'You don't want to go there, do you?' He said come back in a half hour and we'll try again."

Dressed in black slacks and a bright, almost festive white jacket colored with flags from around the world, Nancy Paul's mother spends two hours in that godawful depressing courthouse waiting to see her daughter's admitted murderer. She will get to sit and watch a tape of him hanging her half-naked daughter. Thin, so sad-looking Grippi can't resist hugging her when it's over, Shirley stands her ground. She tells Grippi and everyone else that no one will get her to change her mind about seeing that tape, no matter how long she has to wait.

When they finally get assigned to a judge Grippi thinks is okay, the defendant's attorney takes the victim's mother aside for another try. "I told her I'd never seen anything like this and that I didn't even tell my mother that I had the case," John Perkins tells Grippi in the hallway. "You don't want the last image of your daughter to be one of you seeing her being hanged. I tried, but she insisted." In one last attempt, Detective Minter shows Mrs. Paul a written summary of what is on the tape so she can at least be better prepared. I'll be fine, the mom says. The worst has happened already. Her daughter was murdered.

After several police witnesses testify about the contact they had with Lane and the victim, Grippi is ready to roll the tape. The boorish deputy dims the lights and stares at the screen. The judge leans forward from the bench to get a closer look. The court attendant leaves. She wants no part of this. The aide from the DA's Victim/Witness unit stares at the floor. Nancy Paul's mother and sister leave their seats at one end of the courtroom and move to another side to get a better look at the TV screen.

They watch Lane caress Nancy Paul and carry her over to the chair. Her arms and legs are wrapped around him. Lane, who's grown a full head of hair and put on fifteen to twenty pounds since the killing, sits at the defense table and sips water from a paper cup. He asked a bailiff to refill it two or three times during the hearing but he seems to know it's suddenly different in that room, and now he just spins the empty cup around in his hand. He watches himself on video as if for the first time.

Nancy's mom and sister gasp when the rope is placed around Nancy's neck. The tears start to flow down their cheeks again. Lane is seen jumping off the chair and they shriek as he kicks it away. Nancy's mother sits stiffly in her seat, her fists clenched tight to the middle of her waist. Her entire body convulses. This is what Detective Minter told her everyone was worried about. Is she going to collapse? Her frail hands shake like wind chimes in a summer storm, yet the only noise is from the VCR. The only words are her daughter's sudden moment of terror when she says: "I'm gonna die."

To finish her off, Arthur Gene Lane grabs Nancy's ankles and pulls her legs to make sure she is properly hanged. Grippi is off in a corner, eyes darting at the video, over to Lane to see how he's reacting, over to the mom and sister to see if they will make it through this six minutes of something so horrible that no one in the room can understand why Nancy's mother would want to subject herself to it.

Lane, subdued, fidgets slightly in his seat, as much as the waist and ankle shackles will allow. He reaches for his paper cup of water again. It's still empty. He tries to drink from it anyway but he knows better than to ask the bailiff to fill it up just now. The lights come back on. Shirley Paul's fists are still in a ball but she has stopped shaking. Nancy Paul's sister is wiping big, moist tears from her eyes.

After a moment, the judge asks the attorneys if they wish to sum up. It is a few minutes before noon, and before they can answer, he says, "Let's cut to the chase." There's ample evidence to believe a murder was committed and that the defendant committed it, the judge says while making a motion with his face toward the defendant that lets everyone know he realizes the absurd level of understatement in his remarks.

Let's use the remaining few minutes to talk about the special circumstance, he says, and he asks each lawyer to sum up his argument. He comes down on the only side he can in this case: with Grippi.

"Concealment of purpose is enough," Judge Talmadge Jones says. "The victim goes willingly into the arms of the defendant. They look even romantic as they take their place in the chair. It is clearly apparent to the court that the victim was very surprised and shocked after the chair was kicked out and after she had an affectionate relationship with the defendant."

Bound over, special circumstance intact. Grippi walks out of the courthouse into the sunlight with Nancy's mother and sister. It's hard not to feel dirty after watching this tape. All he can do is give the woman a slight hug and tell her that as long as he has anything to do with it, Arthur Lane will never get out of prison.

Way back when, even before the essay contest, O'Mara decided against seeking the death penalty on Lane. "I just didn't think it was a death case," he said after the prelim. Unless pressed, that's often about as much explaining he cares to offer about these life-and-death decisions he has been making for more than twenty years now.

Dangerous as Lane is, he had no significant violence on his record. Only one plea to conspiracy to commit an assault with a gun, a charge Grippi said he's never seen before that stems from an attempted-murder allegation that couldn't be proved.

With a long psychiatric file from the time he served in prison, O'Mara figures some defense lawyer could get at least one wishy-washy juror to vote against the death penalty. The district attorney and the victim's family would have gone through a penalty trial for nothing. Fifty to life or life without parole is good enough for this guy. It is an easier case than most that come into O'Mara's office. It is certainly easier than the Tison case, which he is just about ready to make a final decision on.

9 Great Bodily Injury Resulting in Death

He's either going to fight when we approach him, or pee his pants and lie down. —District Attorney Investigator Dave Duckett

MARK Curry never got caught up in all the craziness surrounding the Art Lane case. He didn't write an essay. He didn't angle to be assigned to prosecute the bizarre killer. Curry rarely participates in the Four o'Clock Follies or wastes time with office gossip and schmoozing. It's not that he's uninterested. He just prefers to work his cases and get home at a reasonable hour so he can horse around with his two young children. He does a lot of work at home late at night, after they've gone to bed, something he might find harder to squeeze in when they're older and stay up later themselves. For now, he seems to have a singular ability to balance the needs of his family with the demands of his job. O'Mara doesn't care how early Curry leaves the office each day, as long as he gets his work done.

Much of that work in May and June consists of continuing to develop a more complete picture of Tison and bugging O'Mara for a decision. No one will admit it, but the case of the doctor murder suspect is treated differently around the office than, say, the gangster or meth freak who tweaks out and kills some character from the street he had a beef with. There is no rush to file. O'Mara wants to be certain of as much as he can before he signs a 187 warrant on this guy. He's got standing in the community, a pricey lawyer, and a lot of reasonable doubt about exactly how his baby died. The boss is more stubborn on this one than on a lot of the so-called garden-variety murders the district attorney prosecutes.

O'Mara has been hiding out in his office, reviewing piles of material on the SLA and the Myrna Opsahl case. He hasn't told anyone in the office, but he's virtually certain that he will finally file murders charges in the 1975 bank robbery and slaying. He's still telling anyone who asks that the plan is to wait and see how Patty Hearst does when she testifies in the Los Angeles case against Kathleen Soliah, but he doesn't believe that is actually going to happen. He's convinced there will be a negotiated settlement of the case down there and then he'll have to get off his chair and make a decision. When he does file, he's thinking of assigning it to someone else. It would be easier for him to step out of the picture and let another prosecutor try to repair all the damaged relationships that surround the case.

Maybe he'll give it to Curry, since Curry feels so certain he could make something out of it. It's probably a job for two prosecutors, so the question in O'Mara's mind then becomes who'd work best with the aggressive and intensely focused forty-year-old prosecutor who puts so much into his cases and is such a restless sort by nature that twice in his time here he's taken leaves of absence to indulge his real passion in life—world travel. Before his kids were born, Curry took time off to hike in the Himalayas, bicycle through India and Asia, and bounce around from continent to continent. He still fantasizes about quitting the DA's office and trying to become a local or federal prosecutor in someplace new, Florida maybe, or Montana. Sitting still in one place has always been hard for him, but he knows if he does get the SLA case, he won't be going anywhere for at least a few years. That one could take forever to get into court.

Rob Gold is a strong candidate for the other spot, though O'Mara doesn't mention this to Gold or anyone else he works with. Gold used to do homicides for O'Mara and was rewarded for his good record with a promotion to a job he's terminally bored with, supervising other attorneys whose goal is to settle as many cases as possible without taking them to trial. It's a desk job; Gold misses the action of the courtroom. He's best known around the courthouse for his work prosecuting a fifteen-year-old murder that turned into one of the more combative and protracted cases in the history of the district attorney's office, involving two defendants and four defense attorneys who, if Gold blew his nose in court, would file a motion about prosecutorial misconduct. Both defendants got a death sentence and Gold, who worked that case with two other prosecutors, has an ability to be both tenacious and affable at the same time. Always even tempered and unflappable, he's had some of the judges across the street talking him up as a strong candidate for the bench for several years now, and O'Mara knows if Curry and Gold are assigned the SLA case they'll wring every drop of justice out of it that they can and be able to give what will certainly be top-notch defense lawyers all they can handle.

Curry still has DA Investigator Duckett and Detective Gay looking into Tison's past, but their pace has diminished. O'Mara is less skeptical than he was, but he's not sold yet. Especially on a homicide charge. He's leaning more toward something that appears in the Penal Code as 273 (ab), Assault on Child with Force Likely to Produce Great Bodily Injury Resulting in Death, which carries a twenty-five-to-life sentence. O'Mara has a hard time believing a jury would buy that or murder against a doctor who looks more mousy in demeanor and appearance than he does menacing. The head of Major Crimes is favoring something along the lines of involuntary manslaughter. Curry thinks that would be a miscarriage of justice, but he's confident he can sway O'Mara in much the same way he's confident he'll eventually be able to sway a jury.

"Let me read the autopsy report and look at the photos," O'Mara tells Curry one morning in June. "Is there any possibility that she fell back and he grabs her and kicks out the window by accident?"

"I don't think so," says Curry. "Besides, he never said that. He said she leapt like a cat toward the window."

As usual, everyone in the office has an opinion on the case. Word has gotten around about O'Mara's skepticism as well as Curry's lack of doubt. It sets up the usual dichotomy of opinion: the cautious boss versus the superaggressive deputy.

"We can't have a hundred eighty-four independent cowboys around here," Frank Meyer says while hanging around the office on a Friday afternoon. "O'Mara says he wouldn't file it as a homicide? I thought that's what he gets paid the big bucks for and that we all have to genuflect to him. You have to have consistency. You can't have one hotshot going off on his own because he thinks he can do it. You have to know this case is a 187 and the other one isn't."

Finally, the first week in July, O'Mara's seen enough and heard enough about the case, about Curry's experts, his reenactment of the crime scene and the baby toss and all the dirt his investigators have dug up on Tison, to file charges. He's got staunch confidence in Curry, who, before he came to Homicide, prosecuted dozens of Asian gang cases and became known around the state as somewhat of an expert on the culture and how to prosecute tough cases where no one wants to cooperate.

He gives Curry what he wants—charge the doc with murder and arrest his ass—but boss and deputy also disagree on how to bring him in. O'Mara is inclined to have Curry call Tison's lawyer, Don Heller, and tell him what the DA is doing and have him bring his client in for arrest. Treat him like a gentleman, O'Mara figures. Curry disagrees. The guy's a nut, he tells O'Mara. He has tons of weapons. He's not stable. If he knows we're charging him with murder, he may do something stupid. Just charging him and letting the press know can ruin the guy financially. His clinics are liable to fold. Curry wants to have federal Drug Enforcement Administration agents, sheriff's deputies, and DA investigators all show up at the doctor's three clinics early one morning to seize his drugs, question employees as they scatter, and cart the doctor away in handcuffs.

Gay and Curry write up a warrant, and after O'Mara signs it, Gay takes it to the courthouse to get a judge's signature. Then it will be entered into the computer by the clerks who do all the warrant work on the first floor of the district attorney's office. Law enforcement all over the region will know Dr. Dennis Tison is wanted on a no-bail 187. Curry's glad to have finally reached this point, but by the end of the day Friday, July 6, it becomes clear that he has a big problem on his hands. The sheriff's department had said it would assemble a team of its top warrants detectives to go out and arrest the guy. Maybe with help from a SWAT team in neighboring Placer County. But the warrant takes all day to get done. Gay took it to a judge earlier in the day but the judge said it needed more detail, so Gay had to come back to Curry's office, fix it, and try again later. By the time Curry is ready to have Tison picked up, the sheriff's warrants officers are done for the week. This can be a disaster in the making; there is no denying a certain Keystone Kops feeling about it.

By 4:30 P.M. Friday, there's a warrant in the system for Dr. Dennis Jay Tison's arrest for homicide, but there is no one to arrest him until Monday. What if he gets pulled over for a driving infraction over the weekend? What if he's drinking and driving? The poor unsuspecting cop runs a check on his license and sees there's a no-bail murder warrant for the guy. O'Mara's not at all comfortable with the situation and deputies in his homicide squad can't avoid taking delight in this screw-up.

"If he gets stopped for speeding and the patrolman sees a no-bail warrant for a one eighty-seven it will be a full felony take-down," Ernest Sawtelle says with a broad grin on his face. "Face down on the pavement and the officer with his gun drawn until backup shows up. This will not be good." In Homicide, it's sometimes an even bet whether the deputies get more pleasure from winning a big case or seeing someone else in the unit get a face full of shit.

O'Mara imagines the same scenario, but he's not joking. This is fucked up, he knows. "If the guy gets stopped and something bad happens and he gets shot or a cop gets shot, I would be very uncomfortable with that," he tells Curry.

Gay, who by this time has left his job at the sheriff's department and is a full-time investigator for the district attorney's office, is also not happy. The whole thing was supposed to be coordinated with the sheriff's department and now it's a joke. "We're in a position where we don't know where he is. We were going to be running all this surveillance to make sure we got him at the right time, and I call to the sheriff and they say we have to go now. They were all gung ho when I talked to them earlier. They said they had a team all set up to rip him off and now it's like, Yeah, we have a team, Monday through Thursday from eight to four if we're not at lunch."

"It's gotta be a special team," Curry says as the clock approaches 5:00 P.M. "Knowing what we know about this guy, if it was just Jason and me over there, he could come out with a machine gun or something."

Gay is still calling to the sheriff's department to see if he can raise anyone. No one is around. He finds Al Chidester, his immediate superior at the DA's, and asks what he should do.

It's a Sac Sheriff Department case, Chidester tells Gay. The warrant's out. If there's a screw-up, it's on them. Call Placer County and Rocklin

PD. "Let them know if they go out for a noise complaint or something and a guy comes out of the house with an AK-47 there's a reason for it."

Rocklin police, as it turns out, are more attentive to the case over the weekend than the Sacramento Sheriff's Department. They stake out the doctor's new place on a golf course in the leafy suburb by pretending to be carpenters at a house next door that's under construction.

The weekend passes without incident and Curry, Duckett, and Gay try to get things moving again first thing Monday morning by going over to see the Knuckle Draggers, a half-dozen big cops assembled around a table waiting to be briefed on the case. When they want to arrest someone, they arrest him.

Gay and Duckett fill them in on the doctor and why they need to pick him up. He could be dangerous, Gay says. He has a shitload of guns. No one knows for sure where Tison is, because he doesn't appear to have been home in the past twenty-four hours. His wife was due to have a baby by caesarian section over the weekend, so he might be at Mercy Hospital in Folsom, the same hospital where he took Isabel after the fall.

Mary Lee Cranford, who was Gay's superior at the sheriff's department, is in the meeting and underscores what Gay has said. "The guy had three hundred fifty thousand rounds of ammo at his house," she says. "A gun in every drawer and closet you can think of. The guy is ready for war. He has gas masks, knives, and bayonets. We don't want to take him at his house. We want to get him at one of the clinics or in his car." She supervised the case for the sheriff's department and she says she thinks Tison likely hit or slammed the kid in a fit of anger, then threw her out the window to cover it up. If he did, he threw his daughter out the window alive, because she was still breathing and conscious when he got to the hospital with her. Curry believes a more likely scenario is Tison hurt the kid in a flash of rage and then carried her to the deck so he'd have a cover story.

Gay tells the warrants officers Rocklin PD is very concerned about Tison and doesn't understand why a Sac sheriff SWAT team isn't on the case. The Rocklin chief is so worried about Tison's arsenal that when Tison's house was being watched around the clock this past weekend, he sent members of his SWAT team to spy on the house. The chief even had his team draw up a diagram of the property in case something happened. Gay's having a hard time figuring out why his old department seems so blasé about the guy.

"This guy is involved in everything sleazy under the sun," Duckett tells the warrants detectives. "We believe he has trafficked in pharmaceutical crank. He's either going to fight when we approach him or pee his pants and lie down. I don't know. But I consider him dangerous. And he could well be armed."

One of the warrants officers has a question. If they bust in on this guy, whose names at the top of the department will he be throwing around? Gay says he doesn't know, but he's certainly been dropping Blanas, McGinness, and Hess in the past.

The warrants team is ready to go. Not one of them looks as if he's shaved for several days. They like going after a high-profile guy with a bad reputation. Makes for a fun day. As one of them says only half in jest: "Child-abusing neo-Nazi cranksters. That's our specialty."

We should have him in custody in a couple of hours, one of the detectives says as the meeting breaks up. These are not guys you want to have out looking for you. Gay and Duckett feel good about where things stand as they walk back to the DA's office and look for Curry so they can fill him in.

About an hour goes by and Gay gets a call from one of the detectives who was just briefed. Someone at the sheriff's department has called off the warrants guys. They don't want the doctor arrested. Tison should be allowed to turn himself in after all. Gay is livid.

"I don't get why they called the team off," he gripes to Curry. "Any other penny-ante criminal with a no-bail warrant for one eighty-seven and the Knuckle Draggers would have to be pulled off the street. They'd be all over the guy. If they did call this off, it speaks volumes to me about what's going on over there."

Everyone in the DA's Major Crimes unit is suspicious now. Why is the sheriff making things easy for this guy? They have to know what kind of weapons he has. O'Mara wants to know what the fuck's going on. First they send everyone home just when it's time to arrest him on Friday and now they disband their own team that was going to hook him up. Though O'Mara was never keen on a big show-of-force arrest, the sheriff's department's behavior is not sitting well with him.

At 10:40, Duckett, who's known McGinness for years, pages him.

"You guys don't want to pick him up?" he says into the phone when McGinness calls back. "We think he can pose a real problem if he's not handled right."

Duckett runs through the list of weapons Tison has at his house, though he's pretty sure it's information McGinness already has. After they talk about it for a few more minutes, McGinness agrees to bring the Knuckle Draggers back in. Tison is arrested that afternoon, without incident, outside one of his three clinics. He had just dropped his new son off at home. The cops test his blood after the arrest, and the doctor who told Gay he can no longer even look at booze on a supermarket shelf without getting ill has a blood alcohol level of .09. He is legally intoxicated. Curry and O'Mara are relieved the arrest was finally made without incident, but the whole turn of events does nothing to strengthen the relationship between the sheriff's department and Sacramento DA's Office.

The first story about Tison's arrest hits page one of *The Sacramento Bee* on Tuesday, July 10: "Father Arrested in Toddler's Death: Authorities Allege He Threw Girl Out of a Second-Story Window." In it, defense attorney Heller is quoted calling the baby's death a tragic accident. He says he can't believe the district attorney would file murder charges in the case.

When they entered the clinics in pursuit of Tison, an FBI agent who participated in the raids saw a familiar face sitting at a desk in one of the doctor's three clinics. "Hey, I remember you," FBI Agent Matthew Perry said to Roger Dean Matthews as he sat behind a desk with only a prescription pad on it. "When did you get out?"

Matthews was a doctor released from prison on parole just a few months earlier, after serving a short time for Medi-Cal fraud. Heller had been his lawyer and helped him retain his license. When Tison got in trouble, Heller recommended Dr. Matthews to run the clinics and keep the business—and the income—flowing. Heller is a high-priced attorney, not a county-paid public defender.

Now that he's got the doctor in custody, Curry's next concern is to make sure he doesn't get released on bail. He's convinced Tison is dangerous and worried that he might flee rather than stick around and take his chances in court.

"For some reason, I'm more nervous about this hearing than I am before a closing argument," Curry says on Wednesday, July 18, the morning of Tison's bail hearing. Curry has prepared a fourteen-page memorandum that argues Tison should be held on no bail, which is almost always the case when a defendant is charged with murder.

"In addition to the facts of the charged homicide," Curry's motion says, "there is also evidence that the defendant has a history of mental instability, threats of violence, and drug usage. Therefore the prosecution requests the court to keep bail at a 'no bail' status to ensure public safety." Everyone else might be inclined to give this guy a break because he's a doctor, Curry figures, but he's not about to.

Heller argues that the DA has no case. The blood on the deck is from a dog, not a child, he tells the judge. Curry is momentarily embarrassed when he has to admit to the judge that the blood was never tested to see if it came from Isabel Tison. Judge Pat Marlette, a former prosecutor and longtime friend of District Attorney Scully, orders Curry to get the blood positively identified.

The district attorney's office is waging a "smear campaign" against Tison, Heller tells Marlette and the row of reporters watching him from the jury box. "I know Mr. Curry has searched and searched and searched for evidence that Dr. Tison was abusive to his daughter. There is none." (This is before Curry and the sheriff's high-tech crimes detectives discover the incriminating e-mail from Mrs. Tison.) Heller says, "I would urge the court to set bail in this case at ten thousand dollars, the bail that's normally set in negligent homicide cases."

Marlette is not going for it. He calls the doctor's explanation of how his daughter died "improbable." He seems determined to punish him for putting her in harm's way in the first place. "Why anyone with common sense would have a fourteen-month-old child playing on the desk is beyond me," Marlette says. "The child did not move after she hit that deck. That means the child was propelled, if you use common sense, out that window. I'm going to hold Mr. Tison without bail pending the preliminary hearing."

Elena Tison, the doctor's wife, is visibly distraught, her hands shaking as she insists to Ramon Coronado of the Bee that her husband is innocent. "So much of him died when she died. That was his whole world. He would never harm her. He would never harm me."

Curry walks back to the DA's office from the jail, where Marlette's court is located. This, he knows, is just the beginning. He's got a prelim to look forward to, where he'll have to convince another judge there is probable cause to keep holding Tison and that there is good reason to believe he committed the crimes with which he's charged. If the judge agrees with the district attorney, then it would be on to a trial. Because Tison is going to remain in custody and is professing his innocence, he and his attorney are likely to push for a trial as soon as is practical. If he were on bail or everyone was convinced of his guilt, everything would slow way down, but Curry knows Heller will push to get his guy out as soon as possible.

"I feel relieved more than anything else," he says on the way back to his office. "I was thinking of saying to the judge, if you set bail set it at five million. But then I thought that might seem like I really did think bail was appropriate. You know how you start thinking. But until he actually said the words *no bail,* I was pretty nervous. I had no idea what he would do. I'll tell you one thing, though: If that was dog blood on that deck, I'm going to ask to be sent to the Consumer Fraud division and just hide."

10 Trial by Jury

Things have really changed in the homicide business. We used to have all these amazing murders. Now it's drive-bys, gang killings. Or it's some drug dealer killing another drug dealer. Crack, crank, hard looks, drive-bys. It's not like it used to be. The homicide business has really changed.

—John Cabrera, Sacramento police detective

SOMETIMES, it's better to be lucky than good. Prosecutors will take any break they can get in a murder trial—in any trial, for that matter—and on this late-June morning in court, Harrold and Bladet are unwrapping a gift presented to them by Bobby Dixon.

Big signs posted throughout the county jail notify inmates and visitors that all phone conversations are monitored, but they still claim to be caught off-guard when confronted with something said on a phone call or to a visitor on a two-way phone. Even Karol Repkow, a woman with an education and a law degree, is indiscriminate enough to conduct conversations at the jail or on the phone with an inmate that anyone with an ounce of discretion would not want to share with the rest of the world, especially jail guards.

In Dixon's case, he was caught sending incriminating letters to a friend on the outside from whom Dixon wanted a favor. Letters to and from the jail are routinely monitored for contraband. Deputies are assigned to shifts at the jail consisting of nothing more than monitoring mail to see if anything suspicious comes or goes. If a prosecutor has the slightest reason to want to see what an inmate is trying to communicate to someone on the outside, she can also get a judge to sign an order and the DA will then be forwarded every piece of mail sent to or from the inmate. Every con with any experience in the system knows this. Dixon knows this. That's why he went to what he surely thought were elaborate lengths to cover up what he did.

Sheriff's Deputy Antonia Ruiz was monitoring mail on April 29 at the county jail branch known as R–Triple C, for Rio Cosumnes Correctional Center. It's a smaller branch jail at the south end of the county, about twenty miles from downtown. Dixon was being held there in protective custody, at his request, after it became apparent to his co-defendants in the Bread Store case that he was a little more talkative with detectives than his pals might have liked. As getaway driver, Dixon could say he never went into the store. Nor did he lay a hand on anyone. He would have been a likely candidate for the DA's deal that went to Trevor Garcia, but Dixon told so many lies to detectives that it was impossible to even consider putting him on the stand as a prosecution witness. When he finally snitched off his buddies, he asked to be sent to R–Triple C, but Bobby wasn't done trying to extricate himself from the mess he was in.

Ruiz came across an inmate letter addressed to someone named Reggie Miller. The return address was from John Crawford, an inmate in the jail whose county x-ref number, the jail identification tag attached to all inmates, had been obtained by Dixon and placed on the envelope of the outgoing letter as part of Crawford's return mailing address. When DA investigator Teresa Kahl, a former L.A. cop with a bachelor's degree in political science from UCLA and a master's degree in criminal justice from Chapman University, went to interview Crawford at R–Triple C, Crawford told her he didn't know Dixon. Nor had he ever given him his x-ref number or agreed to mail a letter for him. Inmates are always asking other inmates to mail things for them, since they know the mail is monitored, but in this case, Crawford surmised Dixon must have heard him yell out his x-ref to a guard when he asked to be put on sick list one day. Or maybe someone got it off a letter he left lying on a table in his cell, since inmates are always snooping around any kind of paperwork another inmate has in his possession, and traded it to Dixon for something.

Crawford was known around the jail as "somewhat 5150," in the words of his parole agent, Jeff Wells, for the section of the state Welfare and Institutions Code regarding people believed to be a danger to themselves or others due to a mental disorder. "Crawford is the kind of guy who would write a letter for another inmate," Kahl's report quotes Wells. "He would probably write whatever the other inmate told him to write and then mail the letter in Crawford's name. I feel that Crawford would also mail out a letter written by another inmate under Crawford's name. Crawford is not real sophisticated."

Dixon had found someone dumber than he was and set out to take advantage of him. When they met on the restricted ward at the jail, Crawford said Dixon asked point-blank for his x-ref number. "This inmate told Crawford he wanted to hook him up with a girlfriend," Kahl's report said. Crawford didn't fall for it and said Dixon got agitated.

Deputy Ruiz opened the letter that appeared to have been sent by Crawford, read it, and became immediately suspicious. As is the custom, she made a photocopy and mailed the original. The idea was to see if the instructions in the letter would be followed, which could prove criminal action not only on the part of the writer, but also the recipient and the others involved in the plot Bobby Dixon was trying to hatch.

In one of the "Dear Reggie" letters, rife with misspellings and grammatical errors, the writer begins: "What Upper Player! How are you doing out there? I hope maintaining and staying sucker free. As for me, I am doing okay considering the circumstances.

"Liston, Reggie, I need you to do me a favor and get at these fools. I grew up with these fool [sic] and they is kinda young and need some pulling up under the wing! But I need you to tell them that when they come to court they need to say that Detective Overton kept shuting off the tape and telling them with his own words to say Bobby was the driver and Rick B. was the shooter!

"And also go over with them about they statement they made! Tell them when the DA tell them did you say this or that in your statement! Tell them to say yes I did but it was a lie! Why did you lie? Because I was scared of going to jail! It all was lies! I need you to do this as soon as you get this letter because they is coming pretty soon!"

The letter is signed: "From Too Teeze Beezee! Highland Lane!" At the time it was confiscated, Harrold and Bladet were just getting ready to call the young Southside Park punks who told Overton and other detectives after the Bread Store robbery and shooting that they had heard the defendants talking about it, planning it, saw them getting ready, saw them with masks, the Mossberg.

The second Dear Reggie letter in the same envelope intercepted by Deputy Ruiz was more specific:

"What Upper Player?" it began, this time using a question mark at the end of the salutation. "Listons, I need you to get at these cats for me, which is kind of blind to the law and need schooling. Look all these fools were underage and without there parents when they got questions! I grew up with these fools and have already got at them in the beggings [he seems to mean "beginning"] and they came to the preliminary hearing and did halfass alright!"

In addition to repeating his request that Reggie tell the witnesses to say Overton turned off the tape and instructed them on what to say, Dixon said they should testify that whatever they knew about the case, they got out of the newspaper. "And that nobody ever came back and told them anything." Whatever they told the cops was a lie, Dixon said they should testify. He provided names and phone numbers of all the "cats" he wanted Reggie to "get at."

The list included Carlos Cervantes's two younger brothers, Anthony and Al, and Willie and Chris Stephens. If Reggie couldn't find them, he should ask for "there" dad.

"Make sure that you say that you calling for Rick B. and that you need to make sure this message get to Anthony and Al [Cervantes]," Dixon wrote.

Telling Reggie the message was coming from Rick B. would leave nothing to the imagination. If it did, Reggie Miller, age forty-one, who'd been in and out of prison and knew Dixon from time they did at the state prison at Solano, would clarify things just by his appearance.

"Hell, yeah, I know him," Miller told DA investigator Kahl. "He's got a murder case. When I was getting out, I slid him my address. He was going to court."

He told Kahl that Dixon, whom he knew by his prison nickname of "Slim" or "Stretch," asked him to talk to some dudes about his case and promised to write with more details. "I'm not going to lie to you," Miller told Kahl. "He told me that I had to tell the witnesses to change their stories." But Kahl's report says Miller insists he never got a letter and never did what Bobby asked.

"Never. I'll take a lie detector test," Miller told Kahl. "I never contacted nobody for him."

Whether he did or didn't was almost beside the point for Harrold and Bladet. The letters, if they could prove Dixon wrote them, showed "consciousness of guilt," which juries are instructed to consider in their deliberations. Also, the instructions followed exactly what the Stephens boys, the young Cervantes brothers, and a few other kids from the neighborhood testified at both the prelim and the trial. These witnesses, with an assist from the defense attorneys, tried to make Overton out for an ogre and a bully who intimidated them into saying what he wanted them to say. Bladet's playing of the Overton-Cervantes interview tape put a lie to that defense theory. Dixon's letters reinforced the idea.

When the letters first surfaced, Peters tried to show his client didn't write them, but Harrold got a search warrant to obtain other letters Dixon wrote and kept in his cell. He then called a prosecution handwriting expert, whom the judge allowed to testify, and put sections of the letters on the visualizer for jurors to see. All the letters were in Dixon's childlike scrawl, and the expert testified that they all came from his hand.

Before the jurors are allowed to hear any of this, Peters argues that the letters are prejudicial and not germane. Peters even snaps at Dixon while the jury is out, and one of the bailiffs says later he heard Peters call Dixon an idiot. Dixon immediately asks the judge for a closed hearing to complain about his lawyer, so England clears the courtroom to take up Dixon's beef in chambers.

Karowsky, thankful his client is not as dumb as Dixon, says he can't believe that some sergeant at the jail read the letter, saw it contained explicit instructions to commit perjury, and told Deputy Ruiz to mail it anyway. "Our good Sergeant Dunbar, in protecting our liberty and motherhood and apple pie, says, Go ahead, send the letter on," Karowsky fumes out in the hallway while the judge listens to Dixon say why he wants to fire Peters. "But what if the letter says, We're going to escape tomorrow—have a car and cigarettes ready? And Ruiz testifies, Oh, that would be a crime. Fuck," Karowsky spits. "What is it with these people?"

Bladet argues that the letters did exactly what Dixon intended. Every witness named by Dixon testified as Dixon asked. They were all scripted.

Repkow wants to make sure the Brewer jury never hears any of this. England is inclined to agree with her. "There is the danger the jury will assume, no matter what the court says about consciousness of guilt, that it will be applied to Mr. Brewer," Repkow tells the judge as the jurors wait in the hallway. "I think it's obvious to everyone in this courtroom that the credibility of these witnesses has been questionable from the get-go." She goes on to say that there's no evidence anyone received Dixon's letters or acted on them. "For all we know, Mr. Dixon could have been boasting," and if the jury hears any of it, Brewer's Sixth-amendment right to question and cross-examine any and all witnesses against him will be violated, because Dixon is not going to testify and subject himself to questioning.

Peters has dirt all over him and he's not sure how to get it off. He tries by citing two reasons the letters shouldn't be admitted into evidence. First, the originals were mailed out, he says. The copies are barely legible, so they aren't good evidence. He also makes what's known as a 352 motion, a section of the evidence code that says "the court in its discretion may exclude evidence if its probative value is substantially outweighed by the probability that its admission will (a) necessitate undue consumption of time or (b) create substantial danger of undue prejudice, of confusing the issues, or of misleading the jury."

"There is no question the prejudicial effect on Mr. Dixon is strong," Peters argues. "There is plenty of other evidence in this case where we don't have to muck around with this letter, where there is no evidence it was received or it was acted upon. It's not relevant, Your Honor."

Harrold and Bladet love this. They're like little kids who torment a beetle by rolling it over on its back and watching it struggle to right itself. England's expressive face is frozen in disbelief at what he's hearing.

"That is so incredibly relevant it's unbelievable," England lectures Peters. "And as you said, it's incredibly prejudicial. It's about the most prejudicial evidence that can come into court except for a direct confession. All relevant evidence will be admitted by this court. If it prejudices the jury in any way, it's by his own hand. The probative value far outweighs any prejudicial effect for Mr. Dixon. By his own hand, he wrote them. He will have to deal with them."

England agrees with Repkow's contention that Dixon's comments about Brewer being the shooter shouldn't be shown to Brewer's jury. He instructs the prosecutors to redact the references to Brewer from the letters when it comes time to put the evidence before Brewer's jury. England says the Glica and Martinez juries can hear testimony about the letters in their entirety, since there's no reference in them to those two defendants.

"There's a straight version and a cynical version of what happened,"

Karowsky says back out in the hallway. "The straight version is these people at the jail are just stupid. The real cynical version, and I don't share this, is cops don't think lying on the stand is wrong. They have a word for it. It's called testi-lying. The second cynical reason is they don't consider suborning perjury in a murder trial to be a crime."

Lippsmeyer is resigned. "Why bother with the letters at all?" he says on his way out to the street for his customary lunch of black coffee, a Snickers bar, and another cigarette. "Everyone's going to make the same assumption the punks did: that it's Brewer's gun. He had it in the house the day after the shooting. The letters don't change anything."

On their way out of the building, Repkow passes Harrold and says, "Steve, will you be a man and stop letting her call all of the shots?" Repkow's implying it was Bladet's decision to introduce the letters into evidence, but there's not a prosecutor in the world who wouldn't use them.

Harrold is carrying a little sticky note Bladet slid over to him while Repkow was talking in court this morning, one of many she passes throughout the trial that poke fun at Brewer's attorney. "She operates in slow motion," this note says, "especially for a crankster. Is she like that with you in bed?" It's a joke, something Harrold would not do. But when it comes to using Dixon's letters, as well as their contempt for the defendants and their lawyers, Harrold and Bladet have no differences. When they get to their office for lunch, the two prosecutors enjoy telling everyone how they shoved the letters up Dixon's and Peters's ass with England's blessing.

After a quick sandwich, it's back across the street to call Overton to the stand. Bladet sees the veteran detective first and asks what kind of mood he's in. "Just worry about yourself," he snaps. "I'll be fine." "C'mon, Rich, it's important how you come off," Bladet reminds him. Harrold joins in a few seconds later and says, "Now, be a good guy up there, Rich. Remember, you're everyone's dad."

Before the afternoon session can begin, Dixon tells the judge he wants to file another motion to fire his lawyer. He's done this a half-dozen times already. The courtroom's cleared again and the session's held in private, with just the judge, Peters, Dixon, and a court recorder. No one but Dixon knows what he's upset about this time, but when court's reconvened in fifteen minutes, Peters is still Bobby Dixon's attorney and Rich Overton is on the stand soft-pedaling how he treated and questioned the Southside punks.

Overton tells Harrold that he never once turned off his tape recorder when he interviewed any of the young boys from around the park. The juries see more segments from the tapes of Overton interviewing the Stephens boys, despite Peters's objections that the repetition is cumulative and amounts to legal piling on.

Tempers are wearing thin. When Harrold's finished with Overton, Peters gets up and says he's going to cross-examine him now. It's fine to cross-examine Overton with all three juries present, Bladet says. England seems to resent the notion that he just became expendable somehow. The judge glares at Bladet, reminding her and the other lawyers that he'll make such decisions.

"I was just telling you what was in the transcripts," Bladet tells England, suggesting there's nothing in the Overton interrogation transcripts that all three juries can't see and read. "I assumed you would make your own decision."

The judge has heard enough. It's time for a break, England says, excusing the juries. He quietly reminds Bladet, an old friend and occasional drinking buddy from when the two participated in a local legal tradition known as Inn of Court, where judges and lawyers meet to discuss ethical scenarios and often go out for dinner and cocktails, that he's in charge, not her. Court's in recess until tomorrow morning, a tired and exasperated judge tells everyone.

It's been a long day, a good one for the prosecution. The two lawyers walk across the street and Harrold heads right for O'Mara's office, but the door is closed. Sacramento police detectives have called and told O'Mara they think they've found the guy who's good for the recent murder of a pizza deliveryman lured out by a phony order and then shotgunned to death in a rough part of town.

They've been investigating for weeks, but don't have much except word in the street about who did it. They've pulled the guy in on some kind of parole violation and have asked O'Mara to sign a request for a search warrant they can then take to a judge. They want approval to monitor all his outgoing calls while he's in custody at the county jail.

I don't think so, O'Mara tells the detectives. He's watched the slow progress in the case. The cops are getting lazy, he says, thinking they'll strike gold on the phone taps when they've got nothing solid on the guy in the first place.

Jail officials are allowed to monitor phone calls for legitimate security purposes; when it comes to developing evidence, case law makes it clear they must show probable cause. O'Mara was asked to sign an order saying probable cause was there. That would enable the city homicide cops to go to a judge and get their warrant.

"Twenty years ago, I would have written the order," he says. "But I don't do their work for them. I don't do windows and I don't write fuckin' orders like this. It means they don't have the guy. They think he's gonna use the phone and call Mom. 'Hello, Mom. I'm in here on this parole violation and, oh, by the way, remember the time I killed that pizza guy and got sauce all over my shirt?'

"Shit, the cops said—he had a shotgun. He's good for it. Fuck, if it was duck season, that would have covered half the population in North Highlands. Let 'em do some police work, then we'll prosecute the case."

Months later, the cops come back to O'Mara and admit that, while they felt certain they knew who killed the pizza deliveryman, it wasn't a prosecutable case. If the cops are saying that, for God sakes, as far as O'Mara's concerned, it *really* isn't prosecutable.

Harrold and Bladet shuffle back to their offices. Their trial is entering its fifth month. They're totally out of their normal life routines. Both live alone, so by the time they get home at the end of a long day, it's usually a glass of wine and collapse on the couch. Maybe they'll grab a bite on the way home, but no one is eating well. Harrold says he's gained ten pounds because he's not running while the trial is on. Bladet is especially stressed, having given up the promise she made to herself at the start of the trial to maintain balance in her life between work, exercise, fun, and diversion. Her grandfather, with whom she's been extremely close all her life, is near death back in Hawaii, where she spent the first fourteen years of her life. She's constantly torn about not being able to go back and be with him. She's desperate for a few days' break so she can go and see him before he dies.

Because her own father never took much interest in her academic or athletic endeavors while she was growing up and her grandfather did, he was the most influential person in her life. A decorated World War II pilot, William Clifford Harr won a Purple Heart and wore a patch over the eye he lost in battle, which gave him a swashbuckling look. He began a small construction company in San Francisco and when he expanded into Honolulu, he went on to become a major commercial developer there. Bladet's father worked for him until he decided he'd had enough. He moved to Minnesota when she was fourteen and he started his own company.

A proud Irishman with a great sense of humor, her grandfather used to brag about her endlessly. He never missed one of her graduations after she moved to Minnesota, nor later, when she went to college at the University of California, Berkeley, where she majored in rhetoric, nor subsequently, to law school in Boston.

He began to get seriously ill just as the Bread Store, Bladet's first murder trial, was about to start. It tore her up that she'd be so enmeshed in trial when he needed her most, after having been there for her all those years. He had come out to Sacramento for Christmas in 1999, and she visited him late in the summer of 2000, thinking it would be the last time she got to see him for a while. As he became more ill, she flew out for a few days in March, before the first witnesses were called, and decided to go see him again over a long July Fourth weekend. She spent the fifth with him at his home, kissed him good-night, and told him she'd see him again in the morning. At sunrise on the next day, he died.

"Excuse me, but I am pissed off I couldn't ask the judge for two weeks off to be with my mom or grandpa. We took two weeks off because Repkow's fucking around with some murderer and I can't take a week off to be with my grandfather or mom.

"You go through a range of emotions in a trial like this," she says. "I was sitting there earlier listening to Hector Montelongo testify when Steve was questioning him, and I could feel the tear beginning to come down my cheek and I'm saying to myself, Come on, get a grip. Most of the time you're putting on witnesses and it can be all very clinical. I'm asking questions and I'm holding the gun, walking back and forth, and I'm not feeling much of anything.

"But when he was on, man, I just about lost it. I said to Steve, We have to ask what he was thinking when he was down on the floor and had the gun pointed at him, because that will play well to the jury. And then we asked him and he said he was thinking of his two daughters and how he may never see them again. Part of you is thinking, Great, he's testifying what he thinks when he's down on the floor and that's really good stuff. It's what you need as a prosecutor. And I'm also thinking, Poor Jack Frost, sitting there listening to this day after day. How do you do it? Jack and Becky sit there and hear how Jason was shot and how Hector says he hears Jason say, 'I'm shot,' and he's bleeding.

"I wiped my face and that's when I looked over at Brewer. I try not to make eye contact. I try not to engage. And he was mad-dogging me just then. I felt totally consumed by rage and I'm thinking, How can you sit there and joke and listen to all this shit that you did? And I hate him. Completely, I hate him."

Prosecutors will talk about how they try not to get emotionally wrapped up in a case. A tough trial is draining enough without your heart being torn up by the same types of emotion being felt, say, by a family like the Frosts. It's too much if you take on their pain as well, but the best prosecutors also know all the talk of detachment is a lie.

"Next week, I have Trevor and when I first met him I remember thinking, Wow, he's so nice and personable. But, shit, I need to hate him. I want to hate him. He's one of them. It's easier for me to do my job if I'm outraged with what he's done. But I can't let the hostility get in the way of getting the story out, so I have to be careful."

Bladet knows she has to do a delicate bit of balancing with Garcia. She wants the jury to be sympathetic to him, but he was in on the robbery, so she can't make it seem like she's blasé about his role. She's worried about his recall of the night of the crime, since it was more than four years ago, but she's determined not to go over his testimony too carefully. She doesn't want him to sound rehearsed. The defense lawyers are going to attack him and the deal the prosecution made with him. If he comes off too slick and rehearsed, it will give them more ammunition.

Next door, in his office, Harrold's also sweating the Garcia deal and how he's going to come across on the stand. He's still pissed over something he heard one of the defense attorneys whisper the other day after Harrold and Bladet had the juries again watch the portion of the police interrogation video, when Garcia and Martinez were alone in the room and Martinez started spewing expletives and said he had no remorse. "Chilling," Lippsmeyer said in a mocking tone. "I didn't get much out of it. I think we've seen enough." It happened the same day Detective Cabrera stood outside the courtroom waiting to testify about the tape and lamented how homicides ain't what they used to be.

"What fucking planet am I on?" Harrold wants to know. "Lippsmeyer is going to have a hard time minimizing his client's role in that place. That little prick, Glica, he's sitting there smirking while the tape is on. And poor Mr. Frost. Rickie's mom's watching that shit and she's laughing. I don't get it. Will somebody tell me what her fucking deal is? I've seen her talking to Mr. Frost like they've got something in common. She's trying to be his friend. Poor Mr. Frost. I'd bitch-slap her right off her fucking feet."

Rickie Martinez's mom is a short, bouncy woman in her forties who sits in the courtroom every day and watches her son portrayed as a cold-hearted thug. She feels genuinely guilty for how she raised him. She's told anyone within earshot, including the Frosts, how she was taking drugs and partying most of Rickie's childhood and living with a series of men who did the same and smacked her and Rickie around for good measure. She has talked often to the Frosts and they are cordial, but uncomfortable. She's inappropriate at odd times, like when the prosecutors played a videotape of Martinez and Garcia alone in an interrogation room and Rickie saying, "Fuck the pigs. I got no fucking remorse." A few minutes later, she's trying to apologize for his behavior by telling a reporter, "You should have seen me in there with him. I was cursing him out a lot worse. I said, What the fuck are you doing? Are you fucking nuts? Fuck this, fuck that. Who shot that boy? He wouldn't tell me nothing."

Harrold knows the defense will, of course, attack the deal he made in March 2000 with Trevor Garcia after Garcia's attorney called him. Building the case around Garcia poses problems. At the time of his arrest, Garcia was twenty-three. He was living with his father in the same dingy apartment building Rick Brewer and Marichu Flores lived together in. He was unemployed, his last job was six years ago, when he was a dock worker. He often felt run down and fatigued from his diabetes and other assorted health ailments, and he was strung out on drugs. Twice in recent years, he told the cops, he had gone into diabetic comas and nearly died. He takes insulin shots twice a day, so he's liable to get tired and become unfocused if he's on the stand too long. He's also on medication for his ailing kidneys and for high blood pressure. He says he smoked marijuana at least four times a week, starting at age twelve. When he was thirteen, he began using methamphetamine. He told the cops he got cranked up twice a week, in addition to drinking a couple forty-ounce malt liquors virtually every day.

When the cops came to arrest him January 8, 1997, for his role in the Bread Store robbery and shooting, they found a color photo in his bedroom of Garcia and another young man holding a gun to Trevor's head. He had what police said were two gang-style ink sketches, one of which said, "187," the penal-code section for murder. A black-and-white poster was also found that said, "Norte VIV," a neighborhood Latino gang, and the number 187.

As soon as he takes the stand, before he is asked a single question, the defense lawyers move to get the judge to allow them to ask Garcia about his past crimes, his drug use, gang affiliation. England says no, there will be no references to gangs, colors, nicknames, and insignia. None of that is germane to this case.

Bladet counters by saying she wants no questions asked about where Garcia is being held during the trial. He's serving his time at an undisclosed location and since the trial began, he's been in protective custody.

Bladet tells the judge of Garcia's medical condition and need for insulin shots. How he gets light headed and sick if he goes too long without food. He has two escort officers, usually investigators from the DA's office, assigned to take care of him and transport him to and from court.

Jack and Becky Frost are anxious about Garcia's testimony. They know he is the key to the case. That he can pull everything together and make the story a clear narrative for the juries. Megan, Jason's girlfriend, comes in just before the session is to start. Becky tells a friend seated next to Megan that Jason had planned to propose on Christmas, two days after he was shot, and Megan lets out an audible gasp. She says she never knew he'd planned to ask so soon.

Garcia starts answering questions from Bladet at 10:00 A.M. He seems relaxed, even though all the defendants are staring at him from their seats just a few feet away, just as they stared at Carlos Cervantes while he testified. There are six bailiffs in the courtroom this morning, in addition to the two investigators from the district attorney's office. Each one is armed. Garcia's attorney, Stacy Bogh, who negotiated the plea arrangement with Harrold, is seated off to Garcia's left. Margaret Bladet, Dawn's mother, is in the gallery. She wants to watch her daughter's pivotal moment in her first murder trial. As the trial wears on, Harrold has faded more and more into the background. On March 19, he delivered back-to-back opening statements. But his role has gradually shrunk every week since then. Everyone in the office knows Bladet is doing most of the heavy lifting on the case.

She starts with the plea deal, reminding Garcia that if he doesn't tell the truth, he's facing life without parole. It's part of his contract. She wants the jury to know from the start that the People made a deal with Trevor Garcia. Some months later, though no one can forsee this coming at the time, the Ninth Circuit Federal Court of Appeals will throw out a murder conviction from the Sacramento DA's office, in part because the judges believed the prosecutor was less than totally forthcoming about the exact nature of his arrangement with a snitch witness. It will be a big embarrassment to the office. A woman who served sixteen years of a thirty-two-year sentence will be ordered freed as a result. Neither Bladet nor Harrold intends to make that mistake.

"He asked me if I was down to do a lick in the same place," Garcia says of Brewer's offer to him to rob the Bread Store. "He said there was an easy way in and an easy way out."

"When Rick Brewer asked you to join the robbery, why did you say yes?" Bladet asks.

"I was hard up for money," he says. "It was close to Christmas. I wanted to be cool, I guess." Garcia seems like he's matured dramatically since, by his own admission, he was a no-account punk drinking beer all day and going wherever the buzz took him. He laughs at his answer because he knows how stupid his decision was. Harrold, Bladet, and the Frosts can tell the juries believe him.

Brewer told everyone his role. He'd go in with the Mossberg and intimidate everyone. The rest of us, Garcia said, would put people down and rifle the registers.

As Garcia buries Brewer, Brewer's grandmother sits in the back of the courtroom in a wheelchair, straining to listen. She's got two small children with her and during a break, she says they are Rick's younger siblings. "This is very hard," she says. "This is the hardest day of my life. Rick was a sweet boy."

Rickie Martinez's young wife, Melissa, who met him while visiting him in jail with his sister, is also in the gallery. She's furious with Bladet, calling her "dirty," a "bitch," during a break, out of earshot. She's still steamed over how she played the tape of Garcia and Rickie alone in the cell, when Rickie says he has no remorse and he's calling the cops pigs and says fuck them.

"She made it seem like he freakin' hates cops," says this pretty, plump young woman who decided to marry a man she knew was likely to spend the rest of his life in a maximum security prison.

Becky Frost says during a break, almost in tears, that she really wants to believe Garcia. So far she does. Everyone is worried about press coverage and Bladet keeps looking out for Ramon Coronado, the Bee's court reporter, but he never shows up. She's worried about Garcia, but not for his own sake. She'd love to get through this week without anyone reporting about his testimony. God forbid there's a story in the Bee or on the evening news and someone where Garcia is being held kicks his ass or worse.

The next morning, Bladet and Repkow begin to spar as soon as they walk into court. Looking toward Bladet, Repkow suggests Garcia was spoon-fed his testimony by the DA.

Repkow also objects to a new security arrangement that is keeping all the defendants separate, claiming it is retaliatory and for no good reason. There's even more tension in the room than usual this morning, but none of it seems to affect Garcia.

He's talking about how the robbers pulled up to the store, which was decorated for Christmas. "Everyone started putting on their masks and stuff," Garcia testifies. "Rick Brewer said if we were gonna go, let's go. Rick Brewer put on the devil mask. I put on the black mask with the white face on. My decision was Do I want to go or not? I decided to go. I wanted to be down."

When he gets to the part about Brewer holding the gun, Bladet reaches down below where she was sitting and pulls it out. She holds it up in the air. "Do you recognize this?" she asks.

"It's the shotgun," Garcia says.

"What shotgun? Rick Brewer's shotgun? And he had it with him that night when he got out of the car?"

"Yes," Garcia answers, destroying his friend Rick Brewer with a single word.

The witness describes how he fell getting out of the car but still went into the store, even after he heard a shot. "There was smoke in the air," he says, "and to my left, there was Jason Frost lying on the ground. I saw Rick Brewer standing over the victim and the victim was lying in a fetal position. They were to my left, behind the counter. The shotgun was in [Brewer's] possession and he had the devil's mask on."

Back at the district attorney's office, Harrold is buzzing about an offer of a deal from Karowsky and Lippsmeyer. Bladet and Harrold weren't the ones approached. It turns out that Karowsky quietly asked the Frosts during a break how they felt about the possibility of Brewer agreeing to plead guilty to first-degree murder with a special circumstance, which would put him in prison for life without a chance for parole. In exchange, everyone else would get fixed, nineteen-year sentences. This would be Brewer's one noble gesture, Karowsky implied, even though it's not clear Repkow or Brewer are part of the offer. The other defendants would still be young men when they got out.

The Frosts were offended; they refused to talk about it. They listened politely but said, no thanks. Karowsky had gone to them hoping he could convince them it was unfair for the other three defendants to get the same penalty as Brewer, since Brewer was the only one who shot anyone and the others were just along for the ride. Karowsky hoped the Frosts would see their point and then work on Bladet and Harrold.

"I would entertain discussions like that," Harrold says later in the day. "My partner wouldn't. I am ambivalent about the others spending the rest of their lives in prison. Should Rickie Martinez die in prison? Should J. D. Glica spend the rest of his life in there? Is it fair for what he did? Should Glica die in prison for what Rick Brewer arranged and pulled off? You heard Trevor say he decided to go along because he wasn't a punk. I knew I didn't want to see Trevor go away for life. I like him. He doesn't have a record behind him. These are things I think about. We're not a factory putting out widgets here. Bobby Dixon, I have no problem with him going away for life. He's a facilitator. He stole that car and he knew what it was going to be used for. The others are followers.

"My partner's attitude is Fuck you. You made us go through all this. We put on a case. It's too late. Fuck you.

"I have absolutely no compunction about Brewer. He should go away forever. He should have been a capital case. It was a bad decision from over there," he says while pointing in the direction of O'Mara's office. "It's okay, but this guy deserves to die for what he did to Jason Frost and the Frost family."

For Trevor Garcia's cross-examination over the next week or so, the defense lawyers have asked if Harrold and Bladet would be kind enough to edit out the various parts of Garcia's taped interrogation with Detective Winfield that each jury can't see. When Bladet and Harrold say, No, we don't think so, the defense asks for a two-day break to do the work themselves.

"We're running weekends and nights to get our tapes done," Bladet says angrily. "We're all scrambling to get those stupid-ass redactions done and now they come in and ask for two days. That's a crock of shit."

Karowsky calls Harrold after the session on Thursday and asks if he'd edit the Garcia video. "Fuck them," Harrold's telling Bladet, who's proud she's finally rubbing off on her boss. "I'm not doing that tape."

Bladet also weighs in on Karowsky's suggestion of a deal. She's amused he came to the Frosts, not to the prosecution. Harrold might have talked to him; Bladet would have cut him off at the knees.

"Fuck them," she says. "We've been in trial since November. Can you imagine how those poor jurors would feel if we did that now? You sit through five or six months or trial and then you find out, on the eve of closing arguments, they just pled guilty.

"It bothers me that there's a lack of differentiation between Brewer and what he did and Glica and Martinez and what they did. I think Brewer should get the death penalty. No question. I think fair for them is twenty-five to life. The defense attorneys are incompetent. Their clients made full confessions and they turned down the DA's offer of twenty-five to life. What were they thinking?"

She's done. Next week, Garcia gets cross-examined. Harrold's going home to relax. He's seeing a woman and he says it's time to get laid, but no one knows who it is. He likes to be mysterious and private, so people in the office have stopped asking. Bladet says she's going to Nordstrom to shop. She's not sure for what. Then she's going to get a pedicure. Go to the gym, go swimming. They can see the end. They know they're kicking ass. For the first time, they can start to relax and think about their closings. If only Garcia can make it through the cross.

11 | Kidnap, Rape, Murder, Justice

Other sins only speak; murder shrieks out:/The element of water moistens the earth/But blood flies upwards, and bedews the heavens.
— John Webster

No matter how much energy and time is put into one trial like the Bread Store, a good-sized prosecutor's office never has the luxury of concentrating on just a few cases at a time. The four-story building and the six-floor courthouse across the street are always busy. Battalions of young prosecutors, some still on their year-probationary status, fan out from the district attorney's building each morning and then again after lunch, lugging black, boxy attaché cases with them as they try to dispose of the dozens of prelims, motion hearings, and trials they may be balancing at one time. Law-enforcement squad cars pull in and out from the streets around the district attorney's building for quick meetings with prosecutors about cases already in progress or those the cops are trying to get the DA to file.

With July coming to an end, the Bread Store is nearing completion. Curry and Investigator Duckett are preparing the Tison case for a preliminary hearing sometime in the fall. O'Mara's still hunkered down in his office, reading everything there is to read about the Opsahl murder. Los Angeles and Sacramento are continuing to snipe back and forth about the case in the news media.

With everything going on, a high-profile sex assault and murder that galvanized the California capital just six months earlier is starting to fade from public consciousness. Courtney Sconce, a twelve-year-old girl who disappeared the prior November while walking to a neighborhood liquor store to buy some candy, had been found naked on a remote riverbank some sixty miles northeast of Sacramento. She'd been kidnapped, raped, and strangled. The killer left a number of promising clues, but in the summer of 2001, he was still at large and the crime had stopped attracting media coverage.

Sheriff's detectives had recovered several items of clothing and a pair of sunglasses they believed were left by the killer—good, solid clues that the FBI was helping trace back to where they were bought. But the sad reality of life in urban America, declining crime rate or not, is that Courtney is no longer on everyone's mind at the district attorney's office. She's not forgotten by any means, but too much else is competing for attention. Given law enforcement's increased fascination with science and DNA, the emphasis at the outset was on getting and testing samples from anyone who may have had contact with Courtney. Good old-fashioned pick-and-shovel police work was, for a variety of reasons, a secondary priority.

O'Mara is hoping the sheriff's department comes up with a suspect, but he's not optimistic. He's watched old cases turn into unsolved cases more times than he can recall. The trail invariably seems to go dry in a matter of days. He at least knows sheriff's detectives and the FBI are working it harder than the typical scumbag-murdered-by-scumbag caper that takes up so much of the system's resources.

The victim was a young girl from a good family with lots of friends and people who loved her. Literally hundreds of sheriff's department patrol deputies canvassed the neighborhood where Courtney lived, looking for anyone who saw something suspicious. Because a black BMW was reported cruising slowly through the area on the day she disappeared, dozens of young men who drove black BMWs were stopped, questioned, and asked if they would voluntarily supply some DNA to be tested.

Almost every time Scully sees O'Mara on the fourth floor of the district attorney's building—their offices are at opposite ends of the floor, so they might go days without crossing paths—she asks if there is anything new on Sconce. Not really, O'Mara answers. Craig Hill, head of the sheriff's homicide team, comes to O'Mara's office with periodic updates.

Unlike the district attorney's office, two blocks west, inside the sheriff's department at 711 G Street, Sconce is an all-consuming obsession.

"We were scared to death he was still out there and could take and kill some more young girls," Hill said. "There was tremendous pressure here to find this guy and bring him in."

Hill is one of the few homicide cops in the city or county who enjoy a good rapport with O'Mara. In the three years he's been the sheriff's head homicide supervisor, Hill has differed from his two immediate predecessors in that he loves to hit a crime scene and play detective along with his team. He doesn't live behind a desk. He's also different because he puts time in to cultivate O'Mara, walking over to his office several times a week to keep him abreast of cases, to get his advice.

When Hill started in homicide, "O'Mara was a four-letter word around here," the detective says. "John caused so much dissension over here that these detectives wouldn't go over there until the case was all done. They don't like my having a relationship with him. There have been comments like 'He wants every case to be perfect so he can cherry-pick only the ones he knows he can win.'

"I've had talks with John too. I said, 'Hey, lighten up. You want the best cases possible. You gotta work with people.' I think he's mellowed out the last few years."

O'Mara concedes that Hill is different. Ever since Ray Biondi, who set the standard for hardworking and creative homicide detectives, retired from the sheriff's department in 1993 after seventeen years in the top job, O'Mara would be as likely to say something good about any of the detectives who work homicide as he'd be to hug one of his own troops for a job well done. Until Hill came along.

Hill's a big, beefy cop who wears tight-fitting polo shirts and talks straight. He's a celebrated detective who doesn't talk down to suspects and usually gets what he wants out of them as a result.

Almost every week since Courtney was murdered, Hill has been coming to see O'Mara about the various DNA comparisons the sheriff's department has been ordering. What began as a small task and a favor by the state crime lab in Berkeley to process them quickly became an overwhelming burden, as detectives engaged on a fishing expedition to check DNA on more than one hundred possible suspects. Most of it was done without warrants. Hill and his detectives would identify someone

they wanted DNA from, and because none of them killed Courtney, virtually all agreed to supply samples of saliva, blood, hair, swabs from
their mouths.

Detectives drew from a wide range of potential suspects. Although
the news media portrayed her as a young innocent, there were reasons
to believe Courtney was a little mischievous.

Her best girlfriends told detectives she talked all the time about some
nineteen-year-old guy named Tommy who used to meet her Friday nights
when her parents dropped her off at a roller skating rink. They said she
started buying pot from him, flirting. Several of her friends said she
claimed he was her boyfriend. The cops tracked down a couple of
nineteen-year-old guys named Tommy, but there was nothing to the leads.

At one point in the investigation, Hill felt pretty certain he had a solid
suspect. He led O'Mara to believe an arrest was imminent. A young man
matched the physical description given by two fishermen who found
Courtney's body on the riverbank. He drove a black BMW and, even
more tantalizing, had been arrested for sexually molesting a young girl.
The DNA didn't match, though. Not much was generated in the way of
leads for several months.

The FBI had been quietly trying to track items from the murder
scene, left there when two fishermen who were trolling past in a small
boat startled the killer, who had just dragged Courtney out of the water
after washing her vagina and skin in the river. The killer ran off naked,
disappearing over a levee, where his black BMW was parked.

The FBI spent most of its time on the black Adidas visor left behind.
It was determined that only a handful of retail outlets in the area carried
the item. Agents identified twenty customers who bought them and paid
with a check or credit card. It was a tedious process, taking several
months, until one day, two FBI agents went to El Dorado Hills, a Sacramento suburb, to ask a twenty-year-old by the name of Justin Weinberger why someone using his credit card had bought such a visor a few
months before Courtney was killed.

As soon as they saw a driver's license photo of Weinberger, FBI
agents Jeff Rinek and Ken Hittmeier recognized him. They'd been to his
red brick ranch house on November 6, 2000, two days *before* Courtney
was killed, to question him and to execute a search warrant in a child
porn case. Weinberger had been discovered trading pictures of naked

young girls on the Internet. The FBI arrested him and seized his computer. Rinek also remembered the house because Weinberger's father was a high-ranking member of the state attorney general's staff. Michael Weinberger, a well-respected supervisor in the California Department of Justice, managed a team of assistant attorneys general who worked on appeals of death-penalty convictions from around the state. At one time, Dawn Bladet worked for him and considered him a great boss.

The feds actually had started paying attention to the younger Weinberger the prior July, according to court records, when a sheriff's deputy in Tampa, Florida, who had been searching the Internet for child pornographers, came across one of Weinberger's postings at a child porn site and in a chat room. The FBI traced the postings back to Weinberger's computer. In September, a federal judge issued a search warrant to seize the machine and search Weinberger's house in El Dorado Hills, an upscale suburb off Interstate 50, in the rolling country on the way to Lake Tahoe, where he lived with his father.

The feds, however, didn't act right away. According to news reports, the federal magistrate who signed the warrant recognized Justin's father's name, and the original warrant expired after ten days while federal agents decided how to proceed. A new warrant was signed on October 31, and agents finally went to Weinberger's house November 6, 2000—two days before Courtney was killed. They phoned the senior Weinberger at his office to let them know they were at his home. Michael Weinberger met them and allowed agents to inspect his computer. Justin later told Sergeant Hill that he was introduced to child porn when he spied his father looking at it on his computer, but nothing improper was found on the dad's hard drive. On Justin's computer, agents said they found more than three hundred pictures of underage girls in pornographic poses.

The U.S. Attorney's Office then made an important decision that later convinced O'Mara, Hill, and other DA and sheriff's department officials that Justin was given favored treatment because of his dad's position in state law enforcement. Instead of making him answer the charges in federal court, where the minimum penalty if convicted is ten years, the district attorney in El Dorado County said his office was taking over the case at the request of the feds. The maximum penalty for the charges in state court is three years. Weinberger was charged in El Dorado in

May 2001—six months after Courtney was killed but before anyone suspected him in her death—and released on his own recognizance.

In another bizarre and troubling twist, a well-known local psychologist, Shawn Adair Johnston—hired by John Duree, Jr., the Sacramento defense attorney retained by Michael Weinberger to represent his son in the child porn case—examined Justin on November 15, 2000. This was exactly one week *after* Courtney was raped and murdered, but at the time Weinberger was still not a suspect in the Sconce case. Johnston's report, confidential but widely discussed at the courthouse and inside the district attorney's office, found him to have a variety of personality and sexual disorders, including pedophilia. Johnston concluded he was not dangerous.

"I do not believe this is the type of individual who would sexually act out against a real child in the real world," the psychologist wrote. "I am doubtful he would ever act out against a child." By this time, Weinberger had indeed already acted out in a very significant way. He had murdered Courtney Sconce.

Months later, when O'Mara meets with Scully and Chief Deputy Besemer to discuss whether the office should seek the death penalty against Weinberger, he can barely contain himself over Johnston's flubbed evaluation of the admitted rapist and murderer.

"Listen to this," he says by way of introducing Johnston's report. "This is great shit."

With FBI agents back at his door in the first days of July to ask his son for a DNA sample and an explanation of why his visor was found near Courtney's body, Michael Weinberger told them Justin wasn't home. He'd have Justin contact the agents as soon as he returned, he told them. According to what Justin later told sheriff's detectives, his dad immediately dialed Justin's cell phone number and asked him, while Justin was relaxing at Folsom Lake with some friends, what the hell was up with him, the FBI, and this dead girl, Courtney Sconce.

Michael Weinberger had surely been aware of news reports regarding the young girl's death. He must have had a sinking feeling that his son was involved, especially since he had likely seen him wearing the black visor and sunglasses Hill made sure had been all over the news media. It was learned later that not long after Mr. Weinberger sent the agents away in early July 2001 and confronted Justin about what they wanted, the senior Weinberger swallowed a bottle of sleeping pills, put a plastic bag over his head, and waited to die. He was found by a friend and rushed to a hospital.

Weinberger's wife was dying of cancer and his son was a suspect in a murder case. He must have known years of terrible family secrets would be exposed. Among the secrets Justin talked about in his interviews with the cops was a cold, loveless family. Dad was preoccupied with work and career; Mom was said to be depressed, miserable, and a chronic drunk. But there was more. Her two sons by an earlier marriage had both had considerable trouble with the law. The oldest, Calvin Bell, was serving life without parole at Salinas Valley State Prison in Soledad for a variety of crimes, including robbery, kidnapping, assault with a deadly weapon, and prior convictions.

Her other son, Robbie, was on felony probation for drug charges. But the most bizarre of the family's secrets were Justin's revelations to the cops when he was interviewed that his mother, Maureen, had taught him how to French-kiss and at least twice, when she was extremely drunk and he was about thirteen, had sexual intercourse with him. Once, he told Hill and the other detectives, his dad interrupted them just as they finished.

Michael Weinberger became involved with another woman following his wife's death. She was the one who found him, comatose, just about dead, with the bag over his head. He was revived and sent to a psychiatric hospital. A state appeals judge who was a close friend got him released, and he and shocked friends who worked with Weinberger at the attorney general's office kept an eye on him around the clock. By October 2001, he was back at work. According to logs at the county jail, he had visited Justin several times. Instead of running an important appeals team, he was reassigned to the attorney general's purchasing department.

After being contacted that second time by the FBI, Justin, aware that his dad was suicidal, decided not to hang around. He left a message on his best friend's phone that said the FBI was after him for something he didn't do. He announced that he was going on a road trip. He recorded a similar message for voice mail on his cell phone and later he would tell Hill that he'd planned to drive to New York, go to the Empire State Building, and jump to his death. And, yes, he told Hill in a videotaped interview, he probably would have abducted another young girl to rape and kill on the trip out.

Weinberger was in Raton, New Mexico, when a missing-persons bulletin went out from the Sacramento Sheriff's Department, which badly wanted to question the young man and obtain a DNA sample. Thanks to Weinberger's acting out in a variety of self-destructive ways, he was caught within days after vandalizing his motel room and pulling a "dine-and-dash" at a Denny's restaurant. He had two hitchhikers with him at the time. After cheating Denny's out of a meal, Weinberger went to a closed liquor store in a strip mall that turned out to be under video surveillance and tried to break in, according to police reports. It was as if he wanted to get arrested. Within minutes, local police accommodated him.

A tall, gangly kid with reddish-brown hair, some scraggly growth around his chin, and the geeky demeanor of a shy computer nerd, Weinberger began to behave even more bizarrely once in custody. He was told nothing about being wanted in the Sconce case but when he was alone in his cell, he began to bang his head against the sink. A video camera alerted jail guards to what he was doing. They rushed to his cell and told him to knock it off. He was being monitored. They could see everything he did. Don't make us come back, they told him.

A few moments later, he stood up near the sink in his cell, pulled down his pants, and masturbated, his back to the camera. This was all recorded by the jail surveillance video. "He's jacking himself off," a jail deputy is heard to say. Afterward, Weinberger reached up and wiped his ejaculate on the video camera. The image went blurry. This was clearly a very troubled young man. O'Mara knew the crime was the type of horrible act the community would expect Jan Scully's office to seek the death penalty on, but he also believed Weinberger's behavior and upbringing would make it virtually impossible for a jury to vote 12–0 to put the young man to death.

On July 14, Hill sent detectives Lori Timberlake and Marci Minter to New Mexico to interview Weinberger in jail. He calmly told them he had had nothing to do with Courtney's death. He said he'd decided to leave town because both his dad and the FBI seemed convinced that he had. He said his father was hysterical when he left home and was thinking of taking his life rather than facing the publicity that would surely follow his son's arrest for rape and murder. When he was first arrested in New

Mexico, Justin had voluntarily allowed local police, who never asked about Sconce, to take samples of his DNA.

When Timberlake and Minter showed up and started asking about Courtney, telling Weinberger they could prove he had owned a visor identical to the one found with her body, he refused their request for a second DNA sample. They wanted another sample to make sure there were no "chain-of-evidence" questions at a future trial, but they ultimately relied on the samples taken by New Mexico authorities to make their case.

Justin eventually told the detectives that when the FBI had come to his house back on November 6, 2000, to ask about the Internet child porn, he and his dad tried to commit suicide together at that time, with his dying mother in the house.

"Me and my dad both talked about it and we tried it," Weinberger told Timberlake in his Raton cell. "We drank lots of whiskey. We both went out in the car in the garage and turned the cars on and tried to kill ourselves, but it didn't work. We ended waking up and just went in the house and went to bed. Dad said later it was a cry for help." Two days later, Justin Weinberger abducted Courtney.

When the detectives searched his car in New Mexico, they found personal belongings one would pack for a trip and copies of *Hustler* magazine. Weinberger had cut the faces off some of the naked models and pasted faces of young girls over them. He smoked marijuana all the time, every day in recent years, he told detectives. He took LSD a lot too. He said he had dropped acid, in fact, sometime on the day Courtney was killed, though he couldn't remember exactly when.

What a whack job, O'Mara thought as Hill laid it all out to him. "I'm sure this is our guy," Hill said. "It's his visor, he was in the area where Courtney was killed, and he drives a black BMW. Let's get a warrant and arrest him for Courtney."

O'Mara is confident, too, but he's in no hurry. The kid isn't going anywhere. Let's wait until the DNA results come back, he tells Hill, knowing that Blanas is champing at the bit to hold a press conference and announce an arrest in one of the county's biggest cases in recent memory, a case that has parents terrified that a murderous sexual predator is loose in the community. O'Mara reminds Hill that only a few weeks earlier he felt certain he had identified the killer, but lab tests showed the suspect's DNA didn't match.

O'Mara tells Scully and Besemer what's going on, the pressure he's getting to file charges and how he informed Hill that he won't do anything until a positive hit is made on the DNA. Scully is in the middle of a couple of different things at the time and tells Besemer to make sure that if Blanas calls a press conference, to get the district attorney's office involved.

Publicity comes naturally to the sheriff, much more so than it does to the district attorney. The six-foot-five-inch Blanas, who even in his late forties carries himself like the big, affable jock he was while growing up, has canny political instincts.

Scully was miffed on two recent occasions when Blanas's office announced arrests in high-profile cases where the DA had taken the initiative and wasn't even mentioned in the sheriff's press releases. Both officials face reelection contests next year, and while neither would have significant opposition—Scully actually ran unopposed—no district attorney would want to miss out on getting credit for a case like Weinberger, even if the DA didn't have much to do with the arrest other than O'Mara having provided ongoing advice and ribbing to Hill and his detectives as the case developed.

"They got a positive hit on the DNA. They're having a press conference at the sheriff's department in thirty minutes," O'Mara tells Scully and Besemer when he finally opens the door to Scully's office and sticks his head in. Scully and Besemer aren't sure whether Scully should go to the sheriff's press conference and get a little publicity for the office. She's offended she wasn't invited, but it's not her style to crash someone else's party. She winds up not even watching it on TV as officials from several law enforcement agencies other than hers fall all over themselves congratulating one another and heralding this as yet another example of how everyone works so splendidly together when the public's safety is concerned.

The real matter at hand for the DA now is O'Mara being pressured to get the arrest warrant filed with the court by the end of the day. A warrant is a narrative account of all the evidence gathered thus far that adds up to what prosecutors contend is probable cause to arrest someone. If a judge agrees and signs off, the suspect is arrested and charged with the crimes spelled out in the warrant. It's Law Enforcement 101, and according to O'Mara, when you rush, that's when you usually flunk the course. He's seen it happen countless times. In his mind, there's even less reason to hurry, since the target of the warrant is already in custody.

Timberlake is in O'Mara's office, seated in one of those cheesy red chairs that she and so many others have warmed before. He's putting together a narrative of the case, struggling with the precise language, while she's on the cell phone to her partner so she can answer O'Mara's inevitable questions.

Weinberger is in a New Mexico jail without bail. He's not getting out. O'Mara hasn't seen an actual police report on the case. Hill and his two detectives have briefed him verbally a number of times, but he wants all the details before they're recorded into a document that will go to court and become part of the permanent record. Any mistakes and the defense will pounce on them. Why not wait a day? O'Mara asks Timberlake. He knows the answer. Blanas doesn't want to be a liar when he gets up before the press and public and trumpets charges being filed.

"The whole thing made me very nervous," O'Mara says the next day. "I just started cutting shit out because I wasn't sure how they got it. Then I started putting shit in to make up for what I took out."

For instance, the sheriff's department had contacted the bank issuing Weinberger's Visa card so it could verify his purchase of the visor. Even though no warrant was sought or served, the bank turned over Weinberger's credit-card statement, dating back more than eight months.

Even a suspected killer has the expectation of privacy under the United States constitution, O'Mara likes to point out to the sheriff or police detectives whenever he can. "You can't get all that just because you ask for it," he tells Timberlake. "There has to be a judicial order for it."

What's important about that is detectives took the bank records and saw that there was a credit-card transaction at a gun store near where Courtney lived dated the same day as her murder. Weinberger had been in the store and tried to buy a handgun, apparently to assist him in his abduction plans. When he was told there was a waiting period, he ordered a shotgun instead, though he never consummated the transaction or took delivery of the firearm.

That's a hell of a piece of evidence because it takes this kid from El Dorado Hills, maybe thirty miles east of where Courtney lived, and places him within a mile of her home the afternoon she disappeared.

Strictly speaking, the information was obtained illegally. O'Mara figures he could make a straight-faced argument to a judge that Weinberger was suicidal and therefore at risk, so there was no time to seek a warrant. While there is no California case law exactly on that point, he believes he or one of his deputies could bluff a judge and get away with it if they have to. If the judge balked, the DA could still argue the much-tested-and-upheld legal doctrine of "inevitable discovery," which means the information would have been produced legally in the inevitable development of the case, so no real harm was done.

Timberlake's account of the DNA test is also less than complete, because she was told of the results over the phone. O'Mara's initial impulse is to remove that section from the warrant until he can inspect the state crime lab's full report. He doesn't want anything in there the defense can challenge. But after he's removed information on the bank records, the warrant feels thin. So back in goes the DNA reference, incomplete or not. It's not the way O'Mara likes to do business, though, and he resents being manipulated by the sheriff's department. Detectives often make up their own rules as they go along, O'Mara has learned over the years, but it gives defense attorneys too much ammunition he doesn't like them to have.

"I don't see why we have to do everything at the eleventh hour and fifty-ninth minute. It's nuts. Whenever I rush one of these through, I think about it all night. What if I left something out or overstated something that wasn't nailed down? If it's for the record, you like it to be accurate.

"Everyone is so worried around here about being scooped by *The Sacramento Bee* or Channel Three that it drives everything else. It happens more and more, whenever there is a high-profile case. It's got nothing to do with the family either. It doesn't do anything to deal with or lessen the grief or loss they feel. All the rest of it is for politics.

"Shit, Sutter County wanted to prosecute the case up there because that's where she was killed. The DA up there was running for reelection, too, so he wants to try the case. Jan called up there and it was worked out. We'll handle it, but that's how it works on the big cases.

"The next pissing match will be over who goes first, us or the feds," O'Mara predicts. "Jan will be on the warpath about that. The fact is the Sacramento district attorney should go first. If the feds do the child porn case first, there will be so much publicity that for sure the local case will get a change of venue. Which is a waste of time and money for the taxpayers. The murder should be tried here."

One day after the press conference dominates the evening news, Weinberger is brought back to Sacramento and booked in the county jail. Timberlake and Minter go see him the next afternoon.

"I don't need to speak to my lawyer," Weinberger tells Timberlake according to a transcript. "It's not going to make a difference, and the real reason I lied before was because I really want to honestly seek the death penalty. I don't want to do life in prison without parole."

He goes on to tell her that he was determined to abduct a young girl back in November. Courtney was his second choice. A girl he initially saw walking home was his first target, but she went into her house before he could act.

When he saw the tomboyish Courtney on the street, he pulled his car over and got out to ask directions. They talked awhile. She told him she liked his car, Weinberger says. Only two weeks earlier, she had bought a poster of a BMW and taped it to her bedroom wall. Weinberger was not carrying a weapon, but he said he told Courtney he had a gun and she should get in the car.

Her family and friends told sheriff's detectives that Courtney was too much of a fighter and a free spirit for them to believe she got into Weinberger's car without a fierce struggle. Weinberger eventually told detectives she got in "willingly," which is not exactly true if she believed he was armed. But the initial information from the family led detectives to believe Courtney knew her kidnapper. That's why they focused so intently on obtaining DNA from all those potential suspects and didn't immediately concentrate on the clothing and other items left at the scene.

With Courtney next to him, Weinberger drove north out of Sacramento for more than an hour. He says they talked about music and school and sat silent for much of the time. He soon found himself at a remote part of the Feather River and decided to stop the car. He swears he'd never been there before, that he just happened upon it by chance, but authorities say the area is so isolated, it's been used in the past as a dumping ground for dead bodies.

They walked from the road into a thickly wooded area. He says he asked Courtney to remove her clothes. According to him, she did so willingly. To Hill, it sounds as if Weinberger believes they were on some sort of mutually consenting date. She liked his car; they went for a ride, made small talk. He asked her to take off her clothes. She consented— so Weinberger says—and they had sex. It was her first time.

He performed oral sex on her and they had intercourse in a variety of positions, Weinberger says. Finally, on the beach, they were having sex again when she complained he was hurting her.

"That's when I started thinking I had to kill her," he tells the detective in his videotaped statement. "I wanted to get away with it. Looking back, I don't think she would have even told her parents. I wasn't thinking clearly. I was kind of insane. I was imagining people coming after me. I was thinking of sketches of people who aren't known, being in a lineup and her identifying me.

"I was thinking during the painful sex about rape and what that entailed. Something came over me and that's when I started choking her.

"She was trying to get away. She was struggling. I was crying. I knew what I was doing when I was doing it."

Perfect, O'Mara thinks when he sees the videotape. There goes any chance of an insanity plea. He knew what he was doing when he was doing it.

"I knew I had to finish it," Weinberger goes on. "I knew I didn't want a rape charge. I was choking her and looking at the ground crying. Her arms were flailing about and hitting at me. I was on top of her, straddling her, I think. She couldn't really scream because I was choking her. I didn't put anything in her mouth.

"I remember having my hands around her neck a lot longer than I had to. I remember looking at her and she was gone for at least a couple of minutes. I was crying. I got off of her."

A week after the interview in his cell, Hill and Detective Ron Garverick take Weinberger out of the county jail, put him in a van, and ask him to show them where he abducted Courtney. They drive for more than an hour to the remote river area where Weinberger says he had sex with her and strangled her.

O'Mara has a crowd in the office as he watches a video of the tour. Several deputies make light of the exercise. Grippi, who used to work for O'Mara in homicide, says the tape allows Weinberger to tell his story the way he wants it crafted.

When he claims the sex was consensual, Grippi and everyone in the room groan in disbelief. She was twelve, a cute and well-adjusted girl, a virgin. She would never agree to have sex with geeky, socially inept Justin Weinberger. It was the same old crap. Even when confessing, the defendant has to minimize what he's done. Makes him less of a monster in his own eyes.

Nor does anyone buy it when Weinberger tells Hill he'd had sex with twenty women in the past. Once Marge Koller gets the case, she works with DA investigator Shawn Loehr, a former cop in the northern California city of Redding, to fill in the blanks of Weinberger's life. O'Mara wants a more complete picture of the guy so he can have a better sense of whether it's a death case. His initial instincts are that it probably should be, but given Weinberger's youth, lack of criminal record, and his nutty family life—sex with Mom and all that, which can't be proved or disproved now that she's dead—he thinks it's a virtual certainty that he'd never get twelve jurors to vote for lethal injection. All it takes is one to vote against it and you have a mistrial on the penalty phase. Then you have to decide: Do you want to retry that portion of the case? Do you want to subject Courtney's parents and family to all that? Life without parole is good enough, O'Mara believes, if Weinberger would agree to a plea. And if the Sconce family could live with it.

While they're walking along the riverbed, Hill tries to rough out an image of a girl in the sand so Weinberger can kneel down and demonstrate how he choked her. When what he sketches with a stick doesn't look like anything, Hill finds an empty soda can, tosses it at Justin's feet, and tells him to use that.

Weinberger breaks down and begins to bawl, but he does it. He's down on his knees pretending to choke a Sprite can. He puts up no resistance. Never once asking for a lawyer, never evading, willing to do anything Hill asks, Weinberger seems weak and pathetic. There's no swagger or menace in him, like in so many murder defendants. The kid's too lame, too fucked up, to be a death case, O'Mara's becoming convinced.

"I know I could save this guy's life if I was defending him," he says a number of times.

"I dragged her body to the water to wash her off," Weinberger is informing Hill on the video, spitting juice as he speaks from a mouthful of chewing tobacco the detective gave him. "I was still naked. She had blood on her face from being choked. I never hit her.

"I wanted to wash off semen, sand, and blood. I made sure the water went all the way over her. I remember air bubbles coming out of her mouth. I dragged her back to shore. She was a lot heavier. I tried to drag her up the levee. I had no strength. The adrenaline was going through my body.

"I heard the fishermen coming. I was behind a small tree near the cove. They came right up. I grabbed my boxers, sweatshirt, pants, and shoes. The keys were in my pants. I started running toward the car."

He got away. Despite the fishermen giving police a partial description, Weinberger was free. He didn't become a suspect for eight months, when his name showed up as one of the customers buying a black Adidas visor. All that time, his original child porn charge was pending but no one considered him a killer. His court-appointed shrink certainly didn't.

The case is first-degree murder with special circumstances—murder committed in the act of rape and kidnap. Weinberger would be eligible for the death penalty or life in prison with no chance of parole if he were convicted of both the murder and the special. If Courtney really consented to the sex, which no one believes, that would make the sexual assaults statutory rape—sex with someone underage. If she got in the car willingly, which no one believes, there was no kidnap. Hill played it perfectly, and Grippi voices his strong approval, saying, "Good question," when Hill asks Weinberger what crimes he thought he had committed after the first act of intercourse.

Kidnap and—Weinberger says after a long pause—I guess rape. The kid knows the law. His dad's a prosecutor. He knows kidnap and rape are special circumstances. That murder committed in the act of either crime can bring him the death penalty, which he tells Hill he wants.

It was a good idea to get the kid to lock in his own special circumstance and eligibility for the death penalty, Grippi says. For the first time in a long time, there's a conversation in O'Mara's office about a Sacramento homicide detective doing a good job. That's almost as newsworthy as the positive DNA tests.

O'Mara can't help but like Hill. He knows the detective took the kid for In-N-Out burgers before the trip and ordered him a double cheeseburger and fries. He washed it down with a chocolate milkshake *and* a large lemonade. When they went to the drive-through window, it was probably the only order that day the clerk took from a kid in handcuffs and an orange jumpsuit who was facing a potential capital-murder beef.

At the river, Hill takes off his cuffs and tells the kid, "Justin, if you try to run I'm gonna look pretty stupid." Then Hill pulls out his chewing tobacco, placing a moist gob between his teeth and his right cheek. Ever had any chew? he asks Justin. When the murder suspect says no, Hill enables him to have a new life experience. He tells him how to chew and spit and Justin does just that, chewing and spitting nonstop for the next ninety minutes. The kid turns paler than he is usually under the hot July sun when the chew gets to him, but he seems to enjoy sharing some of this new stuff with the sheriff's chief of homicide.

"How come you never asked her to give you a blowjob?" Hill asks Weinberger at one point, trying to learn all he can about what he did to the young girl. "Guy to guy, that's one of the first things I'd think."

"Fuckin' Craig," O'Mara says. "Giving him chew. Double doubles at In-N-Out. Talking shit." O'Mara knew the kid couldn't resist him.

The interview and video accomplish their purpose. One of the worst and most high-profile murders of the past year has been solved. All O'Mara has to do now is decide who should try the case and whether to recommend, as Hill thinks he should, that Justin Weinberger be given the death penalty.

12 | Closing Arguments

For a deputy district attorney, a jury trial is never a game or a contest of clever skills. It is rather an earnest effort to repair the damage done by violent crime—to reclaim a sense of calm and security in the community and to restore the victim's humanity. Whatever the defendant has taken, the prosecutor tries to return.

—Deputy District Attorney Mike Savage, from a speech at the DA's 2000 Prayer Breakfast

JACK and Becky Frost have been in court nearly every day. She still has nightmares about Jason's murder and occasionally cries herself to sleep. Jack says he's still so angry much of the time, he'd love to wring the neck of one of the defendants just to let out some of his hostility.

Becky misses most Wednesdays in court because that's the day she baby-sits her little granddaughter. She needs something besides the dimly lit courtroom, where all anyone's talking about is the murder of her much-loved son. As the trial nears a close, Jason would have been twenty-eight in a few days. He and Jack had been growing closer, after some typically tough teenage years when they had trouble getting along, and would likely have continued repairing their relationship. Jason would be married to Megan. Who knows, maybe they'd be expecting a baby of their own.

Back in court, Lippsmeyer gets the first crack at Garcia. He shows the defense-edited tape of Garcia's interrogation by the cops. The video is a mess. So much was edited out and the copy is of such poor quality, it's nearly impossible to follow. The defense lawyer does manage to illustrate a few of Trevor's lies when he first talked to the cops. He never saw Brewer with a gun. No, never been in a black Jimmy. Don't know nothing about no robbery at a Bread Store.

Lippsmeyer has a tendency to ask questions in a meandering, all-over-the-place manner that witnesses and jurors have a hard time following. Jurors' shoulders begin to slump as if their bodies pick up the signal: Lippsmeyer's asking questions. The defense lawyers in this case are as strong as any of the lawyers on the county's Indigent Defense Panel, but none of them, Lippsmeyer included, have much to work with. Two defendants confessed to being involved in the robbery, and there is ample evidence against the others. In this cross-examination, Lippsmeyer makes no tangible point other than reaffirming what the juries and everyone else in the courtroom already know, that Garcia was not truthful when the cops first talked to him. It almost plays into the prosecution's hands. He was scared. He didn't want to rat out his friends.

Repkow is next. She at least gets Garcia to admit a few points he left out during his direct examination by Bladet. No, he wasn't forced to participate in the robbery. Yes, he was excited by the prospect. You saw the victim after he was shot, bleeding profusely. You saw someone else holding down another employee. Yet you still yelled, Where's the money? You told Steve Harrold and Detective Winfield when they offered you a deal that you never yelled for the money.

"When you denied to Mr. Harrold that you participated in yelling, 'Where's the money?' it was a lie, was it not?" Repkow asks.

"Must have been," Garcia says.

"You didn't want Detective Winfield or Mr. Harrold to think, when you were talking to them last year, that you were an active, willing participant in the crime. Mr. Garcia, the reason you have been given a deal by the prosecution in this case is because you are coming across relatively clean in all this."

"Objection," shouts Bladet.

"Objection sustained," says England.

Unlike Lippsmeyer, Repkow knows the point she wants to make and how to make it.

"You want the jury, the juries that are here, to see you as relatively innocent in this crime, don't you?" she asks Garcia.

"Yes," he admits.

"Can you explain why, after seeing one man down, apparently shot, and one man being held down, you still participated in yelling, 'Where's the money?' Can you explain that?"

He has no answer, and then she states the obvious, but it causes all three juries to mutter to themselves. "You were scared. You could get caught. You say you were scared for Jason, but not enough to stay and help him."

"Yes," Garcia answers softly.

She's finished. Garcia is somewhat wounded. She's made him out for an opportunist. Now it's Peters's turn. He wants jurors to think Garcia is getting a free ride while his guy, Bobby Dixon, is getting screwed, even though he didn't do as much as Garcia.

"You were a named defendant facing the same charges before you made the plea agreement," Bobby Dixon's lawyer says. "Then all those charges went away. And you pleaded guilty to manslaughter."

Peters puts part of the DA's three-page agreement with Garcia on the overhead projector. He points to where it says the deal is null and void unless he tells the truth.

After a brief sidebar, the judge excuses the Brewer jury so Peters can ask about threats Brewer is supposed to have made against Garcia and the others. "Rick Brewer said he would have Bobby Dixon killed when he got to prison," Peters says to Garcia.

"Objection," Bladet blurts out while rising from her chair. Peters is looking for sympathy with the jury for his client. Bladet is determined to head it off.

"Sustained," England says without looking up from a laptop computer, where he's able to follow the testimony as the court reporter transcribes it.

Peters tries another approach. "Do you think you're more guilty than Bobby Dixon?" he asks Garcia.

Bladet is livid. These defendants aren't judged on a curve. She's got to defend the deal with Garcia even if she's not crazy about it.

"Objection!"

"Sustained."

Peters is unfazed. "You did more than he did, didn't you?" he asks this time. Once again Bladet is out of her chair objecting. She knows that by Peters harping on Garcia's penalty being lighter than the rest of the defendants', jurors can guess pretty accurately what Dixon would get if convicted, and jurors are not allowed to consider penalty when they deliberate.

Sustained, England says. The attorneys are getting on each other's nerves. It's been a long day. England decides this is a good time to adjourn until morning.

"Big fucking deal," Bladet stammers on the way back to her office. "That doesn't mean Rick wasn't there. That he didn't put Jason down on the floor and shoot him. The whole thing was sleazy by Peters. Talking about how Rick Brewer threatened them. It doesn't have any relevance at all. Now you're going to get one woman on Dixon's jury worried that if they convict him, poor Bobby's a dead man. Peters plays that aw-shucks-I'm-just-a-country-lawyer routine and he's a fucking sleazebag. The whole trial, he won't even look at me or talk to me. It's like I'm not there. He talks to Steve. He's not comfortable going up against a woman, especially one who's kicking his ass so bad."

Unlike Harrold, Bladet is not content to merely win. She has to dominate and destroy the opposition, especially when the lawyers get under her skin, as Peters has done for asking questions that don't bear any resemblance to evidence that has been presented.

The following morning, Karowsky is last up for a shot at Garcia and he's doing all he can do: trying to make Rickie Martinez seem like a sympathetic figure and then attacking Garcia's credibility. Wasn't the real reason you finally came clean with the detective, Karowsky asks, because Rickie led you to believe he'd already told the cops everything? Garcia says that did motivate him, yes.

Next, he wants to put into perspective the "no remorse" statement Martinez made to Garcia when the cops left the two of them alone in the interrogation room. The lawyer asks Garcia about a rap song by Dr. Dre where he shouts about killing seven people and having no remorse "because I'm the fucking murderer, I drop bombs like Hiroshima." Yeah, we used to like that song, Garcia says. They would play that CD over and over while they got loaded at the park.

With those points out of the way, Karowsky wants to hammer at Garcia. He shows the jury a page numbered 6,214 from the DA's discovery about his typical day of drinking. It's from an interview with the cops in which he says he could drink seven or eight forty-ounce malt liquors. As he's talking, Karowsky takes a can of Olde English from his briefcase and sets it on the witness stand so it sits right in front of Garcia's face. It seems designed simply to embarrass and fluster the witness.

How much do you really drink? Where did you drink? Didn't you say at one time you only drank two of these a day but here you said you might drink seven or eight? The jurors are shaking their heads, muttering again. They don't know what to make of this. Garcia's been on the stand nearly two full weeks and he's not deviated from his essential story. He's not been consistent all the time, but he has been believable. Karowsky seems to be mocking him, trying to paint him as some kind of drunken idiot. It's not working; the juries aren't buying it.

"Are you making some of this stuff up as you go along or was it your recollection?" Karowsky asks.

When it's his turn to ask Garcia if he continued into the store even after hearing a gunshot, Garcia answers calmly: "Yes."

"You can't get any more honest than that," Harrold says during a break. "Trevor's unflappable."

When Karowsky's finished, Bladet has one question on redirect. It requires England to remove all but Dixon's jury.

Bladet wants to know if Brewer ever told Garcia, when they were in the tank together, that if the case came to trial, he had a defense.

Yeah, Garcia says. He was going to blame it on J.D. and Rickie. He was gonna say they came to the apartment, took his gun, and did the deal themselves.

One more trick up Bladet's sleeve. It violates the rules of evidence, but she doesn't care. "You don't have a criminal record, do you?" she asks him.

"Objection," Repkow snaps, and the judge calls over the lawyers for another sidebar. Bladet wants the jurors to know the district attorney made a deal with Garcia because he was not a convicted criminal. By inference, she hopes they'll think the others are. Such testimony is strictly off limits.

Evidence is over. The next week will be spent working on jury instructions, with closing arguments set to begin in less than three weeks. The end really is finally in sight.

Harrold's been ready to go for days. Hell, he wanted to go to closings by the time Trevor Garcia finished explaining what had happened the day of the crime. He didn't need to hear more.

The two prosecutors had decided some time ago that Harrold would close for Glica and Martinez. Bladet would argue Dixon and Brewer.

She's expert on accomplice law, and both Dixon and Brewer present more challenges. Harrold isn't ashamed to admit he's taking the easy way out, hammering on the two guys who confessed to cops right after they were caught.

Harrold and Bladet figure the defense can guess which of them will close on Brewer and who'll take the two young defendants, but the prosecutors can't resist fucking with Peters. They've grown increasingly offended by his demeanor as the trial has worn on. They've not forgotten the insult they felt at the offer Peters made when the lawyers met with Presiding Judge Richard Park before the trial began.

Harrold knows Peters would prefer that Harrold do Dixon's closing. Peters is far more comfortable with Harrold than with Bladet. She makes him uneasy. Like Peters, Harrold is low tech. He prefers a legal pad and some notes as his tools. He'd never use a PowerPoint.

Bladet uses PowerPoint presentations for her closing, as do a growing number of the younger, more techno-conversant deputies. Load everything into a laptop—photos, witness statements, and evidence—jazz it up with snappy graphics, and you can put on a multimedia presentation for the jury with the click of a mouse. Mike Savage, formerly of O'Mara's Major Crimes unit, is the office PowerPoint expert. He spent hours helping Bladet scan in her photos and other evidence. He showed her how to put on a dazzling sound-and-light presentation that does everything but vote to convict. It's an awesome tool and a puzzle more attorneys don't use it.

Harrold's been preparing for days. "I want to be short," he says, realizing almost at once the lunacy of the statement. His being short is like Brewer being warm and cuddly. It's against his nature. Both he and Bladet know it.

"This is a different gig for me," he says while pacing between his office in Gangs and O'Mara's lair in Major Crimes. It's 8:00 A.M. Harrold is due to hit the stage and begin his performance at 9:00. An hour to fret and pace, to scribble notes on his text.

In a closing, neither side wants to be out of character. You don't want to suddenly present the jury with a different personality up there. If you were low key and even keeled during the trial, it's not wise to stand before the jury and suddenly start waving your arms, reenact the murder, and begin to quote Shakespeare.

Harrold comes into court on the morning closing arguments are to start, wearing his thousand-dollar blue Polo pinstripe suit. He's immaculately coiffed. The white shirt and red tie make him look like a candidate for office.

He could be his father ushering a customer into his office to close a deal at Harrold Ford. "You know how it is when you're the sales manager," he says while picking up his papers and beginning to head out for the walk across the street. Car-dealer shtick is in his blood. He is nothing if not eminently likable.

Bladet is subdued. She's been the star of the trial and knows it. The Diva has dazzled. Harrold's the first one to say so. But today, it's his day. She's wearing a black suit, with black pumps and a double strand of white pearls.

"That's all I have to do today is sit there and look pretty," she says. She appears calm but she's probably more nervous than Harrold, worrying whether he'll remember to cover every important element. Hoping he's on point, that he doesn't ramble too much. "It's the hardest thing for me to do," she says to a co-worker. "Just sit there and be quiet."

"I'm ready to go," Harrold says moments before the judge comes in. "I've lived with this a long, long time." He pauses before realizing how ridiculous it sounds for him to complain about anything he's been asked to endure. "But not as long as the Frosts," he quickly adds.

When Mr. and Mrs. Frost walk in before any jurors are seated and the judge has gaveled the session to order, Harrold and Bladet take turns giving them hugs. Jason's girlfriend, Megan, is with them. The large courtroom seems tiny today. A tall, striking blonde who arrived with Harrold is beaming in the gallery, waiting for him to begin. His mother, a stern-looking woman who thought her son should run for district attorney a few years back, has come to watch. Harrold's sister, Ann, an accomplished Berkeley artist, shows up to see her brother perform. It has the feel of a social event. Friends and family greet, embrace, exchange offers of good luck. A few moments later everyone will be seated and Harrold will be talking about shotgun pellets and muscle tissue sprayed against the bakery wall.

The defendants and their lawyers are seated and waiting. Peters is in the gallery. He doesn't have to be here, but it's certainly in his interest, and in his client's interest, to see how Harrold approaches this closing.

To hear what he says about his client. To hear what Lippsmeyer and Karowsky offer in contrast. Repkow—everyone considers this strange, given the import of what's about to begin—is absent. She never misses a chance to sit in court when Fred Clark, her confessed killer-lover, has an appearance so they can make eyes at one another, but she doesn't show up for the first closing argument in her murder trial, which is her only case.

As he did for his opening, Harrold has placed the menacing sketch of a man in a devil's mask on an easel next to the jury box. Josh Christian, one of the employees who was able to run out of the store to safety that night, drew it. It's been a long trial, Judge England tells the jurors. He tells everyone it's probably a good idea to refresh everyone's memory by having the clerk read the exact charges.

Count One is the biggie, 187 (a). Murder. They killed Jason Frost, whether they pulled the trigger or not. They were principals and they were armed. The People also allege a special circumstance: murder committed in the act of robbery. He doesn't tell the jury this, since punishment is not to concern them, but conviction brings automatic sentence of life in prison with no chance of parole. It would also make them eligible for the death penalty, had the People of the state of California, through the district attorney of Sacramento County, sought the ultimate punishment.

Count Two, 664/211, is attempted robbery and use of a firearm. Count Three, 182 (a) (1), conspiracy to commit robbery. To prove conspiracy, the People must show overt action taken to further that conspiracy. Overt Act Number One: stealing the truck. Overt Act Number Two: wearing masks.

And Count Four for Mr. Rickie Martinez and John David Glica: 245 (a) (1), assault with a deadly weapon, for the knife and Mace attack on Bread Store employee Hector Montelongo. According to the original criminal complaints, they are crimes committed "against the peace and dignity of the People of the State of California."

"Did you ever think we'd get here?" Harrold asks the jurors with a smile. "We are here."

This, he begins, was a Christmas murder.

He takes the jurors through the crime, showing some of the defendants' statements to the cops on the visualizer screen.

"All I did was run in, just ran in, started yelling, and then ran out. Hop back in the ride, that's what I did. That's really what I did." This was Glica.

To Harrold, prone to mix metaphors when making a point, Glica was "like a piranha describing a meal that turned sour."

"He didn't put me here," he said about Rick Brewer. "I chose—you know what I'm saying? It—I—regardless of whether I was intoxicated or not. I'm not stupid. I knew what I was doing. I could have said no. [Those last two sentences are underlined for effect, the fatal words for J. D. Glica.] I could have stayed out of that car. You know what I'm saying? He didn't put me to do shit. You know what I'm saying? It's on me and now I gotta face the consequences. And I—one of them—one of them things is I wouldn't say shit and I've already said too much."

He shows the jury Glica's statement of how he threw an employee on the ground "Hella hard, for no reason . . . And then I remember hearing, 'There ain't shit. Fuck.' Then we all turn around, just ran out. I hear two gunshots."

"With these words," Harrold tells the jurors—their eyes and ears are focused directly on him now—"Glica convicted himself of first-degree murder with the special circumstance as a major participant in a robbery. With the realization that there was no money, that instantaneously became the murder of Jason Frost with the sound of the shots."

"Take it like a man and get what's coming to me, that's what I want to do." More Glica words on the screen. In Harrold's narrative accounting for the jury, Glica's minister father is in the cell now. He asks if he'd been drinking. "A little bit," the son said. "Not a lot. I knew what I was doing. Just bring it on. I don't even care no more. Fuck."

This kid's finished. Now it's time to complete the job on Rickie Martinez.

Harrold reminds the jury how "Little Rickie" started out "in a denial mode."

"He said he was drunk and didn't see a gun in the G-ride because he was blacked out, and then started providing details as to his participation, peppered with lies, most noticeably, at all times refusing to identify the shooter or acknowledge his awareness of a gun going in. At one point, he tells Overton that the gunman had the weapon down his pants or up his sleeve. That raises an interesting point about the Mossberg.

Not a handgun, a throwaway, a Saturday night special, or hunting de-vice. This is a mean, vicious killing implement. By all accounts, this weapon was an appendage to Rick Brewer, a body part. The sum of evi-dence shows that Martinez was aware of its existence, its lethal nature, and the fact that it was in the truck that night."

Overton asked Martinez if he knew, when he got into the truck, that they were headed to a robbery. Like his partner's, his own words on the screen continue to sink him.

"Oh, yeah, I kind of figured that out when everybody had masks on and walked in. And we was in a stolen car. I put two and two together."

Harrold scribbled a note in the margin of his closing but didn't read it to the jury. "A brilliant deduction, Holmes," it says.

Martinez won't give up the shooter, but Harrold tells the jury the de-fendant did speak to Brewer's state of mind when the robbery occurred. "He was going crazy because he lost his kids," Martinez told Overton. "I just know he was fucking mad about losing his kids and was fucking upset about it."

"This statement tattoos Martinez with the reckless indifference to human life specified in the special circumstance," says Harrold. "He is a major participant in an attempted robbery with someone who is wearing a devil's mask, armed with a Mossberg, and who is, by Martinez's words, 'fucking mad.' These are things he knows and understands. This is the grave risk of death he is exposing Bread Store patrons and employees to. This is textbook reckless indifference."

One wonders what Martinez is thinking. Steve Harrold, a slick Berkeley-educated lawyer in a suit that no one Martinez has ever known could afford unless they stole enough money in some lick, is destroying him word by self-incriminating word. He'll have the rest of his life to re-member the bad choice he made on December 23, 1996.

"I don't give a fuck." This is what Harrold has up on the screen now. It's what Martinez said to Garcia when the cops put the two of them alone in the room. "I'm going to do some years. So fuck it, fuck these fools. They can fuck off, them and their fucking badge, fuckin' bastards. They can fuck themselves. . . . I don't give a fuck no more. I don't got nothing to lose. I don't give a fuck. I have no remorse."

While the words are on the screen, Harrold also slips in the photo of Jason Frost that was shown in February, when the trial was just beginning. He's reading a *Fodors: Great Britain* travel book, sitting on a porch, shorts, T-shirt, sunny disposition, his dad's round face, his whole life in front of him.

"I don't give a fuck. I have no remorse." Jason daydreaming about taking his hard-earned money and traveling to England with the young woman he wants to marry. It's a sledgehammer juxtaposition. Harrold knows the jury will carry it into the deliberation room.

Rickie's mom is in the audience dying with her son. Her head is in her hands. She is shaking it from side to side.

"This has been going on so long, I'm almost numb," Rhonda Ybarra says during a break in Harrold's ninety-minute closing. "I don't see Rickie the way they do. He's my son. He's loving. He never acted that way around me. I told Mr. and Mrs. Frost, I think Rickie should do time. But he shouldn't go to prison for life. He would never kill anyone."

Melissa Lopez, Rickie's wife, walks over. She's friends with Rickie's sister and when she was asked one day if she wanted to tag along on a jail visit, she said sure. It's not an unusual invitation in the part of town where she grew up. She and Rickie started corresponding. The letters got warmer and warmer. Eventually, even to the shock and chagrin of Rickie's mom, when he asked her to marry him she again said, sure.

"Rickie's the type of guy where if you're upset, he wants to take your mind off it," Melissa says. "There's more to him than what they say in court. Rick Brewer hates the world and is angry and bitter about his life. He's the one who pulled the trigger. How is it fair that he and Rickie get the same punishment?"

Harrold's set to begin again. During the break, Bladet slipped him two notes. They're not the same kind of notes she passed him during the trial about Repkow's sex life or Lippsmeyer making no sense. "Go get um," one says. "I have complete confidence in you." The other one says, "Bossman is on fire! Wow! Very impressive!" After chewing on him for nine months, she means it.

Harrold wraps up. "Was he truthful in the courtroom?" he asks of Trevor Garcia, the robber-turned-snitch-turned-star-witness. "While he admitted lying to Detective Overton, much along the lines of Martinez and Glica, and being untruthful in some parts of his interviews with law enforcement, trying to minimize and protect himself from being a snitch, I would submit that based upon his affect and appearance in the courtroom and the information he provided, that he was quite credible.

"Moreover, he was calm, his answers were short and to the point and rarely, if ever, confusing or contradictory. He was never argumentative. Remember, he was not coached nor had he reviewed any written materials for at least the past sixteen months. Remember this exchange from cross-examination.

"You were screaming at a man who is down, mortally wounded, 'Where's the money?' " Harrold has those last three words on the screen.

"His answer: 'Yes.'

"In fact, Trevor Garcia was brutally honest.

"There you have it. A Christmas Story. Christmas in Sacramento. Christmas at thirteen twenty-four G Street. Christmas in Southside Park. Christmas on J Street. A story you will never forget. A story that will haunt the Frost family and loved ones forever. A story that will torture Hector Montelongo for a very long time.

"Merry Christmas!"

"Ladies and gentlemen of the jury," the judge says, "we stand in recess until one-thirty."

After lunch, when Lippsmeyer gets up to try to argue that his client should not spend the rest of his life in prison, he argues the only point he can: "These defendants were not key. They were not major participants. You could take them out of the case and you'd still have a murder."

He speaks for only thirty-five minutes and he agrees with Harrold's characterization of Jason Frost's killing as "an execution." But it wasn't carried out in furtherance of a robbery, which would make it a special circumstance. The murder, he says, in no way facilitated the robbery.

Karowsky gets up at 2:05 P.M. He reads what he says is the motto of the United States Department of Justice. "The government wins when justice is done."

When he offers his own novel definition of reasonable doubt, one that bears no semblance to the judge's explanation in his instructions, Harrold wants to leap from his seat. "You jurors are reasonable," Karowsky says. "If you have any doubts, therefore it's reasonable."

He goes after Garcia. Why was he so deceptive about how much he drank the day of the crime? "His mind is so hazy from the drinking, he can't remember," says Karowsky. "He's making it up. He can't remember details from the most important day of his life."

Garcia will get out of prison in 2006, Karowsky tells jurors. He'll be thirty-seven. "A deal of a lifetime for a lifetime. He originally faced life without possibility of parole, the rest of his life locked up in California prisons."

Then he tells the jury what all defense lawyers tell a jury when they know their guy is about to be found guilty. "It is you who make these decisions. You have to live with whatever you decide."

13 | Serial Killer

August comes on not like a month, but like an affliction.
—Joan Didion, "Notes from a Native Daughter"

AUGUST is still "so hot that the air shimmers and the grass bleaches white and the blinds stay drawn all day." The biggest town in California's Great Central Valley remains a place that, as Joan Didion once wrote of her hometown, "grew up on farming and discovered to its shock that land has more profitable uses."

Sacramento will always be part of the "other California," the antithesis of the image people around the world have of languid southern California beaches or the hip, hilly streets of San Francisco. Sacramento has always been a Valley town, an urban outpost in a vast stretch of farmland that is the richest and most productive piece of earth in the world. It is a place where just a few years ago, it seemed like everyone you knew was either growing rice or selling real estate or was somehow in the employ of the state of California. It was a small, provincial place where you could listen to the hog report on the morning radio show and spend the afternoon at a hearing at the Capitol held to determine the fate of a billion-dollar state water or highway project. People who moved there from someplace else said it reminded them of Middle America, a farm community with two mighty rivers and a whole lot of common sense running through it. There was no Hollywood or Haight-Ashbury here. This was Peoria on the West Coast.

The small, insular Valley town where state politics, agriculture, and real estate were the only businesses that mattered is gone, replaced by the face-less, no-character ambience that could be any Sunbelt boomtown with big-league ambitions. Skyscrapers and malls have gone up so fast here, it's hard to keep track of them all. As housing prices in and around Los Angeles and San Francisco began to reach the obscene level they rose to in the 1970s and 1980s, Sacramento became known as a spillover place. A place of sec-ond choice. It was a town suddenly struck by explosive growth. Many of the newcomers were refugees from L.A. or the Bay Area who grew tired of two-hour commutes and sending nearly their entire paychecks to the mort-gage companies. Companies from those areas flocked here because Sacra-mento had cheap land and no earthquakes. Asians, Europeans, Latinos, and refugees from the former Soviet Union were attracted by many of the same qualities: there were jobs, Sacramento was relatively affordable, it was a friendly, open community that seemed to welcome newcomers. All the growth made Sacramento a tremendously diverse place where, as in the rest of the state, more languages are spoken than natives of the place even knew existed. It may be the quintessential modern California metropolis after all, so diverse and multiethnic that *Time* magazine in 2002 declared it "America's Most Integrated City."

Like any rapidly growing American city, Sacramento has always drawn more than its fair share of crime. And the month of August 2001 was one of the bloodiest in the city's history.

The phone rings early this morning in John O'Mara's office, the first of what will seem like a hundred calls that pour in today. "Fuck it," he says. "This one I better answer."

A half-dozen deputy DAs are jammed into his small office. They're hovering over the TV behind O'Mara's desk, watching live coverage of the arrest just a few minutes ago of Nikolay Soltys, a twenty-seven-year-old Ukrainian émigré with a history of mental instability and domestic violence. Ten days ago, on August 21, he joined the FBI's Ten Most Wanted list and became the target of an international manhunt after sheriff's deputies say he slit the throats of his pregnant wife, an aunt and uncle, two nine-year-old cousins, and his own three-year-old son. A $120,000 reward was put together from a variety of sources, including Governor Gray Davis. It's all anyone in Sacramento and much of the rest of the state seemed to be talking about: Where was Soltys and what made him kill so many family members?

The murders caused an international sensation too. "Mad Immigrant Murders Family"—that was the tone of much of the media coverage, from CNN to *The New York Times* and newspapers in Europe and across the former Soviet Union. One popular radio news station in Sacramento, KHTK, actually described Soltys as a "maniac killer on the loose." Within minutes of his being arrested after deputies found him, disheveled and disoriented, hiding under a discarded desk in his mother's backyard—he had a potato peeler in his pants pocket and was carrying a ragged sleeping bag and backpack—O'Mara starts getting calls from sheriff's department homicide detectives.

Laurie Earl is the first deputy in Homicide to inform everyone that Soltys has been caught following ten days of speculation in the news media that he either had a big bankroll and had fled the country, was out looking to settle some old scores with other members of his family, or had taken his own life and was waiting to be discovered lying dead somewhere.

"He's alive," Earl says when she sticks her head in O'Mara's office and sees the slight, stoop-shouldered man in the back of a patrol car.

"Unfortunately," O'Mara groans without taking his eyes off the television screen. He immediately thinks two things: Now we have to try the son of a bitch, and here comes a change of menu. That's right, change of menu. Everything is some sort of a joke in Major Crimes. Actually, when he hears Soltys was caught while hiding at his mother's house, O'Mara thinks a third thing.

"We got his mom too," he cracks to everyone in the room. "We're gonna lay a big old fat thirty-two on her. We'll just nail her butt."

Penal Code 32: Accessories. Every person who, after a felony has been committed, harbors, conceals, or aids a principal in such felony, with the intent that said principal may avoid or escape from arrest, trial, conviction, or punishment, having knowledge that said principal has committed such felony or has been charged with such felony or convicted thereof, is an accessory to such felony.

If his mother helped hide her son from capture, the district attorney's office would have two new cases on its hands, but O'Mara knows from the outset that's not going to happen.

The first call to O'Mara comes from Will Bayles, a homicide detective who's been working the Soltys case from the moment a neighbor called 911 the morning of August 20 and said a crazy guy had just cut his wife's throat and chased her next door to another neighbor's apartment. Less than an hour later, after driving off in his silver Nissan Altima, Soltys showed up at his aunt and uncle's house and slashed their throats. He chased his two cousins into the street and did the same to them. One of the children died in his mother's arms when she came running into the street after hearing the screams. Soltys then drove to the home of his mother, who had been watching his little boy, and insisted she turn his son over to him. Then he drove off again.

Later that night, after fearing he had left the area with the child as a hostage, detectives found the boy in a debris-strewn field not far from Soltys's apartment, his throat brutally slashed. Soltys had apparently lured the little blond boy into a box that once held a TV set by placing some children's toys in it. Police were led to the scene after recovering Soltys's abandoned car and finding family pictures and a crude map he had drawn showing the boy could be found under a large radio tower. On his wife's face in one of the pictures were the words *For her tongue* written in Ukrainian.

O'Mara had given the sheriff's department a heads-up a few days earlier that if Soltys were caught, federal law required the Ukrainian Consulate in Washington, D.C., to be notified immediately. Only in this country five months, Soltys remains a citizen of the Ukraine.

"You have to call the consulate," he tells Bayles while four deputies banter about what they're watching on the news. "He should be advised independently and you're required to call the consulate. You can still get a statement out of him. If it becomes an issue, we'll litigate the shit out of it and we'll win, but it would be good to avoid all that if we can."

The issue is important because as soon as he's arrested, Soltys starts talking. Not quickly or in any great detail, but he does freely confess to detectives that he killed his wife, aunt, uncle, two cousins, and his son. His recitation is extremely difficult to follow, but it's a confession nonetheless.

The detectives who interrogate him use a Russian-speaking deputy as an interpreter, but Soltys is Ukrainian, so the translation is difficult at best. Even with the right interpreter, the interview would have been painstakingly slow, as O'Mara will see for himself when he watches a videotape of it in a few days. With every question, Soltys stares off into space, obsessively rubs his hands together, stammers, and emits barely audible half answers. His family was always on his back, he says. It started in the Ukraine and never let up once he moved to California. He seems to suggest he killed everyone to stop the abuse and because they had been plotting against him. When he's asked about his son, he mutters something about being out of his mind at the time and not expecting to be taken alive, but he explains no more.

Everyone in the office groans when the TV cameras show deputies removing Soltys from the squad car he's been in and putting him into another. It's impossible to avoid thinking this is being done just for the cameras. Sheriff Blanas and his top men have been on TV nonstop for ten days. Now they're showing an international television audience that Big Lou's prey has been bagged. The story kicked off a giant media circus in town, with Blanas and detectives appearing on every national news show imaginable while Sacramento and its large Ukrainian community grieved and fretted about how it was being portrayed.

Giant tractor-trailer rigs that the TV networks and cable outfits like CNN and Fox News move to the scenes of big national stories surround the sheriff's department, which is on the same street as the district attorney's office, two blocks to the west, down near the Sacramento River as it flows along the edge of downtown. The sheriff's department has been holding around-the-clock press briefings even when there is nothing to report or when the only thing to report is information that turns out to be wrong.

He's a cunning criminal. He has tens of thousands of dollars he stole from relatives. He's on his way to kill more family members who live out of state. He's traveling with a mystery woman. His son is with him. Members of the local Ukrainian community are harboring him. He's headed back to the Ukraine. It went on like this for ten days, until his arrest, which was equally surreal.

Sheriff's deputies provided twenty-four-hour surveillance of his mother's house in suburban Sacramento. They also put a special panic alarm in the house for the surviving members of the family to use if Soltys showed up. Around 7:45 A.M., just as a new shift of detectives was about to begin its stakeout, relieving deputies who had worked all night, the family's garage door flew open and several members of the Soltys family drove off in a panic. Detectives thought Soltys might be in the group and immediately gave chase. It turned out they were running from Nikolay, who had been was spotted under the old desk in the yard while the family was eating breakfast. He put a finger to his lips, as if to ask his brother, the first to notice him, to remain quiet. When the family drove off, leaving Soltys in the yard, his brother, Stepan, the one who had spotted him, frantically tried to call for help at a nearby shopping center. He was so nervous, he dialed 1-1-9. A clerk came to his aid and helped him dial the correct numbers. By that time, sheriff's deputies were in the yard calling for his surrender. He immediately got out from under the desk and put his hands in the air as detectives handcuffed him.

"The cunning, crazed maniac is in custody," O'Mara mimics the breathless TV reporters. The phone rings again. It's Will Stomsvik, another homicide detective O'Mara enjoys needling.

"When are you guys gonna get him out of there? We keep seeing him moved from one car to the next. Why the fuck don't they have the detectives driving him back to the jail? What's the point of all this? We know you've arrested him."

Grippi pipes in: "Okay, who's gonna go to the Ukraine now to do the background on his childhood and how miserable of an upbringing he had so we shouldn't put a needle in him?"

"Shit, the brother jumped out of the house, called 911 and turned him in," cracks Sawtelle. "He's gonna get the hundred-twenty-thousand-dollars reward. Finally, he says, 'I have realized the American Dream.' "

A TV reporter asks the sheriff if he has anything he wants to say to the community, now that the long Sacramento nightmare is finally over.

"A vote for me," Sawtelle says, "is a vote for safety."

"It would be great if he busted out right now," Grippi says as TV shows the patrol car with Soltys in it starting to move but somehow stuck in traffic. "Pow! Pow! Pow! They blast him. Job done. Hey, how'd he get unhooked?"

"Here comes Tommy," O'Mara says of Tommy Clinkenbeard, a deputy public defender known for his love of the camera, who is certain to be all over his case. "Don't talk. Don't talk. Invoke your rights."

"Now," O'Mara says a few seconds later, "we design the elaborate procedures about who will get the case in this office. Maybe a geography test. Whoever can name the most former Soviet republics wins a trip to Oakland to try the case."

At 10:00 A.M., the scene shifts to Scully's office, where the district attorney wants to know if O'Mara sees this as a capital case. She's also wondering whether she should attend a press conference called by the sheriff for 10:30 A.M.

"I think it's an easy call," he tells her. "When you have that many bodies, the background of the guy doesn't matter. I think it's a DP case. I've already thought of some of the arguments I'd make if I was representing him but with this many bodies, I think you've got to let twelve people decide. Tommy was in Department eighteen on something else and I guess he already announced it's his case. He said he was going to go to the jail and try to see him. I called over there and told them he was going to try to make a stink but for God sakes, let's not have a four fifteen in front of the sheriff's department."

Penal Code 415: Fighting, Causing Loud Noise, or Using Offensive Words in Public Places.

Clinkenbeard isn't the attorney of record, since a lawyer can't be appointed before arraignment. So legally, he has no right to visit Soltys, O'Mara told the homicide detectives when he talked to them earlier.

"He'll just bait the shit out of them and make them arrest him," O'Mara tells Scully. "We don't need that."

All that is sideshow to Scully, whose main concern right now is that she wants O'Mara to put out an amended complaint that includes the unborn baby as one of Soltys' victims. She knows this is bound to be a big issue for right-to-lifers and conservatives and she'd just as soon get it out of the way. Soltys's wife, Lyubov, was three months pregnant. Under a 1970 state law that's rarely used, prosecutors can file murder charges against someone for taking the life of a fetus.

Scully wants the complaint amended to include "Baby Soltys" before this becomes an issue. O'Mara, however, doesn't think like a politician. He's a prosecutor. He doesn't share Scully's desire to rush.

"These people don't have names like Jan Scully or Mary Smith," he says. "Their names have like forty-eight consonants in them. The last thing in the world I want to do is do it wrong. I don't want any of the names misspelled. We can wait until next week and do it right."

Kerry Martin, who runs the victim/witness division of the office, says the coroner gave her all the correct spellings. The complaint can be filed right away. Martin will become heavily involved with Soltys's relatives over the next few weeks, trying to explain to them how the American criminal justice system works and why the news media is so aggressive, and helping transport the bodies back to the Ukraine for burial.

"Okay," O'Mara says, reluctantly. "As long as you got all the right shit. It's definitely going to be a change-of-venue motion, so we shouldn't make anything about this a spectacle. No one else cares about this shit, but I for one don't want to spend six months in San Mateo County trying this case."

This is the first hint he's given since Sacramento was mesmerized by the killings that O'Mara might try this case himself. He knows the pool of qualified homicide deputies who can do the case is small. For one thing, deputies with small children probably wouldn't want to live out of a suitcase for however many months it takes to hold the trial.

As he did when the Sconce case came in, O'Mara makes a quick mental note of the pool he can choose from. Tom Johnson's busted his ass all year in trial after trial and he's got young kids. Todd Laras and Andrew Smith have new babies, and—though he doesn't ever ask how they feel about it—O'Mara assumes they'd not want to be away from home. Ernest Sawtelle's a possibility, though he's never handled anything this big. Curry's got the Tison case. Tim Frawley's done three change of venues already. Earl is too new to the bureau and untested. Frank Meyer's a possibility. His kids are a little older, he's solid. He's doing the Fred Clark case and his two accomplices, but the timing might be right. He makes the short list. Koller has Sconce. Her husband, Paul, is a good candidate, but Besemer and Jeff Rose, a bureau chief whose responsibility includes overseeing the Misdemeanors unit, have been making noise how one of O'Mara's people needs to go down to Misdemeanors and become a lead, someone who can mentor the young, inexperienced deputies. Durenberger's already been told he's got the inside track on that dubious honor.

So what the hell, O'Mara begins to think. He lives alone, except for all his animals. A change of venue wouldn't be as hard on him as it would on some other lawyers in his unit. He has no other cases to juggle. Maybe he should keep Soltys for himself. He'd enjoy going head to head against Clinkenbeard.

O'Mara doesn't think it's going to be a hard case, but it will be contentious. Soltys confessed on videotape within hours after his arrest. There's already plenty of evidence. Of course, as O'Mara will learn when he watches the videotape interrogation, it's not exactly pristine, as various sheriff's department higher-ups contend.

For starters, they fucked up reading him his rights. Anyone who's watched a cop show on TV knows the drill. They have to say you have a right to remain silent and anything you say can and *will* be used against you in a court of law. Well, the detective who advised Soltys, through a Russian interpreter, even though Soltys's native tongue is Ukrainian, forgot the part about anything you say *will* be used against you. Stomsvik said "*can* be used" and left out the *will*. It's not fatal, but Tommy will make it an issue. O'Mara doesn't want a rookie to be tied in knots by the guy. He'd like to find a way to prosecute Soltys without using the confession, since it seems clear the Ukrainian never fully understood what his rights were when he started talking.

The toughest part, as it almost always is in a capital murder case where the evidence of the actual crime is strong, will be the penalty phase. A portrait of Soltys is already emerging from news stories—and he backs this up in the interview with cops—of someone who's long been unstable, who's paranoid, who came to this country and had a very difficult time assimilating. He's been miserable, lonely, and depressed in America and wanted to return home. It would be easy to find one juror who, as Grippi says, doesn't feel comfortable voting to put a needle in the guy's arm and removing him from this world forever.

O'Mara doesn't share his thoughts about trying this one himself with Scully right now. He's just trying to get out of the meeting and back to his office.

Should we have a press conference? Scully asks.

"I'm not giving any interviews," O'Mara, who's wearing his faded gray Dockers with the holes in the rear, says. "I'm not having any press conferences."

Scully wants to talk about liaisons between her office and the Ukrainian community, which has been effusive in its praise of Blanas and his staff. O'Mara doesn't give a shit. All he wants to do is prosecute the guy for seven homicides. When Scully asks him a question, he gives one-word answers, barely looking up. He's like a witness who's been prepped not to say anything more than absolutely necessary. Come on, John, you can almost see Scully thinking. Work with me here.

It's all a bunch of crap to O'Mara. He doesn't care how the office looks in the community. He doesn't care if Blanas gets all the credit and is anointed Sacramento Law Enforcement Deity of Deities and the DA gets no air time. All he wants to do is get back to his office, close the door, and do his job.

Scully's frustrated, too, if for different reasons. "Everything coming out of the sheriff's department is, to put it kindly, less than reliable," she says. "This is an opportunity for us to develop some type of relationship with the community."

Some months earlier, in a vehicular-homicide case Scully and O'Mara think was botched by a deputy district attorney believed by the higher-ups to have a highly inflated opinion of his legal skills, some members of the Ukrainian community—the same community suddenly in love with Sheriff Blanas—became furious with the district attorney's office. Scully saw the Soltys case as a way to repair some of the damage.

Scully wants to say something to the news media after ten days of Blanas soaking up all the attention, but there is no reason for her to attend Blanas's press conference. The DA's day in the sun will come later on in this case, she knows. "We may end up making a statement that we're not making a lot of statements or media contacts in this case, because we'll do everything in our power to not contribute to a change of venue. Because at least if they don't like it, at least if we say it upfront, they'll understand."

O'Mara doesn't care. If Scully wants to make a statement that says she'll have nothing to say, that's her decision. He wants to go.

"And you'll be in search of a prosecutor?" She turns to O'Mara, who's pale by now. "And tell us if you have certain needs that can't be met."

You'd love to hear him say what he's really thinking, but he bites his lip. "I think it will be a pretty straightforward case," he says, and gets up to leave.

No one at the DA's office watches the start of the televised press conference, so no one hears Blanas refer to Soltys as a "vicious criminal." Scully called him before he met the press and asked him to keep details and hyperbole to a minimum. Nikolay Soltys is innocent until proven guilty, she reminded the sheriff, so lets not fan any flames that require the trial to be held out of town. Scully genuinely believes a crime against the community of Sacramento deserves to be heard in Sacramento, where a jury of local residents can determine guilt or innocence. She doesn't want it heard in San Mateo County—at ten times the expense— or who knows where. She also knows telling Blanas to keep his lips sealed is like asking a beagle not to howl. He can't control himself.

"At the request of the district attorney," Blanas tells reporters crowding the front of the sheriff's headquarters building at the same time his detectives are interviewing Soltys a few floors up, "they do not want us to talk about the interview or the 911 tapes. We are obliging her and not releasing that."

When he's asked what Soltys is telling his detectives, Blanas again sounds like he's behaving just as DA Jan Scully has asked him to.

"We are interviewing him and the interview is going well. This is going to be a very high-profile case here in Sacramento and the district attorney is asking us not to discuss it at this point."

O'Mara and the rest of the deputies in his office now watching know the score on all this joint-cooperation garbage. They know Blanas can't stand the FBI honchos he's patting on the back and that the FBI honchos can't stand him. The deputies watching TV in O'Mara's office know nothing said at this press conference will help prosecutors obtain justice against Nikolay Soltys, even as it makes the parade of backslappers up on the podium look good.

The prosecutors also know something when Blanas says he is withholding details of the arrest and Soltys's behavior at the request of District Attorney Jan Scully: it's more than even money that many of the very details she has in mind will leak out of the sheriff's department in a torrent.

Their fears are confirmed the next morning when a front-page article in The Sacramento Bee has this headline on it: "Sources Say Soltys Admits to 6 Killings."

Scully's furious the next day, and it's not because the actual number is seven. O'Mara considers it par for the course. The story says Soltys claimed his family might have been trying to poison him and was spreading lies about him. So much for not convicting the suspect in the media.

The sheriff-department muckety-mucks finally let the actual arrest officers speak, and it's easy to see why they'll never become chief of police or sheriff. They're humble, soft spoken, understated. When they mention the potato peeler, O'Mara squeals with delight: "He was going to skin his next victim alive." As if on cue, some reporter asks the arresting officer if the potato peeler was a murder weapon and everyone in the office cracks up at the answer. "No," he says, "I believe he was going to peel potatoes if he was camping out."

A few days later, on the morning of Tuesday, September 4, Scully finally gets to have her face time on the Soltys case, with a press conference in front of the DA's building. She wants to draw special attention to the charge of homicide for the death of his wife's unborn baby. She also wants to tell the press her office, unlike her friends at the sheriff's department, won't be discussing the case. None of the reporters can recall the last time they were summoned to a press conference to be told the person calling it wants to announce she won't have much to say.

Scully makes a brief statement that Soltys will be arraigned this afternoon on seven counts of murder with special circumstances, which makes him a candidate for the death penalty. She reads the brief statement and then she's asked whether she's concerned Soltys was interviewed by sheriff's detectives without an attorney present. It's not a problem as long as the suspect was fully advised of his rights, she says. This is mischief already being stirred up by the public defender's office, she knows, which is angry because detectives sat Soltys down for an interview before their lawyers were appointed to the case. Clinkenbeard pressed the issue so far, he demanded an emergency hearing before Judge Morrison England, Jr., the judge in the Bread Store trial, to argue that Soltys's rights were denied because jailers wouldn't allow Clinkenbeard to visit him immediately after his arrest.

The hearing is a classic face-off between Clinkenbeard and Glenn Powell, an extremely high-strung and intense deputy who's a lawyer and former deputy district attorney and who holds his onetime employer in generally low regard. It comes the same day England will hear a jury verdict against Bread Store defendant Richard Brewer. O'Mara makes it a

point not to have anyone from the DA's office attend. This is a fight between the sheriff's department and the public defender's office. O'Mara
has enough battles of his own; he doesn't need to go looking for more.
Clinkenbeard files a motion that demands immediate arraignment and
access. Soltys was arrested August 30 but O'Mara didn't move to arraign
him until today, the day after Labor Day. As far as the sheriff's department is concerned, since he hasn't been arraigned, no attorney has been
appointed. So when Tommy and three or four other private lawyers
from around town showed up to talk with Soltys in the hours and days
before his arraignment, the sheriff's department, at the behest of
O'Mara, took the position they were social visits. Sorry, boys, Soltys isn't
accepting social visits just yet.

Powell and Clinkenbeard can't stand each other. Each one is what the
other detests. Powell is a muscle-bound deputy who could give a shit
about Soltys or whether he gets to see Clinkenbeard in his cell. He
waived his rights to a lawyer, Powell tells the judge, and until he's arraigned, Clinkenbeard and the PD have the same right to see him as any
other lawyer in town, which is none. Clinkenbeard is a short, wiry bug
of a man in a ponytail who thumbs his nose at convention and authority.
He'll play as rough as he needs to in defense of a man he believes is having his rights trampled on by people like Powell and the district attorney's office. The dislike each man has for the other is palpable as they
argue before Judge England and a courtroom filled with reporters from
all over the state and members of Brewer's jury.

"We can't pick and choose, out of simple fairness, who goes in and
sees him, because a great many attorneys would like this case," Powell
tells the judge. "The sheriff's department cannot play favorites."

England rules that Clinkenbeard has no inherent right to visit Soltys,
but that the sheriff's department is obligated to inform the Ukrainian
émigré that a public defender would like to see him, and is available to
him, in anticipation of being appointed to represent him once he's been
arraigned. When Clinkenbeard says Soltys might not understand the
offer of a government lawyer being available to him unless a fluent interpreter can explain what this means—this has a different meaning, obviously, in the Ukraine—England orders that an interpreter explain to
Soltys what a public defender can do for him.

Powell doesn't believe this is necessary. He suggests Clinkenbeard can send a letter in the mail to Soltys just like any other lawyer, but England is in no mood to referee a spat between two headstrong lawyers who loathe each other. He's got enough of that in the Bread Store trial. He adjourns the hearing after giving both sides adequate time to express their views.

As aggressive as Clinkenbeard has already been, Scully knows the PD will try to get the confession tossed out of court. She feels strongly that leaks from the sheriff's department about his confession will make the prosecutors' job infinitely more difficult. But she also knows that O'Mara feels confident there's ample evidence against Soltys to make the case even if the confession is suppressed.

As for a possible change of venue, which is question number two at her press conference, she points out that it's not enough for a community to be saturated with general knowledge of a crime. Sacramento's been bombarded by news of the case, but the defense will also have to show that the potential jury pool is predisposed toward guilt. That may not be tough, given all the hoopla attached to the story. But as Scully and the rest of the world will find out a week later, when terrorists attack the World Trade Center and the Pentagon, the story will have a relatively short shelf life. She tells the press crowded onto the grass and sidewalk in front of the district attorney's building—two blocks to the west, the sheriff's department remains surrounded by giant satellite TV trucks—she's hopeful the case will be tried in Sacramento. It belongs in Sacramento, she says. Her office would vigorously oppose moving it.

Despite O'Mara's strong feeling that Soltys is a virtual poster boy for the death penalty, she says no decision has been made on whether to make this a capital case. The last thing she wants to do is have anyone believe these questions aren't subjected to deep and vigorous review inside her office. The truth is, O'Mara develops a gut feeling the day the case walks in the door and goes with it—unless something comes up to make him change his mind.

Clinkenbeard, who will be appointed to the case this afternoon at arraignment, is a fierce opponent of the death penalty. People who work with him say one reason he's stayed away from death-penalty clients is because his moral opposition to capital punishment is too strong to even take on such a case. Later in the year, he'll call O'Mara and say he's developing information about Soltys's past that will mitigate against the DA seeking the death penalty. O'Mara, as he's done many times before, will agree to meet with him and hear what it is. It's got to be more than, gee, the poor guy had a rough childhood and couldn't assimilate or find meaningful work in this country.

"He took the three-year-old out to a fucking field and slit his throat in a field with a box of toys," O'Mara says the day after Scully's press conference. "I'm sure it took him a little while to die, even if he went into shock. I'd be all over that fact in the opening and closing. That will offend the shit out of the jurors. It was the worst part of the crime, as far as I'm concerned. Even if you buy all the bullshit about his being mad at his family and they're trying to poison him and all that. The three-year-old had nothing to do with any of that."

Afterward, upstairs in her office, O'Mara lets Scully know he's not filing against Soltys's mother unless someone above him orders it. The cops have no real evidence she harbored him in any way and O'Mara can't imagine putting her through it.

He's already in a bad mood, wearing a suit because Scully and Besemer want him to attend a meeting this evening with the Ukrainian community at the giant Bethany Slavic Missionary Church, a former health club out in the southern sticks of the county. He tells Scully and Besemer he'll be there, but he doesn't intend to go. His house is only a few miles from the church; once he's in the area, he'll just zip past the church and head home to feed the animals and listen to the ducks quack.

The meeting turns out to be as boring as a legislative committee hearing. It goes on forever. Scully makes many of the same points she made at her press conference earlier in the day. The next morning, when Besemer asks O'Mara why he didn't show up, he says something about getting out of the office late because he was working on the case. By the time he got out to the church, there was so much traffic backed up to get into the parking lot, he just said screw it. No one seems to mind. He's been behaving this way forever.

There's some value to the meeting, though. Even O'Mara can admit it. Many in the Ukrainian community have a profound distrust of government and police. They think when the police or a prosecutor want to talk to you, you're about to be taken out back and tortured or shot. Defense lawyers say it's nearly impossible to get clients from the former Soviet Union to plead guilty, even when it's clearly in their best interest to do so. Scully answers questions about the process and does a lot to allay such fears just by showing up and being cordial and pleasant. "This is certainly one of those cases that will be remembered and thought of sorrowfully by all members of our community," she tells them. "I can assure you the district attorney will work hard to achieve justice for all."

The next morning, O'Mara, Besemer, and Scully meet in Scully's office to discuss who'll try the case. They've made it clear to O'Mara they'd rather have someone else do it. He does his best not to make it appear like he's annoyed or taking it personally, but he is offended. Scully gives him three reasons: He's too valuable to send out of town for six months if the expected change of venue is granted; he's already tried more than his share of big cases and they should be spread around more; and she'd like him to assume more of the role of her special assistant, almost like another chief deputy for policy and related issues.

"I don't subscribe to your theory about spreading the wealth around," he tells them. "I believe in going with the sure bet and picking someone with the experience in these change-of-venue trials."

Later, with O'Mara out of earshot, Scully explains her thinking. "I'm just trying to find out if John really wants to try the case or if it's some sense of obligation with him. John's done a number of these big change-of-venue trials and I want to see why John wants to do this one at this point, and I think part of his thinking is not to burden a young prosecutor. I look at these young prosecutors, and a case like this is the reason some of them are here."

O'Mara tells Scully he never had a burning desire to do any of these cases. To him, it's a job and as bureau chief for homicide and major crimes, it makes sense for him to try the case himself rather than force someone else to do it. "I'm not itching to try a case," he tells her. "I'm itching to solve a problem."

As for the assistant-chief-deputy role, he's got too many rough edges, he tells her. He's not politically correct. He has a knack for going into a meeting and stewing over the bullshit he hears being slung around the room until he can't stand it anymore. He speaks his mind and then pisses off people.

The truth is, O'Mara hates to think he's tried his last case, that he's stuck in an office for the rest of his career giving advice, signing complaints, asking for warrants and charges, cutting up, watching the cooking channel. He talks like one of these career civil servants who swear the day they become eligible for full pension, they're gone, retired to relax and enjoy the rest of life. People who work for him say he's full of shit. That as much as he complains, he loves the place and doesn't have much to trade it for. They have a hard time imagining John O'Mara sitting on his front porch watching the world go by, but he says he's not worried about finding satisfying things to do.

Usually, after a long trial, he trudges out to some spot on his property with a half-formed plan in his mind and starts building just for the therapy of it. For the desperate need to do something as far away in mind and spirit as he can get from the months of dankness and drudgery he's just immersed himself in. "That's the Morris Solomon dock," he says of a redwood pier he built near the peaceful little duck-and-frog lagoon. It went up just after his trial against a laborer convicted of murdering prostitutes and leaving them buried in shallow graves all over town. Pointing to a barn he built for his goats and sheep to get out of the rain and heat, he says, "That's the Dorthea Puente memorial barn." She's the grandmother O'Mara convicted of poisoning old men at her boarding home, so she could steal their government pensions, and burying their bodies in her yard. Building something with his own hands, something he starts and finishes in some reasonable amount of time, is a soothing activity, in stark contrast to the complex cases that never seemed to end. A murder case, with all the delays and built-in appeals, is never really finished until the bad guy dies. He could easily see himself on his small spread, building things, taking time off to travel, enjoying life. Today, he's sick of killers, lawyers, supervisors, pointless meetings, and work.

So what does he decide? Eventually, he will give the case to Tim Frawley, one of the most experienced and seasoned prosecutors in the office, a veteran of three tough change of-venue trials already, a prosecutor so seasoned, he's applied to the governor's office to become a judge and is a good bet to be appointed. This is no up-and-coming eager beaver looking to make a name for himself on a big case. This is O'Mara's way of giving it to the deputy he thinks best equipped to win. He also is thumbing his nose at Scully and Besemer on what they said about giving the young attorneys a chance. When they don't register a peep of opposition to Frawley, O'Mara's suspicions are confirmed. They like the idea of giving young deputies a chance, but their biggest concern is keeping O'Mara in the office, where he can help them make smart decisions and steer clear of dumb ones.

There's another reason he will settle on Frawley. As much as anything these days, O'Mara lives to be amused. Movies or books may provide that for most people, but entertainment for him is to watch people squirm. He loves to watch people blush, get flustered, stumble. It's an odd trait but there's no denying it. Inject him with a truth serum, or just catch him on a day when he doesn't feel like expending the energy to hide his true intentions, and he'll admit he wants Frawley to try the case because Frawley and Clinkenbeard are like a cat and a rat. They'll fight over anything.

When Clinkenbeard is in the courthouse, prosecutors say he's self-righteous, obnoxious, and dogmatic. Frawley is hardly Mr. Popularity at the public defender's office. Lawyers over there say he's sneaky, aloof, combative, and that he fights dirty.

Tall, impossibly fit from all the marathons and triathlons he still runs now that he's in his early fifties, Frawley is a bit of a riddle. He has the erudite good looks of a professor at Dartmouth, where he got his undergraduate degree. Women seem to fall head over heels for him. He seems easygoing and unflappable, but O'Mara knows he's intensely competitive, that he won't let his adversaries get away with a thing. He's also seen Frawley's temper blow on more than one occasion, and knows this is not a pretty sight.

The very first day Frawley and Clinkenbeard are in court together for a routine appearance—someone else handled the arraignment while O'Mara was weighing whom to assign—Frawley has no trouble getting under Tommy's skin. O'Mara roars with delight when he hears about it, not because it produced any great sparks but because it presages what's ahead. The two lawyers are sitting near the lawyers' table waiting, with at least a dozen other lawyers, for their case to be heard. Frawley begins to tell someone how he intends to push for an early preliminary hearing, which all by itself will piss off Clinkenbeard. Making no effort to be discreet, he says Clinkenbeard will stall and delay, like he always does. Clinkenbeard hears his name, turns to Frawley, and asks, "What?" Without even glancing in Clink's direction, Frawley nods to the person he spoke to and says, "I was talking to him." In other words: *Mind your own fucking business Tommy. When I have something I want you to hear, I'll let you know.*

"This is going to be an ugly deal," O'Mara, with a sly smile on his face, says of the Frawley-Clinkenbeard contest over Soltys. "No doubt about it."

14 | Doctor on Trial

> Wherever a man commits a crime, God finds a witness. . . .
> Every secret crime has its reporter.
>
> —Ralph Waldo Emerson

BY the time Tison's preliminary hearing rolls around in October, Mark Curry is as confident as he's ever been. With all the lies Tison has been caught in and the experts willing to testify that Isabel could not have died the way her father said she did, Curry believes the preliminary hearing is little more than a formality.

On the eve of the hearing, Duckett and Curry are seriously considering whether to have Elena Tison arrested for witness tampering. A former employee at the weight-loss clinics told Duckett that Mrs. Tison called her and threatened to sue her for talking to investigators. Curry tells Duckett to write a memo for the file and he'll send a letter to Heller just to let him know what he's been told. Then we'll see if she chills out, Curry says to Duckett.

Little new evidence is presented at the prelim, which unfolds over three days. Heller hammers at Curry's expert witnesses. He says Dr. Angela Rosas, a University of California at Davis pediatrician and associate director of the UCD Child Abuse Center, is not qualified to testify, as she does, that Isabel could not have simply fallen from the window and sustained the types of injuries that killed her.

Sounding like the former assistant United States attorney he was in Sacramento from 1973 to 1977, the fifty-eight-year-old Heller says to Rosas: "You know you're testifying in a preliminary hearing. You know you're under oath. You know this is a very serious matter." Rosas holds her ground.

"Are you saying she had been thrown out the window?" Heller asks.

"If she was thrown out the window, that would be consistent with the [autopsy] report," Rosas answers.

Resting one arm over the empty jury box, Heller concludes: "I don't think the witness is qualified. I don't think she has the basic expertise to reach a conclusion."

Heller is gentler with Curry's other expert, Dr. Bahram Ravani, a Stanford Ph.D. in mechanical engineering who also is a UCD professor. Ravani concluded in his examination of the case that Isabel would have to have gone through the window at five miles per hour to land where she did.

"Isn't it true that she could have crawled to the actual spot where the blood is?" Heller wants to know.

"It's possible," the professor answers. Heller doesn't cut him off when Ravani adds that since Tison said the screen was on top of Isabel when he got to her, it's unlikely she crawled. Dr. Rosas also had testified that with her injuries, she could not have crawled.

Dr. Donald Henrikson, the county pathologist who told Gay early in the case that he thought it was a homicide until shown otherwise, is a terribly nervous witness. Despite having performed more than 4,833 autopsies and having impeccable expert credentials, he seems terrified to be on the stand. Sweating profusely, he is so cautious, so circumspect, he's painful to sit and listen to. Curry knows Heller will attack him now and in trial. The nervous doctor manages to say a few things Curry would want a jury to hear: that there are strong signs the baby was shaken, that a fall of ten to twelve feet would not usually provide such deadly injuries, and that the child essentially died from blunt-force trauma to the head.

On the last day of testimony, Heller seems to score when he calls Deputy John Lopes, a sheriff's department evidence technician. Lopes testifies that he helped examine the Tison house and found "some disturbances in one corner of the screen that looked like handprints of a small child."

On cross, Curry gets Lopes to add that he saw no evidence of footprints on the thin layer of dust that covered the desk when he examined it, only a few hours after Isabel fell.

"Don't you think if someone had been on that desk, there would have been some evidence?" Curry asks Lopes.

"Yes, I do," the evidence technician answers.

A minute later, one very important difference between the two lawyers is illustrated. Heller, fifty eight, thick in the middle, is not used to trying homicides in court. Curry is a prosecutor who tears through murder trials, doing five or six a year and winning the vast majority.

Heller asks Lopes, "If a kid was thrown through a screen, wouldn't you expect some very significant marks to have been left on the screen?"

"Objection. Speculation, Your Honor," cries Curry. Sustained, says the judge.

Yet when Curry does the same thing—speculate—when he asks Lopes, "Don't you *think* Isabel playing on the desk would have left prints in the dust?," Heller is not there. The question is allowed and the answer hurts Tison.

On the following day of testimony, Heller's second and last witness is Barbara Hall, the Tisons' nanny. She testifies that Isabel was starting to walk in the days before her death. She also provides commentary on the family video Heller plays for the judge. It starts on Christmas, with Isabel pushing a big yellow truck she has just gotten as a gift. Tison is crying now, a beaten-down-looking figure in his orange jail jumpsuit. Inmates rarely dress out—the courthouse term for wearing civilian clothes—at prelims. There's no need to put on a suit and tie and get all cleaned up when it's just the judge you're trying to impress, not a jury. Elena brought a suit and tie for her husband to wear and the judge was going to allow it at the start of the hearing, but Tison never made the change. With two of Tison's brothers and his parents seated with her in the courtroom, Elena dabs away tears while the judge is shown the video. The doctor is sobbing and having trouble drawing a breath. Curry refuses to look at him, trying to never make eye contact with the defendant unless absolutely necessary. No cross, Your Honor, he tells Judge Ronald B. Robie, a thoughtful judge who will soon be appointed to a state appellate court. Curry stares straight ahead, looking confident as hell.

The judge says he's heard a lot of evidence. He wants Curry to sum it all up, something neither side is required to do. Curry tells Robie what he believes the testimony has just shown: Tison's story is not credible;

the baby sustained injuries not in keeping with a fall. If she did come out of that window, someone or something had to have propelled her.

"This was not," Curry says, "a simple fall as alleged by Dr. Tison, but rather an assault on a child fourteen months old in which she died from the injuries. . . . We may not know exactly how it occurred, whether he shook her first, threw her, whether he backhanded, or any type of manner like that. The fact is, when he applies force to a child, that shows a strong suspicion that he committed murder."

Heller is next. He gets up from his chair and walks over to the jury box, using it as a prop of sorts, something to lean on while he sums up. "This is solely a circumstantial case, and the law requires that in order to justify relying on circumstantial evidence to sustain a conviction or sustain probable cause that murder or assault resulting in death of a child under eight occurred, the People would be required to prove by evidence that the facts and circumstances must be entirely consistent with their theory of criminal culpability and completely inconsistent with any other rational conclusion."

Heller shows his rust again. He has just misstated the law. What Heller said about a conviction is accurate: in a circumstantial case, if there are two theories of what occurred, the jury must adopt the theory that speaks to the defendant's innocence. But this is a prelim. All Curry has to do is show, as he correctly tells the judge, "there's *some rational ground for assuming a possibility* the offense has been committed and the accused is guilty of it." At the prelim level, the weight is tilted very much in the prosecution's favor. That's why Curry can be so confident right now. He firmly believes Tison is guilty of murder, though he knows this will be a tough sell to a jury. That's why he has given himself 273 (ab) to fall back on. But the burden of proof for the DA at a preliminary hearing is so low, Curry knows he's going to come out ahead in this round.

Robie takes a fifteen-minute break to go to his chambers, read some case law, and make up his mind. When he returns, he tells Curry and Heller that Curry's reading of the law is accurate. Robie then adds his voice to the chorus of people who find the doctor's behavior unsettling and highly suspicious.

"There are a number of troubling facts which in my mind tend to support a reasonable suspicion of criminal conduct," he says. The fact

Tison did not call 911 and "deliberately drove to a hospital which was where he was told that his child wouldn't get the care that he as a physician obviously knew she needed . . . , certainly raises a suspicion in my mind of criminal conduct, almost as much as anything else that was presented."

Curry can't help but gloat a little on the way back to his office. He finds Heller to be an amusing, rather than worthy, adversary. A good deal about him bugs Curry. He thinks he talks too much. That he wears too much damn cologne. To Curry, Heller seems more interested in telling war stories and talking to reporters about how interesting he thinks the case is than in coming up with a credible defense. The guy seems constantly to be on the news and in the newspapers talking about this case and any other criminal justice matter that comes up. Don Heller, unavoidable for comment, veteran reporters joke.

In this instance, Curry thinks Heller shot the first arrow. He said the DA had been conducting a smear campaign, that somehow he has it in for Tison because he doesn't like him.

Elena Tison can't stand Curry. As far as she's concerned, an obsessed prosecutor is out to destroy her family simply because he doesn't approve of her husband's personality or lifestyle. Her nickname for him is "the Turtle," presumably for the long, slow strides he takes when he carries his case files into the courthouse, where she will glare at him with contempt. During a break in one court hearing she called Curry a "fucking jerk." During another she said Dave Duckett, his investigator, was an asshole. Whether she talks to them or not, Curry and Duckett know from the e-mail they obtained under subpoena that Elena Tison was extremely concerned about her husband's drinking. Curry expects to lose this battle to the defense, figuring a judge will not allow the e-mail to be introduced as evidence, since it might be protected under a spousal privilege that says a spouse doesn't have to testify against her husband. Still, he's damn glad to know about Mrs. Tison's feelings and everything else they've dug up about the doctor, because it puts Tison and his attorney in a box.

It's hard to look at Tison and imagine him tossing his baby out the window or willfully hurting her in a way that led to her death. Curry knows that. Jurors would have difficulty with that idea as well. It's simply not something a civilized man, an educated career man, would be likely to do. Heller by this time has come up with several theories about why Tison is innocent. The baby fell. Her hand marks are on the screen, though it's impossible to see where. The doctors at the hospital killed her by giving her the wrong blood. Only trouble with that theory is it fails to address why Isabel was in the emergency room undergoing brain surgery in the first place.

Heller's best defense, the one he would most like to pursue, may well be "Hey, this guy's a doctor, a loving father. He's an upstanding member of the community. He's got friends in positions of responsibility at the sheriff's department. He's not the type of nut job who'd toss his daughter out a window because his stocks were down, for God sakes. The DA is trying to destroy an innocent, honest man because Mark Curry thinks someone appointed him God and he doesn't like the guy. He doesn't approve of his lifestyle. He doesn't approve of all the guns he has in his house."

Heller claimed at the bail hearing that the case should be dismissed right then because he knew that the blood found on Tison's deck did not come from Isabel. It came from the family's Doberman, Lightning, which had been left alone for a long time and bloodied its own nose from frantically banging its head into a glass patio door. Tison used to have two Dobermans but had given one away a while earlier after it bit Isabel and he had to rush her to the hospital for that injury.

Heller bellowed in court how lab results would show this was dog's blood and that would be that. Curry asked the county crime lab to test the blood after Heller raised the issue, and it came back definitively as the baby's. He was so pissed by the time the results came back, he didn't even give Heller the courtesy of a phone call. Instead, on July 23, he sent him a fax that said, in total: "Tests of the blood on the paper towel show that it is of human origin only. At a later time I intend to test the blood to confirm that it is Isabel's and check paternity. Thank you."

The news media acted as if they forgot the allegation; the blood results were never reported. The dilemma for Heller if there is a trial is how can he portray the doctor as a good man who's the victim of some DA smear job, as he also claimed at the bail hearing, when Curry and his investigators have dug up so much information to the contrary?

If Heller does try to go that route with anything subtler than having the guy wear a suit and making sure the jury knows he's a doctor, that would allow Curry to contradict him. It would open the door to all the character evidence about Tison that his lawyer would surely not want a jury to hear. Aside from Elena Tison's worry about leaving her husband alone with their daughter because she says he abuses medication and drinks too much, Curry and his investigators have dug up enough damaging material about Tison's background and character that Heller has to know that road is closed to him. Which makes Curry feel pretty secure.

Dave Duckett, a former West Sacramento cop and onetime Sacramento sheriff's deputy, now works for the district attorney's office. A savvy and tenacious investigator who loves the thrill of the hunt, Duckett works for the Major Crimes division at the DA. He was assigned to help Curry on the Tison case. He did background checks on the doctor's professional history and, along with Curry, found out that his résumé's claim of being a licensed psychiatrist is bogus. Tison spent about four months in a three-year residency program before dropping out. Duckett tracked down his first wife, who told him stories about drug use, threats, extramarital affairs. She also said that when she began to pack a suitcase one afternoon because she'd decided to leave him after talking to the woman he was supposedly having an affair with, Tison put a gun to his head and threatened to blow out his brains if she didn't stop. "Let me move my clothes away before you pull the trigger," his wife said she told him.

She also told the investigator that Tison, who was insanely jealous, harassed a man she went on to date after they split up. Curry wants all this stuff he can get even if he never is allowed to use it. When he hands it over to Heller in discovery, he knows it will only scare Heller off the My-guy's-a-good-upstanding-citizen-being-smeared defense. Duckett also tracked down young women who worked in Tison's weight-loss clinics who described all types of bizarre behavior: inappropriate overtures to female staff; drug use; offers to give drugs to the women, several of whom said they took them; open displays of weapons by both the doctor and his wife; telephone threats to ex-employees who filed complaints with California medical examiners or resisted his advances.

One of the women, Tamara Glanville, said she was nineteen when Tison met her while she was working behind the counter at his dry cleaner. He called her and asked her to come work in his clinics for more than double the pay. She told Duckett that the doctor soon became obsessed with her. He bought her expensive gifts. Despite telling her repeatedly that she had a great figure, he offered her diet drugs, which she said she took for a while. He said he wanted to take Glanville to Paris, that he intended to divorce his wife because he had fallen in love with her.

He'd come into her office and give her foot massages and neck rubs. He seemed to know an awful lot about her personal life, things she said she'd never told him. A co-worker of Tamara's found an article on sexual harassment in the workplace and stuffed it in Tamara's mailbox, in full view, so maybe the doctor would get the idea, because Tamara said she felt too uncomfortable to confront him. She was a kid and she was terrified of him.

Duckett knew she sounded extremely naïve, that a defense attorney could probably attack her as a willing participant in the doctor's flirtations. But her testimony would only add to the character questions—if she were allowed to testify about these things.

"He would sit with his gun, loading it and unloading it," she told Duckett. "He would come in and ask if I wanted to hold his gun." Elena Tison walked around the clinics with a revolver in a shoulder harness. When Tamara Glanville finally told Tison that his overtures made her extremely uncomfortable, that she wasn't interested in him romantically, she was called in and fired. She later filed a complaint against him to the medical board alleging he "recreationally" took the amphetamine-based drugs he prescribed to his patients. When she applied for unemployment insurance with the state, the Tisons wrote a letter opposing her claim. They said she committed six felonies, including dispensing drugs to a patient without a medical license or Tison's approval.

Despite their opposition, Glanville did get unemployment benefits after a state hearing. It was a pattern Duckett said was repeated throughout Tison's professional life. He would be accused of inappropriate behavior by someone he harassed and he would turn the tables on her and make his own accusations. When his first wife went to police and said she was concerned he might have her killed, he sought restraining orders against her, claiming she was mentally unstable and needed psychiatric help. His brother and mother later would sign declarations in which they said the same things about his ex-wife. Heller was right: Curry didn't like the doctor or approve of his lifestyle. The more he learned about Tison, the more he came to despise him. The more he became convinced he was guilty.

The doctor at the hospital emergency room where Tison took Isabel, Dr. Grant Nugent, said Tison smelled of alcohol and was belligerent. Two months later, on April 11, Tison wrote a blistering complaint to the Medical Board of California claiming it was Dr. Nugent who was drunk and belligerent when Tison got to the hospital.

"Immediately," Tison wrote, "I could tell that this individual was under the influence." He went on to say that Dr. Nugent and another hospital staffer stood around and joked about something while he was trying to get treatment for his daughter. "They began to laugh loudly and openly while my daughter lay dying. At this point I told Dr. Nugent in a loud voice that he was aware that I was a physician and attorney and if any harm should befall my daughter due to his inept actions, he would have to answer for his actions." Tison closed his complaint letter by essentially blaming his daughter's death on Dr. Nugent, though he lapsed into calling him Dr. Grant, his first name, as the letter concluded.

"I believe that Dr. Grant's condition of being under the influence and an obvious substance abuser with all of its associated signs and symptoms prevented him from performing his task of attending to Isabel's condition in the emergency room at Mercy Folsom Hospital. Additionally, he coded her physical examination as only requiring a 'low-moderate' procedure on the attached insurance bill, showing that Dr. Grant did not recognize Isabel's grave condition from which she died shortly thereafter. His behavior of verbally berating me with profanities and laughing in my presence while my daughter lay dying nearby only further evidences Dr. Grant's impaired state. If not for this physician's blatantly impaired state of being under the influence from substance abuse, I believe that the outcome of my beautiful, only child, of the tender age of fourteen months, may have been different." None of this was true, Curry discovered.

Medical board investigators laughed off Tisons complaints. Dr. Nugent is a well-known former alcoholic, active in Alcoholics Anonymous and other treatment programs, sober for more than ten years after having his license suspended for a year in 1981 and hitting bottom. He is also highly respected and admired by his colleagues.

Curry found the behavior of the medical board amusing more than anything else. On several occasions when Tison was running his three diet clinics, employees filed complaints saying he used his own drugs, gave them out freely, and behaved in highly inappropriate and apparently illegal ways. Investigators twice wrote reports in which they said they asked Tison about the charges and dropped the case after he denied them. Now, once the death of his daughter hit the papers, lawyers from the California Attorney General's Office were all over the case, appearing in court to make sure Tison lost his medical license, launching their own investigation, showing their support of the DA. Their support can't hurt, Curry thought, but it's a little ridiculous at this point. Where were they when all this was going on?

After Glanville was fired and Tison learned that she had signed at least one of those complaints to the state board of medical examiners, he started harassing her on the telephone, leaving a series of threatening messages on her answering machine. She happily provided the tapes to Duckett when she met with him

"I never bought your wolves in sheep's clothing, okay?" Tison says on one of the calls. "Um, I knew all about your past. I know all about your future. Good luck, Tamara. That's all I can say, because there is no future for you. You had so much riding and you blew it."

A few minutes later, his voice slurred as if he'd been drinking, Tison calls again. "Hey, Tamara, I forgot to mention. I know you called my wife. You better fucking knock it off. If you call her again, I'd be worried. I'd be very worried. I was very nice to you the first time. If you want to push it, try it, bitch, a second time. No one's going to buy your story the second time. Good-bye, Tamara. No one bought your story."

Six minutes later, it's Tison again. "In other words, Tamara, stop screwing with my family with your lies, okay? I know you've called my wife with your little lies. Okay. If you want to get ugly, I can get real ugly. Trust me. Leave my fucking family alone or I'll fuck with you. Leave it, Tamara."

There are other issues, too, in the doctor's background. Apparently, he had a habit of establishing Internet Web domains with names almost identical to those used by existing businesses and then trying to get them to pay hefty sums to buy him out. In one such case, according to an "administrative panel decision" reached by the WIPO Arbitration and Mediation Center, a world body that regulates Web-domain disputes, Tison set up a Web site similar to *The Sacramento Bee*'s site and then offered to sell his domain to the newspaper for an undisclosed amount.

The *Bee*'s site, sacbee.com, contains the on-line version of the newspaper. Tison's site, "sacramentobee.com," contained a large picture of a bee that resembled the newspaper's mascot.

Once on the site, readers were directed to right-wing political and other propaganda. The newspaper became aware of the ruse when a reader called to complain that she had sent an e-mail to Rick Kushman, the *Bee*'s television critic, using a link on the Tison Web site, and had gotten an e-mail reply from him telling her to go "screw yourself." The international arbitration panel concluded from its investigation that Tison was pretending to be Kushman and that he was trying to extort money from the newspaper by impersonating its Web site. Ruling that Tison had set up the similar domain name and was using it "in bad faith," the WIPO ordered that it be transferred to *The Sacramento Bee,* thus putting it out of business. Tison never responded to the complaint or the panel's findings, and his site was abolished. Curry found out about this one by bouncing around on the Internet and being linked from a hit on Tison to the WIPO ruling. Smart, he thought, the guy tries to rip off the newspaper.

When a trial is finally held the following spring, the district attorney's office won't be able to introduce most of what it dug up about Tison's personal or professional life, although the Elena Tison e-mail will be allowed because the spousal privilege is waived when a child is injured or killed. It will be impossible to prove the exact circumstances that led to Isabel Tison's death. It will be up to the prosecution to convince members of a jury that the slump-shouldered man who by then comes to court in a nice respectable business suit and greets the judge, clerk, and other court personnel with friendly hellos each morning and afternoon should be locked up for a very long time, if not the rest of his life.

15 | Major Participant

"Why may not that be the skull of a lawyer? Where be his quiddities now, his quillets, his cases, his tenures, his tricks?"
—Hamlet

ALTHOUGH it's still two days away, Dawn Bladet is getting ready for the first closing argument she has ever given in a murder trial.

Uncharacteristically for her, she plans to be low key, at least in the beginning. She doesn't want to come off too hostile to Dixon. When you hear murder, she plans to tell the jury, you don't think Bobby Dixon. But like one of the jurors said during voir dire, felony murder is clear and it's harsh. She used the analogy of skydiving. It's a dangerous activity. When you choose to partake of it, you know the risks. When you step out of the airplane, you assume the risk from the choice you've made. You're responsible for the consequences. It's the same thing as a robbery that results in murder, even if you were just the getaway driver and would never have killed anyone yourself.

Bladet has metaphors aimed at the women. Metaphors aimed at the men. For the men, it's baseball. Every team needs a pitcher. Every position is important. If someone doesn't play his position and perform his assigned role, everyone loses. Just like this robbery. Everyone knew his position and role. You can't play baseball with no pitcher. You can't do an armed robbery without a driver.

For the women, it's cooking.

"I started thinking cake," she says. "But I thought, wait. It's the frickin' Bread Store. It's all about bread. I had to call my friend and get the recipe for bread. I'm a very good cook but I've never made bread. You need all the ingredients for a successful robbery. Planning. A way to contend with people in the store, the employees. Instruments of the crime. Disguises. A weapon. And what the robbers need above all else is a way to get away. They need a getaway driver. You don't do a robbery without a getaway driver. It doesn't happen. But for Bobby Dixon, Rick Brewer wouldn't be in that store and Jason Frost would be alive."

What Bladet and Harrold seem to like most about her planned closing is that they get to sandbag Peters with it. The two of them have been telling Dixon's lawyer that Harrold will do Dixon's closing. When Peters walks into court and sees the laptop and understands he's in for a slick Bladet PowerPoint, he'll know he's been had.

Repkow has let Harrold know on several occasions she wants him to do Brewer's closing. "No PowerPoints. No animation," she's told Harrold a few times. That was all Bladet needed to hear. At the first meeting in England's court to work on jury instructions, she said to Harrold, loud enough for Repkow to get it: "Steve, don't you think that animation where we put Rick Brewer's face on the Bread Store and then put the devil's mask on him would look good on the visualizer?"

When everyone arrives for court the next morning, Peters knows what's up. He and his investigator, who dresses like a Vegas mobster—for some reason having to do with his hair, which he wears in a bouffant, Harrold calls him Fluffy—refer to Harrold this morning as "Mr. Devious."

Bladet begins her assault on Bobby Marion Dixon with the customary reminder of the felony-murder rule and why it applies to this case. She goes through the skydiving, bread, and baseball metaphors.

"It's a little Midtown bread shop," she says softly, only warming up. "It's a bakery. They make sandwiches. It was two days before Christmas."

Masked men race in and rob the place. One of them shoots Jason Frost three times. "And who's waiting outside in the G-ride to take them safely away? Bobby Dixon."

While Bobby waited, terror struck inside the store. "Jason Frost is trapped behind that counter," she says while clicking on the mouse and commanding a photo of the crime scene. "He's already dropped the money into the safe that night. But the guys don't know that when they enter the Bread Store. Then the shots ring out. Point-blank range. Three wounds. All within close range behind that counter, where he couldn't go anywhere."

He was in the hospital ten days. He had ten separate operations. Heroic efforts were made to save him. Jack and Becky Frost can't bear to hear all this again, but they know they must.

"Don't lose perspective," Bladet insists to the jurors. "This is a courtroom. The defendants are all dressed up for court. This is a long way from Southside Park, where Bobby Dixon was kicking it with his homies. Where this conspiracy was hatched."

To nail Dixon on the special circumstance that would land him in prison for life, the People must prove—beyond a reasonable doubt, same as the actual crimes—he exhibited reckless indifference to human life *and* that he was a major participant. It all seems obvious to Bladet. They go in with guns and masks and employees in the store. This by definition shows reckless indifference to human life. Bobby had to know. Surely he was a major participant.

"Use your common sense," she urges. "They're not going over to the Bread Store in the G-ride with a gun and in masks if they don't all know what they're doing. And they're not going to let the driver be ignorant."

Because the law on accomplice testimony won't let this jury hear other defendants incriminate one another unless the one doing the incriminating testifies, therefore opening himself to cross-examination, Dixon's jury hasn't been able to hear Martinez's commonsense explanation about how he put "two and two together" from riding in a stolen Jimmy with masks and a shotgun.

She recounts Bobby's letters to people on the outside about influencing testimony. There's no evidence they were ever delivered, but the Southside punks seemed to follow the script. More important, she said, the letters show Dixon's consciousness of guilt. Delivered or not, they all but convict him by themselves.

She covers every possible angle. Why did the punks lie? They were scared, Brewer was right there in court watching them. Why did Carlos Cervantes lie? Same reason.

"Carlos Cervantes could not come into this courtroom and tell the truth about what he saw," she says in a voice that's asking, My God, isn't it obvious? "He could not come in here with Rick Brewer and the other defendants and say what he told the police was the truth. He's out now. He's back in Southside Park. That is a very, very real fear. It pained him to rat on his friends. He knew the consequences of being a snitch."

Then she turns to Trevor Garcia, for whom she holds not nearly as much sympathy as her co-counsel.

"Trevor Garcia should have been sitting in trial as a defendant. That's a given. But he was given a plea agreement. You don't have to like it. But that's not the issue before you. Your role is to evaluate the credibility of Trevor Garcia. Did he tell you the truth?

"He didn't make up stories. He didn't exaggerate. Hate the plea agreement. Hate that he gets twelve years. That's right to do. What isn't right is to use that to determine anything but his credibility."

Bladet likes to say how she can get hysterical and anxious about whether her case is coming together when she's in the thick of it, but none of her insecurity shows in court. She's in command. It's almost as if the jurors can see Bobby Dixon get smaller and smaller as she continues to lay into him and the idea, which she knows Peters will argue, that he was not a major player. That he didn't know anyone was going to pull a robbery when they left Southside and he was behind the wheel of his stolen Jimmy.

"You don't have to be a rocket scientist to figure out when you're in an alley in the dark behind a business and it's closed—you're not there to get a sandwich. You're not there to get bread. They put on masks. They carry a gun. He knew exactly what was going down and he knew what his purpose was in that alley."

He hears gunshots. Does he bolt? No. He asks, "How much did we get?" according to Trevor Garcia's testimony.

"Make no mistake. Bobby Dixon was just as much a part of this robbery as any of the others who went inside. Bobby Dixon shared the same intent of each of his coconspirators, to take money that didn't belong to them by the use of force and fear. Had the robbery been successful, Bobby Dixon would have shared in the victory, the profits.

"Well, the robbery wasn't successful. That's another risk of being a robber, that there may not be money where you think it is, that your timing is off. Well, each of the team members share in their failures. But for Bobby Dixon's decision to be a member of the team—without Bobby

Dixon's participation as getaway driver—there would have been no attempt to rob the Bread Store and Jason Frost would be alive today."

Bladet moves the laptop out of the way after two hours of nonstop talking so Peters has room to begin his closing. "It sure was nice of Bobby to send those letters," Harrold says during the break as Peters sets up. "I might buy him a little gift as a token of my appreciation. Maybe a nice pen-and-pencil set."

Watching and listening to Peters, it's not readily apparent that he's wound as tight as he is. He plods along like an amiable Jimmy Stewart, a lawyer never in a hurry, talking that folksy, slow, down-to-earth patter he favors.

"One person can commit a robbery," he says. "You don't need a baseball team. The district attorney wants you to believe this could not have happened without Bobby. That's not true."

He wants the jury to reflect on the witnesses they heard and how a bunch of liars form the heart of the district attorney's case. "If you people get on a jury a year for the rest of your lives, you will not see the number of lying, untruthful witnesses you have seen in this trial. I feel really comfortable saying that."

Dixon didn't kill or rob anyone. To convict him, he says, you've got to believe he was a major participant in all this. He stole the car, sure. But that's all he did.

"If you make a just decision, no one can tell you you're wrong."

They break for lunch. Bladet is furious. Peters won't look at her or acknowledge her presence. It probably has something to do with how the prosecutors covered up who would deliver the closing, but she takes it personally. This is often how it gets in a long, difficult trial. Personalities grate. Nerves fray.

Peters is back at it after lunch and with Bladet's nasty mood, it's possible to feel something bad brewing.

Peters makes a crack how he hopes the jurors don't fall asleep, since it's especially easy to do that right after lunch. They like him. Harrold and Bladet know this and it annoys them.

"If there are two explanations about circumstantial evidence that are reasonable," Peters tells the jury in a preview of instructions the judge will give them formally in a little while, "and one points to his innocence and one to his guilt, the law says you have to accept the one that points to the defendant's innocence."

Instead of believing the DA's argument that Bobby stole the Jimmy so his boys would have a G-ride, Peters wants the jury to adopt the other explanation: that Bobby jacked the Jimmy so he could pull the engine and drop it into his sick Skylark.

"It seems to me," he tells them as he finally nods in Bladet's direction, "she gives you ten percent evidence and ninety percent theory on what they think Bobby did."

Where's the real evidence on Bobby? In what Carlos Cervantes and Trevor Garcia said? They both lied. Everyone knows that.

"The law says if witnesses are willfully false about one part of their testimony, you can say all of it is false," he says—another preview of the judge's instructions.

Peters is doing a good job sowing doubt about Dixon's exact role. The guy's a fool, anyone can see that. Isn't he too stupid to be a major participant? Peters attacks Garcia again. He's a liar. He's the only one who said anything about Bobby asking, "How much did we get?"

He places a piece of paper on the visualizer. "Testimony of an accomplice should be viewed with caution, especially if it incriminates the defendant."

As for the Dixon letters, Peters treats them the only way a defense attorney trying to save his guy's ass could possibly treat them. They don't show consciousness of guilt, as Bladet and Harrold have said. They show Bobby trying to get the witnesses to tell the truth. That's Peters's spin. Remember, the law also says if there are two ways to interpret circumstantial evidence, one reasonable and the other unreasonable, you must accept the reasonable explanation.

"Bobby Dixon's fate has been in my hands for four years," Peters says, again sounding like Jimmy Stewart. "And that's a big responsibility. Now it's yours."

The idea of reasonable doubt is next, and Peters displays a large chart that depicts a thermometer and headings about "probably guilty," "maybe guilty," and several other categories that stop short of "guilty beyond a reasonable doubt."

If you think he's probably guilty, well, that means there's some reasonable doubt mixed in there, so the only proper verdict is not guilty, he says while pointing to the chart.

Peters's final point: He places several dictionary definitions of *doubt* and *reasonable* on the visualizer to show the jury. Given the homicidal thoughts racing through Bladet's brain right now, it's remarkable she's able to restrain herself until Peters finishes. He's crossed the line. You don't pull definitions out of the dictionary. You rely on the law, jury instructions, and legal concepts. She's disappointed England allowed him to get away with it, but it gives her an opening for rebuttal. She could object, but she'd rather lie in wait, striking back in her own way. Judges don't like objections during closing argument. It's a lawyer's time to make his best pitch to the jury. Unless he's grossly distorting the evidence or the facts, most judges allow tremendous leeway in how far an attorney can go.

They take a short break before Bladet's rebuttal. She's out in the hallway, talking it over with Donell Slivka, a prosecutor and friend she worked with when the two were doing child sex assaults together.

Peters's investigator, the one Harrold calls Fluffy, has removed most of Peters's paperwork from the courtroom, as if he sensed Bladet might do something to it. He left the probable-cause thermometer chart sitting where it was while Peters closed. Before she begins, Bladet asks the judge if she can use Peters's definitions so she can properly respond to them. Those are props, Peters tells the judge. They belong to him. He doesn't intend to share with Ms. Bladet. England tells him to give the paper to Bladet so she can make her point.

It's hot in court. Outside, it's nearly 100 degrees, and it's hard to keep the old building cool, especially inside a crowded courtroom. The court reporter is wearing a sleeveless dress, waving her arms around and fanning her underarms in an attempt to dry off. Bladet brushes her hair off her face and begins.

She strides over to the probable-cause chart Peters used and picks it up. She waves it at the jury. "This," she barks, "is not the law."

She's back at the visualizer now. "Mr. Peters doesn't get to decide what to add to reasonable doubt."

"Objection," Peters shouts.

"Sustained," says a wary judge.

She's got a red felt-tip marker in her hand. The reasonable-doubt definition Peters used is on the visualizer lens, projected on the screen for the jury. She looks across the courtroom at Slivka, who's sitting in the back. The women nod ever so slightly in each other's direction and Bladet, with the sweep of her right hand, takes the red marker and draws a thick, angry line across the paper. It's projected on the screen for the jury to see. "This," she shouts, "is not the law!"

Peters's cheeks are as red as Bladet's hair. He leaps from his seat. "Objection," he stammers, demanding Bladet be cited for misconduct. England is blank faced. He's not sure what to do. He gave Bladet the tools she used to deface Peters's exhibit and his defense. In the back of the courtroom, Slivka is smirking at her pal's audacious move. The judge wants to scold his old friend, but he decides to wait until she's finished. And she's not anywhere near finished.

She bends down and pulls the shotgun out from under the prosecution table. She has the red-and-black devil's mask too. She points to Bobby Dixon, walking right up to him, waving a finger in his face.

"This is not a toy," she says of the Mossberg. "Bobby Dixon is a grown man in his twenties. He stole a G-ride. This gun's not a toy." She holds up the mask, Brewer's mask. "This is not kids playing little league. It's not what this is about."

She reminds the jury she didn't rehearse Trevor Garcia's testimony with him. Sure, he made mistakes and contradicted himself. But he told a true story of what happened that day. Dixon lied so many times he couldn't keep his stories straight. He implicated everyone but took no responsibility for his own actions. All the anger of the past eight months is boiling over. She strides up next to him, her right index finger inches from Dixon's scowling face.

"Bobby Dixon is a cowardly snitch," she tells the jury. "He's gonna rat on everyone but himself."

She's taken Dixon's various statements and pulled the lies out so she can put them before the jury one by one. 1. He didn't know anything about no robbery. 2. He heard about it on the TV news. 3. I heard some downtown dudes did it. 4. I don't know where the Bread Store is. 5. Some chick Alicia told me about it. 6. I don't know no Rick Brewer. 7. I only met him in lockup. 8. I've never even been in an SUV. 9. Okay, I was in a black Jimmy. 10. He ID's Brewer in a photo lineup but says he never saw Brewer in an SUV. 11. I heard four or five Mexican dudes did the robbery. 12. I was never in no car with Rick Brewer. 13. I don't know Rick Brewer's phone number. Carlos Cervantes has it. 14. I did go in the Jimmy, but just to sit in it. 15. Yeah, I needed an engine, but little Rick stole it. I wasn't with him when he did. 16. Then he names all the defendants who were in the G-ride. He saw them all drive off. He wasn't in it. 17. He knows Glica and Brewer stay in the same apartment building. 18. He says no one in the store will fit his description. 19. He said he was lookout when Rickie stole the G-ride. 20. Yeah, that is Brewer's phone number in my address book. 21. I didn't see any of this go down. I just heard about it later.

"Distance, distance, distance," she says. "He keeps trying to put distance between himself and the robbery."

She reels off more Dixon lies, this time from his interview with Detective Winfield. I went to the gas station with the guys. Brewer dropped me off at the park. I didn't go anywhere else with them. Even his father comes into the interrogation room and tells him, Stop lying.

"Listen how he answers these questions," Bladet says, still in Dixon's face. "Is this the mind of someone innocently caught up with someone or is this someone with a guilty conscience?"

She wants to bring up the jailhouse letters once more, not wanting the last word to the jury about them to be Peters's comment that Dixon was simply trying to tell the truth. "Nowhere in these letters does it say anything about telling the truth," she says. "You send lawyers and investigators to talk to witnesses about telling the truth, not Reggie Miller, poster boy for Mr. Convicted Felon." Dixon heard shots. He waits for everyone. He stops so Brewer can stash the gun. He stops while they ditch the masks. When the Jimmy breaks down, they run and he smashes an Asian man in the face and tries to steal his car.

She stands over Dixon now. Two bailiffs are behind him, a third is off to his right. Her right index finger is no more than two inches from Dixon's face, which is locked in the same type of contorted expression he might have if he had just smelled something acrid and foul. She mocks Peters and tells the jury: "Bobby Dixon's fate is not in your hands. He made choices that put him here today."

Everyone in the courtroom has been wondering when it would happen. Now it does.

"I did not make choices that put me here today," Dixon blurts out. The bailiffs stand above him. "Mr. Dixon," Judge England says sternly. "No more outbursts! Do you understand me?"

"I'm in here trying to prove my innocence and she says this," Dixon continues.

"We have been together a long time, Mr. Dixon, and you've been fine," England says. "No more outbursts. Do you understand me?"

"Yes, sir," Dixon answers meekly. She's defeated him; he is broken.

When Bladet is finished with her rebuttal, it's time for the judge to weigh in on what he has just witnessed. He thanks the jurors and has them escorted out for a break, telling them to return in twenty minutes for his reading of jury instructions. Once they're gone, Peters explodes.

"Judge, I want her cited for misconduct. She took a red felt pen and drew a line through the document while it was on the visualizer. She's no rookie. This is a murder case. She's been around awhile. She knows full well what's going on here. She made every attempt to deface that in front of the jury. Then she baits Mr. Dixon, calling him a cowardly snitch, until he finally has an outburst. These are not rookies. These are experienced prosecutors. This is blatant, blatant prosecutorial misconduct and the only way to cure it is to declare a mistrial and cite Ms. Bladet for misconduct."

Bladet is asked to explain. Unlike during her fiery rebuttal, she's now calm and sedate. She knows what the Jesuits used to teach is true: It's better to seek forgiveness than permission.

"I was upset. He was misrepresenting the definitions, like he was trying to mislead the jury."

Props used during arguments, she says, are fair game. What she marked up is only paper. It can be reproduced. It has no value. That's why she didn't deface the exhibit, the probable-cause chart. She wanted to, but she figured that actually took some time to prepare, even if it's a load of crap.

"I apologize for defacing a piece of paper," she says to the judge, not Peters.

She denies she baited Dixon. "The fact he can't sit there and keep his mouth shut has nothing to do with me and everything to do with him," she says. Harrold is simply sitting back in his chair, as he has through all this afternoon's drama, and enjoying the show.

"I've been in this business thirty years," responds Peters. "I have never had anyone deface an exhibit. That piece of paper is a bell that has been rung in front of the jury calling me a piece of crap. She called Mr. Dixon a cowardly snitch several times."

England doesn't seem too upset with Bladet, but he tells her she should have objected when Peters put the definitions on the screen. "I was as shocked as anyone to see a line drawn through that document. There did appear to be some anger related to that which, frankly, I was surprised to see."

Bladet didn't bait Dixon, the judge says. Worse things have been said about him in this trial. He denies Peters's motion for a mistrial, but the red line incident seems to bother him.

"The only issue I have is how this was defaced," he says after ruling on the mistrial motion. "It's not the worst thing that could have happened. It is simply the manner in which it was done. The court does not condone it. The court was, to a certain extent, shocked to see it handled that way, but I don't think it rises to the level of misconduct. The jury saw it all. That could be the best thing. The jury saw it all."

Back at the district attorney's office, Bladet is not the least bit contrite. "Maybe I should have objected. I chose to deface his exhibit instead." In fact, she sees only advantage to her side in the whole thing.

"There are ten women on that jury and I know the young ones notice Peters's little sexist slights," she's telling her colleagues in the after-court ritual of going over the day. "I know they're with me. He knows it, too, so now I'm devious and underhanded. You can talk to defense attorneys who've been in court with me. I'm not slimy. You fuck me, I'm gonna bite back."

Closings for Rick Brewer are the next morning. Jan Scully, who doesn't get to court very often, is in the audience. So is her chief deputy, Cindy Besemer. And Margaret Bladet, Dawn's mother. All the Gangs prosecutors are here, as well as a few defense attorneys. They all want to see closing arguments for Rick Brewer, the guy in the devil's mask.

Repkow is finally here, dressed for the occasion all in black: long black coat, black top, black slacks. Bladet's got on a red blazer, with a black skirt and black pumps.

Before the jurors are escorted in, Brewer, through Repkow, wants to waive his right to be present. His grandmother is here but he'd rather spend the day in the tank. Maybe he heard via the jail grapevine how Bladet manhandled Dixon and doesn't want to go through the same thing. He can't possibly be looking forward to hearing himself portrayed as the devil, a cold-blooded angry-at-life murderer. Request denied, England tells Repkow.

Harrold is hunched over at the prosecution table. On Saturday, he was driving into the office for a few light chores on the case and another motorist ran a red light and slammed into his Ford Expedition. His vehicle flipped over and the other driver took off. Harrold had to crawl out. He was jarred and shaken up, but not injured seriously. "I want to find the guy who hit me and kill him," he says, obviously in pain. His neck and back would give him trouble for several weeks, but he's here, eagerly awaiting Bladet's attack on defendant Rick Brewer.

Since the Glica and Martinez jurors went out a few days earlier, they've sent in questions that make the attorneys think they're hung up on the conspiracy aspect of the charges. They want guidance on the instruction about overt acts. The charges say they "secured and utilized" a stolen truck and that they "secured and utilized" facial coverings—the so-called overt acts the law says are needed to prove conspiracy. The jurors ask what that means and the judge gives them as much guidance as he feels he can without discussing punishment.

The first image on the screen is the devil's mask drawn by Josh Christian, one of the employees. Bladet clicks the mouse. These words pop up for the jury to see: "And who is the man behind the devil mask?" Brewer's face pops up next. Then the quote "Things went sour downtown." Brewer's face is noticeably thinner in the picture she uses. He's been in jail more than four years already; even a few weeks in custody and most inmates get fattened up from all the starch and carbohydrates they're fed.

She uses the bread metaphor again, but for a different purpose this time. It's something wonderful and wholesome, the sustenance of life. "It's really hard to imagine a place like the Bread Store becoming a place where life is taken," she says.

She guides jurors through the crime scene until the moment Brewer encounters Jason Frost behind one of the bread counters. Other workers have been held down on the floor, kicked, maced, threatened with a knife. Brewer is over Frost, demanding money. Waving his trademark weapon, the Mossberg, at his face. A devil with a shotgun about to explode. Where's the money? Where's the fucking money?

"He can't get to it," she says of Brewer, a man she believes deserves to die for his crimes, despite what O'Mara concluded. "It's already been dropped in the safe. His timing is off. So does he decide to leave? No. He decided to shoot Jason Frost. Not once, not twice. But three times."

More evidence is recalled. Spent and unspent shotgun shells in the store. The same cartridges found in the pocket of Brewer's jacket when cops search his place, where they found the Mossberg. Trace evidence—flour on his shoes found in the apartment search.

The jury is reintroduced to the Southside punks. Remember their false swagger when they came to court? Their lies? Don't forget the true statements they also made to the cops when they weren't in court, when Rick Brewer and the other defendants weren't here to give them the evil eye.

"I wish you people were the witnesses," she tells the jury, "but it doesn't happen that way. Brewer's friends are going to be the witnesses."

Each punk's picture shows up on the screen, with points of testimony listed.

Carlos Cervantes: He was like a brother to Rick Brewer. He testified about the G-ride, the robbery plans, the twelve-gauge, how Brewer recruited everyone.

Will Stephens: "If you mess with Rick B. or his family, he's gonna shoot you." Brewer told him, "If you get caught, keep it on the downlow."

Chris Stephens: "Things went sour downtown."

Al Cervantes: He identified all the participants.

Faye Collins, Dixon's sister: She reported him to the cops for driving a stolen vehicle.

Trevor Garcia: Yes, we made a deal with him, but he pulled all the facts together. He was believable because he was there and he knows exactly what happened.

The devil mask is on the screen again. Next to Jason Frost's picture. Savage has tutored her well in the art of PowerPoint closings: he's watching the show with pride.

"The evidence in this case," she tells the jurors, "is compelling. That man"—she points at Brewer—"was a felon with a gun. He participated by his role in that robbery. He is a murderer. He is the man who killed

Jason Frost. He can't hide behind his mask. The truth is the man behind that mask is Rick Brewer."

As she says this, Brewer's face comes on the screen beneath the flashing message: "Guilty on All Counts. Guilty on All Counts."

Now, after two hours, at 11:40 A.M., it is Repkow's turn to close by arguing that her client is innocent.

"The power of accusation is a mighty thing," she says after reminding the jurors of their awesome responsibility. "It's a compelling thing. People who can argue well and express themselves well sometimes have a cloak of being correct. But it's not always true. One thing you don't want to do is compound one human tragedy with another, and that would be to find Mr. Brewer guilty of the charges against him."

Incredibly, there's no one from the news media to record a word of this. That's worked out best for the prosecutors. They've dreaded the *Bee's* Ramon Coronado showing up and writing about Garcia the snitch, or the sweet deal the DA offered, Repkow's sexual shenanigans, or any of the other bizarre twists the case has taken that could make their jobs harder. Fortunately for them, if not the public, who will read or hear little of this extravagant three-jury trial, he doesn't stick his head in the courtroom until the very end. It's like being assigned to cover a baseball game and showing up for only the ninth inning, but the prosecutors are pleased.

During lunch, the Brewer jurors assemble on the front steps of the courthouse. They want to take a group photo and they're laughing as they take their poses. Harrold and Bladet are endlessly entertained by this. Jurors aren't anguishing over the "awesome responsibility" Repkow noted at the start of her close. They're not torn up about compounding one tragedy with the other supposed tragedy she mentioned of finding Rick Brewer guilty of all the charges. Trial attorneys on both sides are always looking for signs that indicate which way a jury is leaning. A celebration out by the fountain in the middle of closings is as clear as anything either of the prosecutors has ever seen.

Over the lunch hour, Bladet and Harrold are notified by the court clerk that the Glica and Martinez jury has reached its verdicts. The judge has ordered them sealed until all the juries are finished, but this is taken as another good sign. The only blemish on the day from the district attorney's perspective comes with the news that the Dixon jury has asked if he can be guilty of assault and robbery if he wasn't in the store. "That works for me," Bladet says, but she knows they're probably hung up on *major participant*.

On the way back to court, she laments advice Savage has given her. "Mike tells me I have to be nice and well behaved in my rebuttal. He says I've told them everything and they're right there with me. All I have to do is avoid a mistrial. He's right, but I'm not very happy about it. I want so badly to fuck with Brewer. He gave me the evil eye this morning."

Repkow drones on so slowly that near the end of the day she asks to approach the bench and tells England what everyone already knows: "I'm putting the jury to sleep." She asks to knock off a little earlier than usual, at 3:40, so everyone can come in fresh in the morning. Bladet, of course, objects strenuously. If Repkow's putting the jury to sleep, that's her problem. She refuses to go along with anything that will help the other side. Bladet tells England she wants to use all the time available. He glares at her with a mixture of displeasure and amusement, but at 3:45, he calls it a day.

Not before Repkow drops her bombshell. The anonymous call that put the cops onto Brewer in the first place, the ones they later tied to Jamie Salyer, who had a beef with Brewer and turned him in, didn't come from Salyer at all, Repkow tells the jury. It came from the real killer of Jason Frost. It came from Michael Smith.

The cops had been told that one man inside the Bread Store during the November robbery was black and unmasked. All the witnesses to the second robbery said the robbers were black. None of them were, if the DA's case is to be believed. They were identified as African-American because they wore masks and gloves.

"I think Mr. Brewer was set up by this call and I question whether it was Mr. Salyer who made the call at all," Repkow suggests to the jurors, who've never heard an ounce of testimony about this scenario. "The exclusive focus of the call is Rick Brewer. He says, 'I know he committed a robbery at the Bread Store in November.' The person who made the call wanted the police to act right away. I think it is Michael Smith who made that call."

Smith confessed to participating in the first robbery with Brewer and Brewer's sister, Angelina, but said he had nothing to do with the December 23 incident. In exchange for his guilty plea, Harrold promised he wouldn't be called to testify against Brewer. Now Repkow suddenly claims Smith made the call to inform on Brewer to get him out of the way. Then, according to Repkow, Smith went back and robbed the store a second time. And he killed Jason Frost.

Bladet and Harrold are not surprised. They've come to expect the unexpected from Repkow. The rules on closing arguments are rather liberal, but an attorney is not supposed to introduce something at closing for which no evidence or testimony has been presented during trial. Repkow is creating this from whole cloth, the prosecutors believe. Maybe it's what Brewer has been telling her all along, but there was no evidence presented that this could be true.

Bladet doesn't consider objecting, though. She'll get another crack at her adversary in rebuttal. For now, she sits patiently as Repkow spins her web. Both prosecutors have heard defense attorneys in past trials come up with elaborate explanations about how their guy couldn't possibly have committed the crime he's charged with, but they almost always offer some evidence to back it up, however feeble. Repkow's plowing new ground here.

"I say Michael Smith put the rifle inside that apartment," she continues. "Michael Smith came to that apartment many times. Trevor Gracia told us that."

It had come up in trial that Smith was in Brewer's apartment when the police came and took Brewer's children from him, but never was it suggested that the gun belonged to anyone other than Brewer. Smith was interrogated by Detective Toni Winfield, in a taped conversation January 21, 1997. He and Angelina Brewer had been arrested a few days earlier while driving around the suburbs looking for a place to rob. Smith said he saw Brewer chase after the Child Protective Services workers with the Mossberg, that he put a round in the gun as he ran down the stairs, but that Smith grabbed it from Brewer and unloaded it before he could do anything.

Smith said he was also in the apartment when Brewer telephoned the agency to ask when he could get his kids back. When Winfield asked Smith if he'd ever borrowed Brewer's gun, Smith said: "No. Rick wouldn't give that shotgun to anybody. He wouldn't let anyone have it."

Repkow now goes after Salyer, who the cops said was the tipster. "Salyer is not a good guy," she says. "He wouldn't have made that call out of conscience. He would have done it for credibility. Mr. Salyer, like

Trevor Garcia, contacts authorities when he needs them and when he no longer needs them, he's gone."

He had a record and he worked with the DA before, she points out. In fact, he'd been paid for his help, a total of $6,000 over the years, on several cases. Her message is clear: Jamie Salyer is a professional snitch. After he snitched on Brewer, the DA put him up in a motel for protection.

"That's not real clear why that was ever done," she says. "Mr. Salyer was never in any danger. In fact, none of the people who've testified in this case was ever in danger, at least with respect to Mr. Brewer."

She's going in circles now, but Repkow never seems reluctant to do herself what she's criticized the other side for. Now she's going to attack Trevor Garcia for something she just did.

The law says you can view an accomplice's testimony with caution, she says about Garcia. "I say disregard it. To someone not intimately familiar with the criminal justice system, it's shocking a young man can come into court and accuse an innocent man of murder. Unbelievable. But it does happen."

Harrold is in agony from pain in his back and neck, but he's oblivious to discomfort as he begins to anticipate watching how Bladet will filet this attorney prosecutors like to call the Reptile.

Garcia is a liar, Repkow says. His testimony shows he is. "And it is in Trevor Garcia's best interest to sacrifice Rick Brewer to save his own life."

Before Repkow started this afternoon, Bladet was feeling a little lost with the trial coming to an end. "Tonight, for the first time in a year, I will go home and have nothing to do," she said earlier in the day. "It will be so weird." Now she'll go home and prepare her final attack.

Before sending everyone home for the night, Judge England tries bucking up the jurors by telling them, "We're close." He repeats his daily admonition that they not talk to anyone about the case, including each other. "See you at nine A.M."

Bladet was worn out and exhausted at the end of the day, but when she comes in the next morning outrage has her once again full of energy. Even the judge can see it. He comes out of his chambers, before the defendants and jurors are brought in, and warns Repkow that it might not to safe to sit so close to her adversary. "I've got an extra chair here," he says, "if Miss Bladet has to be restrained. You two are sitting beside each other during rebuttal. Who knows what's going to happen."

"You haven't seen anything," Bladet tells the judge, who does not look the least bit reassured by this remark.

Repkow resumes at 9:20 A.M. Don't go outside the evidence, she tells the jury. Don't speculate, even though she's done just that. The judge was right to offer that restraint chair to Bladet.

England, one of the few African-American judges on the local bench, is uncomfortable about where Repkow goes next, talking about "black voices, black accents" in the Bread Store the night Jason Frost was shot.

"I can't prove who did this robbery," she says, "and I can't prove who shot Jason Frost. But the shooter was a black man." She tells the jury what it will learn firsthand in a few minutes: "Miss Bladet is going to poke fun at that. She'll mock me. She'll say, 'What else can she say?' She'll say, I'm manipulating information. But remember, I'm presenting evidence and information consistent with raising a doubt.

"If Mr. Brewer had participated in this attempted robbery and shooting, why would he bring that gun home and put it in his apartment? Don't be fooled about how the prosecution talks about how it's hidden so deeply. That they didn't even find it the first time, it was hidden so well away. Why would Mr. Brewer keep the gun in his apartment if he knew where it had been and what it was used for?"

And the shells found in Brewer's jacket pocket? Repkow relies on Marichu Flores, who testified they weren't there. "She's adamant that there weren't shells in the pocket and I can't explain that."

Hallelujah, Bladet wants to shout. Something Repkow can't explain.

She does have an explanation for Marichu Flores's original lie to detectives that Brewer never left the apartment the night of the shooting. She knew the cops would use that against Brewer. A day later, when Flores was "more comfortable," she told Winfield that, oh, yeah, he did leave for ten to fifteen minutes to toss out the garbage. "She knows he wasn't out long enough to commit this crime."

Here comes the chart. Repkow's sown the seeds of reasonable doubt and now wants to water them with Karowsky's thermometer chart. If you think Brewer "maybe" is guilty, that's reasonable doubt. You have to acquit. Possibly guilty, same thing. Even if you find "clear and convincing evidence" that he's "probably guilty," you have to acquit. That's reasonable doubt too.

When Repkow is finished, Bladet looks around the courtroom and gets up slowly from her chair. She takes a sip of water. No PowerPoint. No big presentation. It's pure emotion and anger now. She strides over to Repkow's big probable-cause chart—Oh, shit, Harrold's thinking, here it comes again!—and takes it down. She places it facedown on the floor, where the two prosecutors think it belongs.

"This is not the law!" she says loudly.

"Objection," Repkow says.

"Overruled." The judge looks relieved Bladet didn't do something worse.

"Don't go outside the evidence you heard in this case," she mocks Repkow, as Repkow predicted she would. "Don't speculate. Yet for the majority of her argument, that's exactly what Miss Repkow asked you to do. Speculate wildly about who the real killer is. Michael Smith is the real killer. The case is four and a half years old, thousands of pages of reports. Everyone somehow missed who the real killer is. You could bet if there was one piece of evidence that linked Michael Smith to this robbery and murder, you would have heard about it."

What about Repkow's assertion that Detective Overton somehow forced the Southside punks to say what he wanted to hear?

"Big bad Detective Overton," Bladet says with a tone of disgust. "Was he all that mean and evil? Where was the screaming? Where were the threats? This is not *Sesame Street*. This is a homicide investigation. These kids aren't part of *The Mickey Mouse Club*."

She quotes Repkow: "I think he was set up. I think Michael Smith is the real killer." Bladet wheels to face the jury with the coiled body language of a brawler about to land a punch. She's cocky. Arrogant. Pissed off.

"What Miss Repkow thinks or I think is not evidence. It's not a proper consideration in this case to consider what either of us *think*.

"In order to blame a murder on someone else, you have to have more. All the Southside kids said they saw Rick Brewer go on that robbery. They're all part of the grand conspiracy to set up Mr. Brewer? Trevor Garcia is going to risk his life and plea agreement to set up Rick Brewer?

"Who on earth ever describes Michael Smith being there? Maybe he is in the paper bag with the masks, because he is very well hidden and everyone is covering up, four and a half years later, for Michael Smith. You're going to have to believe the Mossberg was somehow stolen from

Rick Brewer's apartment before December 23 without his knowledge. Michael Smith broke in and got it. He took the gun. He just popped in and took it. No one saw him. He breaks back into the house before the Christmas Eve search and puts it back. And he decided, while he was at it, You know what? I'll borrow his shoes. I brought flour with me and I'll put it on his shoes. It's the Pillsbury Doughboy Theory.

"When you look at the physical evidence, you had to come up with a pretty monumental lie to overcome it. Every person ever accused has the right to a jury trial. To make the prosecutor prove its case. It doesn't give you the right to lie. It just means there's a trial. But you gotta come up with something. This one doesn't make sense. It's not based on anything."

Bladet is restrained. She wants to say Repkow's a lying unethical bitch who has phone sex with her clients and that Brewer is a vicious, cold-blooded murderer who's not facing the death penalty only because O'Mara was feeling charitable the day he reviewed the case. On the way into court this morning, one of the bailiffs whispered into Harrold's ear a rumor that Repkow was caught the other night, outside the jail, flashing her confessed killer-lover, Fred Clark. That she was cuffed and detained. My God, Bladet says when she hears. She figures anything's possible with Repkow. Nothing she heard about her would be a shock. Still, she can't digest this latest bit of salacious gossip about a woman she's in court with and whom she finds utterly reprehensible. There's only so much her mind can take in at one time.

She brings it back to the reason everyone is in the courtroom. Why the Frosts have sat through months of this crap, putting their lives on hold so they could represent their son in the trial of the four young men the police and Sacramento County district attorney have said murdered him for no good reason.

"The real consequences that can't be undone in this case," Bladet says, softly now, her fury spent, "is that Jason Frost lost his life. Your verdict can't undo that. But your verdict can speak the truth. Rick Brewer can no longer hide behind his devil mask and his big, bad gun."

It's a bravura performance. The Frosts are in the back watching; they feel like leaping to their feet and applauding. When she sits down, Harrold's reminded one more time why he asked her to be his co-counsel. Now it's just a matter of waiting to see if the thirty-six jurors see things the same way as the district attorney's office. Anything less than across-the-board life sentences would be a disappointment to the prosecutors.

16 | Life or Death

What is the lot described by God above, the reward from the Almighty on high? Is not ruin prescribed for the miscreant and calamity for the wrongdoer?　　　　　—Book of Job

AS Marge Koller settles into the Courtney Sconce case, reviewing the sheriff's reports, videotaped confessions, and backup material, she's torn. Any homicide prosecutor would love to try the big, high-profile case. If you prosecute homicides for a living, the more awful the murder, the better the assignment. It may seem like twisted thinking, but it's undeniably true. It's like being a newspaper reporter and wanting to be there when the 747 goes down. You never hope for a calamity, but when one happens, you don't want to watch from the sidelines. In this case, however, as O'Mara learned early on, there is a strong likelihood that Justin Weinberger would be willing to plead guilty in exchange for the district attorney not seeking the death penalty. Koller knows a negotiated plea of life without parole serves the family and the interests of justice better than a depressing and emotional trial where the result on the penalty phase would likely be a hung jury. She's also not sure whether District Attorney Jan Scully, elected as a tough-on-crime prosecutor who supports capital punishment, would settle for anything less than the ultimate penalty on a crime of this magnitude.

Koller has been in Major Crimes about two years when Sconce comes in. She's a methodical prosecutor who puts the lie to the idea that you must have at least a little of the macho prick in you to do your job. She's a sweetheart, and one of the few people in the district attorney's office it's hard to find people willing to knock.

Her last interesting case, one that rose above what deputies call "your garden-variety murder," was about a year ago when she prosecuted Forrest Gray. Mr. Gray killed three people with a hammer, two in 1992 and his girlfriend in 1999. He remained free until a few days after the last murder, when he was pulled over by a California Highway Patrol officer for a routine traffic stop and said, "You better check on my girlfriend. I beat her up pretty bad." The CHP went to his apartment and found her dead from repeated blows to the head with a hammer.

Koller didn't want to be a cop like her dad, even though she majored in criminal justice at the University of California at Irvine. She didn't think she had the physical strength the job required, so she took a job working in a bank after college. She was bored to death. A friend told her about a test being given to become a sheriff's records officer, a job that paid much better than her bank position. She took it, did well, and stayed eleven years. When she got itchy for more action, she applied to law school, attending nights for four years at Lincoln Law School in Sacramento, the same school Scully attended. In 1989, she started at the DA's office. "Only place I applied," she says. "Only place I wanted to be."

She's known as one of the more sensitive prosecutors in the office when it comes to dealing with victims, but in O'Mara's macho goon squad she probably wins that one by default. For this reason and more, in 1995 Koller won the in-house award given annually to deputy district attorneys who display the most sensitivity to victims and their families.

Her caseload for the year so far had been light, which was fine with her. Last year she did six trials, one right after the other. She convicted three idiots, grown men and women, including one in his early seventies, for killing an eighteen-year-old boy angry at them because they were harassing his younger brother.

The same year she prosecuted a robber who put a woman clerk down on the ground and the woman, who had a history of breathing problems, died of "positional asphyxia." She had to try the case twice. The first jury hung.

In a drive-by shooting, she prosecuted a defendant who aimed his gun out the window of his car—he was in the passenger seat—and instead of hitting the intended target on the street, killed the driver of the car he was in—his close friend—by mistake.

O'Mara didn't say if any of this flashed through his mind when he chose Koller for the Sconce case. It came to him in the shower one morning, he said, and no one wanted him to elaborate. It was Koller's turn for a big case and now that she had it, she knew the right course of action might mean not going to trial at all.

She talks regularly to the Sconces on the phone during the early weeks of the case. She trades e-mails with Courtney's father, Mark, and meets face to face with both Mark and Cynthia, Courtney's mother, several times.

Courtney's parents confide in Koller that they're worried some unscrupulous defense attorney might exploit their personal lives and the privacy of their two other children, each of whom had their own difficulties while growing up. They're feeling a great deal of guilt for allowing Courtney to walk to that neighborhood store where she met her abductor, even though it's something she did almost every day. They are devastated over losing her.

"All the victims I've had, they all reacted so differently," Koller says as she waits for the Sconces to show up to discuss a possible plea agreement. "I had a little Vietnamese woman, all she could do was cry. She wanted to show me pictures of her son. Then I had the father, all he did was scream at me. He wanted the death penalty and it wasn't a death-penalty case. I wasn't doing my job. Jan Scully wasn't doing her job. I've had people sit in my office who wouldn't talk. Or they may say a plea is okay, and then when we take one, they're all mad. I had one case, the father injected a son with heroin and killed him. His father was introducing him to the drug trade and the victim's mother and the victim's older brother each reacted differently. I had each one testify against the dad. They wanted him to get manslaughter and we offered it to him, but he wouldn't take it. Then we went to trial and he got convicted of murder. Man, were they ever mad at me."

When the Sconces arrive, Koller takes them down to a meeting room on the first floor. Marcia Christian, an advocate in the DA's Victim/Witness Assistance bureau, is there too.

Scully, Koller tells Courtney's parents, will make the final decision whether to seek the death penalty against Weinberger.

"I decided weeks ago," Courtney's mother says.

"He sentenced our daughter to death," adds her father.

These are reasonable people, religious but not eye-for-an-eye zealots. They feel so many emotions, they're not sure what's right.

"I just don't think he should be able to play basketball, wash his hair, eat something he likes," Mrs. Sconce says.

"We don't want him ever to get back on the street. If there is even the remotest chance . . ." Mark Sconce says, without completing his thought.

Don't worry. That's not going to happen, Koller assures them.

What about the status of the kidnap charge? Mark Sconce wants to know. She's still trying to firm it up, Koller says. It doesn't matter as far as the special circumstances or death penalty are concerned. The rape guarantees that. It matters dearly to Courtney's parents, however. They want the world to know she was kidnapped, that she didn't get into the car willingly.

They have more questions. They feel as awful as any two people can feel. They know he confessed. Are the statements admissible? They've heard stories that Justin Weinberger claims his mother sexually abused him. Does that give him license to go out and rape someone?

"Tell me," Courtney's dad says. "How can a defense attorney represent a guy like this?"

"I couldn't do it," Koller tells him. "But I'm glad they are there. We want to win and we want to win on appeal. He needs a good lawyer."

The Sconces are mortified at the prospect that their other two kids might somehow have to testify. Putting family members on the stand helps make the victim real, Koller says. Most judges won't even allow the jury to see the victim's picture. She tells them they can't come to court wearing buttons like the ones they wear everywhere with Courtney's pretty face on them.

"Why?" Mark demands. His naïveté belongs to someone who's never been exposed to the inner workings of the criminal justice system. Koller is patient when he asks, "Is that legal? We're supposed to take all the humanity out of it? They're doing everything they can to protect this jerk."

"Don't take offense at this," Cynthia Sconce tells Koller, "but how long have you been doing this kind of work? Before this happened, I was clueless. You have to ask questions. I'm sorry."

"I've tried a lot of murders."

"Did you win?"

Koller takes no offense. She is calm, clearheaded.

"I've won most of my cases," she reassures them. "This guy's not getting off."

"What about a plea bargain, where he doesn't go to trial?" Courtney's mother asks. "Is that something we'd be involved in?"

You'd be consulted, Koller says.

Koller believes the family would like to see the DA seek the death penalty. There will be many more conversations and questions in the coming weeks. Mark Sconce will send more e-mails wanting to know if Michael Weinberger had anything to do with Courtney's murder, since he knows from talking to the sheriff's detectives that Justin said he first saw child porn on his dad's computer.

"If he was involved at all," Mark Sconce writes to Koller on September 6, 2001, "I want him to pay. Courtney had to pay with her virginity and her life. We are going to pay, in anguish and hate, for Justin Weinberger's crime for the rest of our lives, and I want everyone to go down hard. I feel that there are an awful lot of unanswered questions to this crime and I need answers. Can you help?"

It is a sad, desperate-sounding letter. To the cops, to Koller, to O'Mara, it looks like a straightforward case. A very messed-up kid acts out a long-held fantasy and someone's daughter is murdered.

The girl's father is obsessed. He has all kinds of theories. Very few of them make sense, but Koller understands. These are good people and their daughter was taken from them in a hideously violent act.

There's no evidence the dad was involved, Koller says. The more they talk, the more convinced she becomes that a trial is not in the family's best interest.

The Sconces are divided much the same as Koller. They'd be happy to see Weinberger die for his crimes, but they don't want to feel they're making that decision.

It's not their decision, of course. It's up to the DA whether to pursue the death penalty. The family's views are taken into account, but they carry no more weight than several other considerations. In this case, as heinous as the crime was, Weinberger's youth, his lack of criminal record, and his confession once he was arrested all mitigate against the ultimate penalty in O'Mara's mind. As does his highly dysfunctional upbringing.

Courtney's mother and father are a jumble of raw, exposed nerves. Every slight movement or wrong-headed comment makes them shudder. They were extremely agitated when someone at a makeshift neighborhood memorial dubbed "Courtney's Corner" came to them and said they were at the shrine when a guard who worked at the state prison in Folsom stopped by to pay his respects. They heard him tell another visitor that no matter what happened to him with regard to the death penalty, Weinberger was a dead man when he showed up at the prison. Guards, inmates—they'd all be waiting for him. Based on the inmate code that puts rapists and child molesters at the bottom of the prison social scale, he'd be a certain victim in short order.

On the afternoon of September 12, Scully, Besemer, Koller, and O'Mara sit down in Scully's office to decide whether to seek the death penalty. It is the afternoon after New York's World Trade Center towers collapsed, and they start with small talk about people they knew in New York and whether they were near the Towers.

Scully is sympathetic to Koller's desire to spare the family a trial. If the kid's willing to plead to first-degree murder and accept life without parole, Koller says, that would be best for the Sconces.

We don't make those decisions just based on what's good for the family, Scully says. What would the community want? What's right? In the coming months, California will suffer several heavily publicized abductions, sexual assaults, and murders of young girls. The elected DAs will not only seek the death penalty but, in some instances, they will go to court and argue motions themselves. A case like this is an obvious opportunity for a district attorney to score political points, and while Scully knows how charged her decision could become, this is the time and place—the private confines of her office—to fully weigh her course of action. She's not one to grandstand or do what's politically expedient.

"Say you have a camera in your face or a reporter with a notebook," Scully tells Koller. "What do you say?"

She starts to answer that he's a young kid with no record or crimes, just the dine-and-dash in New Mexico, when O'Mara jumps in.

"I am as sure as I can be it can be hung up in the penalty phase. If I was the defense attorney, I know I could save this guy's life."

You had the sex with Mom, the suicide attempt. "Those are big things for the defense. The fact he comes from an upper-middle-class family and had all the opportunities in the world cuts both ways. He had opportunities a lot of our defendants don't have. He came from an intact family. A perfect environment. Then you go behind the scenes and you find out it's very different."

But, O'Mara tells Scully, a no-death disposition leaves the office open to criticism on at least two fronts.

"People can say if he were black or Asian or Hispanic, we wouldn't be talking about a plea. We'd be talking about going to trial and drilling the kid into the next century. It shows the death penalty is discriminatory and based on color and race and economics."

O'Mara isn't worried. He points to a bunch of recent Sacramento cases where poor black defendants were offered pleas of life without parole instead of being tried for death, but they refused to take them. If Weinberger refuses to plea, the office will seek the death penalty for him, too.

The other criticism, one he seems more worried about, is that the kid is getting a break because of his dad. They're prepared to take whatever lumps may come their way on that one, particularly because they don't have much regard for the dad or the favor apparently shown him at the outset by the feds.

Scully wants Koller to find out a little more about Justin's background and write her memo advocating life without parole instead of death. That's O'Mara's backward style of doing death cases. The deputies write a memo in a first-degree murder with special circumstances if they feel the case should *not* carry capital charges, not when they do think so. All the no-death memos he's collected over the years are kept in a binder behind his desk. That way, if someone claims discriminatory decision-making on the death penalty, he can provide all the examples—white, black, rich, poor—of defendants who got life behind bars without parole instead of being charged as capital defendants.

In a few weeks, Koller writes her memo and feels better. Nothing horrible or violent was discovered. He had two girlfriends, Koller says. "One was a ho and one was a boy." The first one had sex with him and Justin's best friend. She told the DA investigator they had sex all the time and there was nothing weird about him. He was a sweet, polite, quiet kid. The fun ended when she moved to Oregon.

The second girlfriend turned out to be a gay man getting ready to have a sex-change operation. Justin never learned he was not a woman and the man broke it off when Justin began pressuring him to have sex.

The district attorney also has a copy of a twenty-page letter Weinberger wrote a few weeks after being arrested to Mike Vidot, who Weinberger said was his one close friend in the world. He wrote of having sex with his mom, being estranged from his dad, wanting to die for his crimes. Vidot lives near an FBI agent and he turned the letter over to him. The agent then gave it to the sheriff's department. As for Michael Weinberger, he was never charged with any crimes or implicated in his son's transgressions by anyone other than Justin. In the months following his second suicide attempt, he was back at the attorney general's office, working in the purchasing division and refusing to talk with reporters.

"Might be hard to believe," Justin Weinberger writes at the end of the letter to his friend, "but I got some real friends in here even though everyone knows who I am from the papers. Been doing a lot of reading, I'm up to 250 pgs a day sometimes."

By the time everything is in order for Weinberger to plead guilty, it's November 8, a year to the day that Courtney was killed. The courtroom on the main floor of the jail is jammed. Mark and Cynthia Sconce hold hands while they wait for Weinberger's case. For the first time since his arrest, Courtney's brother and sister come to court. So do other relatives and a number of Courtney's friends from school, where later in the day her parents and school officials will dedicate a bench in her memory.

Back in chambers with the judge and Koller, Don Manning, Weinberger's public defender, says his client is ready to plead no contest and accept his fate—life in prison with no chance at parole. Not so fast, says Koller, who has refused for just this reason to talk with reporters about Weinberger's "guilty" plea until it was official. The deal she believed she had made with Manning was that Weinberger would plead guilty to kidnap, rape, and murder, enough guilt with special circumstances that would have allowed the DA to seek the death penalty if it wanted to. What's this no-contest crap? she demanded to know.

Two days earlier, Weinberger was in federal court and "pleaded to the sheet" of charges he faced there—four counts of trafficking in child porn on the Internet. In a highly unusual turn of events, his court-appointed federal defender asked the court to sentence his client to the maximum term possible, fifty-five years, while the United States attorney sought a significantly lesser sentence. Weinberger's attorney wanted him to spend as much of his sentence as possible in federal prison before the feds turned him over to the California Department of Corrections to begin his life term.

It's believed that a sexual predator like Weinberger would likely have a somewhat easier time of it in the federal system. In the state's highest security prisons, where L-WOP prisoners are housed, coming in as a sexual predator is tantamount to a death sentence. Neither the district attorney nor the Sconce family has any say in deciding where Weinberger is jailed. It's worked out between state and federal prison officials. The feds took his plea first, so he's their property.

As Sacramento Superior Court Judge Pat Marlette reads each count and asks Weinberger his plea, the blood rushes to Cynthia Sconce's face. Tears begin to pour down her crimson cheeks. It's moments like this one, the kind that would happen again and again in a long capital-punishment trial, that the Sconces want to avoid.

The jury box and much of the spectator gallery are filled with reporters and television cameras. The family and Koller know they'll have to face them. The district attorney is willing to forgo the death penalty because of Weinberger's young age, his lack of a criminal record, his willingness to admit his guilt to the detectives almost as soon as they confronted him, and his show of remorse, Koller tells the court.

Did he apologize or show remorse to you? reporters ask Mr. and Mrs. Sconce once the short session is over.

"I didn't see any remorse," Mark Sconce says. "He pled guilty and that's all it takes. He's gone for the rest of his life. He has in my opinion given himself the death penalty, because he's going to die in jail. Whether it's in two weeks or eighty years from now. He's going to die in jail."

Now the reporters want another word with Koller. How could remorse have been a factor in the DA's thinking when he never apologized to the family? they demand. Most are civil and accept her answer—that he told detectives he was sorry for what he did. He broke down and cried when he confessed. Hell, as O'Mara will point out back at the office, he got down on his knees and tearfully strangled a soda can because Craig Hill asked him to reenact the crime.

That isn't good enough for a large, redheaded radio reporter, who fairly snarls when Koller says remorse was shown.

Back at the office, with O'Mara holding court and everyone else crowding around to hear Koller tell what happened, Ernest Sawtelle, her pal, gets right to the point.

"So we're gonna get some bad press on this, huh, Marge? They're gonna be all over that no-remorse thing."

"Whaddya mean 'we'?" O'Mara shouts. "It was just Marge out there all by herself. There's no 'we.' "

"Prominent Attorney's Son Given Deal," Sawtelle says, predicting how the story will play. *"Film at eleven. DA Says Killer Shows Remorse. Family Says No."*

All that remains now is for Weinberger to be sentenced formally in both the federal and state courts. Marlette was going to impose the life sentence in December, but the family doesn't want to ruin its Christmas by being in the same room with their daughter's murderer. A January date is mentioned, but Marlette will be on vacation. It's typical for a judge who takes a plea to also be the one who orders the sentence, and there's no way in hell Marlette, a known media hound, would put this off on someone else. He sets a date in February 2002.

Justin Weinberger speaks first that morning, reading a prepared statement that sounds like a eulogy that might come from a family friend, not the person who killed Courtney Sconce. It's hard to imagine this will do anything but add to the family's misery and outrage.

"She was an extremely intelligent person," Weinberger says, "beautiful both on the outside as well as the inside. She was full of life and liked by so many. Courtney was truly caring and outgoing.

"I can only guess what the Sconce family must feel when they see my face. I try to put myself in each of their positions, Mark and Cynthia as her father and mother, Justin as her older brother and Ashley her older sister. Courtney was someone I only knew for a few hours, yet her family and friends knew her for so much longer. I think about how much she must have meant to her family and to others. I try to imagine what if it had been my sister or my daughter."

He says he wants to die. Koller and the Sconce family would be only too willing to oblige him if they could do it quickly and easily, without making the Sconces feel worse than they do already.

Courtney's uncle next tells how his nine-year-old daughter wakes up with screaming nightmares about her cousin's murder. How he won't feel whole again until "I get to see, by God's grace, Courtney in the presence of God." The whole room seems to take a deep breath. The Bible speaks of those who seek justice under difficult circumstances as "ordained ministers of God," he says, "an avenger to execute punishment upon him that has done evil."

Mark Sconce rises to speak of all the torment and loss his family is feeling.

"In the past fifteen months, I've quit my job. I started another one after being away from work for three months. I put hundreds of miles on my cars and my motorcycle looking for the jerk who is now known to me as Justin Weinberger. He looks so young and innocent, doesn't he?

"I also spent fifteen months trying to find God. I was told that He could provide comfort. I've lost faith in that—unlike my parents and my brothers—because I still have not found the comfort that people talk about. Maybe I didn't try hard enough. I don't know. I hit the bottle a number of times because I know that tequila will take it a way for a little while. I was clean and sober for quite a long time before he came into my life."

He tells the judge he doesn't care what's done to Weinberger, that it's up to the courts. What counts for Mark Sconce is his daughter.

"Sometimes I have a hard time remembering what her voice sounds like so I play a video of her every so often just to hear her voice and to see her playing basketball and to see her running around in the neighborhood."

Courtney's brother and sister choose not to speak. When it's Cynthia Sconce's turn, she reads two poems written by Ashley and confesses to the tremendous guilt she feels as a mother unable to protect her child. When it's the judge's turn, Koller is surprised to hear Pat Marlette speak so directly from the heart, since he's not known around the district attorney's office, where he spent years as a prosecutor and confidant to his good friend, Jan Scully, as a particularly deep thinker.

"In the course of a few brutal hours, the dreams that all young people have—of high school, of driving a car, of a career, of love and marriage, perhaps dreams of having her own children—were torn from her and trampled," Marlette says, TV cameras rolling. "And the little dreams of a warm bath, another fifteen minutes in a warm bed on a cold morning, the smell of her house at Thanksgiving, elbowing with her brother and sister for space in the backseat of the car, even the hope of those sweet little moments was obliterated.

"Even the silly little dreams coveted by little girls—scrunchies and 'N Sync and Mia Hamm and Christina Aguilera—were shredded by this stranger taking her away from her street and her neighborhood and her town and her mom and her dad and her brother and sister.

"And out on the cold bank of a river with no one to look to for rescue, no cover for her naked body, her sense of personal privacy—which is never so acute and so essential as in a twelve-year-old girl—was violated in ways abhorrent even among animals. That was Courtney Sconce's last day in this community. But it was also the day that she entered into the fabric of this community, a touchstone for people who had never met her or her family.

"In homes throughout Sacramento, families were reminded how easily our sense of security and safety can be shattered and how precious that security is. This community came together in nightly vigils, first out of concern for Courtney, then perhaps out of fear for the safety of their own children, but ultimately they came together to reclaim their security, or reacquaint themselves with their neighbors, to start buddy systems for their kids.

"In this country and in this community, when our security is attacked, we come together—at first to console, then to rebuild and to remove the threat. We are here today to remove the threat.

"Today, a predator will be taken from this community and forbidden to ever return. He will no longer be free, as he was before his arrest, to go about his day without interference. For the rest of his life, any dreams of career, of supporting a family of his own, of holidays at home, will go unrealized. Little niceties, like a warm bath, a little privacy, a comfortable chair, will soon be just memories and then even memories will fade. And the things we all take for granted, choosing when to eat and when to sleep, what to wear—those things don't exist in prison.

"This predator will be taken to live with others who have also offended this community, and even they will shun him because of his crimes. He will feel for the rest of his life the fear and the vulnerability that Courtney felt for those horrible few hours. The harm that Justin Weinberger has done cannot be undone. The loss to Courtney's family and this community cannot be restored, but we will accomplish a measure of justice today. . . ."

Marlette takes a deep breath. He looks at the defendant for the first time since he started to speak, and puts an end to this part of it.

"Mr. Weinberger," says the judge, who seems genuinely shaken by the gravity of what's before him, "you are remanded to the custody of the sheriff to be taken from this community and imprisoned at the Department of Corrections for the rest of your life."

17 | One Less Case

There is no refuge from confession but suicide; and suicide is confession.
                                                        —Daniel Webster

THERE are two questions the news media want answered about the Soltys case. O'Mara is in no hurry to address either of them. Will the district attorney seek the death penalty and who will be assigned to try the case? On a morning in early September, O'Mara is in his office with the door shut when Sheriff's Detective Grant Stomsvik brings over two tapes of his August 30 interview with Soltys. Stomsvik leaves and O'Mara pops the tape into the VCR behind his desk. It's his first chance to see how the interrogation and supposed confession went.

Ten minutes go by and all that's on the tape is an empty chair in a stark interview room. O'Mara's convinced Clinkenbeard's conspiratorial mind will claim that while Soltys isn't on camera, the detectives have him off in a corner and are violating his rights somehow. "That's why I'm watching every second of it," O'Mara says.

The index at the bottom of the tape reads 9:20 A.M. It was taped less than two hours after his arrest. At 9:32, a bedraggled Nikolay Soltys enters the picture. He's wearing a tattered blue T-shirt that says THE CHEER GYM on the front. According to what's written on the back, he's a member of the gym's STAFF. He's in the chair, alone, nervously fidgeting with the waistband of what appear to be sweatpants.

When Stomsvik and two other deputies come into the room, they pat him down—again. Then they leave again. Off-camera, they were placing a call to O'Mara. Stomsvik has realized the court-approved interpreter they were going to use speaks Russian, not Ukrainian. He wants to know if it's okay to use a Ukrainian sheriff's deputy instead.

"I told him it was okay as long as he made an accurate interpretation," O'Mara says while watching the tape. "Tommy will make an issue out of it. Tommy doesn't want to talk about did he kill six people. He doesn't want to talk about any of that. He wants to talk about all this other stuff, and that's how it will be every time he goes to court."

Soltys sits, head in his hands, muttering to himself. Bayles and Stomsvik are still off-camera. At 9:56, they return. Soltys is just staring into space until Stomsvik comes in and starts the timeless cop trick of trying to make the suspect think they're pals.

"Is he injured?" the detective asks the interpreter with a great deal of concern in his voice. "Does he need water, a rest room? Is he hungry? I don't know from his body language that he knows he's safe here. Let him know, the way we do things here, nobody is going to do anything to him."

The detectives leave again. This time when he's alone, Soltys starts to hyperventilate and shriek. He bobs up and down in his chair. He looks like he's going to explode. He's crying, wailing. He sounds like a wolf who's been wounded.

"Tommy will say it's remorse," O'Mara says. "Doesn't look like it to me. Who's he crying for, the people he killed or himself? If you were a little juror in San Jose and you saw that, what would you think? Nobody's said a word to him and he's crying like that." O'Mara says San Jose because he already knows the killing spree has gotten so much publicity, Soltys's lawyers will want to move the case out of town, maybe even out of state.

Marv Stern, head of SACA, the district attorney's Special Assaults and Child Abuse unit, calls with a question about another matter and makes a halfhearted attempt to kidnap the case for his unit, since it does involve child victims. No way, O'Mara tells him. He's not farming this out to another bureau. Everyone in the world's following this case. It needs to stay close to home where, if he doesn't try it himself, he can at least keep an eye on it. He's not going to let some other unit fuck it up.

O'Mara watches the TV screen as a detective brings Soltys an apple, two boxes of dry cereal, a cardboard bowl, and a carton of milk. "Thank you," he says in a thick Slavic accent. He doesn't touch anything, even though detectives said they doubt he ate much during his ten days hiding in a wooded area behind his mother's house. He's emaciated and vacant eyed. The detectives leave again. O'Mara can see they're treating him with kid gloves.

"Whether he's crying for himself or his family, he knows exactly what's going on," O'Mara says. "Tommy will see this and be disappointed. He's hoping they're all tough and intimidating and treating him like shit. That's not happening."

The phone rings. O'Mara hits the "pause" button on the remote for the VCR. It's Clark Fancher, a sheriff's department homicide detective. The Ukrainian consul wants to visit Soltys in the jail. Fancher wants to know if the sheriff's department should "monitor the conversation."

"Absolutely not," O'Mara says into the phone. "We don't need this to be an international incident. Give them their privacy and don't interfere in any way."

When he hangs up, he shakes his head. "The attitude over there is if there isn't a case that says we can't do something, then why not do it?" he says to someone in his office.

The tape is on again. Soltys stares at the milk and apple where they've been placed on a metal table. It's if he thinks they're alive and will leap out and bite him.

"Eat," O'Mara screams at the television. "You'll feel better. Drink some milk and eat some apple." Soltys just stares.

"Drink the milk, you asshole! You know you want to."

The murder suspect stands, clasps his hands together as if to pray, and mutters a few words to himself. He eyes the food with suspicion for several more minutes before finally picking up the apple and taking a hungry chunk out of it.

"Put that in your fucking pipe and smoke it, Tommy Clinkenbeard," O'Mara says as Soltys tears into the apple.

O'Mara watches with intense fascination as Soltys opens two boxes of dry cereal and slowly eats what's in each one—without touching the milk. It takes five minutes, but O'Mara's riveted.

"This is a great tape," O'Mara says. "They're not asking any questions. They're not doing anything. They're just feeding him. Tommy'll just say it's an inducement to get him to confess."

Finally, Soltys opens the milk, after all the cereal is gone. O'Mara roars with laughter. He pounds the table and smiles like he's won the lottery.

"Now he drinks the fucking milk. This is great. In a minute it will dawn on him. Let's see, where was I in my crying? I'm fucked."

Stomsvik and Bayles finally come back into the room, giving O'Mara and Soltys something more to concentrate on than just the food.

"My impression is the Ukrainian police are very bad and forceful," Stomsvik says to the interpreter, who then repeats it to Soltys in his language. "Tell him we're not going to beat him or anything like that."

The tape counter says 10:42 A.M. Soltys has been in the sheriff's department interrogation room one hour and ten minutes. He's had part of an apple, two boxes of dry cereal, a few sips of warm milk. It's time to read him his rights. "What you say can be used against you," Stomsvik says. "You can have a lawyer present. If you have no money, one will be appointed."

"Tell me your side of the story," Stomsvik says. Soltys appears to be giving the suggestion some thought. "You can see it," O'Mara says. "Nobody's in his face. He doesn't seem confused. He's thinking."

Before he starts, Soltys has a question the interpreter translates this way: What's he going to get?

"Tell him in America," Stomsvik answers, "the police here don't make those decisions. There is a district attorney's office that makes those decisions. Usually, in cases like this, there's prison. There's also a death penalty that can be enforced. But we've not solved it yet."

A big plate of spaghetti is brought in and Stomsvik finally gets to the heart of it. "Why did you kill your wife? We know you must have been very hurt to do that."

There they go again, O'Mara thinks. The detectives love to play social worker. They have to side with the guy. They feel compelled to give him an out.

"Tommy will make the argument that he didn't expressly waive his rights to an attorney and that he didn't understand he didn't have to talk," O'Mara says. "That will be the argument. That if you give a formulistic advisement to a person like this, what does it mean? Plus, they left out part of the advisement. There are cases that say you have to tell the suspect anything you say can *and will* be used against you. It's not good to have left that out, but it won't be fatal."

The interview drags on for six hours. Soltys is asked why he killed someone, what set him off, what was he thinking. Most of the time, he sits there looking lost and dumbfounded. He rubs his hands together furiously, as if they're wood and he's trying to start a fire. He picks at his face, his hands. He takes deep breaths. He can't seem to get enough air into his lungs.

Stomsvik finally shows him a picture of Lyubov, his wife, with the words Soltys apparently scribbled on the back that say he killed her "for insolence . . . for her tongue."

"What did you mean by that?" the detective asks.

Nikolay Soltys, accused mass murderer, sighs deeply. "It happened from the beginning," he says. In a halting and painfully slow stutter, he attempts to explain that his difficulty with his wife and other relatives started in the Ukraine with a fight over an air filter. Yes, an air filter. His in-laws thought he was no good, lazy, a bum, because he didn't have steady work. One day, he was supposed to drive them somewhere but he failed to show up at the appointed time. His car wouldn't start. He said he was working on it and when he took the air filter out to clean it, instead of using a chemical solution he washed it in water. It became clogged. The car wouldn't go. His in-laws later accused him of lying because they'd seen him driving earlier in the day.

When he got to California less than a year ago, after living with other relatives in Binghamton, New York, it was the same thing. His wife was always picking at him. On the day he killed her, they had a fight. She picked up a knife that was by the bed. Finally, he cut her throat. At that point, though he never says it, there was no turning back.

It's a bizarre story. His wife never loved him, he said. She saw other men, both in Ukraine and in America. He isn't even sure if Sergey was his son. But when it comes to explaining exactly what happened the day of the murders, what finally made him slash his wife's throat and then drive sixteen miles across town and kill an aunt and uncle and two young cousins before getting back in his car to retrieve his son and then cut his throat, too, he's all mumbles and sighs.

"You have to let it out," the detective says. "Tell us. It's too much for one person to try to keep inside. It's okay. Don't hold it in. Let us understand. What did Sergey [his uncle] say? Did Sergey say something bad about you? Was it a lie? Did Sergey lie about something about you? Did

Zoya [his aunt] say something about you? Was it a lie? Did the lie have something to do with your wife or your child? Was the lie about Lyubov, your wife? Was the lie about the baby inside Lyubov?"

Stomsvik and Bayles are asking questions every way they can to get something out of him, but Soltys stares or talks in vague generalities that are nearly impossible to follow. Did your family hurt you? Lie about you? Threaten you?

"Sergey said once that he can find someone to kill him for fifty dollars," the interpreter translates something Soltys said.

"Why did Sergey say that?" Stomsvik follows up.

"He doesn't even know," the translator says. "He always tries to be pretty peaceful with his family and with them. I tried to have a good rapport with them and to talk only good." O'Mara and the detectives know this is crap. They know Soltys has a history of physically abusing his wife, that when they came to America the biggest Slavic church in town wouldn't let him join for just that reason.

"But they had something about him, I don't even know," the interpreter continues. "Some meanness. And also earlier, when I used to live in the state of New York, when I was moving here, he kind of said something to me that I will be a California bum or homeless."

So much for O'Mara's admonition about getting the translator to make an exact translation of the interview. Sometimes the translator turns to Stomsvik and sounds as if he's repeating Soltys's words verbatim. Other times, the interpreter paraphrases and puts the answer in his own words.

"Did you kill the two children to make their parents feel bad?" Stomsvik asks about Soltys's cousins, Tatyana Kukharskaya and Dmitriy Kukharskiy.

Soltys mumbles something in his high-pitched, almost effeminate-sounding voice. "No," the translator says. "At that point, I don't know what I did. I feel real sorry about all that."

Remorse, O'Mara's thinking. He's laying the groundwork for remorse, probably giving Soltys more credit than he deserves for thinking clearly.

Why did you kill your own son, Sergey? Stomsvik asks. Detectives had held out hope of finding the towheaded little boy alive. In crime-scene photos taken after they found him with his throat slashed, it's easy to see how stricken they were by their discovery. Garverick is shown carrying the boy in his arms, the detective's face as pale as dishwater.

"At that time, I did not want to live," Soltys says, raising the specter of an NGI defense—not guilty by reason of insanity. "I did not know what I did." The reason he didn't turn himself in to police, he tells Stomsvik, is he wanted to see his mother, which he did the following day.

O'Mara needs a break. The first tape is just about over. He'll watch the rest of it and the second one later, maybe tomorrow. He's got the idea. The defendant is no physics professor. He doesn't make much sense, but it's possible to discern his version of what drove him to kill six people and—if he's the father—his unborn baby.

His family was picking at him for a variety of things. He lost it. Reports have already surfaced in the press that Soltys had a record of domestic violence in the Ukraine. His wife was said to be reluctant to join him in this country. She was afraid of him. People who knew him in Shumsk, the little village where he lived until moving first to Binghamton, New York, and then to Sacramento, described him as a loner, with few close friends and a hot temper.

The *Los Angeles Times* reported that he was suspended from his Pentecostal church in the Ukraine after one violent incident with his wife. When he came to Sacramento, the Pentecostal church there wouldn't let him join. He's a bully, a violent man, who snapped. It's happened a million times before. What makes this one interesting is the guy's from another world. His lawyer will figure a way to incorporate that into some kind of defense. O'Mara's not particularly worried about it.

Just as O'Mara is turning off the VCR, Albert Locher walks in, sees the end of the tape, and can't resist offering his take on the case. He's been at the DA's office twenty-five years, about as long as O'Mara, and has tried a number of big, high-profile cases over his career. He's prosecuted two judges, one for fixing traffic tickets for his pals, the other for cutting trees off his property illegally. He's done murder trials and death-penalty cases. He prosecuted a white supremacist who firebombed a Sacramento synagogue, the local NAACP, and an Asian city councilman's home. He's gone after big-time embezzlers and a vigilante who chased down someone who slashed his car tires and then murdered him. He's a bureau chief, just like O'Mara, overseeing Special Investigations, which includes all cop shootings. He's also over high-tech crimes, and real-estate fraud; juvenile prosecutions; and domestic violence, the office's largest unit with seven full-time prosecutors. He's got a couple of dog units, too, that don't generate much and where no one with any ambition ever wants to go, such as the consumer- and environmental-protection divisions.

Locher is an adjunct professor at the McGeorge School of Law, a well-respected Sacramento school that many future prosecutors attend. He loves to talk legal theory and arcane issues of evidence and strategy. He's one of those people who never seem to age, although he turned fifty this year. Loving to talk as he does, he offers some free advice to O'Mara on Soltys.

"It's a case that has to be won," he says in obvious understatement. "But it's a case that can be fucked up. There are six or eight people in this operation who could do it without fucking it up, but there are a lot more people in the building who would fuck it up." O'Mara thinks Locher is being stingy on the number of people who'd be up to the task of prosecuting Soltys, but it's not easy stopping Locher once he gets going. O'Mara shifts in his chair for what he knows will be a lengthy dissertation.

"Somebody's going to have to tutor themselves on all the psychological issues and how to cross-examine the psychiatrists," Locher says, "and tutor themselves on all the cultural differences. It's not that complicated. You've got six autopsies, three crime scenes. It's still not all that complicated. What's going to be complicated is all the psychiatric and cultural differences. You have all those cards to play. You have to make sure you don't lose those cards. You have to play defense attorney every step of the way on all those issues. They'll probably use some type of psychiatric defense. Frawley has all the tools, but he hasn't done a complicated psychiatric defense. Frank Meyer would worry himself to death. He could do it. The glass is always half empty with Frank. He'd probably have a stroke before it's over.

"One thing you could do as prosecutor is not put on any psychiatrist at all and just attack theirs. Juries are skeptical of psychiatry anyway. You've got the horror of the crimes going for you. Just attack his credibility and you'd score points. Or, you could use whatever psychiatrists who become available to you out of the court system."

If Soltys goes NGI, the judge will likely appoint several psychiatrists whose written reports would be available to both sides. If he uses a diminished-capacity defense, which allows his lawyer to argue that Soltys might be guilty of something less than first-degree murder, the court doesn't appoint psychiatrists. The defense typically plays "hide the expert," where they may have one or more psychiatrists examine the defendant but not write a report, especially if the psychiatrist sizes up the defendant in a way that could help the DA. That way, there's nothing to turn over in early discovery. DAs sometimes monitor visit lists—they can do this by gaining access to the jail's computer visitation logs without leaving their office—but it's risky, because the defense attorney can find out about it and raise a ruckus in motions.

"I'd expect Soltys to go NGI," Locher surmises, "because the defense attorney will be afraid not to. Or, option number three, you can use the court shrinks and your own. That may be problematic, because it will be tough to get court approval for a direct examination of the defendant by your guy. If you do, your guy would be late to the exam. The defense will get the earlier shot. As a practical matter, your guy wouldn't be able to examine the defendant until after the defense put on its experts and made its argument about his psychiatric condition. That's a disadvantage, too, because your guy would examine him quite a long time after the crimes occurred, whereas the defense would have been able to do that much closer to the actual crimes.

"You need to educate yourself on the Slavic, Ukrainian culture as much as the psychiatric. There's the whole translation issue. Do you use an English-speaking psychiatrist and interpret? Do you find a Ukrainian psychiatrist, and how many of those are out in the universe you can choose from? So you end up dealing with all those issues, and they can be tricky. You have to be very precise and meticulous."

It's noon. O'Mara would like to get lunch. "The biggest argument they'll make is he really didn't understand in a meaningful way what his rights are," he interrupts Locher, hoping this will bring their talk to a close. "I think there's a lot for the defense to work with on that point. But I'm making the assumption the case will be strong enough without the confession. There are some good things in the confession, but there are some things I wouldn't want the jury to see. The crying. Is it remorse? His answers are monosyllabic. He seems out of it. But the motive is clearly suggested by what I'd seen on the tape, and it's 'what everyone thought.' Everyone was leaning on him to get his act together, to get a job, to quit sloughing off, and it ate at him for a long period of time. So the tape is good, but maybe you can get at it in some other way.".

By the end of the week, O'Mara is bored with the Soltys tape and needs a day away from it. When he finally gets back to watching it, he just leans back and stares.

Soltys sounds even more pathetic as the interrogation goes on. He had no help eluding arrest, he tells detectives. He didn't know he was all over the news. He found the clothes he was wearing. He ate food from garbage cans. Each time he's asked why he killed a particular person, all he comes up with, after minutes of fidgeting and sighing, is that they were saying false things about him.

"I simply did not know what I was doing," he says a number of times.

When he fails to explain exactly what sparked his attack on his wife, Stomsvik treats him with the kind of gentility that O'Mara knows will drive Clinkenbeard nuts.

"Tell me," he pleads. "Tell me, Nikolay. Why this day?" He pulls his chair closer to Soltys, who never looks up. He's staring at his shoes. The detective places a hand gently on Soltys's back.

"Don't hold it in. Help us understand. Why this day? What started all this?" Finally, he begins to mumble at an excruciatingly slow pace. The interpreter translates.

"Before that, I found a knife near her. I asked why she needed it. She said—she said, just because. She was saying to him she doesn't need a husband like that."

"You're doing a good job," Stomsvik tells him, and the interpreter translates for Soltys. "Let it all out. Go ahead, tell me. Go ahead, Nikolay, tell me."

"I took it away," he says of the knife. "I took it to the kitchen and left it there."

"Okay," Stomsvik says. "What happened next, Nikolay?"

"It seemed to me there were a lot of reasons," Soltys tells him. Their chairs are inches apart. Soltys continues to look down at his shoes, but Stomsvik won't let him disengage. The detective is so close, Soltys must be able to feel him breathe.

"Tell me those reasons, Nikolay. I want to understand."

"She hid me of the knives"—this is what comes from the interpreter's lips—"and I saw, quite a few times, the knife near her. I simply was asking her where the knife was. She did not say."

O'Mara squirms in his seat, his chin resting in the palm of his hand. It's as hard to watch as any interview he's ever seen. The words come so slowly that Soltys never builds up momentum. The tape drags and drags. Kerry Martin knocks on his door and rescues him.

"The family wants to know what he said in the interview," she tells O'Mara, who can only think of answering, "He said lots of stupid things." They talk briefly about whether the Ukrainian Consulate has been notified. O'Mara tells her Marci Minter, a homicide detective, says she sent a fax to the consulate a few days ago. He's tired of the subject. Martin leaves and O'Mara turns the tape on again.

"When you first cut or stabbed Lyubov in the bedroom," Stomsvik asks, "was she standing up or was she lying down?"

"I don't know," Soltys says. "Simply, she was probably walking."

On the morning she was killed, Lyubov was to start a job as a checker at a nearby grocery store. Soltys says he was planning to enroll at a nearby community college. When she seemed to be running late for her first day at work, the arguing escalated. Soon they were wrestling and grabbing each other, he says. "He ripped the knife out of her hand and cut her," the interpreter finally says.

"Where?" Stomsvik wants to know.

"In the bedroom," says Soltys.

"Where on her body?"

Soltys says he doesn't remember.

Somehow, he says, he got the impression she was going to kill him. When Stomsvik gives Soltys a spoon and asks him to act out how she threatened him and what happened next, Soltys puts down the spoon and stares at it. Finally, the words "I don't care" crawl out of his mouth.

O'Mara bolts up in his chair and shuts off the tape. He's seen enough, particularly if he's going to assign the case. The guy's not very bright. He's certainly not articulate. He's not the cunning criminal sheriff's officials made him out to be. The longer he remained at large, the more cunning authorities seemed to make him. In the coming months, Soltys will behave bizarrely in the county jail as well. He'll stab himself with a pencil. In a November incident jail officials will call a suicide attempt, he will leap over a second-floor railing rather than return to his cell. His broken heel will require surgery. Some at the DA's think Soltys is too pathetic for the death penalty. O'Mara had determined some time earlier that the office would seek it and, if he's convicted, leave it to a jury of his peers, if twelve peers of this guy could be found.

In the meantime, Clinkenbeard has called and says he's developing information that might change O'Mara's mind about the death penalty. I'm willing to listen, O'Mara tells him. Come on over when you're ready. No need to make an appointment. O'Mara is always there.

In a few days, the Soltys rampage would be pushed out of the spotlight when a Sacramento security guard went on his own twenty-four-hour killing spree, murdering five people, including his ex-girlfriend. Joseph Ferguson, twenty, killed himself in a stolen car as police closed in on him. On a videotape he made and left at the home of a man he held hostage and eventually killed, Ferguson said he wanted to kill one more victim than Soltys.

It was impossible to recall a bloodier month in California's capital city. Prosecutors were delighted when Ferguson extended them the courtesy of taking his own life. No defendant means no case for the district attorney to concern itself with. Some in the community lament the fact that suicide means no one will ever understand what prompted the violence, but the prosecutors could care less.

In the DA's office, it's just the way Andrew "Gio" Giobberti, a homicide prosecutor in the noir thriller *Hollowpoint,* by Rob Reuland, an assistant district attorney in Brooklyn, says it is.

"People die for a lot of reasons here, and most of them are really shitty reasons," he instructs a young colleague. "You try to figure it out and you lose your mind. Stop thinking about *why* people die and spend more time on *how* they die and *when* and *where* and who the fuck did it—that's all you have to prove. That's all that matters. You're not a goddamn philosopher. You don't have to prove *why. Why* is for TV. It's for movies . . . Fuck *why. . . .* We never know why people die—they just do."

Two days after his murder spree, Ferguson's desire for lasting infamy is dashed anyway when loaded jetliners are flown into the Pentagon and World Trade Center towers.

The Ferguson case, however, does affect the DA's office after all.

During a brief break in the Bread Store trial, Dawn Bladet was in Hawaii attending a memorial for her grandfather when Ferguson went on his rampage. She knew all about Ferguson the minute she heard his name. Several years earlier, she had prosecuted his mother on charges she sexually molested Ferguson and another son over a period of years. The case against Susan Ferguson could have gone either way. Sexual molestations with a female perpetrator and male victims—let alone a mom molesting her two sons—are notoriously hard to prove. On the eve of trial, Bladet was anxious about whether she'd prevail. But Susan Ferguson suddenly decided to plead guilty and was sentenced to fourteen years in state prison.

The September 11 terror attacks also left their mark at the DA's office and courthouse, just as they did everywhere else. Most of the results were predictable. Judges dismissed juries who were too upset to continue with their work. Everything seemed to stop for several days as people tried to absorb the news and what it meant. American flags were suddenly everywhere. But the most novel response came in a fax sent within hours after the attacks by a psychiatrist from San Luis Obispo, along the state's Central Coast, by the name of S. Miles Estner. He was under subpoena to testify in a murder case as a defense witness.

The defendant, Jeffrey Kiehm, a twenty-year-old man with a history of mental instability, told detectives he was planning to rob a bank because he needed money. He didn't know whether he had the guts to use a gun if security personnel or police got in his way, so he decided to test himself. About the same time, Kiehm bought some marijuana from a dealer by the name of Legion Dobbins. He told the cops he was angry because Dobbins shorted him, giving him less pot than he paid for. Pissed at Dobbins, eager to test his mettle if he ran into armed resistance during a planned bank robbery, he did what so many of the people who make up the district attorney's clientele do: he used a gun. He shot Dobbins twice in the head with a .40-caliber Glock on May 21, 2000.

"I cannot and will not be available to this court in the matter of Jeffrey Kiehn for a period of at least several weeks," Estner said in a fax sent to Judge Jimmy Long within hours of the September 11 attacks. "It goes almost without saying that we are in a National Crisis and that my family and friends on the East Coast look to me for guidance and need me to be there right now.

"I was born and raised in Pittsburgh, Pennsylvania, where my elderly father still resides, alone, a handicapped widower, and where I attended Medical School. As you must know, one of the terrorist plane crashes occurred nearby. He needs my help more than any criminal defendant or criminal defense attorney, despite their interests.

"In addition, a substantial portion of my medical education and training were in New York City and Washington, D.C., where I also have family and friends to whom I must and will attend.

"In the hopes that you will understand my predicament, I hope that the Kiehm trial can be delayed or—retried, and, frankly, [the defense attorney's] unprofessional and illegal attempts to compel my appearance, despite my personal tragedies, have soured me on that matter altogether.

"Furthermore, it seems clear that there will be no air traffic to allow my travel from this distant location. I am not sure roads leading to Sacramento from here are accessible.

"I apologize for any inconvenience to the Court, the Jury, or the Defendant, with his right to speedy trial. As for [the defense lawyer] he has been so unsympathetic to my predicament that I plan and hope to have no further dealings with him.

"Thank you in advance for your appreciation of my predicament and conflicts in these regards. I hope that Justice will be served and apologize for my inability to participate in it at this time."

For God sakes, Andrew Smith, the prosecutor in the case, is thinking when Judge Long shows him the fax. Is the guy a shrink or a 5150 candidate?

The defense lawyer in the case, Daniel J. Russo, was far more exercised about the matter, particularly since Dr. Estner was his witness. The psychiatrist, whose practice was in Sacramento when he was assigned to the case, had already examined Kiehm, who was using a psychiatric defense. Estner had spent considerable time reviewing the facts of the case.

"I was informed by my office that Dr. Estner was refusing to appear in court because of fear that the courthouse would be the target of terrorists," Russo said in his own fax to the judge and prosecutor. "When I learned that, I requested that my partner, Amy Morton, call Dr. Estner and explain to him that he had to be in court.

"Dr. Estner told her he would not appear in court and he repeated over and over, 'It's not happening.' When Ms. Morton asked him why, he said he wouldn't travel until things were settled down. He was described as whispering as he told her roads were closed and 'it's not happening.' In spite of telling him how important his testimony would be, he continued [about] refusing to appear and he sounded extremely distressed."

Russo told the judge he then called Dr. Estner himself on his cell phone and at his home and got the following message on the doctor's message service: "Hello, it's Dr. Estner. It's approximately eight A.M. Tuesday, September eleventh. I believe the country is in a state of crisis. I will not be receiving or returning calls until the matters have been clarified. Thank you so much. Bye-bye."

Judge Long granted a mistrial, at Russo's request, figuring that even if Estner did show up, he and Russo were so much at odds, his testimony would be tainted.

Like so much of what goes on in the dim corridors of the county courthouse, the proceeding was delayed for months. A new trial was put off until sometime in the spring of 2002. By that time, Smith had been told by Scully and Besemer, he was going to be transferred out of homicide and down to the Misdemeanor division, where he'd help young prosecutors with their first trials as deputy district attorneys. Smith, like Durenberger before him, was promised he'd stay in Misdemeanors no more than eighteen months. On the day he goes down, if not sooner, a new round of jockeying will begin among deputies anxious to take his place at the top of the hill in Major Crimes, prosecuting people like Jeffrey Kiehm and reacting to whatever bizarre turns a case might take.

One case they won't have to deal with is Nick Soltys. Despite being on suicide watch the entire time he was in the county jail, Soltys was found hanged to death in his Sacramento County Jail cell on February 13, 2002. He had made a crude rope braided from cloth and a piece of plastic. He tied it to a light fixture on the cell wall that was about five feet off the ground and pulled against the rope until he lost consciousness.

His body was in a corner of the cell that once held Unabomber Ted Kaczynski and was apparently out of range of the surveillance camera. "I can't put two thousand officers over there to hold the hand of every inmate," the sheriff said after his death.

Clinkenbeard demanded an investigation by an outside agency, saying he couldn't understand how an inmate on twenty-four-hour suicide watch could still take his own life. "This was not an instant death," he said. "He was essentially choking to death."

There were conflicting reports, too, about whether Soltys was taking antidepressants. Clinkenbeard said he was refusing to take them, but a few weeks before his death, he got a judge to order that Soltys be given no medication. According to prosecutor Frawley, Clinkenbeard did this because he didn't want anything to interfere with clean psychiatric exams of his client. Following his death, Clinkenbeard said he had been planning to use an insanity defense in the case after discovering that Soltys had grown up near the Chernobyl nuclear accident in the old Soviet Union and suffered a number of maladies as a result.

Over the next few months, the jail would have a suicide epidemic, averaging one a month for the first seven months of 2002. It was an embarrassment to the sheriff's department, which runs the jail, but no one at the district attorney's office—or the sheriff's department, for that matter—shed any tears about an inmate's death. It just meant one less case to worry about.

One less case was particularly good news for O'Mara. Though Sacramento's weather often stays hot well into October, the summer was over. Rain was finally starting to appear in the weather forecasts and the days were getting shorter. So, he knew, was the time that he had left to delay his final decision on the old SLA case. The time to act was here.

18 | L.A. Blues

They're going to be all over your ass now. The press, the Opsahls, L.A. Everyone.
> —Kerry Martin, head of the Sacramento
> DA's Victims/Witness unit, to John O'Mara

HALLOWEEN Day, Wednesday, October 31, two developments occur that shake the Sacramento County District Attorney's Office from its daily routine. The first comes in the form of an envelope addressed to District Attorney Jan Scully. Inside is a picture of Osama bin Laden and a note that says, "If you opened this, you're already dead." The local FBI office and the California attorney general receive nearly identical letters at the same time. When a DA mail clerk opens the envelope, white powder pours out, getting on the clerk's clothes and hands.

Scully and her prosecutors, clerks, investigators, secretaries, and janitors pace in front of the building and in the parking lot for several hours while county hazardous-materials experts test the powder. The nation is in the midst of anthrax hysteria, the supposed second wave of terror attacks following September 11. Prosecutors and trained investigators are no less susceptible to fear and panic than anyone else. One rumor that buzzes through the crowd is that the powder's already been tested and the results came back "presumptive" for anthrax. It's fifty-fifty, a deputy DA says, that the powder is deadly.

The clerk is severely shaken. She's been through a decontamination process and is convinced she risked her life and the lives of everyone in the building by not being more careful. By 1:30 P.M., Scully gets word that the powder is harmless. Dozens of employees have already scattered and aren't around when the district attorney, who's given a dozen news interviews by now, says, "If you don't feel comfortable going back in today, I understand. But I'm ready to get back to business."

The second routine-shattering event happens 325 miles south in a Los Angeles courtroom. Just before 2 P.M., Sara Jane Olson, after a two-and-a-half-hour closed session that includes her lawyers, prosecutors, and Superior Court Judge Larry Paul Fidler, pleads guilty to two counts of attempting to murder Los Angeles police officers by placing bombs under squad cars. There goes O'Mara's plan to watch her trial so he can see how Patty Hearst holds up as a star prosecution witness.

One charge says Olson placed a massive nail-packed pipe bomb beneath a car parked outside an International House of Pancakes on Sunset Boulevard, where officers John Hall and James Bryan stopped for a late dinner on August 21, 1975. The three-inch-diameter pipe bomb was rigged to go off when the car backed up, but the officers rushed from the scene to respond to an urgent call and the rapid turn from the parking lot forced the firing pin to miss its mark by a fraction of an inch. Police later recreated the bomb and exploded it under a car while videotaping the results. According to detectives, had the bomb gone off, it would have resulted in numerous casualties inside the restaurant and killed the two officers.

Once the bomb was discovered, police searched squad cars throughout the city and found a nearly identical device under a patrol car parked at the Hollenbeck substation. That's count two in Olson's pleading.

In Patty Hearst's book, she tells how Jim Kilgore, Teko (Bill Harris), and Kathleen Soliah were driving around Los Angeles, "arguing over what would make a meaningful and significant target for their super three-inch bomb." Hearst writes that she and Emily Harris were part of a team that staged similar actions in the San Francisco area, including two bombs that exploded under cars parked at the Marin County Civic Center in San Rafael, a long Frank Lloyd Wright building resembling a horizontal spaceship that contained the county courthouse and offices for the local sheriff and a law library.

"While stopped for a traffic light, still arguing, with the bomb still in the car, Kathy in her fury had made some kind of disparaging remark about Jim's sexual prowess," writes the newspaper heiress, who presumably would have testified to the same events had Olson gone to trial in Los Angeles. "He in turn hauled off and socked her in the eye. Teko, at the wheel, tried to avenge the attack, and with Kathy between them, the two men came to blows in the front seat of the car. Meanwhile, the cars behind them began to honk, jolting them back to reality." They finally settled on the police targets, according to Hearst, as part of their plan to avenge the deaths of their comrades in the May 1974 Los Angeles shootout and fire.

"Feeling marvelous," she writes, "they drove back to their motel to await news of their daring attack against the pigs who had killed our comrades in that blazing shoot-out. Teko talked of revenge as they waited for the news of the bombings to be reported. But the news was not what Teko had expected."

Bob Bell, the Sacramento district attorney investigator, was paged early on Halloween morning by an FBI agent in Los Angeles predicting something like this would happen. When he tells O'Mara about Olson's plea shortly after everyone is allowed back in the building following the anthrax scare, the veteran prosecutor isn't surprised. He is defiant.

He doesn't believe reports out of the Los Angeles District Attorney's Office that say Olson pleaded to two counts that could give her a double life term. In exchange for the plea, prosecutors reportedly agreed to drop the conspiracy-to-commit-murder charge, which also carries a life sentence. "Our fear," her lead attorney, Shawn Snider Chapman, would say a few days later, "was that there was probably enough evidence for a jury to convict her on either an aiding-and-abetting theory or a conspiracy theory." She said this despite plans to call witnesses at the trial who would swear Olson was in northern California when the Los Angeles bombs were placed.

According to Olson's lawyers, her plea means she'd serve no more than two and a half years on each count, making her eligible for parole as early as three and a half years from now. She could go back to Minnesota and resume her suburban life with her emergency-room-doctor husband and their three daughters.

Los Angeles prosecutors Mike Latin and Eleanor Hunter insist she pleaded to two life terms and would have to serve at least twenty years, which means that if Olson were to get out as soon as her lawyers maintain, she'd be relying on the ultraharsh state board of prison terms to cut her a break. The nine-member board, whose members are appointed by the governor, is made up of mostly ex-cops and sheriff's officers. These are the people Olson would be asking for early release for trying to kill a bunch of cops. It sounds like a tough sell, but O'Mara suspects some type of deal has been worked out.

Bell says he called Latin and left him a voice mail message to learn more about her plea agreement, "but he's probably out with Eleanor celebrating at the local bar."

"Yeah," O'Mara says. "They're out from under that puppy now. You know how Soliah's going to spin this. She's going to say, 'I'm not really guilty but I was looking at a life sentence, and after September eleventh they would have found a dog guilty.' So she pleads guilty and proclaims her innocence. You can do that under a West plea." That's the name of a California Supreme Court case that says a defendant can plead guilty even while proclaiming innocence if he or she believes there's ample evidence to support a conviction.

By this time, Kerry Martin has come into O'Mara's office and tells him something he already knows. "They're going to be all over your ass now," she says. "The press, the Opsahls, L.A. Everyone."

"I'm going to disconnect my phone," he tells her. "I'll put a message on, " 'Hi. You've reached John O'Mara. He has anthrax poisoning and he's not expected to live. Bob Bell is taking all his calls.' "

He explains to Martin and Bell: "The pressure will be on us to make an instantaneous decision. But there's still a lot for us to do. We need to listen to all those tapes L.A. has. We need to get all the documents and items of evidence they have and make sure we go through it all. Shit, now that L.A.'s out from under this, my suspicion is they'll back the Ryder truck up to the back of the building and pile it all in." The tapes O'Mara mentions are 122 hours of interviews with witnesses around the time of the Opsahl murder. L.A. has been promising for months to send up transcripts but they've never materialized.

O'Mara is dead on about Olson's spin. Newspapers everywhere report the next morning that the ex-revolutionary-turned-soccer-mom pleaded guilty in Fidler's courtroom, then stepped out in the hallway and told reporters she was innocent.

"I pleaded to something of which I am not guilty," Olson told reporters in the hallway of the courthouse. "It became clear to me that

[September 11] was going to have a remarkable effect on the outcome of this trial," she said tearfully. "I think it's unfortunate that the effect probably was going to be negative."

Bell comes in first thing and tells O'Mara that Latin called him at home early this morning and said press reports about how much time Olson will get—four to five years—are wrong. Latin said she pleaded guilty to two ten-to-life terms.

"Bullshit," snaps O'Mara. "This is all carefully scripted. Everyone is saying their little part, so everyone is right. They've put a happy face on everyone but me and Jon Opsahl. And don't think Soliah's rolling over on anyone, because she's not. This whole thing speaks volumes about how these people think. One minute, she pleads guilty and the next minute she says, 'I didn't do anything.' "

Protests from the L.A. prosecutors to the contrary, plea negotiations with Olson and her attorneys have in fact been going on for months. On November 7, after Fidler expressed his chagrin over Olson's statements to reporters about her innocence, and after she was called into his courtroom and again said she wished to plead guilty, Latin is quoted in the *San Francisco Chronicle* finally admitting plea negotiations were ongoing.

"September eleventh is way in the background," Latin says in the *Chronicle* piece. "All this was a function of the fact that we were actually going to be starting trial. In the past, every time the case came up for trial it would be continued. Then negotiations would fall apart once they had manipulated a continuance."

Attorney Stuart Hanlon, who had been Olson's lawyer but eventually dropped the case because he wanted to spend more time with his young daughters following the death of his wife from leukemia, was now acting as a consultant to her defense team. In the same *Chronicle* article, he's quoted saying plea discussions had been going on for at least four months, adding "We got serious after September eleventh." He later filed an "under penalty of perjury" declaration with the court that said negotiations about a possible plea settlement began at least as early as 1999. The same declaration says Latin and Hunter always insisted Olson would serve no more than three and a half years. "I can represent to this Court that in all discussions I had with the representatives of the People . . . the People always maintained that they would be satisfied if Ms. Olson did three to four years in custody."

Olson's disavowal of her guilty plea, meanwhile, infuriated Judge Fidler, who angrily called her back into court to explain her flip-flop. On November 6, he quizzed Olson on what she truly believed regarding her guilt or innocence.

"Within minutes of entering the plea," Fidler said, "Ms. Olson publicly disavowed her guilt and proclaimed her innocence. . . . A guilty plea is not a way station on the way to a press conference proclaiming one's innocence. The integrity of the criminal justice system requires that she make a choice. She cannot have it both ways."

In reaffirming her guilty plea, Olson told Fidler: "I want to make it clear, Your Honor, I did not make that bomb. I did not possess that bomb. I did not plant that bomb. But under the concept of aiding and abetting, I do plead guilty."

"Because you are guilty of the crimes?" Fidler asked.

"Yes," she answered.

A week later, Olson had another change of heart. She filed a motion that was unsealed on November 14 asking that she be allowed to withdraw the plea and go to trial after all. "After deeper reflection," she wrote, "I realize I cannot plead guilty when I know I am not. Cowardice prevented me from doing what I knew I should: throw caution aside and move forward to trial. I am not second-guessing my decision as much as I have found the courage to take what I know is the honest course."

The confused turn of events got even stranger. Tony Serra, one of her lawyers, filed papers in court that claimed he bullied and coerced her into the guilty plea and put her into a "psychological condition of coercion" that resulted in her acting against her own better judgment. It's essentially the same defense Hearst used when she was tried and convicted of bank robbery in 1976.

On December 3, Fidler summoned Olson and her lawyers back to court. Shawn Snider Chapman argued that Serra had what the incredulous judge later characterized as a "Svengali"-like hold on Olson.

"He coerced her strongly to do it," Chapman argued. "Mr. Serra screamed and yelled at her and told her—I apologize for the language—she would be a fucking idiot if she didn't take the deal."

Serra failed to show in court, and the judge called his absence "absurd, unprofessional, and inexcusable." Instead of appearing, Serra sent a fax to the judge later in the day, apologizing for not showing up. He attributed his absence "to my karma, not to my volition." In short, he wrote, he missed his flight.

"Therefore, in a state of mind of dank frustration, I went home and went back to bed. I won't ever let this happen again. I will fly the night before. Please accept my heartfelt apology."

Fidler was not moved by any sympathy toward Olson. He refused to let her withdraw her plea and ordered everyone back to court January 18 for formal sentencing. But not before he got a few things off his chest.

"I took that guilty plea essentially twice from Ms. Olson," the judge said. "Were you lying to me then or are you lying to me now? She cannot have it both ways. She pled guilty because she is guilty," he said as the hearing ended. "The facts show she is guilty. The motion is denied."

"I couldn't for a minute accept a guilty plea from a person who I believed was innocent," Fidler also said during the hearing. "I couldn't sleep. I intend to sleep well tonight."

Fidler also castigated Olson and her lawyers for clinging to the terror attacks of September 11 as the reason she pleaded guilty in the first place.

It was fair to be concerned that an act which "absolutely rocked this country might affect this trial," Fidler said, but it was impossible to know whether her right to a fair trial would be compromised until prospective jurors were questioned about their views, something that was to have begun the week after her original guilty plea.

"The constant trying to link this trial to September eleventh is abhorrent. It is unfair to those who died September eleventh and it's unfair to the prospective jury." He said the claim was "ridiculous . . . just another allegation to try to keep this case from going to trial."

Now, O'Mara knows, there's nothing to prevent him from moving forward on Opsahl, regardless how poor of an idea he might think such a move is.

"I have a bad feeling that the Patty thing won't work out," he says of finally casting Hearst in the role of star witness in the Opsahl case. "I hope to God I'm wrong, because I think this case is going to be prosecuted. That's not a good reason not to prosecute, because you have an intuitive feeling it won't work out, but that's how I feel. I wanted to see her in L.A. It didn't matter to me whether the DA won or lost. I just wanted to see how Patty Hearst did. She still maintains she was brainwashed, which I don't believe for one minute. She's never taken full responsibility for her actions. How is a jury going to respond to that? How will a jury respond to her? In the Hibernia Bank trial there was evidence put on in her defense about her psychiatric state. That's going to come back to haunt us."

O'Mara knows the guilty plea turns the news media's attention to Sacramento. He figures he'll announce a decision after Olson is sentenced on January 18. Until then, he plans to be invisible. "I don't plan on answering the phone," he says. "Until January 18, we should keep quiet."

What he intends to do in the meantime is very discreetly talk to the two prosecutors he would want to take the case, if indeed there is a case. So on the morning of November 30, for the first time that Mark Curry can remember, O'Mara pokes his head into Curry's office and wants to know if the two of them can talk. Curry's immediate fear is, Shit, what unit am I being transferred to?

Since the beginning of the year, the prospect of being transferred out of Major Crimes has been hanging over Curry's head. He was boosted up to Attorney 6 early in the year after scoring at the top of the list on the supervisors' exam. It's the highest pay grade in the office short of holding one of the six bureau-chief jobs just below Scully and Besemer, yet Curry seemed to have beaten Scully's system of trying to turn the best trial attorneys into supervisors and potential future bureau chiefs: he was considered a supervisor, his pay was raised to supervisor level, and he didn't have to supervise anyone. He was still trying cases.

The Tison case might be his best insurance. It's not likely to go to trial until spring 2002, and a big case is often the best way to avoid being transferred in an office where people are regularly moved to fill vacancies caused by promotion, retirement or a prosecutor who decides it's time to make some real money and move into private practice.

The best trial attorneys don't want to be removed from the courtroom. They're measured, by themselves and others, by cases won, defense attorneys rolled, and bad guys put away forever. When you supervise, you can take pride in watching your attorneys develop, but there's no adrenaline rush. It's boring. Rob Gold and Mike Savage, two former homicide-team stars, are already stuck in the same mud Curry's trying to avoid. They've each spent a year supervising other prosecutors and are itching to get back in court.

So when O'Mara, perhaps the most noncommunicative supervisor in the building, sticks his head into his office, Curry cannot be blamed for thinking something bad is about to happen.

"How'd you like to try the SLA case with Robbie?" O'Mara says, making the grand gesture of rescuing both Gold and Curry from the rock pile. It's the biggest potential case the office has to offer, and in his own—not always subtle—way, Curry has been angling for it throughout the year. He's talked fairly freely about how he'd do it if it were his. He's made it clear his approach would be a lot different than the way O'Mara had been handling it. Enough time has passed, Curry believes, that it probably makes sense to approach Patty Hearst and gauge her willingness to testify and prepare enough to be effective as a star witness for the People.

With Olson's arrest, Curry had also said many times he would have approached the former fugitive's lawyers soon after her capture to see if there was any possibility she'd be willing to testify against her former SLA comrades. Instead of conducting a low-grade guerrilla war with L.A. over the past year, as the Sacramento DA's office allowed itself to do, Curry has said he would have gone to L.A. and looked for common ground with prosecutors down there. He thought it would be prudent to gauge whether they'd be interested in trying to put together a deal that would wind up with Olson testifying in the Sacramento murder case in exchange for charges against her being dropped in both jurisdictions. Curry knew it would be a hard sell in L.A., where successive chiefs of police wanted someone held accountable for having tried in 1975 to murder cops by putting bombs under their cars, but it was an intriguing possibility.

O'Mara was aware of Curry's thoughts on the case. They'd had a few brief, informal conversations about it over the year, plus there aren't a lot of secrets in a district attorney's office. O'Mara has long respected Curry's energy and legal skills, but he thought he was naïve in sizing up the Opsahl case, that he needed to know more about its intricacies before spouting off about the right way to proceed.

As far as O'Mara was concerned, making overtures to L.A. prosecutors or to Hearst or Olson would only make the Sacramento DA's Office look foolish, weak, or desperate, which is how Curry thought the office has looked for not filing and being more aggressive in the first place. With Gold, another well-regarded prosecutor with a solid record on big cases, on the team, they'd take risks O'Mara wouldn't consider.

For the Sacramento County District Attorney's Office, this is a dog of a case. If one or more defendants are prosecuted successfully for the April 21, 1975, murder of Myrna Opsahl, the family and everyone else can say, 'See, this could have happened years ago if the Sacramento DA had had the balls to go after it.'

If charges are filed and the case is thrown out or lost, the office gets ripped for being incompetent, which is what the critics have said all along. For a hungry prosecutor signed up late in the game, who comes into the proceeding with no baggage, the case could be a career maker, the kind that would make a spot on the bench considerably more likely.

Curry is O'Mara's first choice to give the case file a final review in anticipation of a January 18 decision. When he looks around the building for someone who's got the skills and the temperament to work with another attorney over a long period of time, Gold, a former newspaper sports reporter who went to law school at night and has risen to become one of the most respected prosecutors in town, is a logical choice for co-counsel.

For most of the year, O'Mara has gone back and forth about whether to try the case himself. He knows more about the evidence and the various participants than anyone else in the office. Whoever is assigned to the case will also have to convince a judge that charges are now being filed for sound legal reasons, not just because political pressure has been applied to the office and Scully got tired of hearing about it.

That will be a tough sell for anyone. The so-called "new" evidence that Scully will cite when she announces the filings is subtler and less significant than she will let on or that news media all over the country will report. This is the singular hurdle the office must clear if the case is to proceed to trial and Patty Hearst finally gets to testify. "The day we get Patty Hearst on the stand is the day we win the case," Curry will say later. "It's just that there's a hell of a long and difficult road to travel before we get to that point."

O'Mara knows there are good reasons he should step aside, not the least of which are Scully and Besemer, who each believe he's become an obstacle to the case moving forward. O'Mara has possibly done more soul searching about his own motives and behavior on this case than on any other in his career, and has also came to share Scully and Besemer's view as the year has progressed.

"The minute I file, this case has a life of two, three, four years. You're talking nights, working Saturdays, Sundays. I don't have young kids. My wife has passed away. All I have is the fucking animals and, who knows, maybe this would be the impetus to finally get rid of them. But it's going to take years to get this to trial, especially if everyone is arrested and then let out on bail, which I suspect is what would happen. If they were in, it would move much more quickly. But if they're out, the defense would want all the time in the world to prepare, and we certainly would be in no position to argue that there's some compelling reason to move quickly. I'm not trying to be a martyr. I just think I know better than anyone in the section what's involved and how demanding a case like this will be."

O'Mara knows too: The prosecutor should have a rapport with his star witness. It might be easier for someone else to begin fresh with Hearst. You want to believe your witness, and O'Mara still can't accept the notion that she was brainwashed and never sided with the SLA.

Scully and Besemer have given O'Mara a bad time in the past about not spreading out the big cases among younger deputies. It's been a few years since he tried a case himself, but for years he took the highest-profile and toughest murders that came in. The elderly boarding-home landlady who poisoned nine old pensioners she cared for, a Sacramento laborer who left prostitutes' bodies buried all over town, a Mexican Mafia case that ran the length of the state and took seven years to complete. All were sensational crimes, and O'Mara made his statewide reputation on how he prosecuted the killers. Scully and Besemer make noise from time to time that O'Mara should spread around the big cases, and whenever the subject comes up of who should prosecute the SLA case, they revive their "case hog" criticism. O'Mara is offended by the comments, but he does want he wants anyway.

"The biggest reasons for me just have to do with me," he says in a bit of personal introspection he rarely engages in with anyone else in the room. "I've been doing this a long time. I've just kind of gotten to the point where there isn't much interest in spending Saturdays and Sundays working on this stuff. Part of me would like to do it because, sure, my ego is involved. I've been accused of all kinds of incompetence on this. I would like to answer the challenge. But I feel differently, especially since my wife died. I just don't have the same devotion to want to do a case for so long a time. I still think I have the capability to do it. I don't think I want to spend that much time on a case.

"Truth be known, I have no desire to be a lawyer anymore. If I could make some money doing something else, I'd walk out today. People tend not to believe me when I say this, but it's always been a job for me. I've never seen myself on a white horse or doing some holy work. I'd like to not have to work, just like everyone else."

He knew at the start of the year it would come to this. That outside pressure would force him to reexamine his record on a crime left over from another era. He's spent much of the year doing just what the Opsahl family and law enforcement in Sacramento and L.A. have done: second-guessing his decisions.

"Maybe I should have prosecuted these people in 1991," he says of the grand jury he ran back then. "Had we done that, maybe Patty Hearst would have cooperated. But I doubt it. She's a very different witness than we usually have up here. Most people we have some control over. They're in custody. Or they have some other beef going. She's beyond our control in a very real sense. All the new evidence is fine and dandy, but the people in the bank are masked. So it comes down to having an insider, and the kinds of things we can do to induce people to testify and be cooperative—we can't do that with Patty Hearst. You have to go through her lawyer, first of all, and he's very active in protecting her interests. If I was as wealthy as her and I had two teenage daughters and a husband, why on earth would you be interested in bringing all this unpleasantness up again? Why come to California and spend all that time talking to some donkey DA about a part of your life you want to forget?"

It's not exactly the kind of encouragement a deputy wants to hear when he or she is handed a big case, and the first thing O'Mara tells Curry and Gold to do is make sure they really want this mess. That they're willing to take it on and give it all they have and maybe a little more, because that's what this case will require. O'Mara has faith in both men busting their butts and using solid judgment throughout once they're steeped in the cold, hard facts of the matter. He just wants them to appreciate fully what they're getting into. And he knows they can't. Not until they're in it and the magnitude fully sinks in.

Check with your wives, he says. Make sure they're okay with the amount of time this will take from your families, your children. Gold has already worked on one extremely contentious and tough murder case that took a year to win, so he knows how an assignment like this can take over your life. This is a trial that might easily last six months to a year, especially if there are multiple defendants. O'Mara already has twenty-five thousand pages of discovery from L.A. sitting in boxes in his office. There is bound to be more.

Over the course of the next several months, investigators will discover literally hundreds of thousands of FBI documents stored in various evidence archives around the country that the prosecutors will need to inspect to make sure there's nothing in them that will sabotage the case. The Hearst kidnapping and subsequent SLA crime spree sparked the most intensive FBI manhunt in the history of the agency until the Unabomber started sending bombs to people around the country. It may never be possible to know everything that's out there in connection with the case.

On Monday, December 3, the day Olson's plea is made final in L.A., O'Mara gets more than forty calls from the media. It's only going to get worse. Every time they go to court, TV cameras and reporters will converge on Curry and Gold. Attention in this old crime that has made international headlines off and on for more than twenty-five years will now shift entirely to Sacramento. Curry and Gold will be under scrutiny few prosecutors ever experience. The case will change and affect them in ways they couldn't have imagined or foreseen on the day O'Mara stuck his head into Curry's office and dangled the case of a lifetime before him.

The pile of transcripts from 122 hours of taped interviews finally arrived in O'Mara's office from L.A. a few days before Curry was asked to review the case. Down the hall, in Bob Bell's office, the veteran investigator put together detailed lists of witnesses to be called, evidence to be sorted, leads to run down. They're massive lists, and Bell's not sure of the whereabouts of more than half the people on them.

The workload is just part of it, though. There are other threshold concerns. Defense lawyers will claim their clients' rights have been severely compromised because the district attorney waited so long—a generation—to file charges. They'll file motions seeking to throw out all the charges and accuse the district attorney of filing only because the office was being pressured.

Why did it take twenty-six years to file charges? Some of the top defense lawyers in California will argue that their clients might have known around the time of the crime where the suspects were on a given day, but a lifetime has passed by now. They have families. They've raised kids. They've reformed their ways and have many solid citizens as friends who will testify to the productive lives they've been leading since shedding their foolish and often violent idealism. Why are you prosecuting this case now? You could have done it back then, when our clients had a fair shot. To try them now violates their rights to due process.

Is it because Jon Opsahl put together an impressive Web site and has repeatedly accused the district attorney's office of ineptitude? Did pressure from the sheriff's department cause the DA to charge these clients with murder after deciding time and again there was no prosecutable case? Were you afraid the U.S. attorney would take the case and embarrass your office? What's the matter, did L.A. calling you names finally take its toll? Scully and O'Mara would no doubt be asked by the defense to answer these questions, under oath, at some point in the proceedings.

Curry and Gold confer immediately after O'Mara tells them he wants them to review the case quickly, and they agree on one point. They want to be able to say in court, to the news media—hell, to their wives and kids and to themselves—that charges are being brought now because the case and evidence are significantly different. They need to believe they're trying it for sound legal reasons. Not because Scully and O'Mara are tired of listening to all the critics who said the Sacramento DA has been derelict for allowing Myrna Opsahl's killers to go unprosecuted for a quarter of a century.

The prosecutors agree among themselves never to say or do anything in this case they don't absolutely believe one hundred percent. That they won't put their necks on the line for the office just so it can save face. It's probably a little naïve to state this so explicitly, since prosecuting and defending a criminal case involve some bobbing and weaving around the facts, but the two men are acutely aware that politics and public perception have become part of the equation. They are determined not to be compromised by either.

As they start to dig into the files, they realize that, yes, there is new evidence. When Olson was arrested in Minnesota in 1999 after more than twenty years as a fugitive, detectives in Sacramento were finally able to match her palm print to one found on a padlock attached to a

Sacramento garage. SLA members stored rented and stolen cars in the garage that were used in several bank robberies, including the one where Mrs. Opsahl was murdered. Until Olson was captured, the print on the padlock was a mystery.

The shotgun pellets from Mrs. Opsahl's body that Bell retrieved from storage and sent to the FBI were now tied by advances in forensic technology to the same manufacturing batch as ammunition seized from SLA safe houses in San Francisco when Hearst and the others were arrested in 1975. That's new. The technology, which the defense would surely challenge, has been around for at least a decade, but prosecutors believe it has a better chance of standing up to scrutiny than it did in the past.

The prosecutors are convinced that Olson's guilty plea greatly strengthens Sacramento's hand, because it establishes that she did associate with Hearst and the Harrises. At the very least, she has now admitted in court that she aided and abetted the SLA's cause and its crimes. Though she waffled on her plea, she did finally admit criminal culpability. She later appealed Judge Fidler's refusal to allow her to withdraw her plea, but no matter how that's ultimately decided, Sara Jane Olson is on the record saying she aided and abetted the SLA, Patty Hearst, and the Harrises in criminal activities.

Curry and Gold want more. That's why they're anxious to try some things O'Mara didn't think were worth the effort. At the time O'Mara asked him if he wanted the case, Curry believed Olson was ripe for a deal. Just like in the Bread Store trial, California's felony-murder rule is the law of the day. Even if an accomplice had nothing to do with the actual murder, if you were a major participant in a robbery and someone was killed, you're on the hook for homicide. Olson could be facing twenty-five years to life for the Carmichael robbery and Opsahl's death. She has three teenage daughters to whom she's devoted. She has a husband. If she's convicted in a Sacramento trial, she loses everything. She'd likely spend the rest of her life in prison, no matter who turns out to be right about how much time her Los Angeles guilty plea winds up keeping her behind bars. Would she be willing to roll over on whoever else was in on the robbery? What about any of the others? Are they still devoted to their old comrades?

Curry wants to pursue Olson because he's looking for a quick way to allay his concerns on the delay-of-prosecution question. He knows that if

Olson does turn, the issue disappears. Sacramento prosecutors could argue the case is being filed now because they have an additional insider to corroborate Hearst's version of what took place in the Crocker National Bank.

Olson would be off the hook, but it makes the case eminently winnable if you file just against Bill and Emily Harris. They were the true ringleaders, according to Hearst. Throw in Mike Bortin, who Hearst says was also in the bank, if you feel like it. James Kilgore was supposedly inside the bank, too, but he remains at large. Steven Soliah and Wendy Yoshimura, lookout and additional getaway-car driver in Hearst's account, were given immunity by O'Mara when he ran the grand jury. They're off the hook no matter what, though the DA would certainly call them to testify in the case. Bill Harris set up the plan and pulled everyone in, according to Hearst. Emily supposedly pulled the trigger. "As far as legal and moral culpability," Curry says, "it's imperative that you go after those two."

O'Mara tells Curry and Gold to be as discreet as possible about his decision to put them on the case. If anyone asks, just say you were assigned to review the evidence with fresh eyes. He doesn't want a lot of whispering going on before some of these issues are resolved. If Olson is approached, Curry wants to do it as soon as possible so he and Gold know exactly what they're dealing with. If she tells them they're wasting their time, as her attorney told Bob Bell when approached her soon after her 1999 arrest, you drop it.

Scully will want to have a press conference to announce the charges, but that can't happen until all the defendants are identified. O'Mara has always believed the best course of action is to file only against Emily Harris. Keep it tight. Narrowly focused. Minimize the number of defense attorneys who will cross-examine Hearst and try to make her look like an airhead and a liar.

He knows Scully is going to want to file against everyone possible. She'd have a hard time explaining to a victim's family and to the public that Patty Hearst can only stand one defense attorney cross-examining her. "As prosecutors," she says one day in her office, "we might be able to understand that, but I don't think a community can understand that. She's your case and you can't let her be cross-examined by more than one defense attorney?"

Within days after his initial conversation with O'Mara, Curry begins to look more tense and preoccupied than he has all year. His brain is spinning with questions. He's trying to prepare for the Tison trial, which is scheduled to start in a few months. Before that, he has to retry a tough murder case in which the client was represented by Pete Harned. Harned is a former prosecutor in the office who was fired after he was found to possess child porn on his home computer when he brought it in for repair.

Gold is coming off a capital trial he carried over into his supervisor's job, involving a guy found guilty of raping his next door neighbor and slicing her grandmother in two with a machete when she interrupted him. Gold got his guilty verdict. He withstood the defense motion to void the death penalty on grounds the client was insane. Now he's in the penalty phase of the trial that will end in a hung jury in a few weeks. O'Mara will elect not to retry the defendant on the penalty phase, settling for life in prison without parole. For now, though, Gold is as distracted as Curry. Both men haven't been able to think about the SLA case as deeply as they'd like. A mess would become a disaster if the story about their assignment leaked out before they were versed on the case.

On Friday, December 7, when they each have a break in their schedule, Gold and Curry meet with Hunter and Latin, the Los Angeles prosecutors. Winter, such as it is, has come to the California capital. The air is cold and damp. It seems to rain every other day. If it doesn't, the fog swallows the Central Valley. It's the time of year newspapers carry articles about pileups on the highways caused from cars traveling too fast and banging into one another in near-zero visibility. O'Mara himself never felt like meeting with L.A. He knew what they'd been saying about his behavior in the case. He'd sat with them for an hour or so when they came up one time to show off their PowerPoint on the Sacramento evidence. He was in no mood then to suffer what he saw as their arrogance and desire to pawn off their case on Sacramento.

Curry and Gold come back to Sacramento feeling the Los Angeles prosecutors have been more cooperative than O'Mara is willing to believe. They've been agitating for more than a year to get Sacramento to file, but Latin and Hunter asked Curry and Gold to wait until after Olson is sentenced January 18. That's fine, Curry and Gold told them, knowing that was O'Mara's plan anyway. Besides, they need time to prepare. They haven't even spoken to anyone in the Opsahl family, because Scully and

O'Mara have asked them to hold off. They don't want Jon Opsahl to blab to the news media he's so effectively used to push his cause. The case has been around forever, but it's only been on their desk for a few weeks. They can wait. Their main concern now is keeping things quiet until they file. They should have known with Lou Blanas, the unpredictable sheriff who for more than a year has been questioning O'Mara's hesitancy, that keeping things quiet would be virtually impossible.

19 | Decision Time

*From the first moments of the prosecution's opening statement,
the strange nature of the proceedings made a deep impression.
How did it happen, I wondered, that a practice of truth-seeking
had evolved to divide the job up in all these curious ways? The
asking of questions was reserved to those who would play no role
in judging the answers, while we, the jury, who were supposed to
try to figure out what had gone on, had to remain absolutely
silent. And though it was up to us to decide if the defendant was
guilty, we would have no part in determining the consequences of
that decision: the business of setting punishments was reserved to
the judge; we wouldn't even know what they might be.*
                                    —D. Graham Burnett, *A Trial by Jury*

THIRTY-SIX ordinary people chosen at random, the jurors and
the remaining alternates, have had their lives in suspension for
much of the past six months. Now, Judge Morrison England, Jr., their
godfather for this extraordinary endurance test, is going to command
them how to think about all they've seen and heard. The actual proceedings known as the Bread Store have gone on far longer, but much of the
work was done before the juries were assembled. The arguments about
what could be seen and heard, how evidence was to be presented—
those took place before any of the jurors knew they would be spending
half of the next year of their lives forced to listen to often acrimonious
and combative all-day conversations about robbery, murder, lies, plots,
snitches, drugs, drinking binges, auto theft, assault and battery, Mace,
masks, lawyers, shotguns, blood, massive organ failure, crime scenes,
and all the other nice little subtleties of a murder trial.

All this weighed heavily on them, yet the judge prohibited them from
talking to anyone else—even each other—about what they were thinking.

"Members of the jury: You are reminded that you are jurors of three
separate jury trials which happen to be taking place at the same time in

the same courtroom," the judge begins his instructions. "Each jury is to consider only the evidence relevant to the case which that jury is considering. You are not to be influenced by actions or conduct of any other jury should you hear of them, including, but not limited to, requests for exhibits, or verdicts reached by any other jury. You are serving separate and unrelated functions.

"You have heard all the evidence and the arguments of the attorneys, and now it is my duty to instruct you on the law that applies to this case. The law requires that I read the instructions to you. You will have these instructions in written form in the jury room to refer to during your deliberations.

"You must base your decision on the facts and the law.

"You have two duties to perform. First, you must determine what facts have been proved from the evidence received in the trial and not from any other source. A 'fact' is something proved by the evidence or by stipulation. A stipulation is an agreement between attorneys regarding the facts. Second, you must apply the law that I state to you, to the facts, as you determine them, and in this way arrive at your verdict and and any finding you are instructed to include in your verdict.

"You must accept and follow the law as I state it to you, regardless of whether you agree with the law. If anything concerning the law said by the attorneys in their argument or at any other time during the trial conflicts with my instructions on the law, you must follow my instructions."

The prosecution has a tough burden. It's spelled out very explicitly in what the judge tells the juries. Circumstantial evidence carries as much weight as direct evidence. In other words, a bunch of thugs talking about how they saw the defendants together and heard talk of a botched robbery and shooting means as much as, say, the gun being found in Brewer's apartment. If circumstantial evidence is to count, though, it must be "consistent with the theory that the defendant is guilty of the crime" and "cannot be reconciled with any other rational conclusion."

"Further, each fact which is essential to complete a set of circumstances necessary to establish the defendant's guilt must be proved beyond a reasonable doubt. In other words, before an inference essential to establish guilt may be found to have been proved beyond a reasonable doubt, each fact or circumstance on which the inference necessarily rests must be proved beyond a reasonable doubt."

"If the circumstantial evidence as to any particular count permits two reasonable interpretations, one of which points to the defendant's guilt and the other to his innocence, you must adopt the interpretation that points to the defendant's innocence, and rejects the interpretation that points to his guilt."

And what of "reasonable doubt"? Anyone who's seen a cop show on TV has heard the words. What do they mean?

"Reasonable doubt is defined as follows: It is not a mere possible doubt, because everything relating to human affairs is open to some possible or imaginary doubt. It is that state of the case which, after the entire comparison and consideration of all the evidence, leaves the minds of the jurors in that condition that they cannot say they feel an abiding conviction of the truth of the charge."

Jurors may not find the defendants guilty of murder, robbery, or assault, the judge says, unless "the proved circumstances are not only (1) consistent with the theory that the defendant had the required specific intent but (2) cannot be reconciled with any other rational conclusion."

Did Glica and Martinez have the intent to kill someone or participate in the killing of someone? No one argued that they did. No evidence was presented to show this to have been the case. Their intention seemed to have been to commit robbery. To steal money.

The felony murder law doesn't parse words or ideas. It's why the two prosecutors questioned potential jurors in voir dire if they could apply this tough law to defendants even if they were not the ones who actually pulled the trigger.

"If a human being is killed by any one of several persons engaged in the attempted commission of the crime of robbery, all persons who either directly and actively commit the act constituting that crime, or who with the knowledge of the unlawful purpose of the perpetrator of the crime and with the intent or purpose of committing, encouraging, or facilitating the commission of the offense, aid, promote, encourage, or instigate by act or advice its commission, are guilty of murder of the first degree, whether the killing is intentional, unintentional, or accidental."

Now comes the key language, which was argued back and forth between defense lawyers and prosecutors for several days.

"If you find that a defendant was not the actual killer of a human being, you cannot find the special circumstance to be true to that defendant unless you are satisfied beyond a reasonable doubt that such defendant *with reckless disregard for human life and as a major participant*, aided, abetted, counseled, commanded, induced, solicited, requested, or assisted in the commission of the crime of attempted robbery which resulted in the death of Jason Frost.

"A defendant acts with reckless indifference to human life when that defendant knows or is aware that his acts involve a grave risk of death to an innocent human being.

"You must decide separately as to each of the defendants the existence or nonexistence of the special circumstances alleged in this case."

On the very next page of the jury instructions, the eighteenth of thirty pages that the judge reads separately to each of the three juries, England appears to give everyone but Brewer an out, but they are words the defense never took advantage of.

To find the special circumstance of murder committed *in the act of a robbery*, the juries must find two things: that the murder was attempted while a defendant was engaged in or an accomplice to the attempted robbery, AND that "the murder was committed in order to carry out or advance the attempted commission of the crime of robbery to facilitate the escape therefrom or to avoid detection. In other words, the special circumstance referred to in these instructions is not established if the attempted robbery was merely incidental to the commission of the murder."

Clearly, the robbery was not incidental to the murder. The reverse may be true, but not the former. They went there to rob. That was their primary goal. But was the murder committed, as the instruction says it must have been, "in order to carry out or advance the attempted commission of the crime of robbery or to facilitate the escape therefrom or to avoid detection?" It doesn't seem so. The robbers already knew they would get no money when Jason Frost was shot. The shooting did nothing to advance the robbery. Nor was it done to avoid detection. If that were the goal—to kill witnesses—everyone in the store would have been shot. Lawyers for Glica, Martinez, and Dixon didn't go near this. Maybe they missed it. Maybe they thought it was hopeless.

"You must not be influenced by sentiment, conjecture, sympathy, passion, prejudice, public opinion, or public feeling. Both the People and a defendant have a right to expect that you will conscientiously consider and weight the evidence, apply the law, and reach a just verdict regardless of the consequences."

He goes on to admonish each jury that they're not to discuss or consider punishment or length of sentence. That is for the judge to determine. The juries must decide only innocence or guilt, without regard to how long a defendant will spend behind bars because of what the juries decide.

One last warning, which comes more in the way of fatherly advice than an explicit order. "The attitude and conduct of jurors at all times are very important," England, his voice hoarse from so much talking, says. "It is rarely helpful for a juror at the beginning of deliberations to express an emphatic opinion on the case or to announce a determination to stand for a certain verdict. When one does that at the outset, a sense of pride may be aroused and one may hesitate to change a position even if shown it is wrong. Remember that you are not partisans or advocates in this matter. You are impartial judges of the facts."

Finally, the juries have the case, but juries rarely do everything a judge instructs them to do.

After a few days, Harrold gets a call that the jury in the Bobby Dixon case seems hopelessly deadlocked on the special circumstance.

A large Hispanic woman who brought her Bible to the first day of deliberations is holding out. The other jurors would later say she took every question personally, quoting from the Bible when she was asked to explain. The forewoman sent back a question for the judge that asked about the ramifications of not being able to agree on the special, but he declined to say too much because the answer speaks to punishment, which the jury is not supposed to consider or discuss.

The ramifications are considerable. If the jury can't reach unanimity on the special, the judge will declare a mistrial on that one narrow element. The DA wouldn't retry just that part of the case, so if Dixon were convicted on everything else, he'd get twenty-five to life for the homicide, instead of life without parole. On that charge alone, he'd be eligible for parole in about twenty-one years. With time already served, he could be out—if all he was facing were the 187—in about seventeen years. Hardly a free ride, but it's a shade better than no hope of ever getting out of prison.

"They're hung on the special," Harrold whispers to someone when the lawyers are called to court the next morning. "Our juror with the Bible doesn't think the getaway driver is a major participant."

Bladet tries to explain to the Frosts, who left their home in Grass Valley, about an hour away, and drove down to hear the verdict. She explains that the forewoman of the jury is very thorough and has asked for witness lists, among other things. They want to go over some of the testimony. When the woman, who took six binders full of notes during the trial, scanned the lists and saw that three names from her notebooks were not on the witness lists, Bladet was nonplussed at her thoroughness. "What is this, a test?" she says to the Frosts, frustrated with the jury's inability to see the case the way she does.

By the time they get to court this morning, the lawyers have been notified that the Brewer jury has also reached a verdict. Bladet is confident about Brewer's jury, mildly miffed with Dixon's, anxious to hear from Glica and Martinez.

Dixon's jury comes in first. The judge declares the mistrial on the special and hears the forewoman say guilty to all other counts. Dixon just sits there, blank faced, his shoulders slumped. Jack and Becky Frost appear to be numb, too, holding hands. Letting the words sink in. They can live with this verdict. It's Brewer they want most.

Judge England thanks the jury. It's almost unheard of to keep twelve people together for so long with no remaining alternates. He says he wishes he could do more for them to show his and the county's appreciation for their extraordinary public service and hands them each a certificate of service.

Peters is in the hallway talking to jurors. He's feeling good. He got all he could for his client and he knows it, especially when the jurors start talking. The letters showed Bobby was guilty as hell, they said. He lied about his role and gave everyone else up.

The holdout juror is alone, away from the group. She's still clutching her Bible and she says she stood firm on the major participant because she couldn't imagine Bobby Dixon planning or thinking through anything. Her intransigence in the deliberations made things rather ugly.

"I despise the woman," Lynn Jenner, one of the jurors, an ad saleswoman for *The Sacramento Bee*, says of the holdout. "Any discussion, she took as a personal attack. She brought up Rodney King. She wouldn't look at us. She kept saying she demanded respect as a person. She was against the detectives. She was ready to slap Bladet after she drew the red line. She didn't like Overton.

"It was very difficult in there. She was just unreasonable. She wouldn't listen to our point of view, but we had to listen to her point of view. She felt we all had our minds made up before we came in there. I swear, I was, take it home and stick it up your butt and sleep with it. I almost wanted to bring a picture of Jason in there and throw it in her face."

The judge, as is his custom after a long trial, invites the jurors and the Frosts back into his chambers. Jenner wants to know if a juror can be sued for damages in a jury deliberation. She's let everyone know she and the holdout really got into it.

"I've had juries that went like this for a week and a half," England says with a grin. "Where it was eleven to one and they kept saying, 'We're not done.' It's not like it is on TV. Nothing like that."

He was on a jury when he was practicing law, he tells them, and was the lone holdout until he eventually brought five more to his side for a six–six split and a mistrial.

"It's something you go through that changes how you see things. You know, it's still a pretty good system. It has flaws, but it works pretty well. A lot of places, I wouldn't want to be. Where they hold your hand in the fire until you tell the truth."

The Brewer and Dixon verdicts have come back ten months to the day the case was assigned to his courtroom and he started hearing arguments on evidence. He compliments the jury again for having stayed together since May without alternates. Jurors came to court sick. While some judges constantly miss work with dentist appointments, doctor appointments, and a variety of personal distractions, England showed up the same day he had a root canal.

Life goes on during a long trial. The Frosts' first granddaughter was born on December 11, 2001, and they're expecting another. Several jurors openly weep when Becky, finally able to relate to them as a real person instead of the blank-faced victim who's in court every day, passes around pictures. It's a moment as fraught with emotion as any during the trial. "She's kept us alive," she says of the adorable little girl in the photos.

Out in the hallway now, the jurors can't stop talking. Words cascade from their mouths. A woman named Lisa liked the way Bladet got Dixon to blow his cool during her closing.

"I saw this half smile on his face and it just hit me," she says. "I was very open through the whole thing. The letters really put in my mind the idea that, if he's innocent like he says, why'd he do that? I wouldn't want to be against Dawn Bladet."

The pictures etched forever in juror Carol Parker's mind are of the Southside punks. "The next generation of defendants," she calls them. "These kids can't even read. I was at a restaurant and looked at the busboy and started tearing up. I told him, 'Thank goodness you're contributing to society.' This does that to you."

Brewer's jury comes back at 1:30, but England first must mediate the dispute between the sheriff's department and the public defender's office over who can have access to Soltys in the jail.

The Brewer jury deliberated two and a half days before finding him guilty on all counts. They asked no questions of the judge. No instructions needed to be clarified. All they requested was to watch the Carlos Cervantes interrogation video again. "We just wanted to make sure we heard everything he had to say so we'd be comfortable with this decision ten years from now," one of the jurors says.

Juror Erik Olson, a former news wire-service editor who's now a teacher, calls Trevor Garcia "the glue that held the whole case together. He was the core. Everyone was pretty incredible, not very believable around the edges. But the core truth of the case, which he really pulled together, was very strong."

Tony Makarczyk, a thirty-two-year-old customer-service rep for a local insurance company, says jurors picked up on the dislike Bladet and Repkow had for one another, and occasionally they found it distracting.

"It was very obvious, for whatever reason, that Miss Bladet had issues with Miss Repkow," he says. "While Repkow was speaking, we'd notice Miss Bladet snicker at times. It seemed unnecessary and it was distracting. At times, it was hard to focus on the evidence or information being presented because those two were going at it. But Bladet was very impressive as a prosecutor. If someone would interrupt her, she'd stop and react right away. She missed nothing. I watched the defendants a lot. They seemed too comfortable. They joked a little from time to time. That bothered me. That story Repkow came up with in her closing, not one of us bought that for a second. It was obvious that was not based on anything."

Jurors didn't buy the Overton-as-villain scenario either. "My goodness,"

Victoria Hoff says, "is he ever smooth. He didn't bully anyone. He almost charmed it out of them. He was a total professional. We were very impressed with him."

The Glica and Martinez jury stayed out the longest and doesn't come in until the following Tuesday, the same day the courthouse is swarming with news media to watch Soltys get arraigned. When the jury returns, it's clear its members engaged in exactly what Karowsky and Lippsmeyer hoped they would: nullification.

The term refers to an age-old practice of juries refusing to follow the law or a judge's instructions because they consider the law or instructions unjust or flawed. Instead, they vote their consciences.

Nullification has a long history in the United States, dating back to its use by northern juries before the Civil War to protect runaway slaves. In the South, juries sometimes used it if they didn't feel comfortable convicting whites charged with murdering blacks and civil rights activists. Juries have used it to show leniency toward draft resisters and pot smokers. Court rulings have long held the practice illegal, but if a judge doesn't learn about it directly, there is little he can do once a verdict is reached. Jurors who go this direction often conceal their true feelings if quizzed by a judge. Karowsky and Lippsmeyer made no secret *outside* the courtroom that nullification was what they hoped for, but it was something they had to be careful about saying too loudly. It was nothing they could voice in court.

Jurors felt sorry for the youngest of the defendants and found "not true" the special circumstance that "the murder was committed in the attempted commission of the crime of robbery." The jury's decision was even more astounding to Harrold and Bladet, since both defendants were found guilty of all the charges, including attempted robbery. The practical effect is that the prosecutors again were rolled on the L-WOP. First-degree murder with a special means the rest of your life behind bars—period. No shot at parole. First-degree murder without the special means twenty-five to life, a possibility of parole after serving twenty-one years. It will be up to the judge to impose sentence, but the jurors gave the young defendants a break.

"They won't admit it," Karowsky says out in the hallway, "but what they did was nullify the L-WOP. Deep down inside it was an emotional response to the L-WOP. They just couldn't give it to them."

Lippsmeyer won't use the *n* word, but he certainly appreciates what happened. He feels very good about it. "Like all responsible citizens, they followed the law the best they could. And our strategy was not stupid. At least we saved them from the L-WOP."

The jurors grew very close throughout the long trial, and when they get together for a group dinner a few weeks later at a Mexican restaurant, they aren't reluctant to admit that the defense lawyers are right.

"We felt bad for them because they were only seventeen at the time of the crime," says Kim Jagelka, a criminal-justice student at a local community college who also works for the state Department of Consumer Affairs. The vote for the special against Glica and Martinez never advanced beyond nine to three against it.

A juror who asks not to be identified says the special circumstance didn't apply to Glica and Martinez because Brewer killed Frost simply because he was angry. It had nothing to do with the crime of robbery.

"I didn't go with that," another juror disagrees. "If they go into a building with a powerful, angry guy carrying a shotgun, they knew what they were doing. They had responsibility."

Diana Garcia, another state employee, felt empathy for the two youngest defendants and admits that's what saved them from first-degree verdicts. "They were young. They got no guidance at home. They were looking for someone to guide them and they found it in Brewer. Age was a big problem for us. I think if they were older, I would have felt differently."

After the verdicts are read and jurors retreat to the hallway, Alaina Jordan, an African-American juror with five kids, breaks down and sobs uncontrollably for a good five minutes. She is thinking of her own kids, mistakes they've made while growing up, and is overcome with emotion over what she has just sat through. She is thinking, too, of her own transgressions on the way to adulthood.

"I have a seventeen-year-old and I'm thinking the whole time during the trial, where are the parents? Why did these kids not feel they had an out? That they could say no instead of going with this guy? Every kid needs an out."

Bladet and Harrold weren't as upset about the decision the day it was reached as they would be after they had time to reflect.

"They know they didn't follow the law," Bladet says. "It was not a legal decision. But that's why they're there. That's why we have juries. Twenty-five years is a really long time for them to contemplate what they've done. They have to serve eighty-five percent of the time before being eligible for parole."

"It gives these folks some hope," Harrold says of Glica and Martinez and their families. "That's not a bad thing."

The Frosts and Jason's girlfriend, Megan, have no problem with the verdicts. Even they have some sympathy for Glica and Martinez. Still, Bladet is frustrated. No one says it out loud, but the DA had two defendants confess on videotape to felony murder. The jury found an "attempt rob" and 187 took place. Yet, somehow, the L-WOP, which was exactly what the case circumstances demanded as far as O'Mara and the cops are concerned, slipped away.

"The jurors know what they did," Bladet says the morning after the Glica-Martinez verdicts were read. "They didn't even say anything to me or Steve or the Frosts, but they empathized totally with the boys. They're only seeing part of the picture. They think they are these little cherubs who only made one mistake. You wanna see their freakin' rap sheets? They've been fucking juvenile gangbangers their whole lives."

Harrold's more charitable about it all. "It's okay," he says, realizing the results are short of the district attorney's expectations. "We had this woman in the front row who's a mother of five, for God sakes. I'm disappointed they didn't follow the law and that they discussed penalty, but it's fair."

The last word on each of the four defendants, judgment and sentencing, will be spread out over the calendar through December. When the dates are set, taking into account the time the county probation department needs to write up its presentence report on each defendant, as well as the time defense lawyers say they need to craft their motions for a new trial or reduced sentence, the last sentencing, Rickie Martinez, is scheduled for December 14. Scheduling is so tough that the judge has set a separate session for each defendant, meaning the Frosts will have to sit through four separate court hearings. Karowsky wanted to push it out as far as possible for Martinez. The defense lawyer said he needed more time to prepare motions for a new trial. He'd need at least six weeks, he said, to get a court shrink to examine Rickie so he could include that in his motions.

"It's all about your fucking client," a furious Bladet says after the sentencing dates are set. "They've got to do this before Christmas, the anniversary. The Frosts can't have a Christmas. It's all about Rickie. Forget the fact there are real people out there."

Defendants' families have suffered greatly, too, in all this. Their sons and brothers have been in the county jail four years. Mothers and fathers of the four men on trial are confronted with their horrific failings as parents. As awful as the Frosts feel sitting here day after day listening to testimony about their son's murder, Rickie Martinez's mother has been here most days, too, listening to her son being portrayed as some no-account gangbanger who lived for quick, easy cash and malt liquor. How he went into a robbery with an angry asshole named Rick Brewer and caused pain and tragedy.

Bobby Dixon gets sentenced first on Friday, September 28. It's nearly a year since the case was assigned to Judge Morrison England, Jr., who sits and listens impassively as Bob Peters goes through his motion for a new trial. All the defendants are here, even though it's only Dixon who's getting sentenced *today*. Brewer has come out with a shaved head, which makes him look more menacing. His dark, deep-set eyes take in everything around him.

Before the session starts, Harrold finds Becky Frost and asks how she's feeling. "Would it be cathartic for you to say something at the sentencing?" he wants to know.

"I don't know what it would be, but I definitely want to say something," she says. "Just make sure there's a box of tissues up there."

"I'll make sure they have a case," Harrold reassures her. It's a role he's played from the start, reassuring the family that they'll at least find some measure of justice, some measure of dignity and respect, out of all this. He's got his critics around the office, but to the Frosts, the man is gold.

"I can't tell you all Steve and Dawn have meant to us," Becky says. "They've been so dedicated to this case. They've kept us informed every step of the way. They've done a great job. We think the world of both of them. I can't imagine what this would have been like without them."

Peters asks that the first-degree murder conviction be reduced to manslaughter, since Bobby shot no one and only drove the car. But the judge, who finally gets to speak *his* mind about the defendants at judgment and sentencing, isn't buying it. As an African-American man who has made a great deal of his life through hard work, integrity, and character, England has no sympathy for the young black man sitting before

him at the defense table and his constant harping that he's not responsible for Jason Frost's death. He's heard stories like Dixon's countless
times before.

He will sentence Dixon to twenty-five years for murder, the judge
says. He'll add a year because someone was armed. He adds five years
for conspiracy to commit robbery, which is the maximum he can get for
that count. He tacks on another four years and eight months for the car
theft, assault, attempted robbery, and for being a criminal with a gun. He
is showing no leniency. Altogether, he hands Dixon a grand total of
thirty-two years, eight months.

"Do the people offer any evidence in aggravation of sentence?" the
judge asks. Yes, Bladet says. Mrs. Frost would like to address the court.

Two weeks have passed since the terrorist attacks in New York and at
the Pentagon. The Frosts have been riveted to the news of death and
mourning like the rest of the nation, but they can't help feel some re-
sentment over around-the-clock attention being paid to the victims'
families. They understand how they feel, but they know individual families like theirs are exposed to devastating loss at the hands of criminals
every day of the year. It rarely makes the national news or merits a call
from the White House.

Becky hates that she feels this way, less human than she was before
Jason was murdered.

As she turns to get out of the crowded row of seats she's in, friends
and family surround Becky Frost. She's not sure what she wants to say.
She's been waiting so long to speak from the heart to these young thugs,
who've caused pain and hurt in her life that is beyond her ability to articulate. She knows she'll only be able to scratch the surface. She won't
talk about the nightmares she has, the ones with Jason in the hospital,
hooked up to all the machines working desperately to keep him alive.
Or when she wakes up terrified in the middle of the night certain she
just saw Brewer jump across the defense table to get at her, only to be restrained by deputies.

"You were part of the devastation in my life," Becky, tissues in hand and
tears in her bloodshot eyes, tells Dixon from the witness stand. "The only
way I can express that is the devastation New York is having right now.

"My son is gone. My heart is empty. I have no hate, no love, no feeling, and you were part of it. Right now, I talk about myself, but you

don't realize the hundreds of people that knew my son and how it's dev-astated so many people. So much change. I hope you make better choices in your future, wherever that may be."

Harrold has tears in his eyes, which he tries to blink away. When Becky gets off the stand he whispers in her ear, and people in the court-room can see he's shaky right now. "I love you," he says. "I'll see you every December 23 until my last breath."

Harrold can't explain why he identifies so much with the Frosts. It's not the way most prosecutors behave. "I never knew the kid," he says of the Frosts' son. "They've just been so supportive. I'll take your lead, they said a million times. They took me around where they work. Jack's given me the tour of Grass Valley, where they live. They've been so open and giving. It meant everything to me to do right by them in the case.

"It meant everything," he says again, drawing out the last word slowly. "And I think we did. I know we did. They think we did."

Peters has a few changes he wants made in Dixon's probation report, most having to do with the letters Dixon sent from jail. A reference to them might not look good in a future parole hearing, but England says no, the reference to the letters and the coercing of witnesses stays in.

Peters's client would like to address the court.

"Number one, I want to request a motion for a new trial," Dixon says in an angry voice. "That's number one. Number two, I want to respond to what she said, to what's-her-name, Mrs. Frost."

This ought to be great, the prosecutors are thinking. First thing out of the asshole's mouth is he wants a new trial and he doesn't even know the name of the victim's mother.

"I just want to say," Dixon stutters, "you know, my heart goes out to your family. And like I seriously, seriously, I mean I feel totally sorry for what happened but—and, you know, I am sorry. I couldn't do nothing to prevent it from happening, but I am not responsible.

"And like I said, no man deserves to lose a life, and I am losing my life on account of some monster, basically. You know what I mean? He took my life, took the rest of these kids' lives. I didn't even do anything other than just be there and I am losing my life for this. It ain't right. Jason Frost's life wasn't right. It's just not right.

"But I am sorry I couldn't do nothing to prevent it, but I actually—please don't hold me responsible. Please don't hold me responsible for what happened to Jason Frost. That's all I could ask. Like I said, I am sorry. I couldn't do anything to prevent it, but I am not responsible. That's all I got to say."

Motion for a new trial denied, the judge snaps. Now it's Morrison England's turn to weigh in on how he feels about Bobby Marion Dixon. Harrold and Bladet desperately want to hear the judge lay Dixon out.

"Mr. Dixon," he begins, "it's really difficult sometimes to go through these types of proceedings. This is no different than any other time." England pauses, carefully selecting what he wishes to say.

"I have heard the words that you just said to Mrs. Frost and the family and friends of the victim in the matter, and I hear those words, but I have to tell you, Mr. Dixon, those words are still hollow. You still are not accepting responsibility for the actions that you took that night.

"If it were not for you, Mr. Brewer, as you call him, 'the monster,' and the other defendants, would not have felt so safe and secure to enter into a store with a shotgun and attempt to steal money through force and fear from the employees.

"Maybe at one point in your life you will be able to take responsibility for your actions, be accountable for what you have done, and maybe when that occurs, the words you have just said to Mrs. Frost will actually have some meaning."

He also has a few words for Peters, specifically addressing references Peters made in his closing argument more than a month ago about Dixon's tough upbringing.

"The bottom line is, there are a lot of people in this world that have had a lot worse upbringing than Mr. Dixon ever thought of having and never involved themselves in criminal activities to the level that he has involved himself in."

"I agree," Peters says. But the judge isn't looking for a dialogue. This is a lecture.

"It is absolutely unbelievable to me how an individual could be released from a state prison of California on November twenty-ninth, 1996, and then be involved in an activity that resulted in the death of a human being on December twenty-third, 1996. That is twenty-seven, approximately, days after getting out of prison for two years. It is absolutely beyond any comprehension that I have that Mr. Dixon did not know exactly what was going on and was not participating in the planning of this robbery.

"He may not have been planning the robbery from four hours before, but the moment he got into that vehicle and he saw a twelve-gauge Mossberg pump shotgun seated—put between the seat and the console, sticking up, and with masks on, he knew what was happening.

"It's time," the judge says, "for him to be accountable for his actions. I noticed in the last paragraph or so of your argument, or your motion, Mr. Peters, that you indicated it was not the defendant's idea to commit any robbery or shoot anyone. He was not armed. He fired no shots. He gave no direction and did not plan the robbery and then expressed surprise when shots had been fired after the robbery. I would like to point out several points that I have.

"Mr. Dixon stole the car that was used to transport the defendants and that shotgun to the robbery.

"He drove all the defendants to the Bread Store where the attempted robbery was to take place.

"He waited for the defendants in the alley, for the other defendants to exit the Bread Store after the robbery.

"He gave the defendants a safe haven and a way to conceal that sawed-off, twelve-gauge shotgun by putting it into that vehicle. I would like to point out the fact that Mr. Dixon was there waiting with the car running in this alley, allowing Mr. Brewer to come out and conceal a twelve-gauge shotgun, [makes him] very much a participant in the case.

"I think it may have had some more impact on Mr. Brewer if he had to walk down J Street carrying a twelve-gauge shotgun as opposed to running out in the dark and jumping into a waiting GMC Jimmy and speeding away into the night. Mr. Dixon drives all of the defendants and that twelve-gauge shotgun to a place of safety so they can run home. If there has ever been a definition of 'major participation' in a crime, Mr. Dixon is it."

That's the part Harrold and Bladet silently cheer. The jury determined that getaway driver Bobby Dixon was not a major participant. Harrold and Bladet feel vindicated by the judge. One asshole down, they're thinking—down for a long time—and three more to go.

20 | Long Time Coming

There's no excuse why this has taken so long that I can fathom. If there is, maybe we'll hear it. —Patty Hearst

I N late December, Jan Scully, wanting to make sure she's not surprised by any last-minute developments in the Opsahl case, convenes the first of what she says will be weekly meetings to make sure everyone is moving in the same direction. Even during the holidays, when she'll be up at Donner Lake relaxing in her family's vacation house, she intends to phone in for weekly conference calls. For this initial meeting she has one overriding message for Curry and Gold: Be careful whom you talk to, even more careful what you say.

Be careful what you say to the Opsahl family, Scully tells Curry and Gold. They're never going to be on our side. Besides, if you tell them charges are coming, they may not be able to keep it to themselves.

A week ago, Scully told the two prosecutors she didn't think it was wise for them and Bell to sit down with the Opsahls, even after a meeting had already been set up. "The Opsahls are not your friends," Scully told the three of them. Now she tells everyone in the room that she wants Kerry Martin, head of Victim/Witness assistance, to be the family's contact at the district attorney's office. This presumably would minimize—if not altogether eliminate—the need for the prosecutors or Bell to have face-to-face contact with the Opsahls.

Bell was so angry, he didn't sleep all night after Scully nixed the Opsahl meeting. As much as he wanted to be around when charges were finally filed, Bell, only a few months from retirement, told his wife he was going to march into Scully's office, throw his investigator shield on her desk, and resign if she didn't relent. He did meet with Scully alone and convinced her that sitting down with the Opsahls was something he and the prosecutors needed to do, especially given the family's less-than-wonderful relationship with the office up until now.

Bell felt strongly that the Opsahls needed to be aware of what was coming. He didn't share Scully and O'Mara's concern that Jon Opsahl would immediately put news of the charges on his ever-changing Web site or call someone in the news media and wind up being quoted anonymously as "a source close to the investigation." Scully doesn't want to do anything to alert the defendants. They haven't been hiding all these years, but she doesn't want them to start thinking about that now, with murder charges finally about to be filed.

"If you talk with them, tell them that if they want to be that undis-closed source or publish it on their Web site, if your mother's killer isn't punished, you have yourself to thank," Scully tells Curry and Gold. "The Opsahls have to be on our team. I know they've never been happy with how we handled this, and we can't unring the bell. But they also have to understand, the easiest thing for us to do is nothing. It always made sense for us to wait to see how Patty Hearst did in Los Angeles. That was our strongest hand in this case. John was always right about that."

Martin has talked to Jon Opsahl before. She thinks he'll do what's best for the case. He feels his mother's murder has been given such short shrift by the district attorney's office over the years that he wants to be reassured Scully is truly committed to making the case work. "He wants someone to say, 'We're going to take the case to trial and we're going to win it,' " Martin says.

Bell agrees the young doctor can be hard to predict. About six months from now, though no one can imagine this at the time, he will have his medical license taken from him by the California Board of Medical Examiners because he's prescribed drugs, including the antibiotic Cipro and the painkiller Vicodin, after simply asking patients a few questions in an Internet medical-history survey. "But I really don't think he'll violate our request to be quiet," Bell says.

Curry and Gold simply want to introduce themselves to the family so the Opsahls don't hear Sacramento's intentions from other sources, such as the Los Angeles District Attorney's office.

"Okay," Scully relents, "but I would hope when you meet them you don't give them the idea that somehow this case wasn't important to this office or that John hasn't done anything. From a timing standpoint, I don't think it ever made sense to make a decision on this case before the L.A. case was final. I'm not concerned that the Opsahls don't agree with that. I don't want you to win them over by saying we didn't think the case was important, because it's not true."

"We found we don't talk about the past," Curry, with a smile, says of himself and Gold. "We talk about the present."

Don't get too cozy with the prosecutors in Los Angeles, Scully adds. "They've tried to run this case from the beginning. It's the height of arrogance to say they'll prosecute if Sacramento doesn't, or that some other prosecutorial agency would step in. I believe they want the same results we do, but they want to call the shots on what we do and we will not let that happen. This is a new case and a new place. We should treat them like we're the federal government and they're the state government."

She knows Curry and Gold went down to meet with prosecutors in Los Angeles and tells them she's glad they did. She still doesn't trust them down there and never will. She doesn't need to add that she can't stand Steve Cooley, the elected district attorney in Los Angeles. She can't forget the condescending and arrogant letters she received from Cooley earlier in the year about what a district attorney's responsibility is to the public and how he demanded a decision on the Sacramento case within thirty days.

Curry and Gold know they'll find their own comfort level in dealing with everyone. For now, the main thing they need to do before charges are filed is make sure they know exactly what evidence is preserved and which witnesses are available. After all this time, they'd look like fools if they filed charges and learned later that certain evidence was lost or witnesses they wanted to call were dead or incoherent.

Have you decided how, or when, to approach Patty Hearst? Scully asks.

"We thought we'd go out to Connecticut and meet her at some café," Gold jokes. "Or maybe by the pool at the Hearst castle." Everyone in the room knows Hearst is not the typical witness to murder, but Gold believes she'd be more than willing to cooperate if she's approached differently than she was in the past.

"I think she feels somewhat bitter about how she was treated by the government," he says. "All the way through. I do think she does have some emotional commitment to this case. That she wants to do right by what happened here to Mrs. Opsahl. We want to tell her we're here to start fresh and that we believe her."

"L.A. was just going to throw her up on the stand," Scully says. "They didn't care how she looked."

"They said they didn't think they had to spend much time prepping her," Bell says. "They believed she wouldn't want to embarrass herself and that she had a lot of motivation to prepare on her own."

Fine, O'Mara says, but there's a real difference between how she and her lawyer might prepare to testify and how he believes she must be coached to testify in such an old case where it's certain the defense is going to attack her every way that it can. Not coach her to the point she's told what to say. Coaching so she recalls every detail, can foresee every defense attempt to trip her up, can withstand the furious attempts the defendants' attorneys will make to confuse her, to make it appear as if she has an agenda, that she lied many years ago about what she did and what she knows, and that she is lying still.

Gold shares something from L.A. that everyone finds amusing. Mike Latin, one of the prosecutors on the Olson case, told Gold and Curry that they didn't want to get too close to Hearst because they were afraid of a public backlash similar to the one their office suffered when they made racist cop Mark Furman a key witness against O.J. Simpson.

"Latin told us they did some polling and found that many people in Los Angeles didn't believe Patty or like her very much," Gold says, "but at the same time they didn't like her, the more they thought Soliah was guilty."

Only in L.A., Besemer cracks, do they take a public opinion poll before trying a major case. Scully doesn't share L.A.'s view. She tells everyone in the room she wants to treat Hearst with respect and that her office should work as closely with her as possible so she can be effective in court.

"We don't have to excuse what she did, but we don't have to judge her," she says. "She's already been judged."

The main thing to remember, Scully says, is that from now until you file, the prosecutors should be wary of everyone. "I don't think you have much of a base of support from anyone outside this office," she tells them. She leaves unsaid the fact that she includes on her list of nonsupporters the Sacramento Sheriff's Department, where officials have been openly second-guessing the district attorney's judgment on the case—especially O'Mara's reluctance to file earlier.

As anyone who's been around the criminal-justice system for very long knows, the idea that all law enforcement agencies are brothers and sisters in arms united in their fight against the bad guys is a myth. Much of the time they're stabbing each other in the back for credit, press coverage, resources, control.

Just one day after Scully's warnings to her deputies, the office is whipped into a frenzy over Sheriff Lou Blanas's intention that morning to arrest all the SLA suspects right now, before charges are filed. Everyone at the sheriff's department knows the DA plans to charge as many as five defendants in the Opsahl case. Blanas is tired of waiting. It seems his impatience has been triggered by something he read in the morning newspaper.

On the front page of *The Sacramento Bee* Tuesday December 18, there is a story by Los Angeles bureau reporter Laura Mecoy that carries the headline: "Victim's Son Presses DA on SLA-Linked Slaying." The story goes on to speculate that Sacramento is about to announce whether it will file charges, quoting Craig Hill, the sheriff's homicide chief, who in response to a question from the reporter says he expects the decision to come down around January 18, when Olson is sentenced in L.A.

This made Blanas nervous. If he read it in the newspaper, the defendants probably did too. Even though his opponent has no chance of dethroning him, Blanas is in a reelection campaign. The last thing he wants is SLA defendants to flee because Sacramento law enforcement is in no hurry to arrest them. Besemer got a call from somebody in Blanas's shop early that morning that he was going to have all the defendants arrested immediately. Emily Montague (her new name) and Olson are in the Los Angeles area. Bill Harris lives in Oakland, where he has worked for years as a private investigator for lawyer Stuart Hanlon. Bortin lives in Portland; he runs a wood-floor restoration business there, with his wife, Josephine, who is Olson's sister, and the couple's four kids. Kilgore is still a fugitive after fleeing San Francisco the same time Kathleen Olson disappeared in 1975.

No charges have been filed, no warrants issued, but Blanas wants everyone brought in on probable cause, which he knows there's plenty of. He thinks the murder suspects will flee, even though they've known for months that intense pressure was being applied on the Sacramento DA's Office to charge them with murder and they've not run yet.

At the DA's office, the top officials suspect it's all about Blanas wanting to hold a pre-Christmas news conference that shouts to the world: "25-Year-Old Murder Solved; Sheriff Hero Again." Scully is still annoyed over how much glowing media coverage Blanas and the department got when Nickolay Soltys was caught, never mind the fact Soltys sneaked back into his mother's house while it was under twenty-four-hour surveillance or that it was a call from one of his startled relatives that led to Soltys's capture.

After a brief and angry session in O'Mara's office—he scolds Gold for thinking Blanas could be trusted to stay quiet until warrants are actually prepared—O'Mara calls Hill. He and O'Mara have enjoyed a good relationship all year, but O'Mara immediately starts yelling at him.

"Shit, Craig, that's stupid paranoid cop shit," O'Mara barks into the phone about Blanas's argument that the defendants might flee. "This is crazy shit."

The suspects in the Carmichael bank robbery have been looking over their shoulders for twenty-five years. Michael Bortin told the *Los Angeles Times* in a January 2000 article that the talk of old SLA crimes was "like a deranged relative knocking on your door every few years." They have families, new lives, and, as O'Mara shouts into the phone to Hill, this is 2001, not 1976. It's not as easy to go underground these days. The rebellion-is-cool era of the 1960s and '70s is gone, O'Mara shouts into the phone. It's been trumped by September 11 and its aftermath. The country's mood is solidly pro–law enforcement.

Standing in O'Mara's office, it's possible to hear Hill through the phone—when O'Mara stops shouting, that is. "John, you're yelling at me," Hill says. The sheriff's homicide chief also tells the district attorney's homicide chief he knows O'Mara's right, that waiting until the DA is ready to file charges in a few weeks is the proper thing to do. O'Mara also knows Blanas is pressuring Hill to pressure O'Mara.

"It's a big fat bluff," O'Mara tells someone in his office. "Think about it. I'm a police officer in Los Angeles or St. Paul. It's been twenty-six years and I don't have a warrant, but you want me to go out to Kathy Soliah's house and arrest her? This is twenty-fucking-six-years old. They're gonna say, you got a warrant, we'll be glad to help you."

O'Mara makes it clear to Hill that no warrants will be filed by the DA's office until charges are ready. We're waiting until Olson is sentenced January 18, he tells him. There's no rush. Blanas has made noise about going directly to a judge who's a friend of his who, Blanas says, will sign a warrant prepared by the sheriff's department, bypassing the district attorney altogether. Typically, suspects are arrested after a district attorney has filed a complaint and declaration of evidence in the case. An arrest warrant is prepared and taken over to the courthouse so a judge can sign it. You don't arrest people on probable cause without a warrant unless there's a damn good reason, like they are about to flee or are a danger to themselves or others. Or they've been caught in a criminal act.

At one point in this very heated day, Blanas has Ed Newton, one of his deputies assigned to the case, write an affidavit of the facts to present a judge. But no matter what Blanas has told his deputies, O'Mara doesn't believe any judge would actually sign a warrant that the district attorney is not a party to, especially in a case with this high of a profile.

All the yelling and lectures about arrest procedure don't do much good. Hill tells O'Mara he sees his point, but then he shows up a short time later to continue arguing. At the same time, Sheriff's Captain John McGinness walks over to see Scully at the other end of the fourth floor.

Look, Scully tells McGinness, we've put two of our best deputies on the case. You guys can read between the lines. You know what we're going to do. Just be patient. When we're ready to file, you'll be the first ones we tell.

By the end of the day, much of which has been taken up with phone calls and meetings back and forth on Blanas's plan to make arrests, the sheriff finally backs down.

"I told Craig if Lou came up with some arrest warrant or filed something to have these people arrested, there would be problems," O'Mara says when it's all over. "I told him, You do what you have to do, but that's not something we'd forget anytime soon." Just be patient, he tells everyone. We've waited this long, a couple more weeks won't hurt.

He's right, and everyone in the room also knows it will be like this—insane—for as long as this old case is alive.

Almost one month later, on the morning of January 16, 2002, the Sacramento County District Attorney's Office is finally ready to begin making good on the 1975 murder of Myrna Opsahl. The plan to wait until Olson's formal sentencing in Los Angeles on the eighteenth is ditched when a reporter from the *San Francisco Chronicle* starts calling around with questions about imminent arrests. O'Mara isn't about to protest at this point. He got Blanas to back off for nearly four weeks. He knows he is out of time.

Emily Montague, fifty-four, is first. The woman known long ago as Emily Harris—Yolanda to her SLA comrades—once was a rage-filled radical committed to overthrowing the United States government. According to authorities, who base their account almost exclusively on what Patty Hearst has testified to and written took place in a Sacramento suburb on the morning of April 21, 1975, it was Harris who pointed her shotgun at Myrna Opsahl during the Crocker Bank robbery in Carmichael and fired the shotgun blast that killed her.

At 8:02 on the morning of Wednesday, January 16, 2002, Montague is driving a green Chrysler Sebring about a hundred yards from her Spanish-style home in southern California when Sacramento County sheriff and California Highway Patrol officers pull her over. "I asked her to get out of her car and she did," CHP Officer Vincent Bell tells the *Los Angeles Times*.

Her house, a favorite with neighborhood trick-or-treaters, sits near a country club in an upscale neighborhood in Altadena. She shares it with Noreen Baca, her partner of more than ten years. There's a perfect lawn, a cactus garden, and a small American flag hanging outside. Montague has the quiet, demure look of a high school librarian. For nearly two decades, she's lived an obscure but busy and productive middle-class life with her friends and family.

Years ago, in the wake of Vietnam and the Kennedy assassinations, Harris, a former social chairperson of Chi Omega, a University of Indiana sorority, had become so convinced the system was hopelessly corrupt, she was willing to plan kidnappings, murders, bank robberies, and bombings to ignite a revolution.

On the morning of her arrest, she is on her way to work as a management consultant for the entertainment industry. Her clients have included such American icons as Disney, MGM, and Paramount Pictures. She offers no resistance and says hardly a word on a flight to Sacramento, where she is jailed awaiting arraignment for murder.

"I made choices," she told a *Los Angeles Times* reporter in an interview a year before her arrest. "Looking back now, I think some of those choices were extremely reckless and ill conceived.

"We were reacting to the war in Vietnam, the assassinations of John Kennedy, Robert Kennedy, Martin Luther King, the Black Panthers, government surveillance. We felt a revolution was going to happen. By 1972 and '73, we realized the world wasn't going to change."

Sixteen minutes later, at 8:18 A.M. in a quiet residential neighborhood near scenic Lake Merritt in Oakland, Bill Harris—SLA field command name General Teko—is driving his green Honda Passport SUV. Cody, seven, and Shane, thirteen, his two boys, are seated in the back. Harris, who helps coach his sons' soccer teams, is taking them to school. Police allow him to use his cell phone and call a friend, who comes and finishes transporting the boys while their father is arrested for murder.

Chubby, gray in the beard and temples, Emily Harris's former husband is fifty-seven now, an investigator for prominent San Francisco criminal defense attorney Stuart Hanlon. In another lifetime, the incendiary Vietnam veteran, a Marine, in an SLA "communiqué" he hoped would galvanize millions into action, called for "unleashing the most devastating revolutionary violence ever imagined."

According to what authorities believe, Harris waited outside the Crocker National Bank in Carmichael as an armed lookout. He did this, Hearst said, because he was the best shot in the group. They also believe he masterminded the robbery so his band of revolutionaries could raise cash for a string of bombings that remaining SLA members were planning—and carried out—on various police targets around the state.

Neither of the Harrises had ever been charged in connection with the Crocker Bank robbery or Myrna Opsahl's death. They each spent about eight years in prison after pleading guilty to kidnapping Patty Hearst and other SLA crimes. Divorced while behind bars, they remain close and hold on to their left-leaning politics, but they long ago disavowed their violent pasts.

"Everyone's interested in how we've changed and haven't changed," Bill Harris told a reporter in the spring of 2001. "I'm older, no longer self-destructive, and unwilling to go to jail."

In an interview with the *Los Angeles Times* about two years before his arrest, Harris engaged in a soliloquy reminiscent of Hamlet. "Did I accomplish anything? Yeah, I accomplished ignominy."

As for his revolutionary ways, Harris said: "If you do something and you succeed, then you're a revolutionary of high quality and you get to be George Washington, the father of the country. But if you challenge power and you're rubbed out, you're in the trash bin of history."

Harris went to work as a receptionist in a law firm after being released from prison and eventually became a private investigator, though the state refused to grant him a license because of his criminal past. He has spent the past few years working for Hanlon. In 1988, he married Rebecca Young, an attorney in Hanlon's firm and a San Francisco law professor.

Some six hundred miles up the Pacific Coast, in a working-class neighborhood of southeast Portland, Michael Bortin is getting ready to start another day at Zen Hardwood Floors, a company he founded and owns.

Police, who've been staking out his home for several days, telephone the fifty-three-year-old Bortin and tell him they have his place surrounded. He is ordered to come out and surrender. In the driveway, there is a pickup truck parked with a bumper sticker on it that says, VI-SUALIZE WHIRLED PEAS.

Wearing bulletproof vests and with guns drawn, police order Bortin to the ground. As neighbors watch, they cuff him. He and his wife, the former Josephine Soliah, have four children. The youngest is Rebecca, twelve, a star soccer player and the apple of her dad's eye.

"All I know is they did a bit of overkill," Josephine Soliah-Bortin tells the Portland *Oregonian*. "We weren't going to come out with guns a-blazing. We're just two middle-age, middle-class, hardworking people who were not expecting this."

At the time of the bank robbery, Bortin was on probation for his role in an alleged 1972 Berkeley bomb plot. When his probation was revoked in 1975 for associating with known criminals, he failed to turn himself in and remained at large for nearly eight years, hiding for much of that time in Boston. In 1984, after spending the night with his dying mother, who urged him to surrender, he turned himself in and spent a little more than a year in prison. She died of cancer the next day.

"It wasn't like I was going to get caught," he was quoted at the time. "I've prospered. Being a white fugitive in this country is an easier life than being a Third World person who is law abiding."

Around 4:30 P.M., fifty-five-year-old Sara Jane Olson, who is scheduled to show up in court in two days for formal sentencing on the Los Angeles bombing charges, surrenders to police in connection with the Carmichael case. She again denies knowing anything about the bank robbery. She has said many times she was not anywhere near Sacramento at the time.

A fifth suspect, James Kilgore, fifty-four, who was Olson's lover at the time, is also charged with murder for the Opsahl slaying, but he's been a fugitive since 1975. In February 1976, witnesses said they saw Kilgore in a tour group at San Simeon, the Hearst castle that is now a California state park, moments before a bomb exploded and caused $1 million in damage to an ornate guesthouse at the landmark.

An angry communiqué from the so-called New World Liberation Front, an SLA spinoff, was sent to Hearst's father, seeking a $250,000 defense fund for the Harrises. The communiqué said Patty Hearst would not have lived to appear at her federal bank robbery trial had she been released from prison. Kilgore, who police say is married and has two children, has not been heard from since. They do believe, however, that he's been in touch with one or more members of the group over the years.

"Our family has waited twenty-six years for this day," Jon Opsahl says at a press conference in Sacramento on the afternoon of the arrests. "And to District Attorney Jan Scully and Sheriff Lou Blanas, I have one other thing to say: It's about time."

The fact that Sacramento authorities moved up their plans to make the arrests by two days gives prosecutors in the Los Angeles District Attorney's Office one more reason to be furious with Sacramento. A top official in the DA's office in L.A. threw a fit when Sacramento officials called and said the arrests were taking place on the sixteenth, before the Olson case was closed.

"You don't do anything for twenty-five years and now you can't wait two more fucking days," a senior Los Angeles prosecutor yelled at a Sacramento investigator.

Scully and Blanas, with the Opsahl family at their sides, address a horde of reporters at the Sacramento Sheriff's Department the afternoon of the arrests. Blanas, towering over the district attorney, nods for Scully to go first.

"We all agree," she says, "after almost twenty-seven years, justice has not been served. The state of the evidence today has convinced me now is the time to seek justice for Myrna Opsahl."

Scully cites "forensic testing procedures not available until recently" as the principal reason her office believes charges can now be filed. She is referring to the lead pellets taken from Opsahl's body matched with ammunition seized from SLA safehouses. She also mentions Olson's palm print and the fact that she pleaded guilty to aiding and abetting the SLA in its Los Angeles bomb plot.

"Mission accomplished as far as I am concerned," a relieved Jon Opsahl tells a roomful of reporters. "This is very therapeutic in a sense. Her death did matter. . . . It was the kind of parallel life Kathleen Soliah assumed that was disturbing. She took my mother's life and assumed the life she'd been leading when she was murdered."

A day later, Olson's lawyer, Shawn Snider Chapman, previews what essentially will be the defense argument, in demanding the case be thrown out because it's unfair to file charges after so much time has passed. Nothing has changed in all the years between the crime, the earlier decisions not to charge, and the arrests, she tells reporters, except "the dogged determination of Mr. Opsahl and the relentless pressure of the district attorney's office in Los Angeles."

Scully bristles at the comment, saying a few weeks later that "I didn't need Jon Opsahl to get us to file those charges." There was no denying, however, that the young doctor's persistence made it virtually impossible for the Sacramento District Attorney's Office not to file in the case.

Two days after the arrests, on January 18, 2002, Olson, Bortin, Montague, and Harris are reunited in a Sacramento courtroom and arraigned on first-degree murder charges. One newspaper account says they look more like retirees than revolutionaries, with their graying hair, wrinkled faces, and girth of middle age.

Earlier in the day, Olson is sentenced in Los Angeles during an emotional hour-long hearing in which she apologizes for the harm she's done and is hugged by her sobbing fifteen-year-old daughter, Leila Peterson, who tells the judge Olson has been "one of the best mothers anyone could ever want."

"I will always be by your side no matter what," the teenager says as the two hug in a tearful embrace.

Jon Opsahl, who is in the courtroom during the gut-wrenching moment, calls Olson's apology "too little, too late."

At a bail hearing, Curry and Gold go to court and ask that bail for all the defendants, who are brought in from the county jail in shackles, be set at $1 million. In the case of Harris and Montague, the DA prevails at yet another emotional hearing in which the former rebels produce countless witnesses who testify to their outstanding character and good lives. Bortin's bail is set a few days later at $500,000, after he's extradited from Oregon.

The court hears testimony about Montague's hard work raising money to fight AIDS and breast cancer. She has no kids of her own, but has done volunteer work with youth groups. In her professional life, she's been a vital resource for the entertainment industry, learning computer skills in classes she took in prison and going on to master arcane high-tech software used for movie and music producers.

Lois MacDonald, a registered nurse and longtime friend of Montague's who is also an air force reserve major and a member of the space shuttle recovery team, says Montague had confided in her about her past. She said she saw nothing to give her pause in the life of a dear friend whom she'd met thirteen years earlier playing in a woman's softball league.

"Emily is a very important person in my life," she wrote in a letter to the court. "When she had surgery eleven years ago, I was at her bedside. When my mother died ten years ago, [Emily] was a great comfort to me. And more recently, during a period when I was recovering from two major and traumatic surgeries, Emily was there, helping me recover both physically and emotionally. Emily is a faithful and generous friend."

Noreen Baca, Emily's longtime companion, also sent a letter to the court, as did several members of Baca's extended family: "Emily has taught me so many different things," Baca wrote. "Her character has impressed itself deeply upon me. I know Emily's heart. She is a woman of grace, integrity, and dignity."

It's hard to believe this is the same person who, according to Patty Hearst, shot Myrna Opsahl and then said afterward that it didn't matter because she was a "bourgeois pig."

Stephanie Brown, a legal receptionist and law-firm office manager who said she'd known Bill Harris for fifteen years, called him "a devoted family man and a wonderful dad."

Nancy Colman, a San Francisco attorney, wrote in a letter to the court: "For many years, Bill has been a responsible, law-abiding, and productive member of society. He has extremely strong ties to his family and to his community, both personally and professionally. For over a year and a half, Bill has been aware of the likelihood that charges would be brought against him in the Carmichael bank robbery case. Yet he has remained in his community, with his family, and he has stood ready to face this prosecution and defend himself against these charges."

In short, Yolanda and General Teko were buried long ago. For the past two decades, Bill Harris and Emily Montague have been exemplary citizens, the kind of people who make great neighbors.

The testimonials are impressive. Gold and Curry seem caught off-guard by the large number of upstanding citizens who vouch for the two accused murderers. But Gold, who does the talking for the district attorney at the bail hearing, is not swayed.

"Ironically," he tells the judge in what became the sound bite of the day, "the Harrises have become now the people they used to despise. Not long ago, these people would have been issued a death warrant for the people they have become."

Sacramento Superior Court Judge Tani Cantil-Sakauye says she has seen little evidence to believe the defendants are flight risks, but she agree to set the bail at $1 million, as the prosecution urged, rather than the $250,000 requested by Montague's lawyer and the $200,000 requested by Harris.

"While the case is twenty-seven years old," she tells a jammed courtroom, "the offense is very serious."

She's read all the letters that were submitted, the judge adds, and was impressed. "But while I was driving home I realized I could also be reading those letters about Myrna Opsahl, who at forty-two was gunned down in a bank."

Bortin enjoys the same kind of testimonials at his hearing. Friends speak of his extraordinary work ethic. How years of carpentry and floor installation and reconditioning had left him with a broken back that had to be repaired several times by surgery, two hip replacements, carpal tunnel syndrome, and chronic pain.

The most moving testimony comes from Rudy Nehrling, Bortin's twenty-two-year-old son by a woman he lived with before he met his current wife. The young man, a senior at New York University, loves his dad fiercely and tells the judge how he taught him to drive a stick shift and to recondition floors so he could make some money during summers off from college.

"While I was at school, he would call me every single week like clockwork and we would talk for hours on end," Bortin's son tells the judge. "He paid my child support to my mother consistently, never missing a payment for twelve years, and then he put me through college at New York University, where I will be graduating this spring."

"His energy and love is endless and inspiring," he says.

After spending about three weeks in the Sacramento County Jail, the three defendants are all freed when friends and family put up cash, property, and their homes to raise bail.

The Opsahl murder is a case now, with its own rhythm and timing. It may take several more years and many twists and turns before it gets to court. If a "simple robbery gone bad" like the Bread Store case took more than four years from charges to testimony, there's no telling how long it will be before the first witness is sworn in case Number 02F00525, *People of the State of California* v. *Emily Montague Harris; William Taylor Harris; Sara Jane Olson; Michael Alexander Bortin; and James William Kilgore.* It is a twenty-seven-year-old murder that probably should have been charged when it occurred. O'Mara and those before him were convinced the prosecution would have failed. That's why they never filed charges in the first place. Now O'Mara gets to sit back and watch, offering advice when asked, as two of his most capable prosecutors try to make their mark, maybe even get in line for eventual judgeships, by bringing in a guilty verdict and showing him up. There will be days, when they are collecting and sorting through evidence and witness lists about a crime that occurred while they were teenagers, that Mark Curry and Rob Gold will ask themselves why they ever agreed to take this on.

"Ya know," O'Mara says one day in his office, "it's a no-win situation for us no matter what happens in this case. If we win, people will just say, see, you should have done this a long time ago. If we lose, it's because we screwed it up. We're incompetent, like they've been saying all along."

21 | The Frosts

Rickie, your mother is going to be able to see you through bars for the rest of your life. Thank God she can still see her son, because I can't.

—Becky Frost

LIKE the other defendants in the Bread Store trial, James David Glica had a lousy childhood. His father, James Chavez-Glica, wasn't around very often in his son's life. He and J.D.'s mother divorced in 1985, when J.D. was six. When he was sixteen, his mother took him and his siblings to Arizona so she could get her son away from his gang associations in Sacramento. In March 1996, about nine months before he helped rob the Bread Store, J.D. moved back to Sacramento and stayed with his father until his arrest.

"The defendant characterized his formative years as rough, noting he had very little money," his probation report says. "His mother was always depressed and used methamphetamine, his older sister was suicidal, his father was gay, his best friend was shot, and he was always in fights."

A short, somewhat pudgy kid with a round face and piercing blue eyes, J.D. Glica was the mystery of the group. He'd sit in court with an impassive look on his face, as if the proceedings were about someone else, and would create elaborate and highly detailed pencil drawings of cars, motorcycles, animals—whatever popped into his imagination. At one point, his father said, he had a chance to get a scholarship to an art academy in San Francisco but kept getting in trouble instead. At eleven, he was arrested for arson. Soon after that, it was burglary. He stole cars and was found guilty of grand theft auto as a juvenile.

When he was a kid, he told a psychologist who examined him at the request of his defense attorney, he got into a lot of fights with kids who made fun of his dad being gay. Because he was small, he often came out on the losing end.

The psychologist, Shawn Johnston, the same expert who examined Justin Weinberger a week *after* he killed Courtney Sconce and said in his report that Weinberger would never actually harm another person, seemed to think Glica had been transformed since Jason Frost's murder.

"He is engaged in painful and self-punitive introspection regarding his life in general and his involvement in the instant offense in specific," Johnston wrote in a confidential report dated October 23, 2001. "It seems clear from James's statements that even in the face of an expected long-term prison sentence, he is trying to find a sense of meaning, if not actual salvation."

While reading the report and scribbling angry notations in the margin, Harrold was not surprised when he came to the punch line, since the report was prepared at Lippsmeyer's request: "In terms of sentencing alternatives available to the Court, the numerous and important mitigating factors described above may augur against the necessity of imposing the maximum possible punishment against him."

Though they both concede Glica has talent, is brighter than his co-defendants, and has some other redeeming qualities they can't seem to find in the others, neither Harrold nor Bladet feels terribly sympathetic about the kid.

As far as the two prosecutors are concerned, Glica and Martinez have already been shown leniency by the jury, when it didn't find for the special. They do sit quietly and listen as Glica's father talks about his son and begs the court for mercy and understanding.

"You know, I look at my son, twenty-two years old, and I think back to years ago when these mistakes were made, and to me, as horrific . . . I cannot imagine anything worse than the Frosts' loss. There is nothing worse in my mind than what they have experienced, and yet there's so much more that defines my son, to me, the father.

"You know, J.D. was famous when he was growing up for never being able to tell an untruth. Well, he tried sometimes, I will tell you, he tried.

It was big neon on his forehead because there was a—there was a grain of integrity, a truth about that child when he was growing up that was inherent, innate in his being.

"He had just been commissioned by the American Legion High School. He had just been invited to do a mural for the school. He was attending regularly, which was great. His grades were improving. He worked with me at the Sacramento Opera Association. I was so proud of that. I was managing director and he was invited by the general director to come and do some of the artwork for the set. I was so proud of him. So these are the things that probably were never spoken in court. I don't know.

"J.D. didn't want me here. I wanted to be here. He didn't want me to see and hear everything that was going on. That's the kind of people I guess we are, and as many mistakes as we make, and sometimes we do, we take responsibility for them, and we stand on our own two feet about them.

"J.D. is no different. That is the way he was reared. I am not always proud of J.D.'s actions, it's true. I am his father and that's my prerogative, but I am proud of my son, and I stand before you to tell you that I am proud of my son.

"I say these things being mindful in my daily prayers and my thoughts of the Frost family. Every day I think of you.

"I look into my daughter, Rita's, eyes, and I see her grief. I look into my ex-wife's eyes, J.D.'s mother's eyes, and I see her grief and sadness.

"He is more than this moment. He is more than this act. He is a whole human being who has so many good qualities and has made a mistake. I don't know what it is your option to do. And I don't even know what I have a right to ask. But to me, justice is seeing things as they are and responding accordingly, and I know that is what you will do."

Almost everyone in the courtroom, save the judge, perhaps, is teary eyed. Bladet maintains her composure. She has a job to do. She must now jump into the emotion of the moment and unleash her own cold argument that says: Don't be fooled. He doesn't deserve nearly as much empathy as his father would have us believe.

Her heart is only half in it because she, too, has seen a glimmer of humanity in young Mr. Glica. She has a job to do. Who knows, after all, how the judge will react if Bladet doesn't argue against a reduced sentence? What if he surprised everyone and cut Glica an even bigger break than the jury already has? How would that look in a high-profile murder case?

348 / THE PROSECUTORS

"This is someone who is above-average intelligence," Bladet says. "This was not a stupid kid. Dr. Johnston observes he has a tendency to disregard and even disdain social norms and has adopted an arrogant attitude. His interpersonal relationships are likely to be strained, competitive, and maladaptive.

"When he gets bored, he likes to stir up some excitement and is seen by others as hotheaded and has very few fears. He often exercises poor judgment. He believes he's being punished without cause.

"Throughout the report, what struck me was the description of exactly who the criminal system deals with. Not a promising good young kid who made a bad decision on one day, as Mr. Lippsmeyer says. This is a kid who at eleven years old had his first arrest, who continued engaging in criminal conduct, who got involved in a gang, who was selling drugs to make money, who decided on this day it would be a good idea to engage with other people in a violent robbery where somebody was killed. This is not just a bad decision on a single day. This is a course of conduct that is indicative of the type of character that this individual possessed.

"The ability that Mr. Lippsmeyer talked about, and that Defendant Glica's father discussed, about his ability to grow and change in the last four years—it's so frustrating to hear that transition and that change being utilized as a basis to somehow grant leniency or to mitigate a defendant's conduct that he somehow changes when he's been locked up and incarcerated for a length of time.

"The opportunity to change and grow and become a better person was taken away from Jason Frost. He hasn't had that opportunity in the last four and a half, five years. His family hasn't had an opportunity to see the kind of changes and the kind of man that he would become. And the only reason that happened is because this defendant actively and violently engaged with his coconspirators to commit this robbery.

"This was not a kid making a bad call. This was a criminal defendant with a history consistent with criminal defendants we see in this courthouse every day, who made a decision to participate in a violent crime that caused the death of another human being. And I don't think there is any basis to give him leniency or to reduce the jury's findings in this case."

It is the judge's turn once again. His brow is furrowed, his mouth turned down into a frown.

"I think Mr. Glica, the father, spoke very eloquently about his son and very moving as well," he begins. "In this particular case, James David Glica was actually looking at the potential of a sentence of life without the possibility of parole.

"The jury saw fit to find the special-circumstance allegation was not true. With all due respect to the jury, I don't understand exactly how that could have occurred under the circumstances and the evidence that was presented. But that is irrelevant, that is, the fact that the jury found it to be not true. So Mr. Glica is therefore no longer looking at the possible sentence of life without the possibility of parole. The system worked to that extent, and I think that must be credited to your ability as a defense attorney, Mr. Lippsmeyer, at some point to get to that point."

Glica was a major participant in the robbery, holding someone down, kicking an employee, which made it easier for Brewer to menace and shoot Jason Frost. As for his relatively young age at the time of the crime, England says he may have been only seventeen but his "street age" at the time was more like twenty-seven. His life had been filled with crime up to that point. He was on probation for a savage beating of a man in Davis for no other reason than the man asked him a question about a party.

The judge has seen the accomplished drawings. He knows the young man has talent and intelligence.

"That talent has been wasted," he says, "and it's been utilized for not the good that it could be. This is a very sad day to have to do what I am going to have to do, but I think that the Legislature has made it clear what the punishment is."

Twenty-five years for the felony murder. Ten for the other crimes, with three of those suspended. Thirty-two years total for J. D. Glica.

"As I sit here this morning, listening to the really eloquent speech given by James Glica's father, it had an impact," Jack Frost says when he's sitting on the witness stand and is allowed to speak. "But you know what, Mr. Glica? My son's death had a hell of an impact on me and my wife and my family and we can never have him back.

"If anything in your life means anything to you or your family, I hope that at some point you understand the severity and total disregard for life that you were involved with when my son was taken from this earth in no small part due to your actions also. I understand that you're still alive and your family is suffering, but they have the recourse of being able to visit you and perhaps at some point in your life you will realize that you're still living, and God have mercy on your soul."

Becky Frost cannot count the times she's driven down from her home in Grass Valley, an idyllic little town in the foothills of the Sierra Nevada, a town on the way to Lake Tahoe and ski country, where tourists stop for the quaint streets and Victorian architecture, so she can sit in the same room as four young men the state of California has deemed responsible for the murder of her boy. She, too, has seen the humanity in James David Glica, but there's no way for her to focus on that now. She feels too much pain to see anything else, and of all the people who address the court, it's her words and her presence on that witness stand as a grieving, heart-broken mother that get to Glica. As she speaks, his eyes shed tears she believes are real. She cries, too, at the sound of her own words.

"J.D.," she says, as if he were her own, "you were a part of it. You made that decision. You laughed and joked about it. You wore a mask. You copped the attitude that you could accomplish what you wanted to accomplish. You had to have that kind of arrogance about you to know that you didn't care about life—all because of money.

"I hope you have an opportunity in prison to do the best you can, and if your lawyer claims that that is a possibility, I hope it will happen. But you still took my son's life. It's true you didn't pull the trigger, but you agreed, all of you agreed, and planned it, wore the masks, took a gun, and shot my son. And the court's decision is just, whatever it may be."

Not by Lippsmeyer, it isn't. He's over at the Indigent Defense Panel offices a few minutes after the sentencing and still livid, unmoved by the compliment England paid him for getting his client twenty-five to life on the homicide instead of life without parole.

"Morrison is full of shit," he says. "Adding seven years to that kid's sentence is adding insult to injury. Our criminal justice system is our criminal system. There ain't no justice here. This is a seventeen-year-old's bad decision. In some respects, there's a pattern if you put together the juvenile actions. But life in prison? Come on."

A long trial not only wears down everyone who participates it. Lawyers on both sides find it nearly impossible to stay tightly focused on the proceeding all the way through. By the time Rickie Martinez is to be sentenced, both prosecutors have other things on their minds.

Harrold just got a phone call from Emily, his oldest daughter, who's twenty-four and lives in New York. She's a public affairs coordinator for the Lifetime cable TV network and has received the station's Lifetime Ace Award for her extraordinary efforts in the aftermath of September 11. She organized the volunteer activities of 150 station employees, and as her nomination for the award says: "Emily has taken the lead on the 9-11 Volunteer Project and she has consistently displayed nothing but grace, professionalism, and smarts in all aspects of her work."

His other daughter, Adrienne, twenty-one, is about to leave for Paris for a semester of study at the Sorbonne. Harrold is mad about both of them and has plans to travel to Kenya and go mountain climbing with Adrienne when she graduates from the University of California at Berkeley, his alma mater. For much of their childhoods he was so wrapped up at work and managing his career that he missed a lot, but it's hard to imagine a father who is closer to his daughters now that they've left home.

Bladet is irritated with the judge, whom she adores and admires. She's throwing a big Christmas party the night of Friday December 14 and he's told her he doesn't think it's appropriate for him to be there, especially while the trial is just wrapping up. She understands, but when she talks to him after this morning's session, she's as relentless in his chambers on the subject of his coming to her party as she's been every step of the way in court or with Harrold. The word *no* is not something she's accustomed to hearing.

When Judge England convenes judgment and sentencing for Martinez, Karowsky has finally surrendered to the inevitable. "Candidly," he tells the judge, "the most I think I can do for the young man today is correct the probation report, because that is going to follow him throughout the system." He wants the reference to Martinez saying he has no remorse stricken from the report. It's out of context, Karowsky maintains, and doesn't reflect Martinez's true feelings. If a parole board years from now reads it in his report, it will be held against him. It's unfair, his lawyer says.

"He said it. It's accurate. It's what happened," Bladet shoots back. She's not about to let up now.

It sounds cold-hearted, Karowsky says.

It was cold-hearted, Bladet counters. Callous too. He said it.

The judge saw the video along with the jury. He has no doubts the comment reflected Martinez's feelings at the time. "He was a defiant, cocky young man who felt he had done his job in keeping the detective from getting to the truth of what had occurred," the judge says. "I don't see how the court can strike those words when they came in as evidence."

Like the other defense lawyers, Karowsky wants the judge to reduce Martinez's sentence. He makes the same argument as Lippsmeyer, that twenty-five to life is too much for a kid who didn't pull the trigger. England doesn't agree; he gives Martinez the same thirty-two years as Glica.

Tonya Marie Cano, Martinez's sister, reads a letter she wrote that sounds like a script from one of those daytime talk shows on TV that highlight depraved, dysfunctional families. With her mother seated next to her, she talks about her mother's drug binges, the bad men in her life, years of physical abuse heaped on Rickie. When they were little, Tonya says, "My mom would have parties just about every night. There would be kegs outside, people smoking marijuana and smoking cigarettes. People making out.

"I love my mother to death, as well does Rickie, but the parenting she did while we were very young had a very big impact on my brother's life now."

She goes on to read a bizarre poem that might be considered a bad joke if not for the real people and feelings involved. Harrold and Bladet sit stone-faced through it all. Prosecutors quickly lose the ability to be taken aback by people's actions, and these two stopped being shocked by human behavior a long time ago.

"Dear God. Please give my brother one more chance at life for he is only twenty years old," Rickie's sister begins.

"Can't you see I'm pleading to you, now before it's too late, please don't make this mistake of making him a ward of the state. With this I leave you now to make a decision that can determine the well-being of a young man's life. Please remember he has a wife and family. Think of them and how they will be if the head of the household is not returned shortly."

I've heard it all, Harrold tells himself. Head of the household, my ass. Shit, he married the woman after he was in jail.

How does Becky Frost continue to do this? Harrold is wondering as she gets up to talk to another defendant.

"Rickie," Becky says, crying again even though she's becoming an old hand at this, "I've met your family. In the past year, your family and my family have shared something. I'm so confused, with the love and support your family has for you, that you chose the path you went on. I can't understand that.

"Rickie, your mother is going to be able to see you through bars for the rest of your life. Thank God she can still see her son, because I can't."

Becky is spent. As she walks back to her seat, Rickie's mother, who sat through most of the trial and has just heard the judge sentence her son to thirty-two years in prison, rises and embraces Becky Frost. Watching the two women hug and hold on to one another in the middle of the courtroom sends shivers of emotion down Bladet's spine. She has a stricken look on her face. It's exhausting to be assaulted by such emotion day in, day out. Thank God, she's thinking, this is finally just about over. It never seems to let up in this case.

Jack Frost's anger is boiling over, still, as he takes the witness stand and says to Rickie, "Unfortunately, you're still living. Our lineage has stopped. Based on what I've sat and listened to in this courtroom for the last five years, I feel you have received a just sentence."

The Frosts have no doubt in their mind that if it weren't for Rick Brewer and his miserable, angry life, their son would be alive today. Brewer has been portrayed throughout the trial as the devil who planned and organized this crime, so there's more than the usual interest on the day of his sentencing. Judge Morrison England's courtroom seems more full than it has been all year. Three bailiffs. Three district attorney investigators. The Frost family. Several of their friends. A vase of flowers sits on Judge England's desk: daisies, dahlias, chrysanthemums. He buys them every Wednesday at the farmers market across from City Hall to add some beauty to this grim chamber. The buzz of conversation stops abruptly when Brewer waddles in fully chained and is seated at the defense table next to his attorney.

The first order of business is Repkow's motion for a new trial. Unlike the other attorneys, she's arguing the trial has been flawed. She cites six rulings made by England that denied her client a fair trial. Harrold and Bladet knew this was coming, but still it annoys them. Repkow's doing her job, but she's lost all credibility. It doesn't matter, though. They expect England to treat her motion with the lack of dignity they believe it deserves.

England mistakenly refused to sever Brewer from the rest of the defendants, which caused him harm and prejudice because the other defense attorneys clearly had different legal strategies than she did, Rep-kow argues. Testimony about Brewer's threat to a social worker about the taking of his kids, about the first robbery and his sister's involve-ment in it, about Brewer's abusive relationship with Marichu Flores, the introduction of Dixon's letters, allowing the jury to view coroner au-topsy photos of Jason Frost—these all added up to deny Brewer a fair trial. She wanted the gun kept out as evidence, too, because, she says, police obtained it without a search warrant.

Brewer was denied a fair trial because Harrold was not objective, she continues. She reminds the judge that Harrold and the Frosts have dinner every year around the time of their son's death. This is "not worthy of crit-icism" on a human level, she says, but as a prosecutor it proves Harrold was not able to be fair and objective. And Harrold called Brewer an asshole dur-ing the trial and openly glared at him in the presence of jurors.

Bladet's written answer to the motion takes exception to each Rep-kow point and concludes by saying that even if she were right, the evi-dence against Brewer was so overwhelming that none of it mattered. The trial results would have been the same no matter how the judge ruled on her various objections. As for the "asshole" comment, Bladet wrote that "the People defy defendant to demonstrate any portion in this case which reflects Mr. Harrold calling defendant an 'asshole.' Although this colorful description of defendant might be fitting, it was never ex-pressed in front of the jury, in open court, or otherwise." The idea that Harrold is guilty of glaring, Bladet argues, is "just plain ridiculous and responding to it is pointless."

Repkow wants a private hearing with the judge to discuss her ongo-ing complaints that her rights to privately communicate with Brewer at the jail have been violated. She's been forced to talk to him through a no-pass, glass window, where inmates received social visitors as well, after the jail clamped down on her access following her various shenani-gans with Fred Clark. He's discussed this with her many times, England says, and nothing has changed. He's not about to interrupt the sentenc-ing to meet again in private.

"Motion for new trial is denied," he says, "and that's denied on all counts and with respect specifically to those issues where the Court has exercised its discretion."

Becky Frost trudges again to the witness stand to speak, this time to the man who pulled the trigger and brutally murdered her son. She needs no Kleenex. She is stronger now, anxious to make this speech.

"This is the second worst thing that I have ever done in my life," she says to Brewer, who refuses to even glance in her direction. "The first one was burying my son.

"You have put me into a world that I never knew or wanted to know. I have learned what bitterness is about, what hatred is about, untrust, no care or concern for people, and it's a horrible, dark world.

"It's where people like you with no soul and a dark heart belong, and I wish that no one would ever go."

The room is rapt, silent. Judge England's face is fixed in a long frown. Harrold and Bladet are fighting back tears. Even Brewer will notice this next comment and turn his head for a brief moment to look in Becky's direction.

"You're not ever going to know how I feel unless one of your children at the age of twenty-three gets shot down cold, one of your own children." She got to him, Harrold's thinking.

"Jason was a very positive person. He always had the better side of life to look at. You have put a hole in my heart that will never heal and I have to bear the pain for the rest of my life. My son will never see a sunset or walk on the beach or hold his own child, and I hope you never will too. And I hope the court sentences you to the maximum. You probably won't ever understand this or care, but at least I got to share it, what I feel."

Jack Frost follows his wife to the witness stand and warms himself up by saying, "Richard Brewer is the name that I have grown to detest. Five years ago, I had a vibrant, loving, growing son who was ready to make his way in the world, and thanks to you, Mr. Brewer, that is no longer a possibility. I wish you all the best in your future misery."

Jason's sister, Shauna, who's so close to giving birth to her second baby, it looks as if she might do it right here in court, rarely came to the trial. It was too much for her to bear. But today is too much of a high-water mark to miss.

She and Jason were very close. It infuriates her that neither of her children will get to enjoy the young man who would have been their sweet, goofy, warm uncle Jason. She said she was so devastated by her brother's murder that she lost her memory for six months after Jason's death.

"Still to this day I often feel lost and alone and wanting so badly to talk to Jason, but I will never hear his voice respond or see him make a silly face just to make me smile."

It feels as if the air has been sucked from the room. Everyone in it seems to have tears in their eyes: the bailiffs, the court reporter, everyone in the audience. The judge isn't crying, but he appears to be drowning in all this grief. These rooms have heard countless tragic stories over the years, but there's little to compare with the emotional release that comes after a long, tension-filled murder trial when the family of the victim finally speaks. None of the people in the courtroom are able to hide the effect this is having on them.

"Megan Gould would like to address the court," Bladet says while she composes herself.

This is Jason's girlfriend. Bright, adorable, still quick to smile after all she's been through. If Richard Brewer hadn't crossed paths with her boyfriend, or maybe if he'd gotten to the store ten minutes earlier, when the money was still in the registers, she'd be married to Jason now instead of taking the witness stand in a courtroom to confront his killer eye to eye.

"My life just stopped there and froze in time for so long," she says. "The ten days that he was in the hospital, I don't know how many bargains with God I did. 'I will never do this again. Just don't let him die.'

"But, um, you know, he did die, and it was terrible coming home after all of this, to a decorated house for Christmas, my Christmas tree still up and lit and all of our unopened presents underneath the tree to each other. It was terrible." For an instant, she's transported back to that moment and she walks unsteadily back to her seat.

Do the People have anything to add? the judge asks the prosecutors.

"At the time Jason Frost was killed, he was trapped, he posed no threat to the defendant or any of his co-defendants," Bladet says. "The killing was just simply cruel and pointless and incredibly brazen. . . .

"He fired those shots at Jason Frost at incredibly close range . . . and the type of weapon he used was so incredibly destructive just in its nature, that one shot could have easily and may very well have killed Jason or any other human who came in contact with a gunshot wound from that gun.

"Yet in that close location, with no threat posed to him, this man shot

Jason Frost three times after, as one of the witnesses described, his sweater opened up. I mean, after the visible results of the first shot could be seen and appreciated by any human being, he still chose to fire two more times, one of those while Jason is on the ground bleeding, in his buttocks.

"That alone, the nature, the location, the number of those wounds, is just a demonstration of the kind of depraved and violent character this person has, character which in all other respects is entirely lacking. And the cruelty and the manner that Jason Frost suffered before he died, no human being should ever have to endure."

When it's Repkow's turn to speak, she says the killing occurred "in the heat of passion, in the heat of anger." The murder was not planned or anticipated, she says, and she asks the judge to make concurrent any other sentences he might impose on top of the one for murder.

"It seems to me that the ultimate sentence which the Court is contemplating, which is life without the possibility of parole, is, I mean, it sounds ridiculous for me to say that it's sufficient, but I think it would be inappropriate for the Court to impose on top of that a ten-year sentence. To enhance the sentence for the use of the gun would be really in violation of the eighth amendment and is really a matter of dual use of facts."

England is not persuaded by her argument. He sentences Brewer to life without parole for the homicide, adds the ten Repkow just asked not be added for use of the gun; tacks on five for the robbery and four more for using a gun in that count, and another ten for the rest of the counts. Total sentence, on top of the life term: twenty-five years.

"As a judge," England begins his sermon, "you give thought to a lot of different things. You hear stories about people saying that 'if I were in a position of being an executioner or the person making the decision, I know what I would do.'

"Those types of statements are really taken in the abstract, because no one knows what it's like to in essence sentence a human being to die in prison. To that end, I have given a great deal of thought and consideration to the sentence I am going to impose today.

"The decisions that I have worked on and have thought about over the last few weeks have not been made lightly. I want to make it very clear to you, Mr. Brewer, and to everyone here, this is something that causes one to lose sleep over any time that you're put in this position.

"But in going through the thought process, as a parent, it somehow put things in perspective. And you, Mr. Brewer, are a parent. You have three children.

"It's hard for me to even comprehend a thought of my child being placed in a position where he or she were trapped and no place to go, and more than likely begging for his or her life, and have all three sides covered by either walls or counters, and having you standing on the fourth side with a sawed-off twelve-gauge Mossberg shotgun as you racked one shell apparently for—maybe for fear purposes, to show that you meant business, and then realizing that you weren't getting what you wanted, to then fire once into the abdomen of the victim, watch the clothing, flesh probably explode, rack it one more time and fire a second shot into that person, again flesh, clothing everywhere. Possibly even on you, you were so close.

"Then to have the person on the ground and think of it as your child. And to think of the cold, callous heart that it takes to then take that shotgun and place it on the buttocks and fire a third time to the extent that the wadding from the shotgun shell actually imbeds in the flesh.

"Ms. Repkow indicated that she felt that this was not a premeditated killing but the intent was to commit a robbery. I disagree. There may have been an intent when you entered that store to commit a robbery, but once you realized that it was not going to go on the way that you had originally planned, you went on your own and decided to show Jason Frost how really angry you were.

"I don't know why you were so angry. I realize from Probation that there had been drugs, alcohol, in your past. There may have been family issues that you were dealing with, and I guess somehow all of that justified your taking the life of another human being.

"Well, in going through this thought process to decide how and what I should do with respect to your sentence, once you go through these thoughts and you think about what the victim went through, what the family and the friends have gone through, and continue to go through, and what risk you pose to the citizens of this county and this state, or anywhere that you may run, if I could say it at all, it makes this job a little bit more easy.

"I have watched as these people spoke to the Court and to you. You did not look at one of them. I don't know, maybe you can't look at them.

Well, I am looking at you, and I am telling you, that what you have done is shown nothing except that you are the most evil person I can comprehend. There is no justification for what you have done. No way, no how, and at no time."

With that, explaining how he's denying Repkow's request to make any of the sentences concurrent, England said he's using the maximum penalty on each count so any appellate court "understands the depth and the feeling that this Court has put into making the decision that it should be upper term. In other words, I have done everything that I possibly can to give you the maximum possible confinement."

It's not the death penalty, Harrold and Bladet are thinking, but it's not bad. They respect this judge, who's just articulated everything they have worked for in the case and all that they stand for as prosecutors. Why they go to court to try murder cases and aren't at some private firm drawing much larger salaries, never connecting in this way with people like the Frosts. They want to stand up and cheer for Judge Morrison England, Jr.

Outside in the courthouse hallway, by the elevators, Harrold and Bladet take turns hugging Jack and Becky Frost. Steve and Becky have shared a little joke throughout the trial. They will embrace, holding each other tight, while Harrold provides a running commentary on the quality of the hug. "That's it. That's good. Yeah, that gets it," he says. As they leave each other's grasp, it is impossible to tell who needs and gets more from the show of affection, prosecutor or the mother of the victim. When they part this afternoon, it's with a promise to get together soon for lunch or dinner, as Harrold has done this time of year every year since Jason Frost was mortally wounded two days before Christmas in 1996.

22 | Epilogue: The Sacramento District Attorney

Does the system actually work? Apparently, not to anybody's satisfaction.

—Lawrence M. Friedman, *Crime and Punishment in American History*

BY the time 2001 has ended, John O'Mara is restless. He's shaved his bushy mustache. The shaggy hair with streaks of gray around the temples is a little shorter than usual. The cherry-red Corvette convertible he bought late in the summer sits in the garage at his house south of town. Occasionally, he'll rev it up for a long drive to the coast, but most of his weekends are spent alone, tending to the animals and his property.

He's bored being in the office so much. For the first time in quite a while, he's actively trolling for a case of his own. He almost takes on the murder of a twelve-year-old boy who lived in North Carolina but was spending the summer in Sacramento with his estranged father, who beat him to death while the child was in his custody. He spent a few days reviewing the evidence and thought the mother was responsible, too, but he assigned it to one of his deputies after charging both parents with murder. It wasn't unusual enough to pique his interest.

For the men and women who prosecute criminals in the Sacramento District Attorney's Office for a living, 2001 ended on a relatively high note. The calendar is everything to a trial lawyer. Always trying to get into court, to find an available judge, mesh your available time with the defense lawyer, schedule motions, subpoena witnesses, and keep the cases moving. You are a captive to everyone else's schedule. At the same time, though, the calendar is arbitrary and meaningless. Holidays are noted with a day off, of course, but the end and beginning of weeks, months, and even years have little distinction. You finish a case, you start another. You finish a year, a new one begins. The crimes and the cases never let up. The crime rate can go up or down, but the trial attorney in a prosecutor's office is never without work.

It takes a certain temperament to become a prosecutor and spend so much time in the dark shadows of humanity. To be around rapists, killers, child abusers, thieves, and con men. To read autopsy reports and study murder-scene photos while eating a sandwich. To spend all that time with victims, to be suffused with so much loss, pain, and devastation. To spend day after day in trial, arguing, engaging in legal combat. Selling your case and yourself to twelve ordinary people you've never met before who will determine whether you succeed or fail.

Yet there are extraordinary rewards. For most of us, when we read of another brutal crime in the newspaper or hear a tearful family member fall apart on the evening news because a loved one was taken from them, we may feel sadness and great outrage, but there is nothing we can do about it. For a prosecutor whose job begins when he hears about a murder committed in his community, it's possible to turn outrage into action. He can make someone pay for that attack "against the peace and dignity" of the people in his community. He or she can repair some of the damage done by a violent crime. The prosecutor can restore a community's sense of security by taking strong and permanent action against someone who took that peace and destroyed it for his own perverse reasons.

The Bread Store case came out, for the most part, the way it was supposed to. Trevor Garcia, the main prosecution witness and snitch in the case, was serving his time without incident in the protective-custody wing of one of the state's largest penitentiaries. When Harrold went to see how he was doing late in the summer of 2002, Garcia was excited because he had just gotten a television set for his cell. Harrold was his first visitor, and Garcia was biding his time toward a 2006 release date. He told the prosecutor he was going to live in the Bay Area and stay the hell out of Sacramento. The other defendants, all of whom filed appeals for new trials, were serving their sentences uneventfully. "He's a good guy," Harrold said after his visit with Garcia. "I like him. He's gonna be okay."

There was no news about Carlos Cervantes or any of the other Southside Park witnesses. Whatever they were doing, it was being done

outside the purview of the cops and the DA, at least for the time being.
Bobby Dixon was serving his time and wearing a snitch jacket, too, even
though he had never testified in the case. Harrold considered it just a
matter of time before Brewer, who was housed in one of the state's maximum security prisons, figured out a way to get back at him for ratting
him out to the cops.

With the case behind him, Harrold took some time off to see his
daughters—a week in France with Adrienne, a few days in New York to
be with Emily during the September 11 anniversary commemoration.
Like O'Mara, the chief of the Gangs unit also bought a fancy new sports
car, a black two-door Thunderbird that set him back $53,000. And at
the end of 2002, after running the Gangs unit for twenty years, Harrold
was transferred by Scully and Besemer to the Career Criminal team,
where prosecutors go after three-strikes cases and there is very little of
the action or prestige that attaches to the Gangs job. If he was hurt or
disappointed by the move, he didn't let on and at a party commemorat-
ing his time in Gangs, more than seventy-five people showed up—the
city council and board of supervisors passed on praise—and thanked
Harrold for making the capital city's streets at least a little safer. "There
are a whole lot of gangsters who are going to sleep easier tonight," an assistant Sacramento police chief told Harrold at the party, "because they
know they won't have to be dealing with you no more."

Harrold's partner, Dawn Bladet, ran her first marathon down in San
Diego and then had her gall bladder removed shortly after waking up
one morning in excruciating pain. After four weeks of trying to rest at
home, she was back prosecuting gangbangers, expecting to move up to
Major Crimes in the not-too-distant future. After she and one of the jurors in the Bread Store case exchanged several flattering e-mails toward
the end of 2002, they got together and actually went out on a few dates
but the relationship didn't seem to go anywhere. In early 2003, when an
opening came up in Sex Crimes, she took it.

Her nemesis, Karol Repkow, took time off to donate one of her
kidneys to her sister, who needed it to survive. An article about some
of Repkow's professional problems finally surfaced in The Sacramento
Bee during Fred Clark's trial for murder, but it just scratched the surface. She got herself appointed to the Indigent Defense Panel, so she
could be assigned cases again, and she was in court making eyes at Clark

during much of his trial. A jury convicted him of first-degree murder, but voted against the death penalty. He was sentenced to life without parole instead.

Steve Grippi took Art Lane, the video killer, to court late in the summer of 2002. After an unsuccessful attempt by the defense to argue that Lane was trying to assist his girlfriend in committing suicide, a jury watched the video and had little trouble convicting Lane of first-degree murder. They also went for the special circumstance of lying-in-wait, so O'Mara got what he wanted out of the case: Lane would be locked up forever, with no chance at parole.

Another relatively easy one for the district attorney's office was Frank Meyer's case against Ryan Kanawyer, the kid who shotgunned his grandparents to death because they refused to keep feeding his drug habit with cash. Eric Newsom, a buddy who police detectives said supplied the shotgun, was eventually charged with second-degree murder, as O'Mara insisted he be; Newsom pleaded guilty before trial and was sentenced to fifteen years to life. A girl and another guy who were in the car—two more O'Mara wanted to charge—were never filed on. Craig Hill insisted that no matter what O'Mara's instincts might have told him, there was no evidence the two others in the car had any knowledge of or involvement in the crime. Just because they were in the car and may have seen Kanawyer get out and retrieve a shotgun from the trunk before going into his grandparents' house, was enough for O'Mara. It wasn't enough for the detectives. Once again, they saw a case differently.

Justin Weinberger, Courtney Sconce's killer, was quietly serving his ten-year federal sentence at the United States penitentiary in Beaumont, Texas. By the end of the summer of 2002, a spokeswoman for the prison said he had had no incidents, but she cautioned that this was no country club. A sexual predator like Weinberger, she said, would have a tough time in such a place. There are thirteen hundred inmates at Beaumont and more than half of them are serving life sentences, so there were plenty of convicts around with nothing to lose. Weinberger refused a number of requests to be interviewed by various members of the news media, including one from a *Los Angeles Times* writer who featured the killer in a cover story in the Sunday *Times* magazine with the headline "Murder Just Because." After serving his federal time, he would be transferred to the California Department of Corrections to spend the rest of his life in a state prison.

"His crime was particularly disturbing because he killed just two days after the FBI came to his home and seized his child-pornography collection," reporter Tim Reiterman, wrote. "FBI officials say it may be the first time that a child-porn search prompted such a tragedy, and the murder left veteran agents agonizing over their handling of the case and wondering how they might better predict when a suspect will act on his impulses. This shy son of a state prosecutor did not seem to fit the stereotype of a pedophile, let alone a rapist and murderer."

With the Tison child murder case set for trial in April 2002, Curry felt he had no choice but to pull out, and it didn't have the best possible outcome as far as the district attorney's office was concerned.

In the end, sloppy police work hurt the prosecution. Because the crime scene was not thoroughly inspected the night of the fall—no search for additional blood was conducted, measurements weren't taken, the house was never treated like a crime scene—Don Heller, Tison's lawyer, was able to sow doubt in the jurors' minds about a number of elements in the case.

The former prosecutor turned out to be far more effective in trial than anyone at the district attorney's office would have expected. His expert medical witnesses were able to discredit the prosecution's notion that Isabel had multiple injuries inconsistent with a simple fall because hospital records didn't support this conclusion. In the end, the jury came back and determined Tison was guilty of voluntary manslaughter, not homicide or child assault resulting in death. Curry and Mike Savage, the prosecutor who wound up trying the case, spent weeks anguishing about the result, and the judge sentenced Tison to six years in prison, a far cry from the twenty-five years to life the district attorney's office was seeking.

Once again, O'Mara had a contrary opinion. He felt quite comfortable with the verdict and sentence. "It was a righteous outcome, given the circumstances," he said. "Anytime you can't suggest to the jury, not just by way of your own theory but also by the evidence, exactly what happened, and you have a defendant who doesn't look like a killer, it's going to be tough. But someone like Tison, a doctor, is going to get a big benefit of the doubt. He lost his kid. He has to live with that and he's getting six years. The judge clearly had sympathy. He saw the incident as just one of those things that happen. I can't complain about what he did."

Curry and Rob Gold spent the first half of 2002 consumed with the SLA case, reviewing hundreds of boxes of evidence, locating witnesses, trying to make sure there were no surprises that would be uncovered at the last minute to embarrass the office. Both prosecutors believed if they could get Patty Hearst on the stand, they'd win. If they got to that point, the SLA case figured to be one of the state's great show trials, a media circus in which the billionaire newspaper heiress was the star prosecution witness against her old captors and tormentors from another generation.

By the end of the summer, however, prosecutors and defense lawyers were quietly discussing a possible settlement. The defendants would all plead guilty and admit their roles in the robbery and murder in open court in exchange for leniency. Kilgore, the last remaining SLA fugitive, would also surrender and be included in the guilty pleas.

Jon Opsahl, who had been anxiously awaiting the day his mother's suspected killers would finally go to trial, was a key to the negotiations moving forward. He'd been quiet of late, with no more sniping at the Sacramento County District Attorney's Office for what he saw as its past failings. He was no doubt distracted by his own legal problems. Alleging that he had dispensed large amounts of antibiotics, antidepressants and narcotic painkillers over the Internet without following a new state law that said patients must first receive a "good-faith examination," the Medical Board of California suspended his license in April of 2002. It was the first such case in California, and the administrative law judge who ordered the action wrote this of the man who'd been such a thorn in the side of the district attorney's office: "Respondent's belief that talking over the phone with patients satisfied the requirement of a good-faith examination is profoundly disturbing and demonstrates a combination of incredible arrogance and a woeful lack of judgment." In early 2003, his license was taken away permanently, despite Opsahl's lawyer's claim that the reopening of his mother's murder case had caused him to be less careful than he should have been.

If the family was okay with it, Scully and O'Mara were willing to settle for something they considered reasonable. Curry and Gold were anxious to try what would undoubtedly be the biggest cases of their careers, but they also realized settling made a great deal of sense. Negotiations continued off and on for several months and finally, on November 7, 2002, an extraordinary session was held in the Sacramento Superior

Court that virtually brought a close to the twenty-seven-year-old case. Defendants Harris, Montague, Olson, and Bortin all stood up, with the Opsahl family in the courtroom, and admitted guilt for the slaying of Myrna Opsahl. "I take full responsibility for her death," Emily Montague said, breaking into tears as she spoke. "I was horrified at the time and am still devastated to this day. There has not been a day in the last twenty-seven years that I have not thought of Mrs. Opsahl and the tragedy that I brought to her family."

Agreeing to a provision insisted upon by the Opsahl family, Judge Thomas M. Cecil said from the bench that part of the negotiated settlement precluded any of the defendants from ever profiting from the case through books, movie deals, or other arrangements. Kilgore, who had been living and teaching under an assumed name in South Africa, would turn himself in and waive extradition so he, too, could plead guilty. By admitting their guilt and thereby avoiding a trial that Scully's office had estimated would have cost Sacramento County at least $4 million to stage, the defendants agreed to serve what would amount to about three and a half years in prison for the murder. "We've always wanted the truth to be known," Jon Opsahl said at a press conference after the court session. "That's what this case has always been about."

Scully, citing problems with evidence and other difficulties in trying to win such an old case, told reporters that accepting a plea deal was "a very difficult decision for me." But, she added, "There comes a time when a wrong, albeit an old one, has to be addressed."

Silent in all this, of course, was O'Mara. He didn't come to the press conference and he didn't take phone calls from reporters. He didn't want to talk about whether he felt vindicated or somehow off the hook at how things finally worked out. He didn't want to say anything at all, particularly since part of the plea agreement gave defendants the right to withdraw their pleas and actually go to trial if the state Board of Prison Terms, which reviews sentences handed down under laws that were in effect as far back as the Opsahl murder, later decided to tack years on to the penalties negotiated between the district attorney, the defendants, and Judge Cecil.

Though pleased that there was no public outcry attacking the settlement and that the Opsahls gave the deal their blessing, O'Mara knew it was an imperfect solution. "I have no problem with it at all," he said during an interview in his office. "It's a reasonable conclusion at this point. It's not justice. Someone was murdered and when that happens most people think the people responsible should pay with their life or spend the rest of their lives in prison. I still think Patty Hearst would have been a difficult witness for us to manage and given everything that has happened, this makes a great deal of sense. These things rarely work out exactly the way you'd like them to."

Having this case resolved finally was a relief, but the murders kept coming in. About a hundred a year in the city and county, and O'Mara finally found one in late 2002 that was different and challenging enough to bring him back to trial for the first time in several years.

A woman who had two severely disabled teenagers, both of whom she and her ex-husband had adopted soon after they were born and cared for ever since, was suspected of overdosing her 18-year-old son with OxyContin, a synthetic morphine painkiller, drowning him in the bath, and trying to make it look like an accident. Homicide detectives in the sheriff's department had no solid motive other than their theory that somehow, after all those years caring for very difficult children, the mom snapped and needed a way out. O'Mara had never seen a case like this in the two thousand–plus murders he'd examined over his career. He knew the mom would be a somewhat sympathetic defendant and that it would take all his skills and powers of persuasion to convince twelve people in the box, as he likes to say, that she was a premeditated murderer of her own son. He has the kind of mind that enjoys mastering complex details of medicine and physiology that a case like this would require. Plus, though he hates to admit it, lest the deputies in his own office and the cops he always gives a hard time conclude he actually has a heart, O'Mara has always been drawn to the cases with the most hapless victims.

"I'm going to be here a while longer," he said one day after making his decision, "I probably ought to do something." This is what passes for introspection by John O'Mara, or introspection he cares to share with the rest of the world.

He was ambivalent about the stage he was at in his career. For him, all the battles and wars, all the energy and emotion expended and the high cost attached to being head of Major Crimes for a generation, had left him reluctant to walk across the street and do battle. The OxyContin case may provide the spark he needs to test himself in that way again, to see if he can summon up the fire and energy one more time. At least he is ready to give it a try. He even lost about forty pounds—he said he did it because he figured his knees would stop hurting if he were lighter—and began wearing suits to the office again, regardless of whether he was scheduled for court.

"I'm now like those guys I despised when I was coming up," he said before filing murder charges in the drug-poisoning case. "I've become one of those people who goes to meetings, writes memos, and doesn't do anything. I'm a noncontributing member of this little society."

For a professional prosecutor, the job is not about meetings and memos. It's all about going to court and trying cases. This is how the good ones measure whether they're worth a damn. O'Mara believes what he's saying on this particular lazy fall afternoon in the California capital. It's a hundred degrees outside in late September. The heat feels like a personal insult at a time of year when much of the rest of the nation is easing into the cool weather of autumn. He denigrates his role as office gatekeeper, mentor to attorneys who want mentoring, and the dominant personality and decision maker in an office of 180 attorneys, because it's never been a part of the job he has particularly enjoyed.

He's good at it, and his boss, Jan Scully, knows the value of a wise old hand. She knows he continues to be the backbone of the place, but she may not be fully aware how in his mind, O'Mara's all but moved on already. He keeps these thoughts mostly to himself, but he has lost his passion for the job and wasn't sure if he could—or wanted to—recapture it. There is no one to impress, nothing to prove. His wife is gone, his children grown. Unlike the younger attorneys who can't wait for the chance to try a big case and make a name for themselves, what he really looks forward to more than anything else is retirement in eight or nine years.

Sitting on the redwood deck he built off the duck pond near his house after one long, exhausting trial, O'Mara sips a beer and sounds like someone weary from the cumulative weight of more than twenty-five years as the capital of California's chief murder prosecutor. "It doesn't really bother me," he said while acknowledging that his once legendary career is a rocket coming down, not one going up. "You start to realize this shit was happening long before I got here and it will happen long after I leave. It's always been just a job to me."